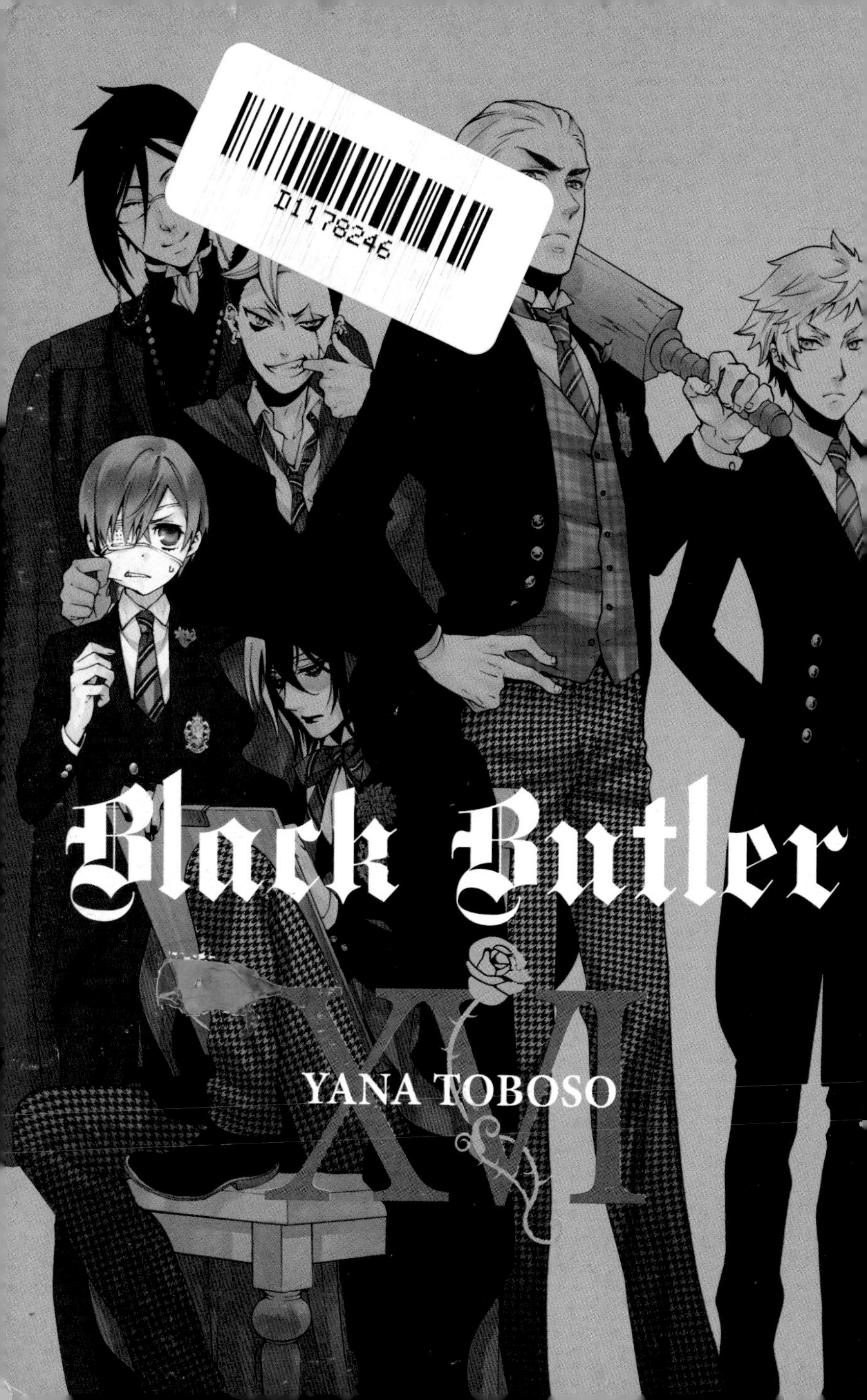
Black Butler
XVI
YANA TOBOSO

Contents

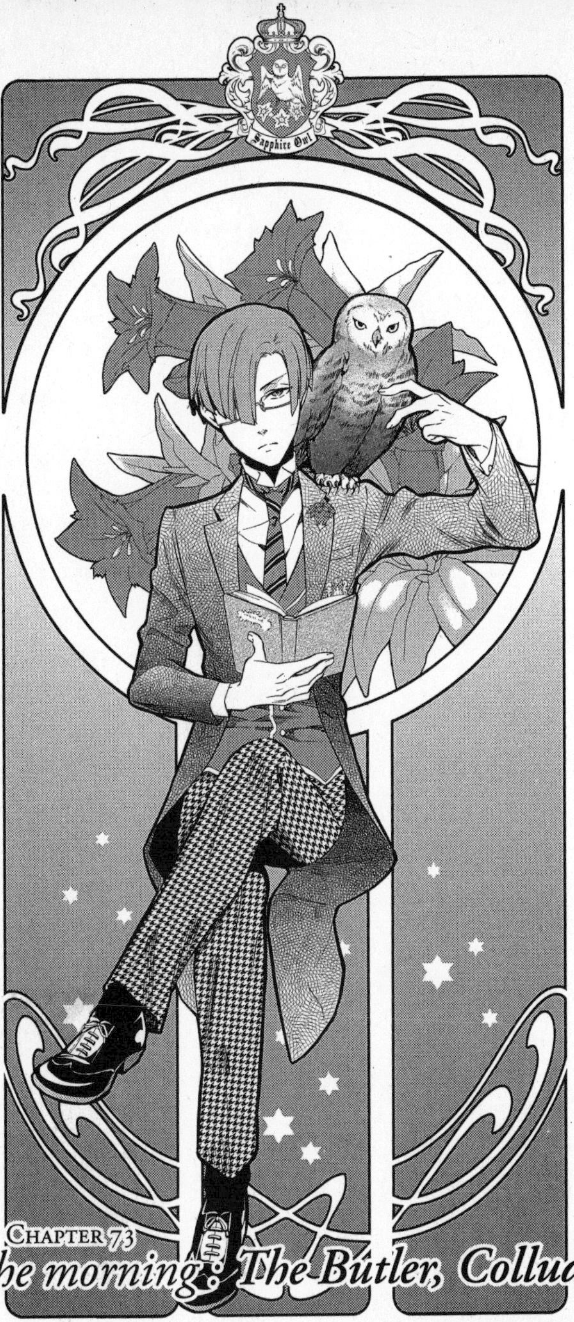
Sapphire Owl

Chapter 73

In the morning: The Butler, Colluding

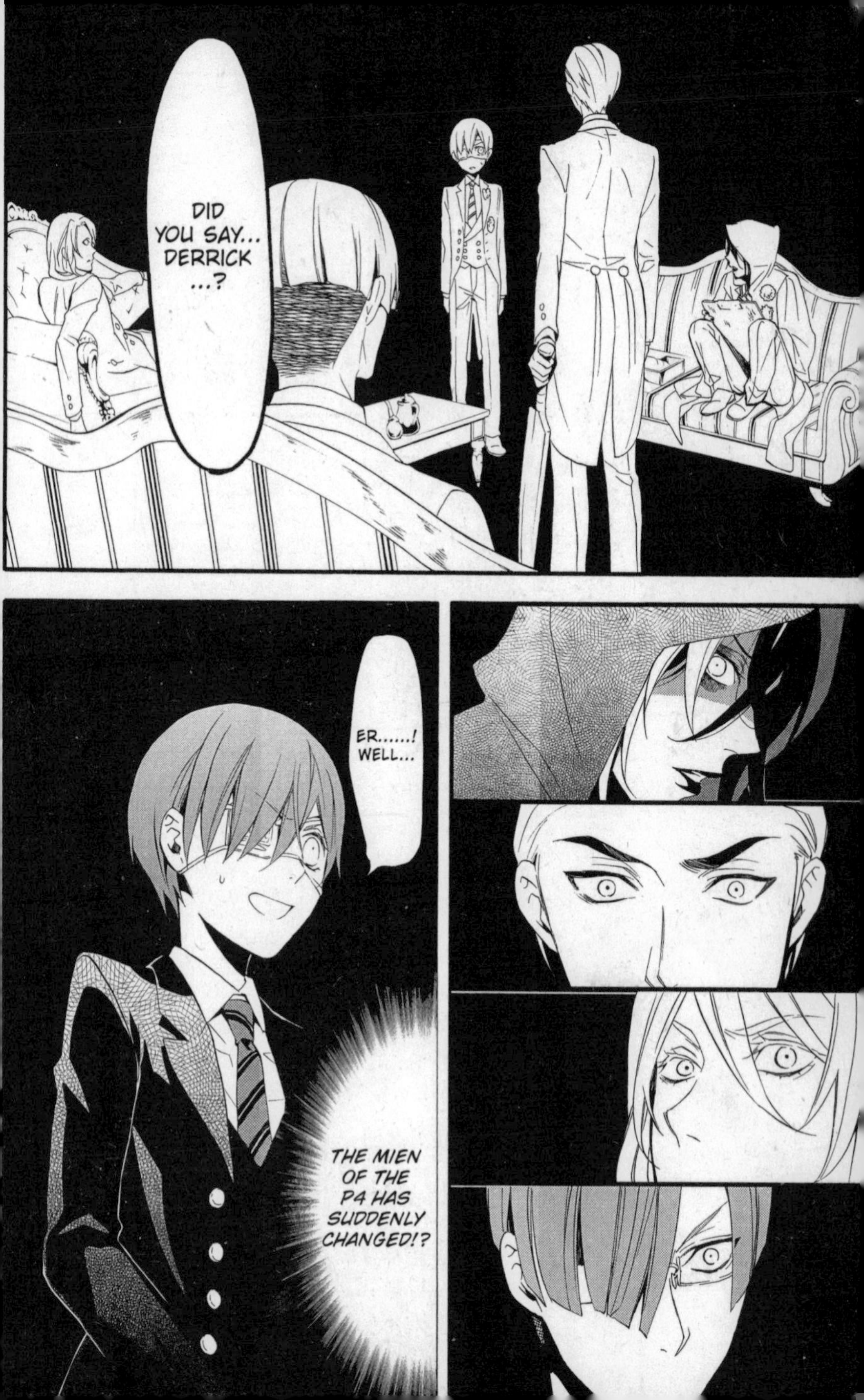
DID YOU SAY... DERRICK ...?
ER......! WELL...
THE MIEN OF THE P4 HAS SUDDENLY CHANGED!?

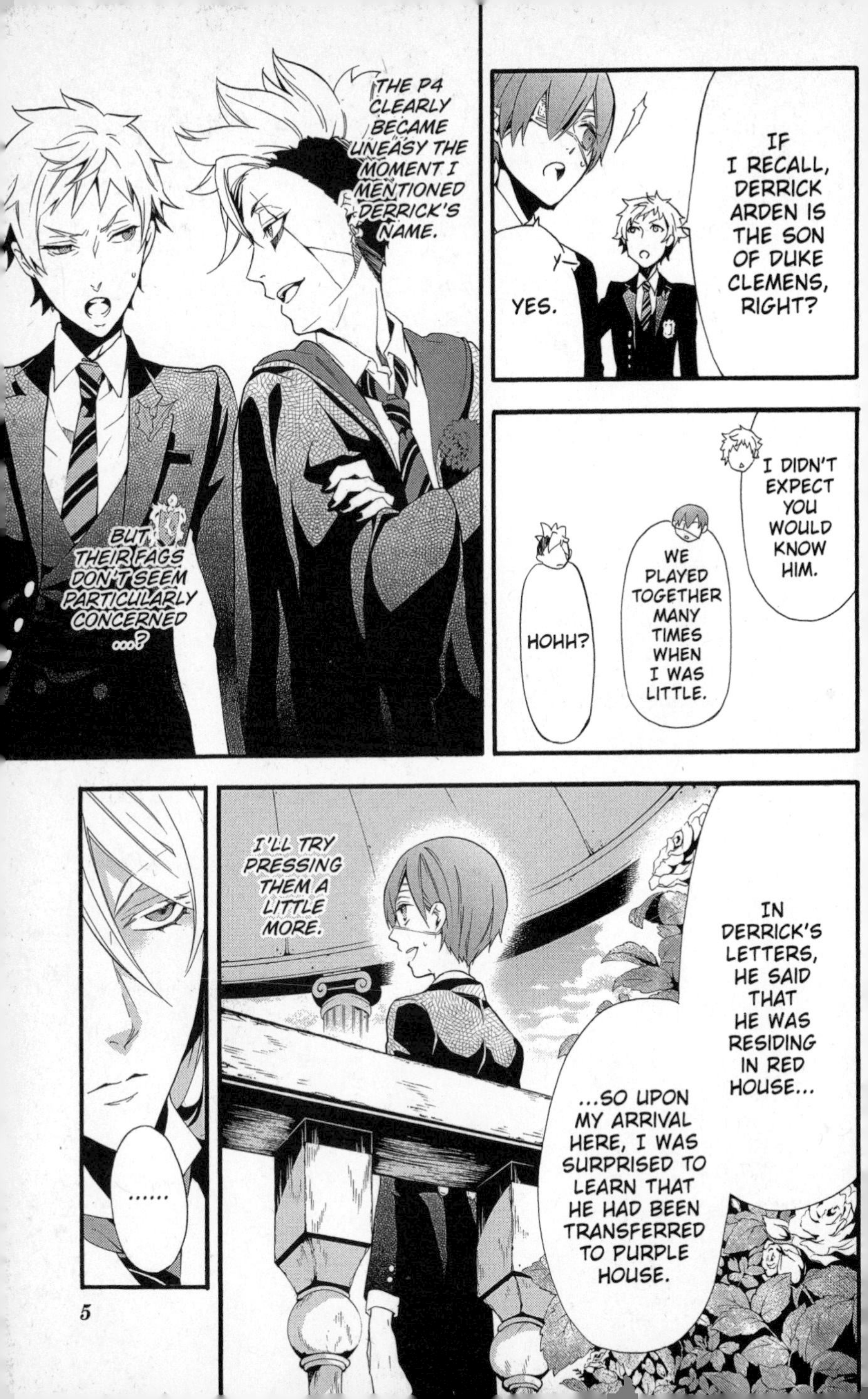
IF I RECALL, DERRICK ARDEN IS THE SON OF DUKE CLEMENS, RIGHT?
Y—
YES.
I DIDN'T EXPECT YOU WOULD KNOW HIM.
WE PLAYED TOGETHER MANY TIMES WHEN I WAS LITTLE.
HOHH?
THE P4 CLEARLY BECAME UNEASY THE MOMENT I MENTIONED DERRICK'S NAME.
BUT THEIR FAGS DON'T SEEM PARTICULARLY CONCERNED ...?
IN DERRICK'S LETTERS, HE SAID THAT HE WAS RESIDING IN RED HOUSE...
...SO UPON MY ARRIVAL HERE, I WAS SURPRISED TO LEARN THAT HE HAD BEEN TRANSFERRED TO PURPLE HOUSE.
I'LL TRY PRESSING THEM A LITTLE MORE.
......

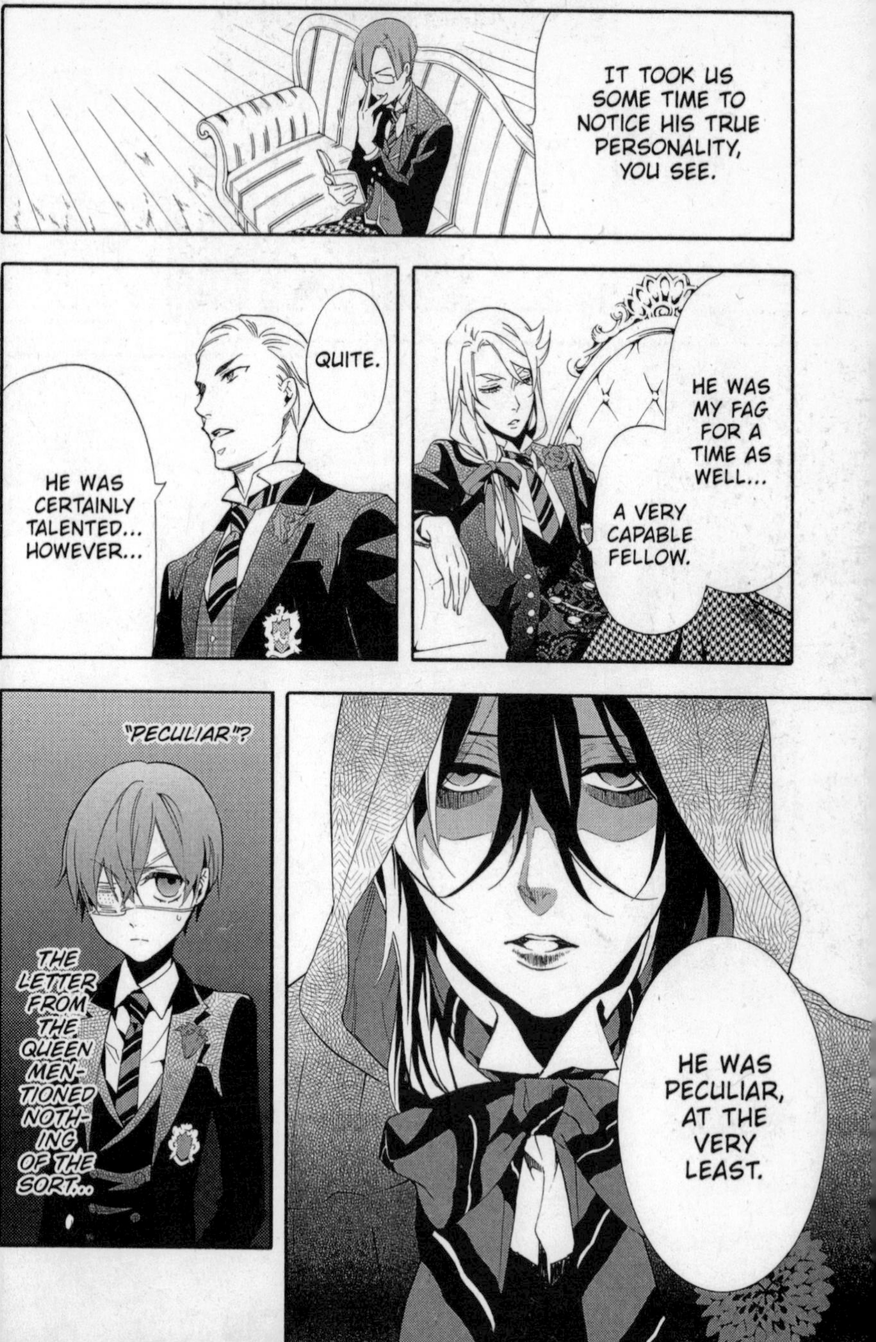
IT TOOK US SOME TIME TO NOTICE HIS TRUE PERSONALITY, YOU SEE.
HE WAS MY FAG FOR A TIME AS WELL...
A VERY CAPABLE FELLOW.
QUITE.
HE WAS CERTAINLY TALENTED... HOWEVER...
HE WAS PECULIAR, AT THE VERY LEAST.
"PECULIAR"?
THE LETTER FROM THE QUEEN MENTIONED NOTHING OF THE SORT...

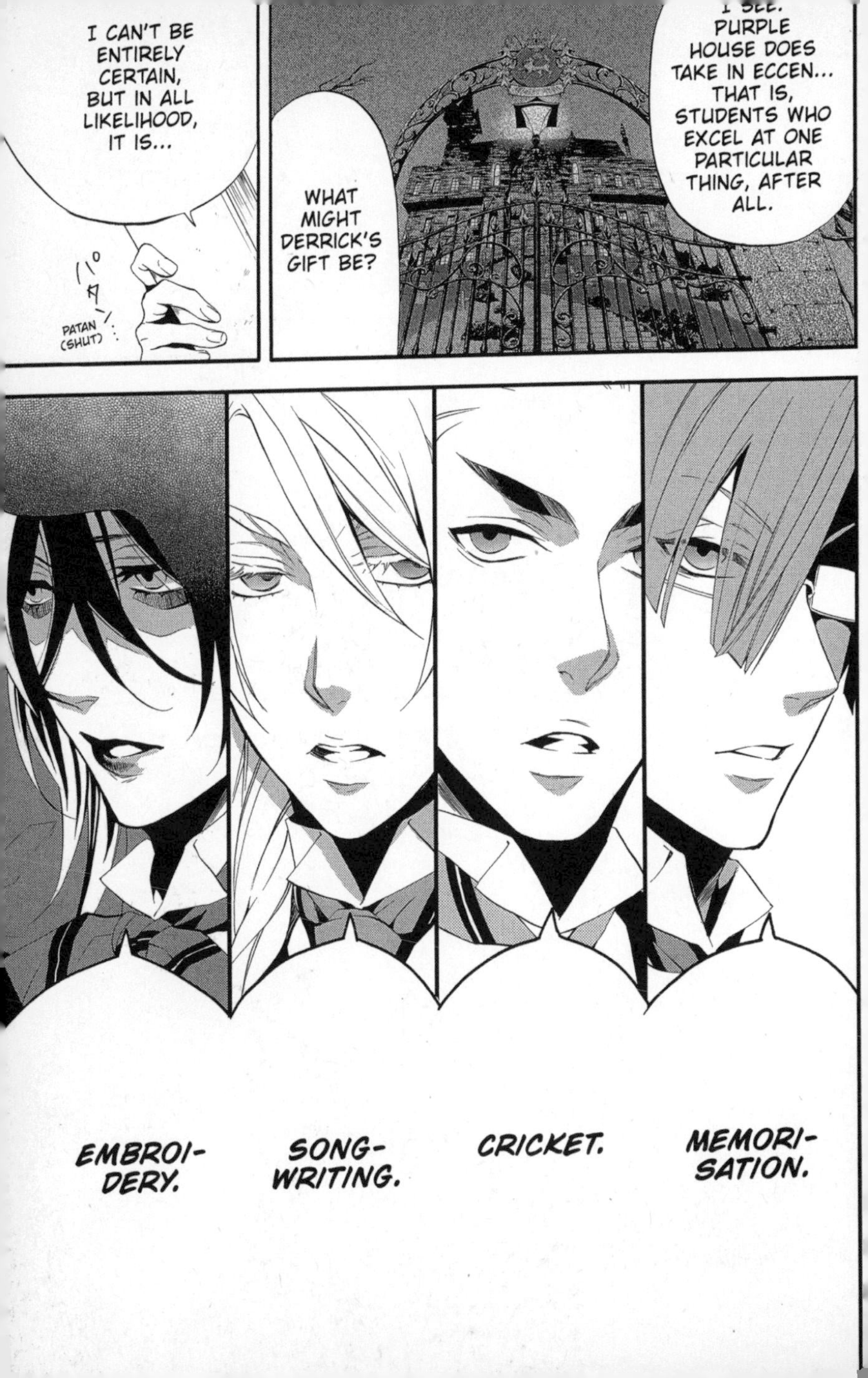

I SEE. PURPLE HOUSE DOES TAKE IN ECCEN... THAT IS, STUDENTS WHO EXCEL AT ONE PARTICULAR THING, AFTER ALL.
WHAT MIGHT DERRICK'S GIFT BE?
I CAN'T BE ENTIRELY CERTAIN, BUT IN ALL LIKELIHOOD, IT IS...
PATAN (SHUT)
MEMORI-SATION.
CRICKET.
SONG-WRITING.
EMBROI-DERY.

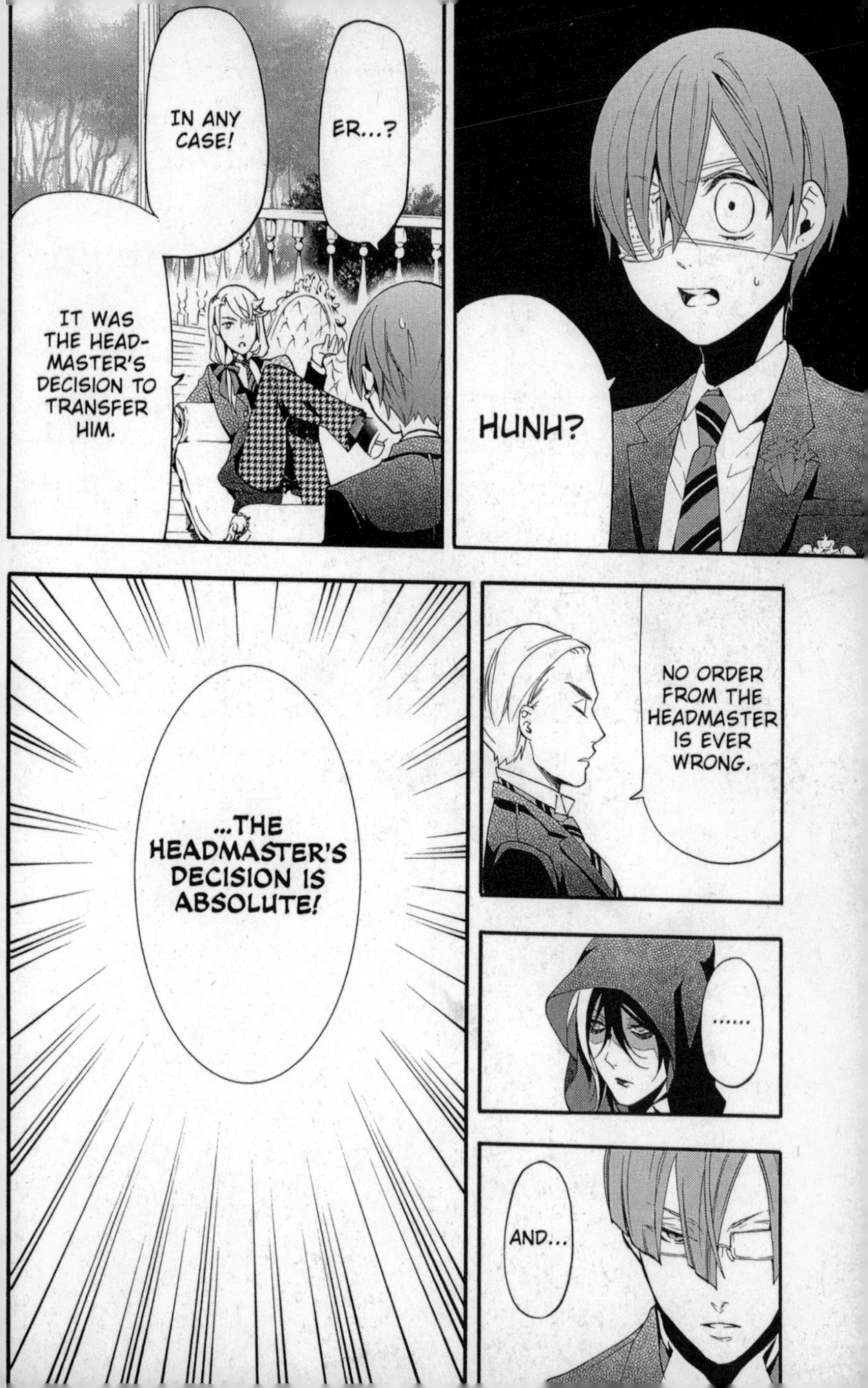
HUNH?
ER...?
IN ANY CASE!
IT WAS THE HEAD-MASTER'S DECISION TO TRANSFER HIM.
NO ORDER FROM THE HEADMASTER IS EVER WRONG.
......
AND...
...THE HEADMASTER'S DECISION IS ABSOLUTE!

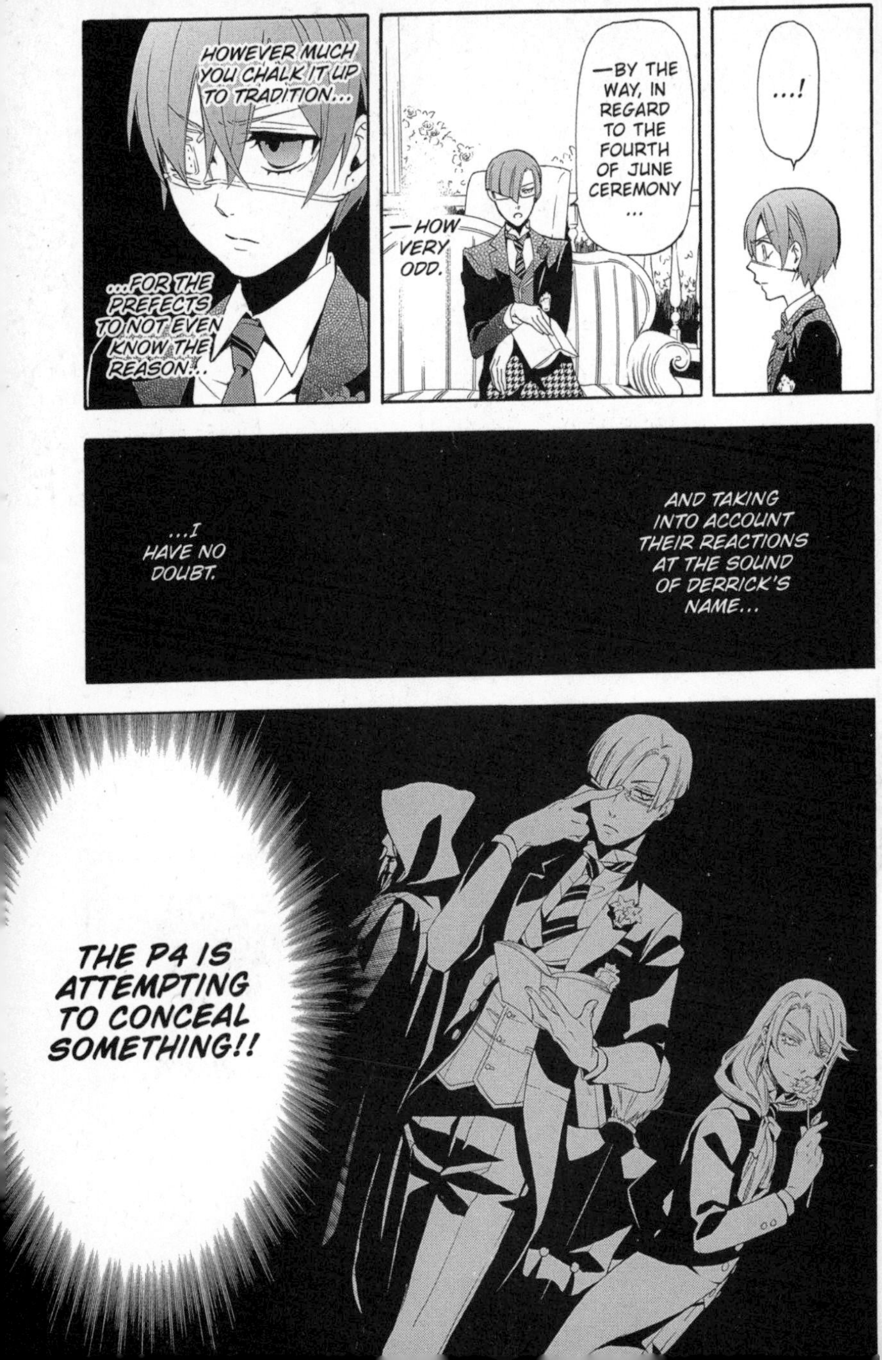
...!
—BY THE WAY, IN REGARD TO THE FOURTH OF JUNE CEREMONY ...
—HOW VERY ODD.
HOWEVER MUCH YOU CHALK IT UP TO TRADITION...
...FOR THE PREFECTS TO NOT EVEN KNOW THE REASON...
AND TAKING INTO ACCOUNT THEIR REACTIONS AT THE SOUND OF DERRICK'S NAME...
...I HAVE NO DOUBT.
THE P4 IS ATTEMPTING TO CONCEAL SOMETHING!!

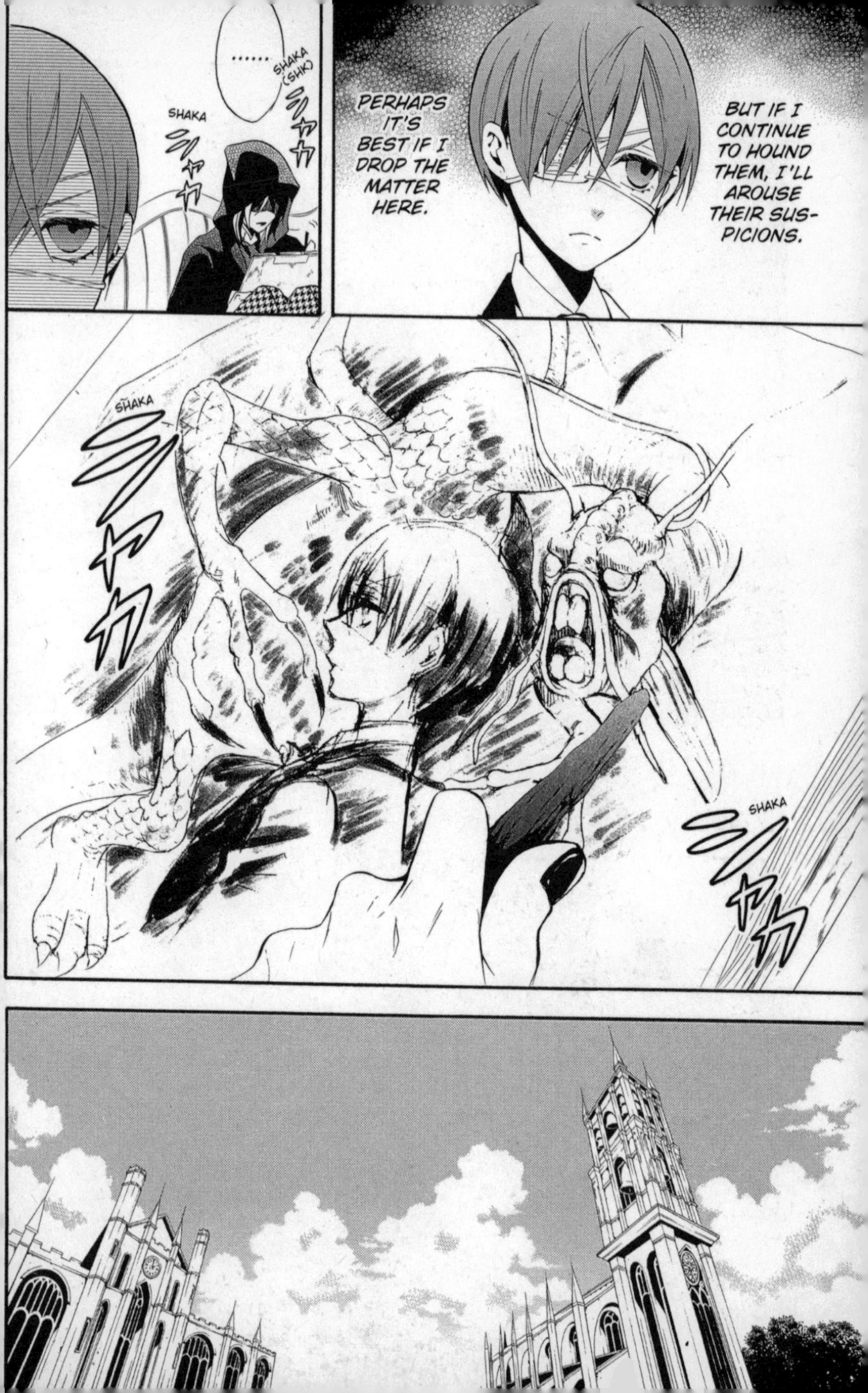
PERHAPS IT'S BEST IF I DROP THE MATTER HERE.
BUT IF I CONTINUE TO HOUND THEM, I'LL AROUSE THEIR SUSPICIONS.
......
SHAKA (SHK)
SHAKA
SHAKA
SHAKA

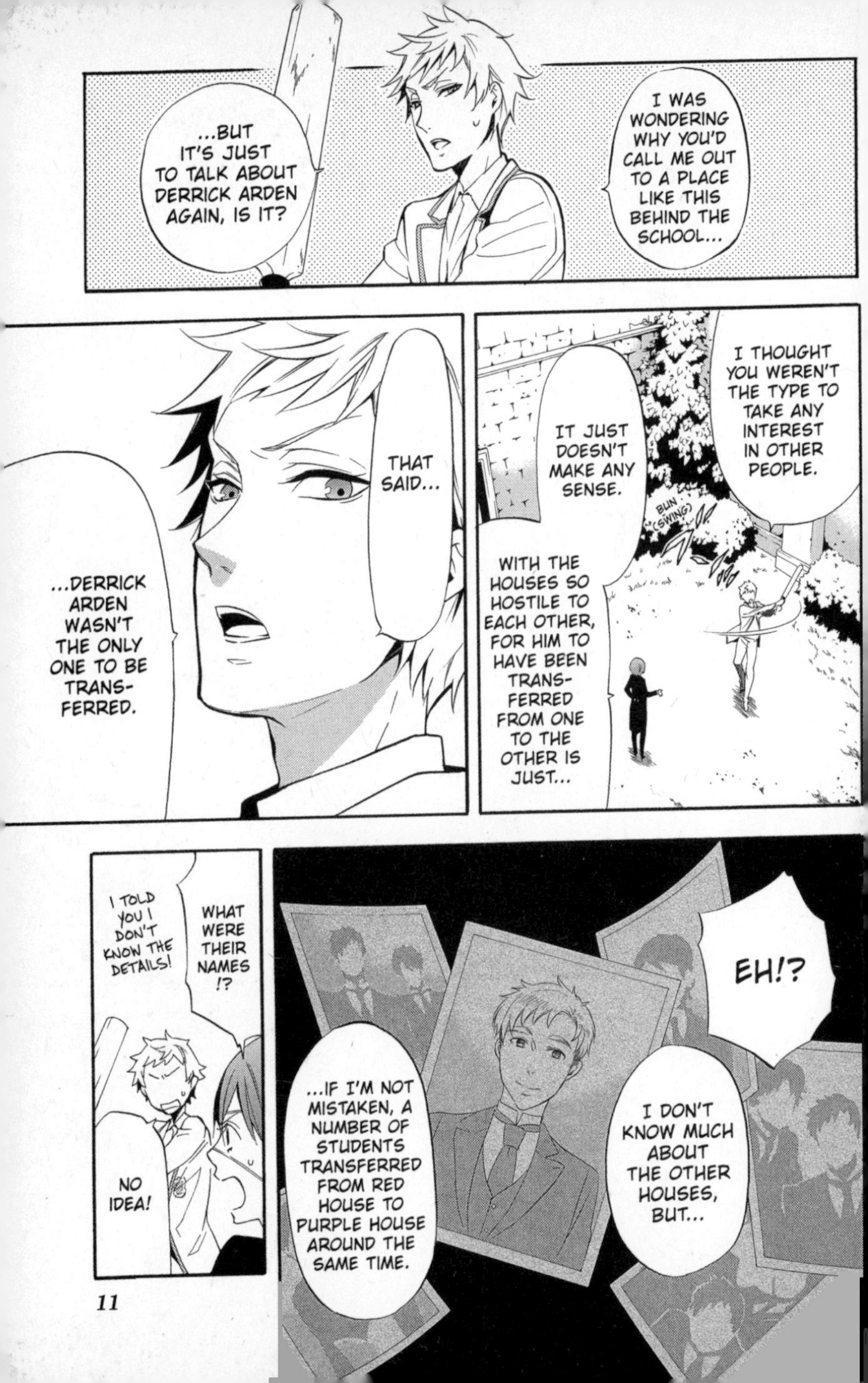
I WAS WONDERING WHY YOU'D CALL ME OUT TO A PLACE LIKE THIS BEHIND THE SCHOOL...
...BUT IT'S JUST TO TALK ABOUT DERRICK ARDEN AGAIN, IS IT?
I THOUGHT YOU WEREN'T THE TYPE TO TAKE ANY INTEREST IN OTHER PEOPLE.
BUN (SWING)
IT JUST DOESN'T MAKE ANY SENSE.
WITH THE HOUSES SO HOSTILE TO EACH OTHER, FOR HIM TO HAVE BEEN TRANSFERRED FROM ONE TO THE OTHER IS JUST...
THAT SAID...
...DERRICK ARDEN WASN'T THE ONLY ONE TO BE TRANSFERRED.
EH!?
I DON'T KNOW MUCH ABOUT THE OTHER HOUSES, BUT...
...IF I'M NOT MISTAKEN, A NUMBER OF STUDENTS TRANSFERRED FROM RED HOUSE TO PURPLE HOUSE AROUND THE SAME TIME.
WHAT WERE THEIR NAMES!?
I TOLD YOU I DON'T KNOW THE DETAILS!
NO IDEA!

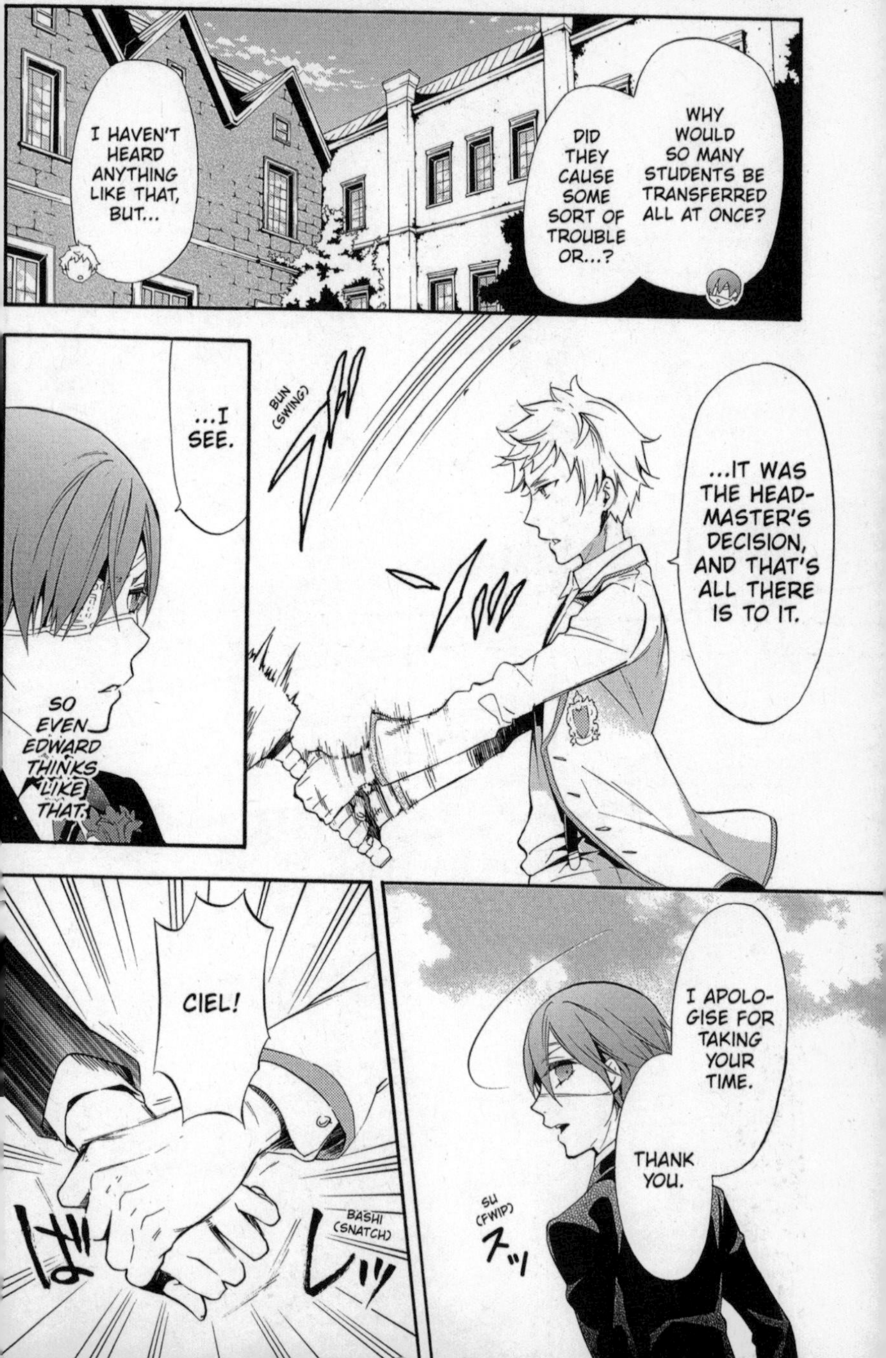
WHY WOULD SO MANY STUDENTS BE TRANSFERRED ALL AT ONCE?
DID THEY CAUSE SOME SORT OF TROUBLE OR...?
I HAVEN'T HEARD ANYTHING LIKE THAT, BUT...
...IT WAS THE HEAD-MASTER'S DECISION, AND THAT'S ALL THERE IS TO IT.
BUN (SWING)
...I SEE.
SO EVEN EDWARD THINKS LIKE THAT.
I APOLOGISE FOR TAKING YOUR TIME.
THANK YOU.
SU (FWIP)
CIEL!
BASHI (SNATCH)

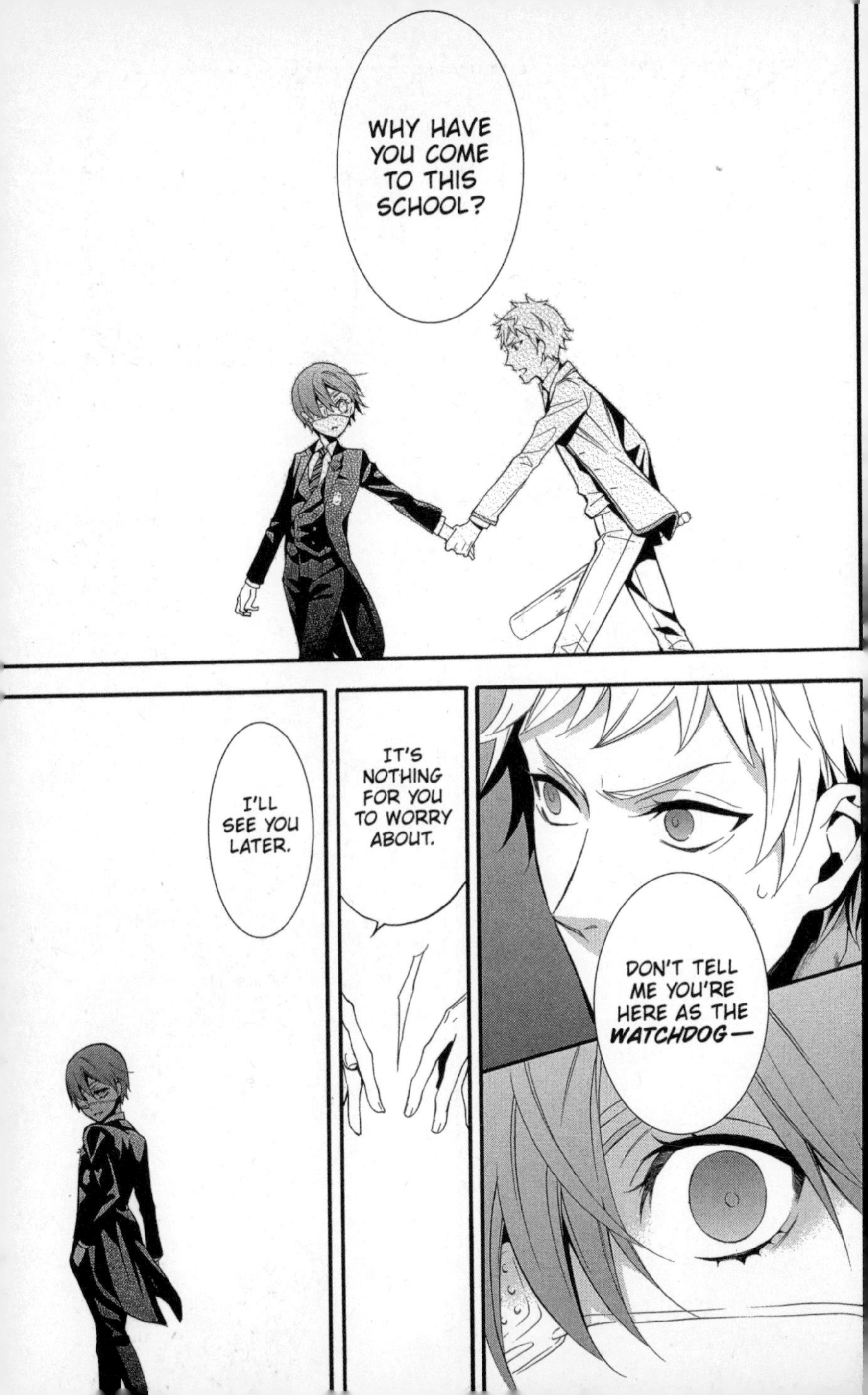
WHY HAVE YOU COME TO THIS SCHOOL?
DON'T TELL ME YOU'RE HERE AS THE *WATCHDOG*—
IT'S NOTHING FOR YOU TO WORRY ABOUT.
I'LL SEE YOU LATER.

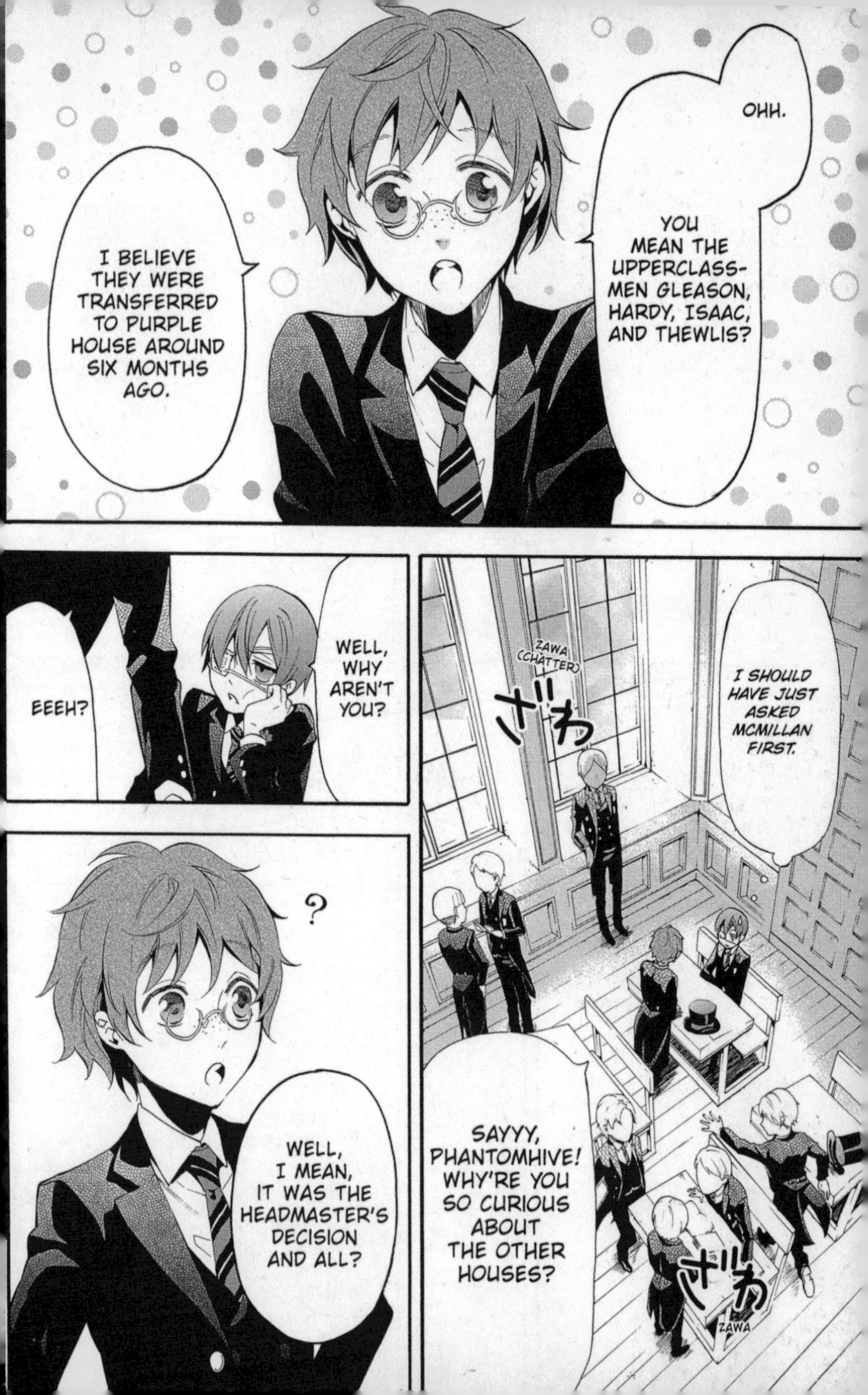
OHH.
YOU MEAN THE UPPERCLASS-MEN GLEASON, HARDY, ISAAC, AND THEWLIS?
I BELIEVE THEY WERE TRANSFERRED TO PURPLE HOUSE AROUND SIX MONTHS AGO.
I SHOULD HAVE JUST ASKED MCMILLAN FIRST.
ZAWA (CHATTER)
ざわ
SAYYY, PHANTOMHIVE! WHY'RE YOU SO CURIOUS ABOUT THE OTHER HOUSES?
ざわ
ZAWA
WELL, WHY AREN'T YOU?
EEEH?
?
WELL, I MEAN, IT WAS THE HEADMASTER'S DECISION AND ALL?

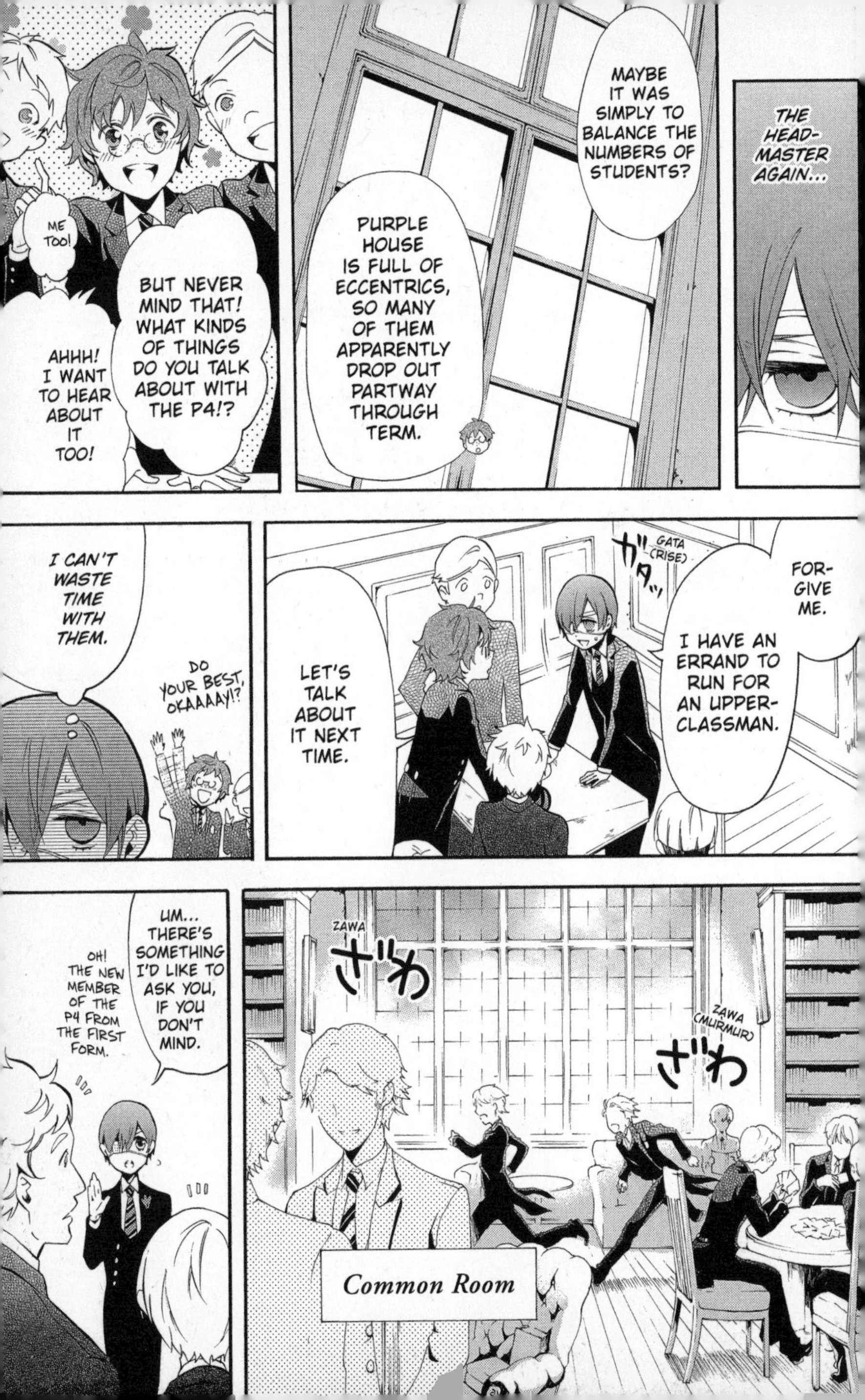
THE HEAD-MASTER AGAIN...
MAYBE IT WAS SIMPLY TO BALANCE THE NUMBERS OF STUDENTS?
PURPLE HOUSE IS FULL OF ECCENTRICS, SO MANY OF THEM APPARENTLY DROP OUT PARTWAY THROUGH TERM.
BUT NEVER MIND THAT! WHAT KINDS OF THINGS DO YOU TALK ABOUT WITH THE P4!?
ME TOO!
AHHH! I WANT TO HEAR ABOUT IT TOO!
ガタッ
GATA (RISE)
FOR-GIVE ME.
I HAVE AN ERRAND TO RUN FOR AN UPPER-CLASSMAN.
LET'S TALK ABOUT IT NEXT TIME.
I CAN'T WASTE TIME WITH THEM.
DO YOUR BEST, OKAAAAY!?
ざわ
ZAWA
ざわ
ZAWA (MURMUR)
Common Room
UM... THERE'S SOMETHING I'D LIKE TO ASK YOU, IF YOU DON'T MIND.
OH! THE NEW MEMBER OF THE P4 FROM THE FIRST FORM.

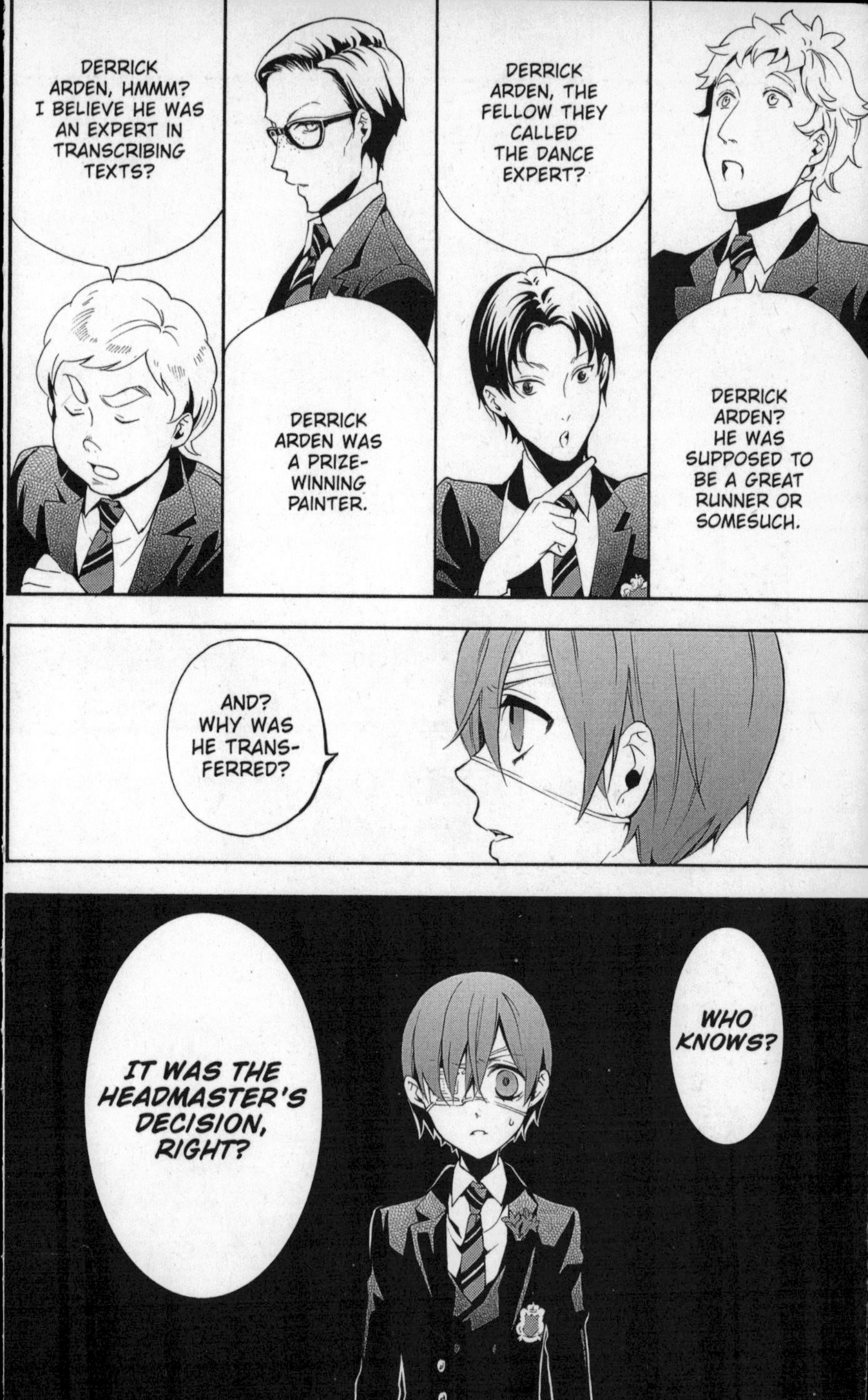
DERRICK ARDEN? HE WAS SUPPOSED TO BE A GREAT RUNNER OR SOMESUCH.
DERRICK ARDEN, THE FELLOW THEY CALLED THE DANCE EXPERT?
DERRICK ARDEN WAS A PRIZE-WINNING PAINTER.
DERRICK ARDEN, HMMM? I BELIEVE HE WAS AN EXPERT IN TRANSCRIBING TEXTS?
AND? WHY WAS HE TRANS-FERRED?
WHO KNOWS?
IT WAS THE HEADMASTER'S DECISION, RIGHT?

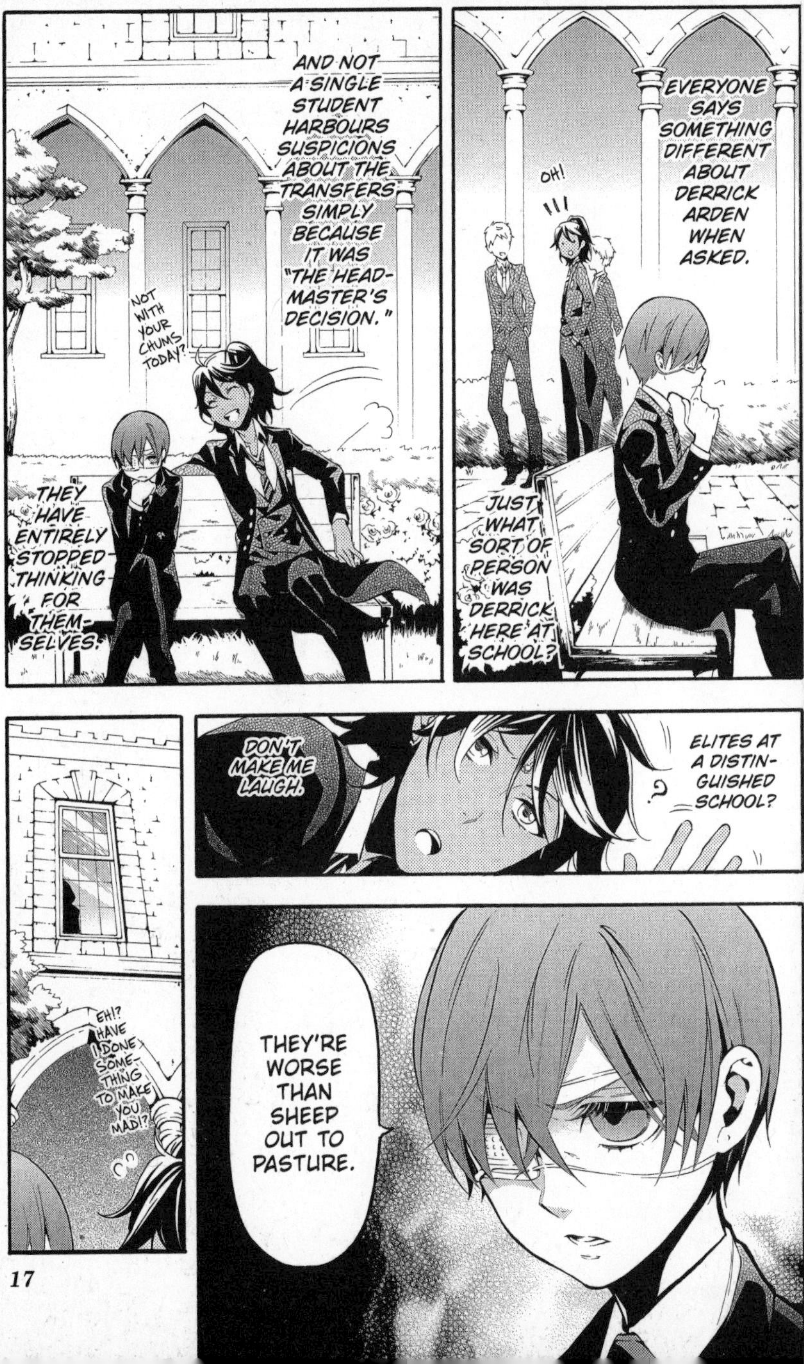
EVERYONE SAYS SOMETHING DIFFERENT ABOUT DERRICK ARDEN WHEN ASKED.
OH!
JUST WHAT SORT OF PERSON WAS DERRICK HERE AT SCHOOL?
AND NOT A SINGLE STUDENT HARBOURS SUSPICIONS ABOUT THE TRANSFERS SIMPLY BECAUSE IT WAS "THE HEAD-MASTER'S DECISION."
NOT WITH YOUR CHUMS TODAY?
THEY HAVE ENTIRELY STOPPED THINKING FOR THEM-SELVES.
ELITES AT A DISTIN-GUISHED SCHOOL?
DON'T MAKE ME LAUGH.
THEY'RE WORSE THAN SHEEP OUT TO PASTURE.
EH!? HAVE I DONE SOME-THING TO MAKE YOU MAD!?

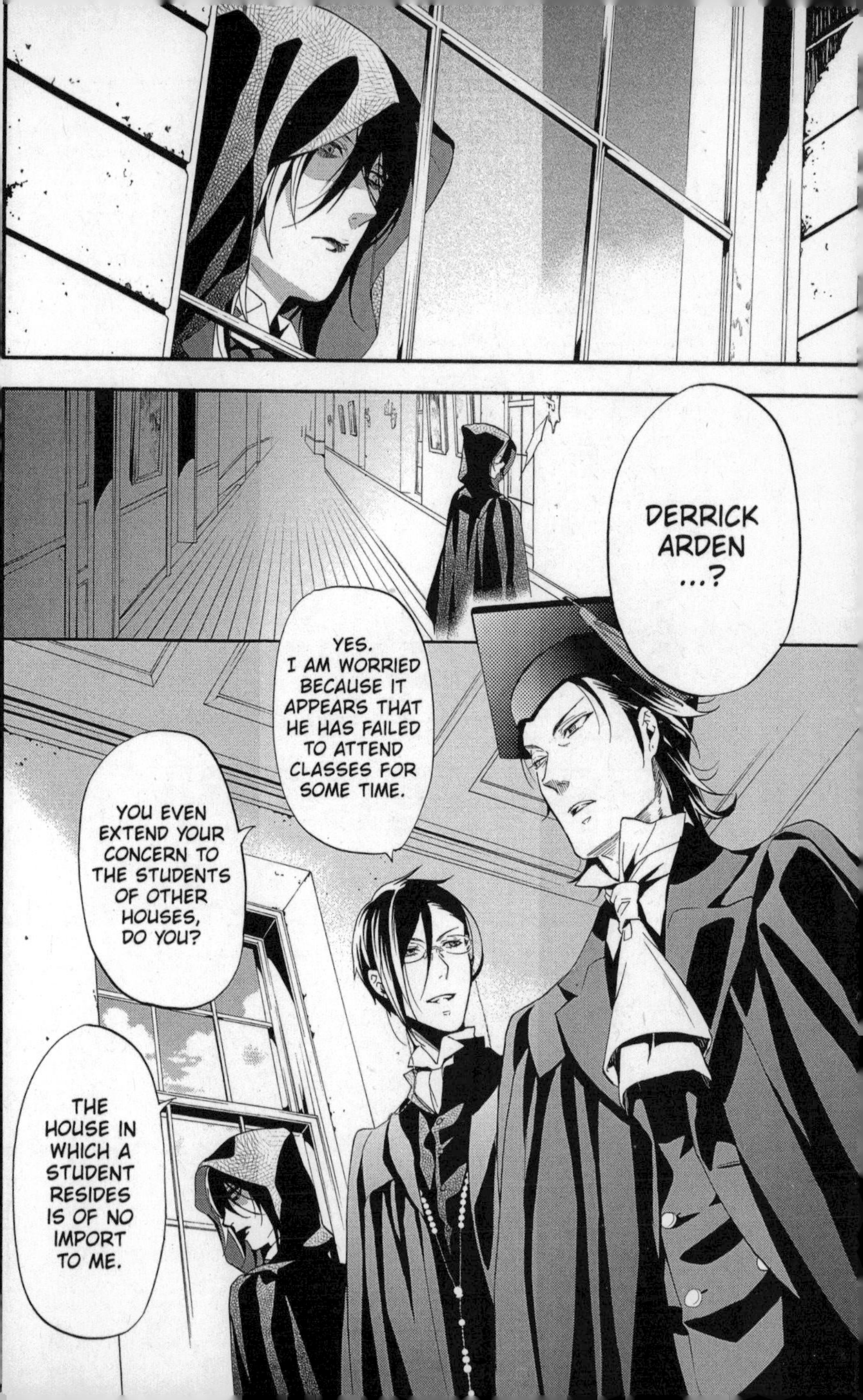
DERRICK ARDEN ...?
YES. I AM WORRIED BECAUSE IT APPEARS THAT HE HAS FAILED TO ATTEND CLASSES FOR SOME TIME.
YOU EVEN EXTEND YOUR CONCERN TO THE STUDENTS OF OTHER HOUSES, DO YOU?
THE HOUSE IN WHICH A STUDENT RESIDES IS OF NO IMPORT TO ME.

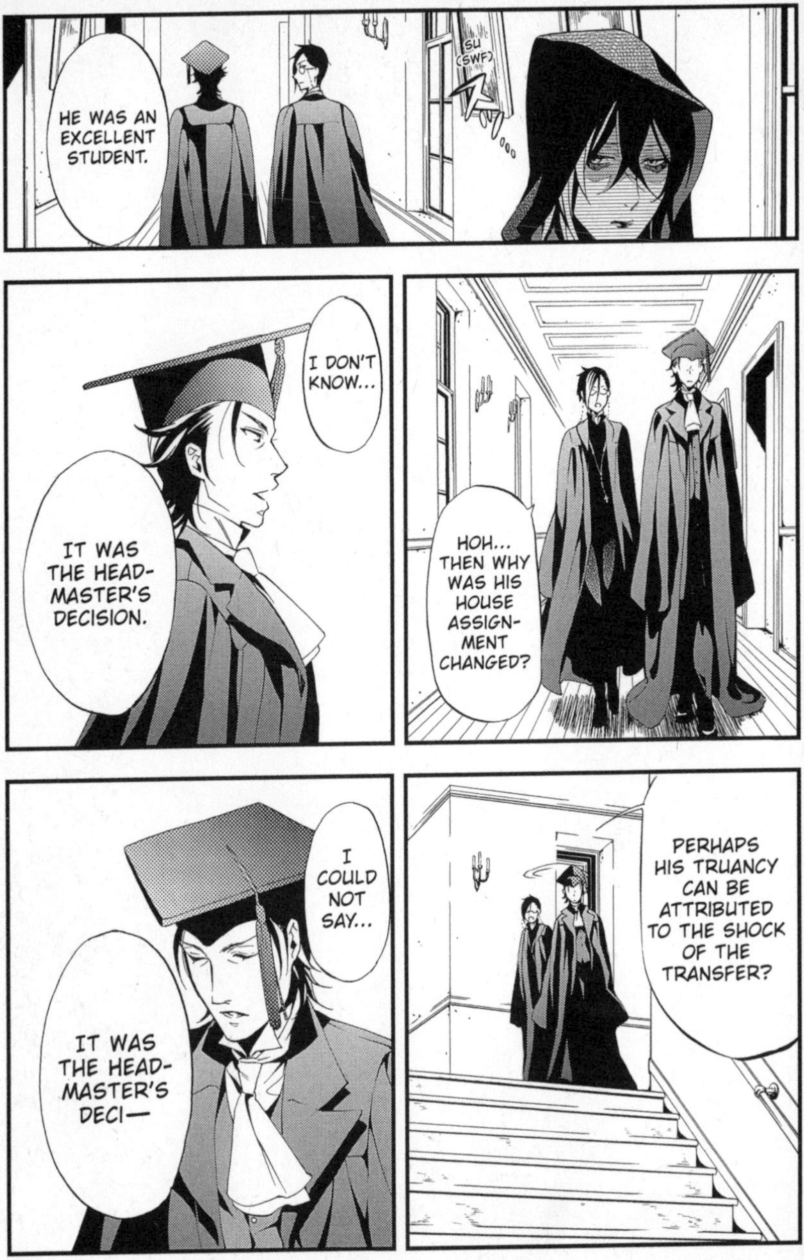
SU (SWF)
HE WAS AN EXCELLENT STUDENT.
HOH... THEN WHY WAS HIS HOUSE ASSIGNMENT CHANGED?
I DON'T KNOW...
IT WAS THE HEADMASTER'S DECISION.
PERHAPS HIS TRUANCY CAN BE ATTRIBUTED TO THE SHOCK OF THE TRANSFER?
I COULD NOT SAY...
IT WAS THE HEADMASTER'S DECI—

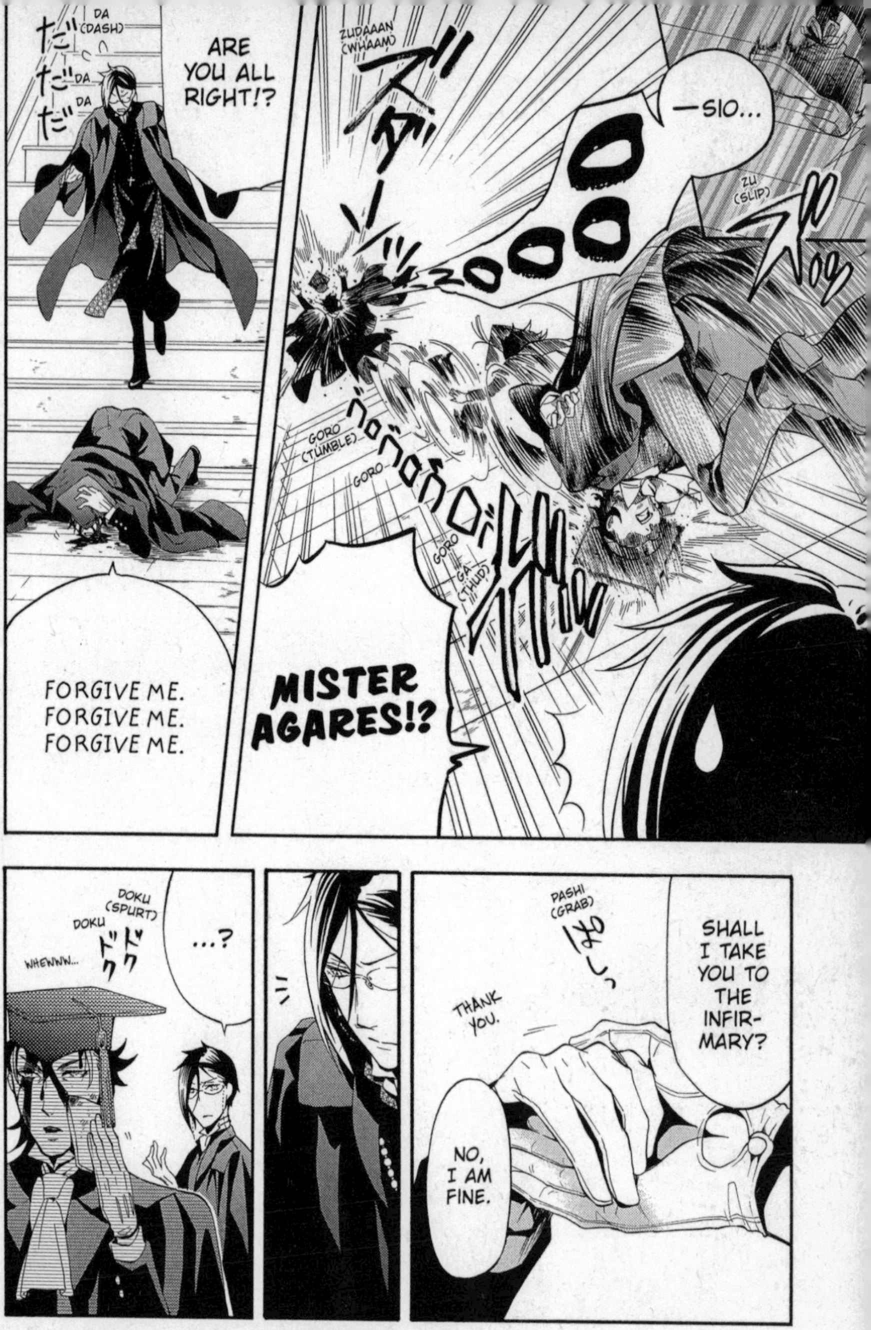
—SIO...
ZUDAAAN (WHAAM)
ZU (SLIP)
GORO (TUMBLE)
GORO
GORO
GA (THUD)
MISTER AGARES!?
ARE YOU ALL RIGHT!?
DA (DASH)
DA
DA
FORGIVE ME. FORGIVE ME. FORGIVE ME.
SHALL I TAKE YOU TO THE INFIRMARY?
PASHI (GRAB)
THANK YOU.
NO, I AM FINE.
...?
DOKU (SPURT)
DOKU
WHEWWW...

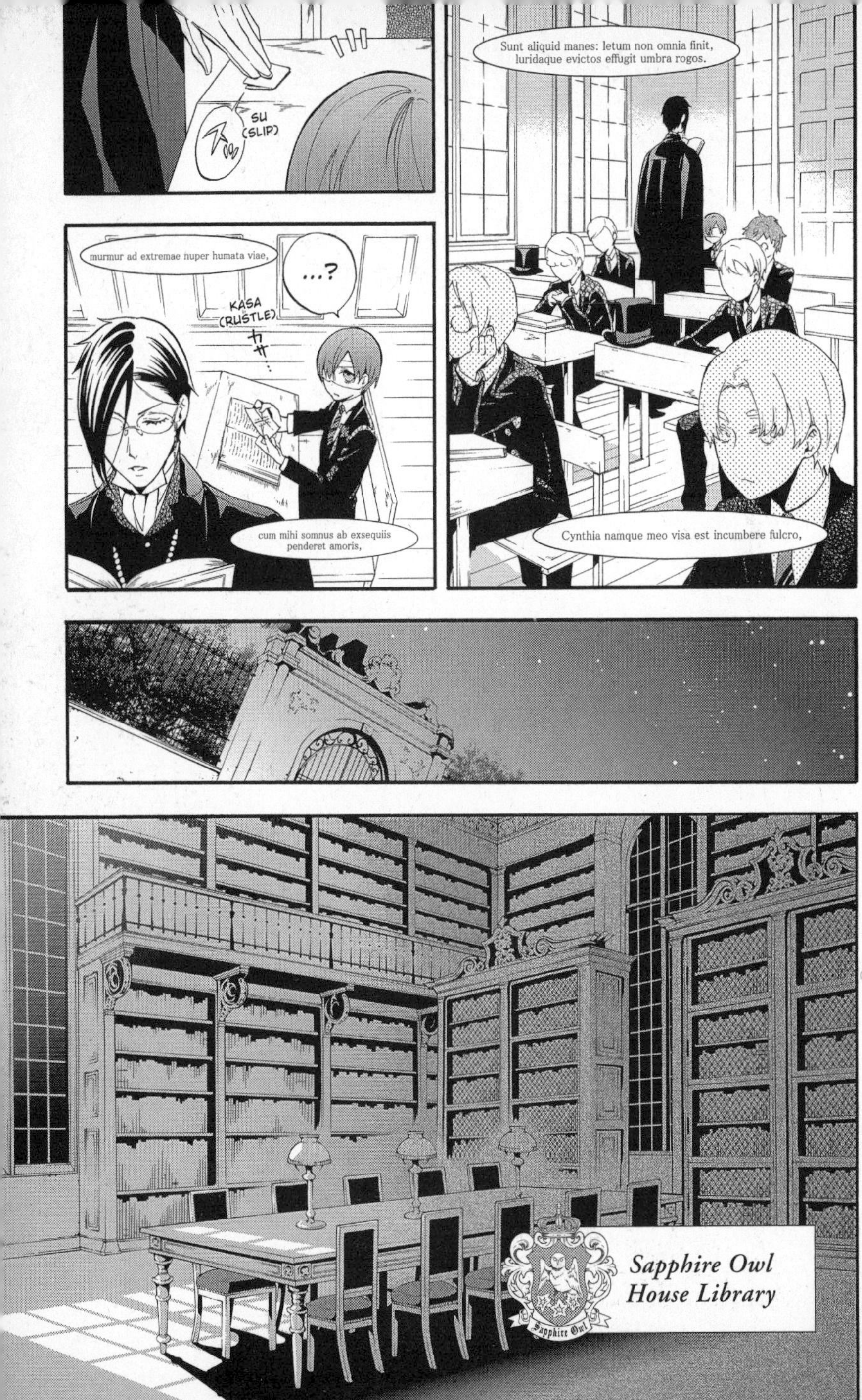
Sunt aliquid manes: letum non omnia finit, luridaque evictos effugit umbra rogos.
Cynthia namque meo visa est incumbere fulcro,
SU (SLIP)
murmur ad extremae nuper humata viae,
...?
KASA (RUSTLE)
cum mihi somnus ab exsequiis penderet amoris,
Sapphire Owl House Library
Sapphire Owl

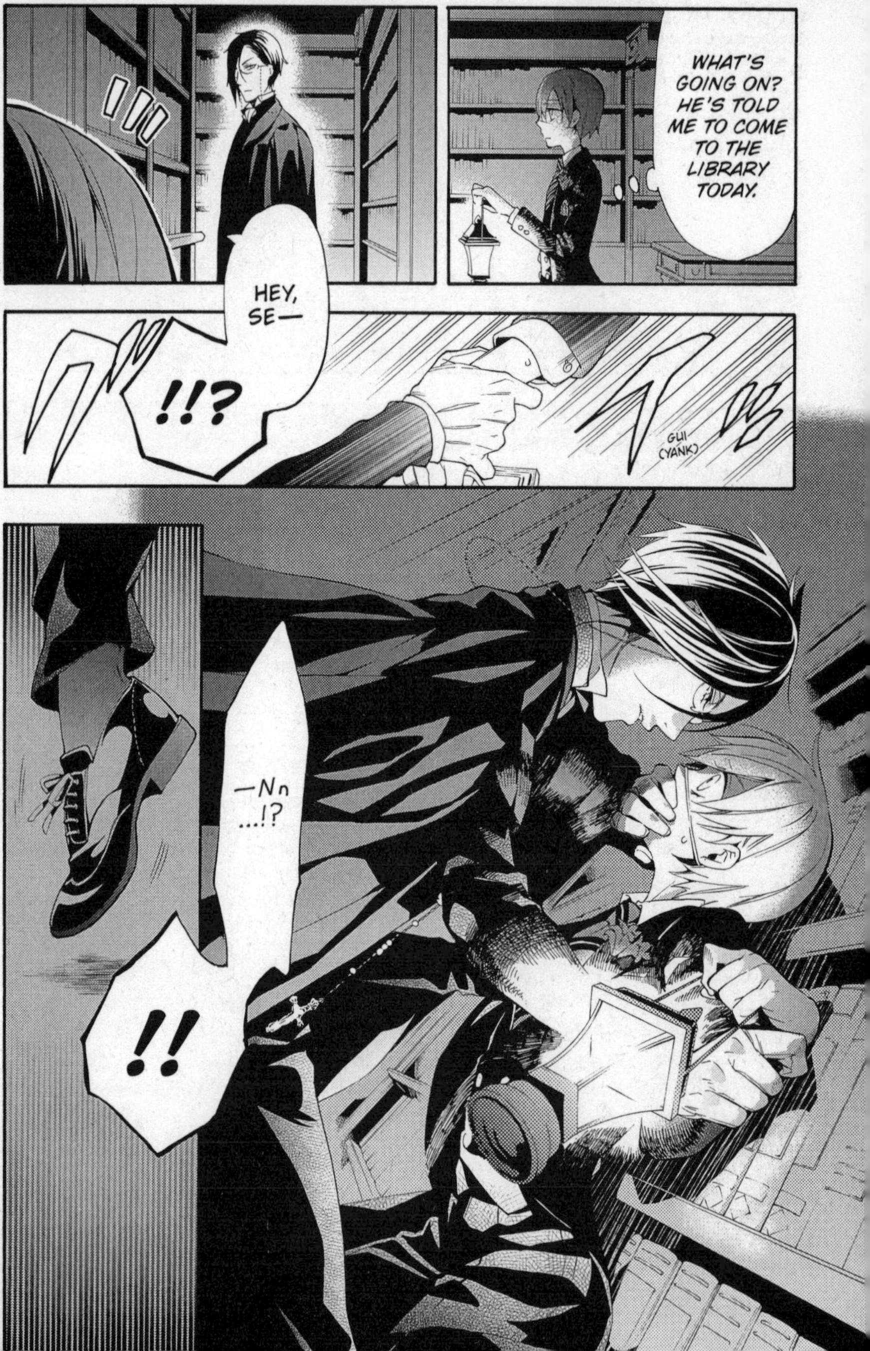
WHAT'S GOING ON? HE'S TOLD ME TO COME TO THE LIBRARY TODAY.
!!!
HEY, SE—
!!?
GUI (YANK)
—Nn ...!?
!!

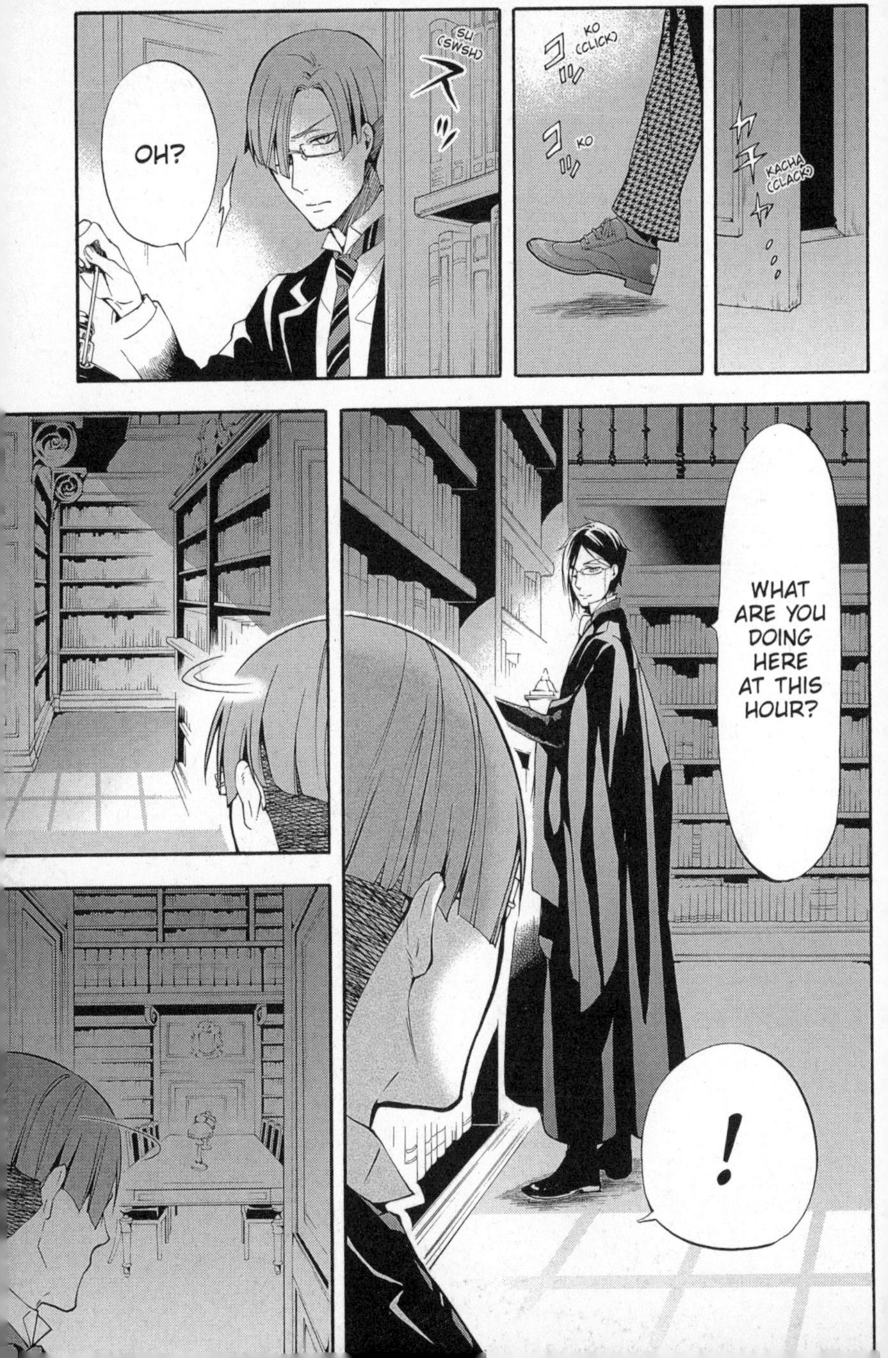
KACHA (CLACK)
KO (CLICK)
KO
SU (SWSH)
OH?
WHAT ARE YOU DOING HERE AT THIS HOUR?
!

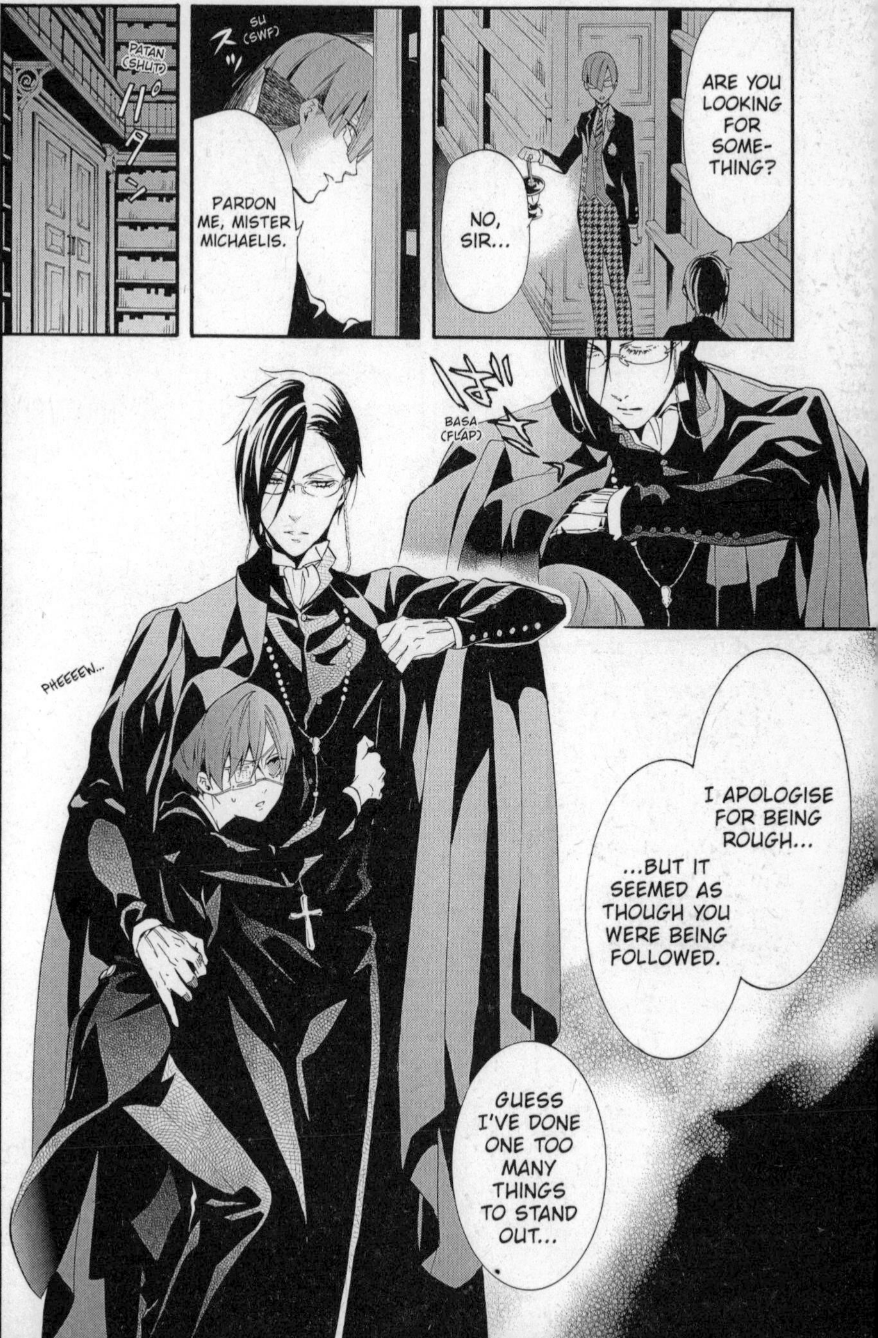
ARE YOU LOOKING FOR SOME-THING?
NO, SIR...
SU (SWF)
PARDON ME, MISTER MICHAELIS.
PATAN (SHUT)
BASA (FLAP)
I APOLOGISE FOR BEING ROUGH...
...BUT IT SEEMED AS THOUGH YOU WERE BEING FOLLOWED.
PHEEEEW...
GUESS I'VE DONE ONE TOO MANY THINGS TO STAND OUT...

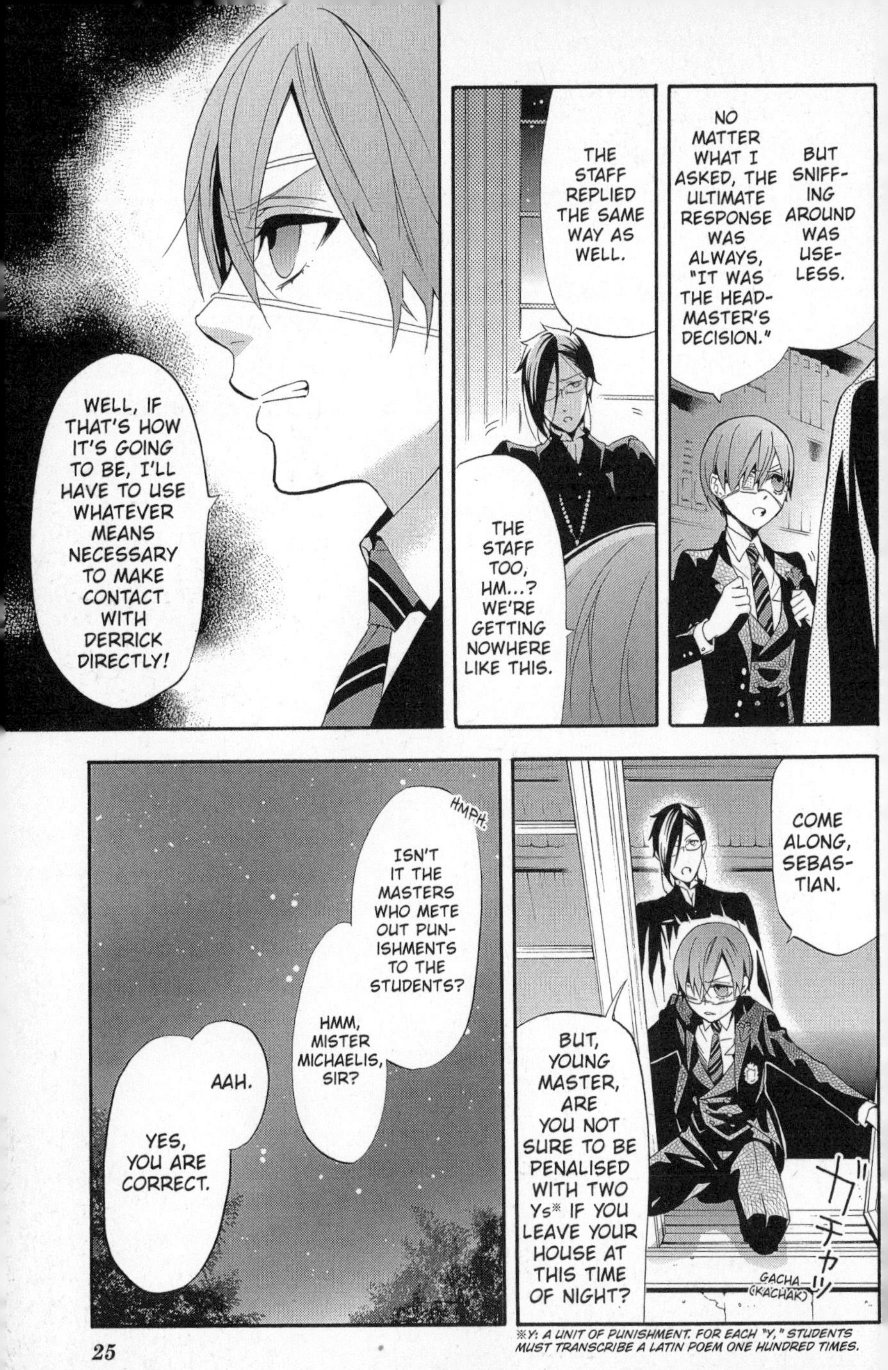
BUT SNIFFING AROUND WAS USELESS.
NO MATTER WHAT I ASKED, THE ULTIMATE RESPONSE WAS ALWAYS, "IT WAS THE HEADMASTER'S DECISION."
THE STAFF REPLIED THE SAME WAY AS WELL.
THE STAFF TOO, HM...? WE'RE GETTING NOWHERE LIKE THIS.
WELL, IF THAT'S HOW IT'S GOING TO BE, I'LL HAVE TO USE WHATEVER MEANS NECESSARY TO MAKE CONTACT WITH DERRICK DIRECTLY!
COME ALONG, SEBASTIAN.
ガチャッ
GACHA (KACHAK)
BUT, YOUNG MASTER, ARE YOU NOT SURE TO BE PENALISED WITH TWO Ys※ IF YOU LEAVE YOUR HOUSE AT THIS TIME OF NIGHT?
HMPH.
ISN'T IT THE MASTERS WHO METE OUT PUNISHMENTS TO THE STUDENTS?
HMM, MISTER MICHAELIS, SIR?
AAH.
YES, YOU ARE CORRECT.

※Y: A UNIT OF PUNISHMENT. FOR EACH "Y," STUDENTS MUST TRANSCRIBE A LATIN POEM ONE HUNDRED TIMES.

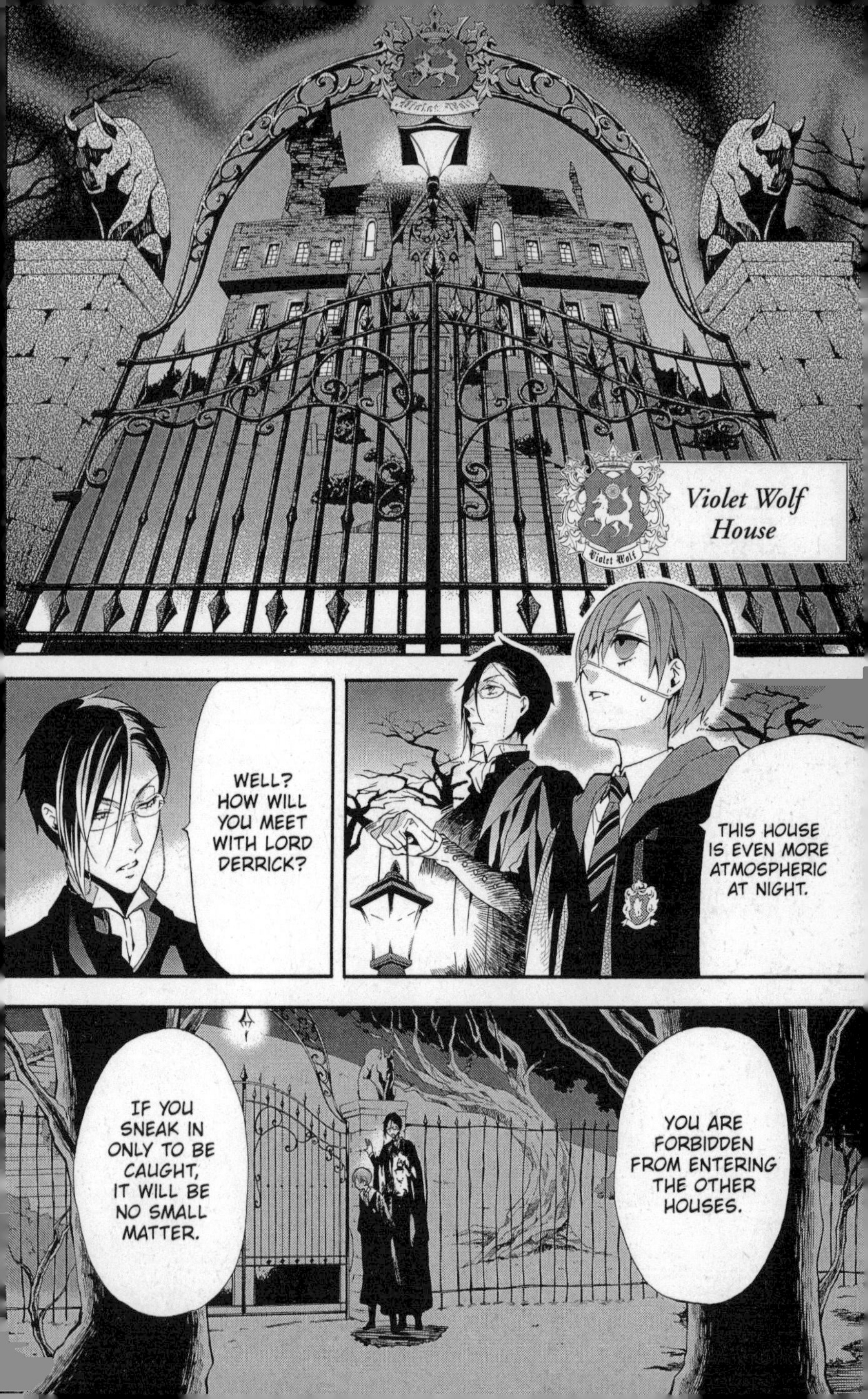
Violet Wolf
Violet Wolf House
THIS HOUSE IS EVEN MORE ATMOSPHERIC AT NIGHT.
WELL? HOW WILL YOU MEET WITH LORD DERRICK?
YOU ARE FORBIDDEN FROM ENTERING THE OTHER HOUSES.
IF YOU SNEAK IN ONLY TO BE CAUGHT, IT WILL BE NO SMALL MATTER.

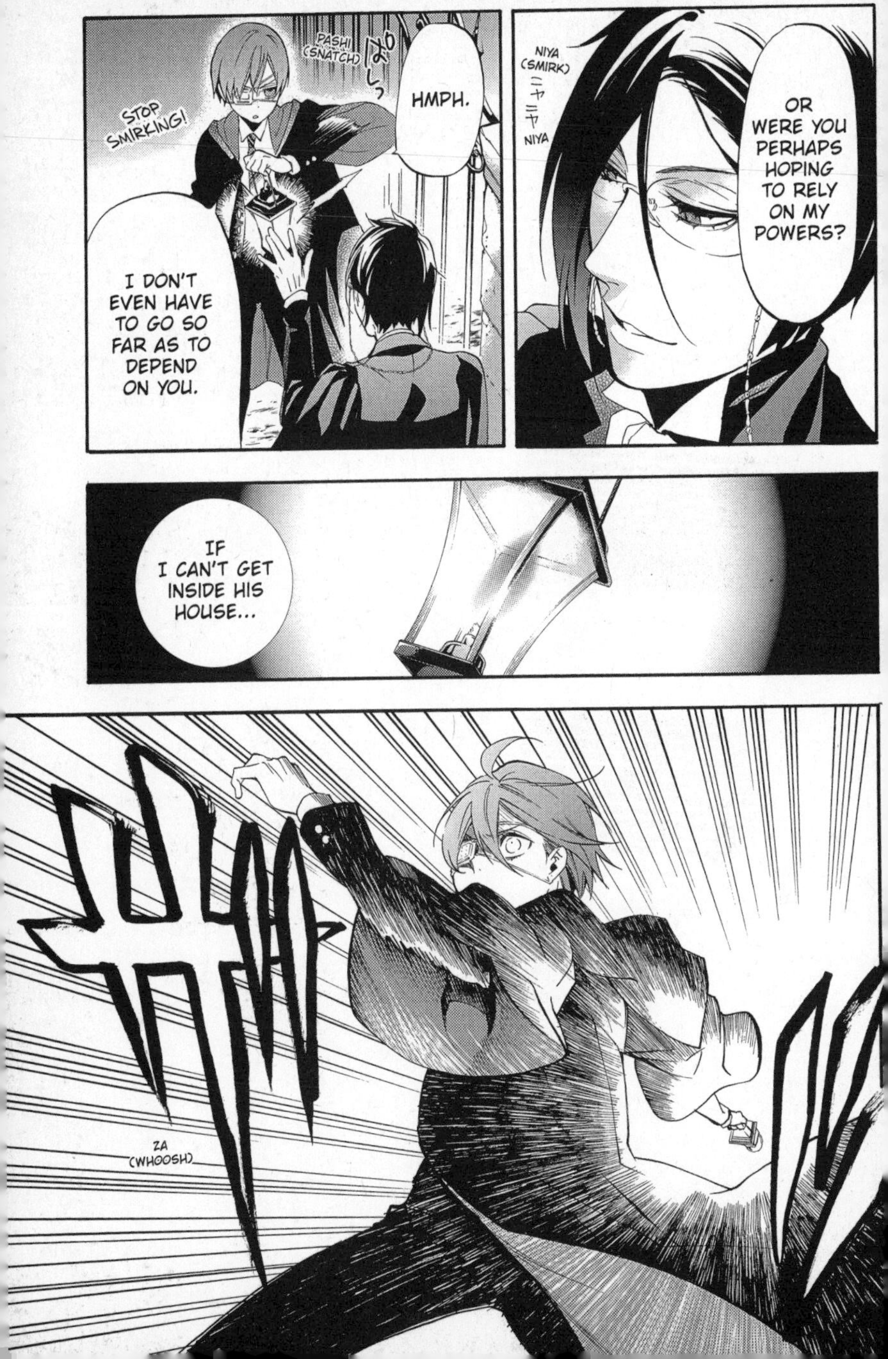
NIYA (SMIRK)
ニヤニヤ
NIYA
OR WERE YOU PERHAPS HOPING TO RELY ON MY POWERS?
PASHI (SNATCH)
ぱしっ
HMPH.
STOP SMIRKING!
I DON'T EVEN HAVE TO GO SO FAR AS TO DEPEND ON YOU.
IF I CAN'T GET INSIDE HIS HOUSE...
ZA (WHOOSH)

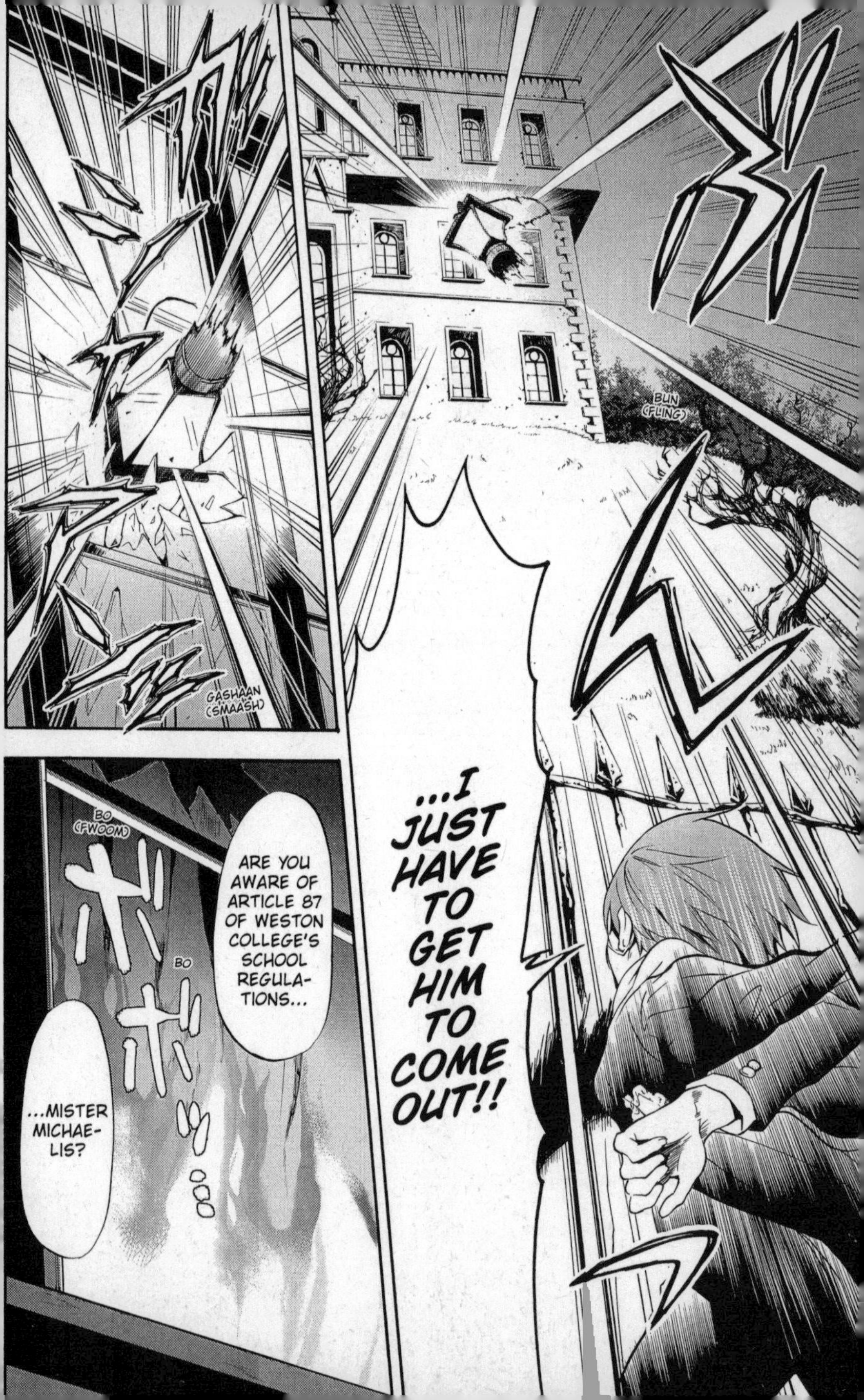
BUN (FLING)
...I JUST HAVE TO GET HIM TO COME OUT!!
GASHAAN (SMAASH)
BO (FWOOM)
ARE YOU AWARE OF ARTICLE 87 OF WESTON COLLEGE'S SCHOOL REGULATIONS...
BO
...MISTER MICHAELIS?

ARTICLE 87 OF WESTON COLLEGE'S SCHOOL REGULATIONS...

"IN CASE OF AN EMERGENCY, SUCH AS THE ONSET OF A FIRE OR OTHER CALAMITY, WITHIN THE SCHOOL BUILDINGS OR HOUSES...

"...ALL STUDENTS MUST PROMPTLY EVACUATE TO THE SCHOOLYARD AND ANSWER TO THE ROLL CALL TAKEN BY THE PREFECTS."

YOUR CONDUCT IS DESERVING OF EXPULSION IF YOU ARE FOUND OUT, PHANTOMHIVE.

HOWEVER...

...AS WATCHDOG TO THE QUEEN, YOUR ACTIONS ARE DESERVING OF GREAT PRAISE, YOUNG MASTER.

PREFECT BLUEWER WAS RIGHT. I SHOULD KNOW THE SCHOOL REGULATIONS BY HEART.

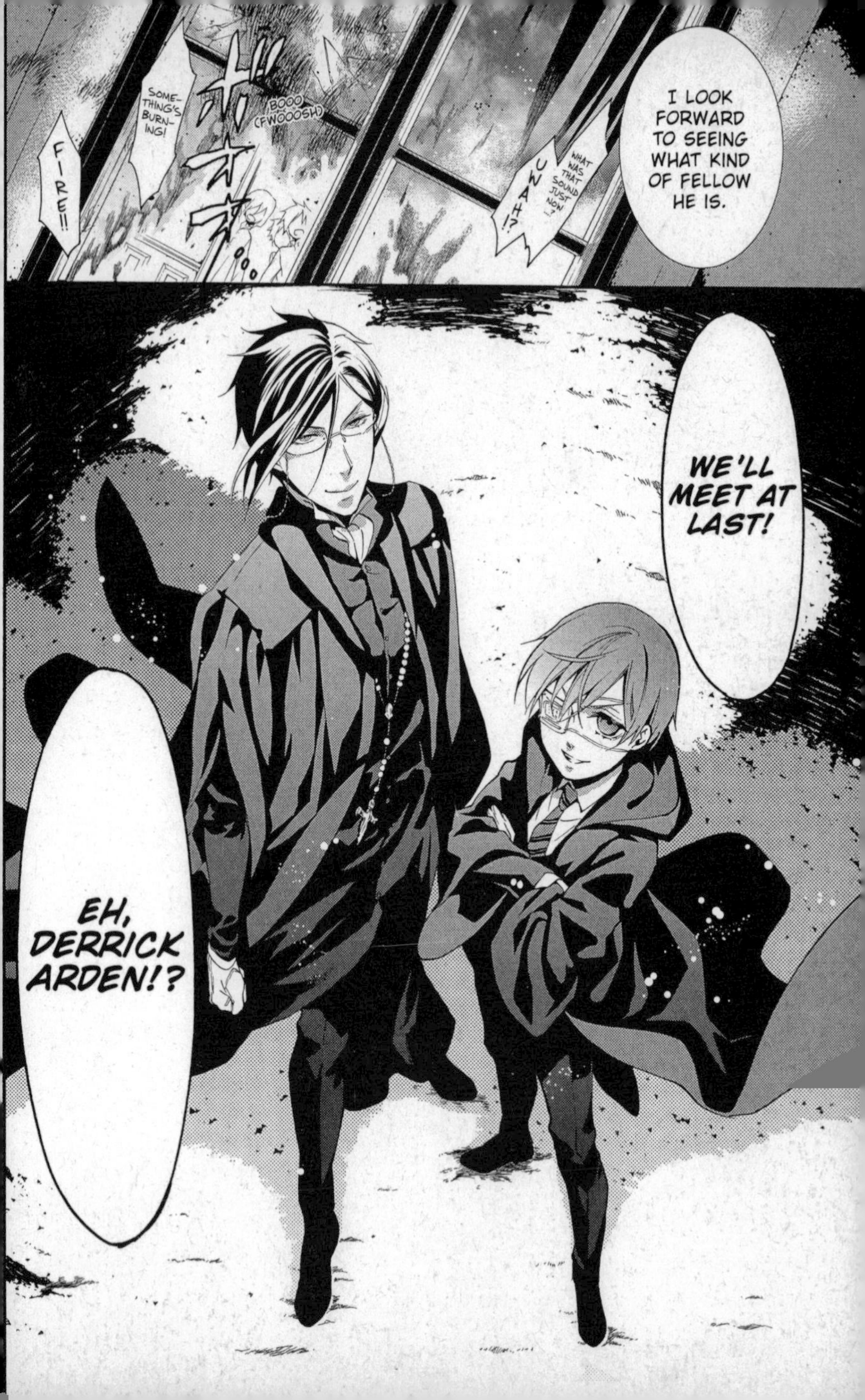
I LOOK FORWARD TO SEEING WHAT KIND OF FELLOW HE IS.
WHAT WAS THAT SOUND JUST NOW...?
UWAH!?
BOOO (FWOOOSH)
SOME-THING'S BURN-ING!
FIRE!!
WE'LL MEET AT LAST!
EH, DERRICK ARDEN!?

Black Butler

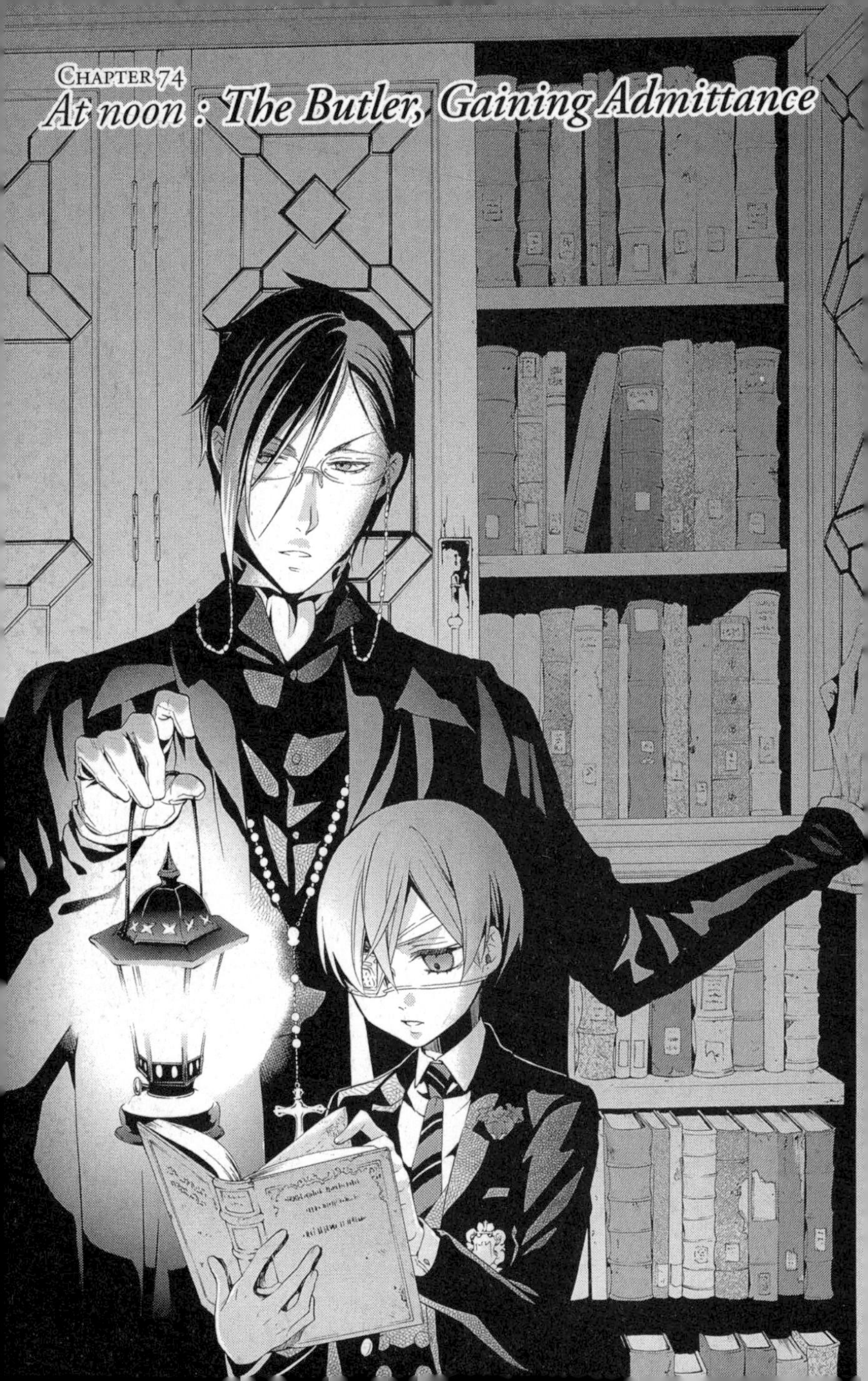
Chapter 74
At noon : The Butler, Gaining Admittance

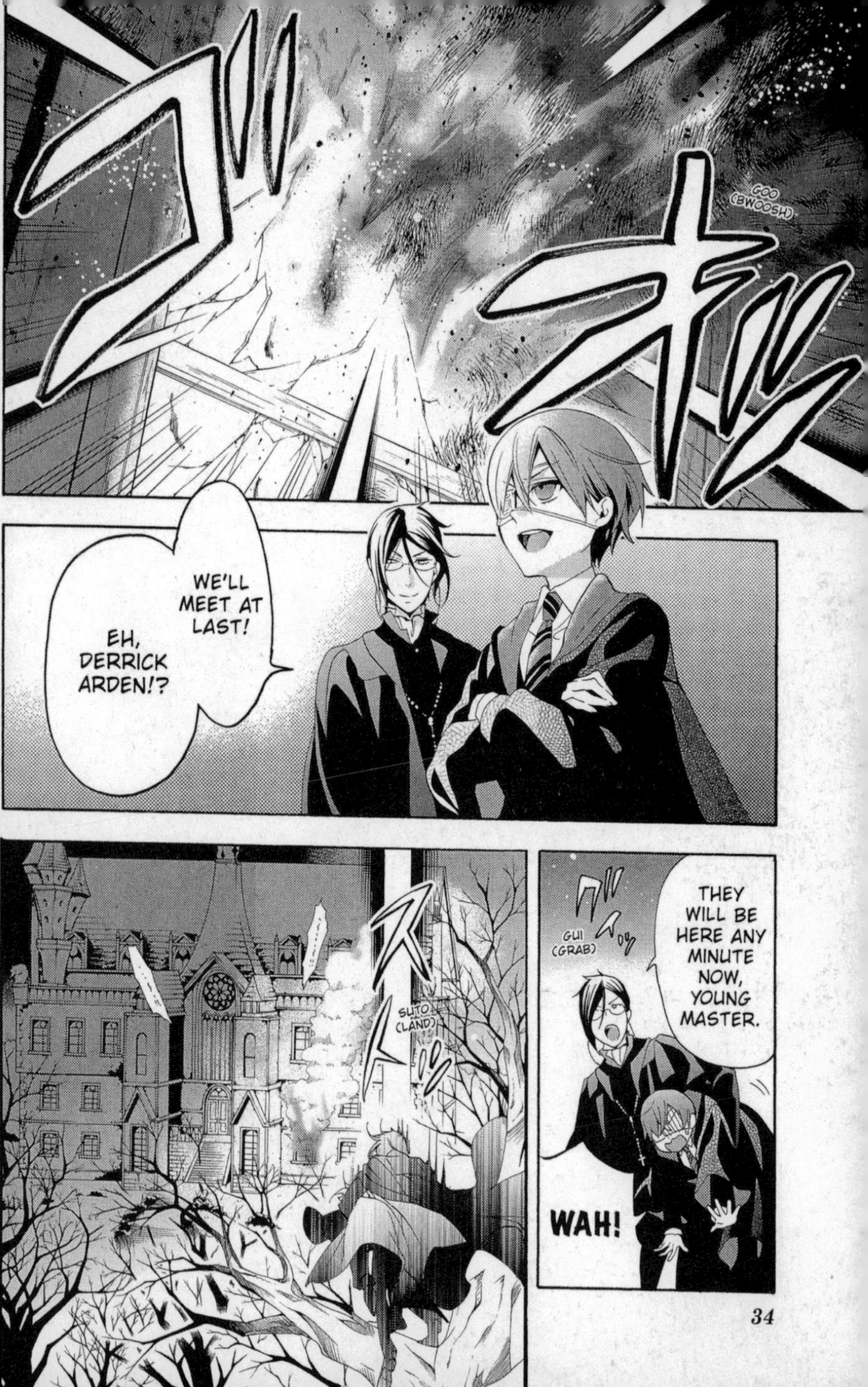
GOO (BWOOSH)
WE'LL MEET AT LAST! EH, DERRICK ARDEN!?
GUI (GRAB)
THEY WILL BE HERE ANY MINUTE NOW, YOUNG MASTER.
WAH!
SUTO (LAND)

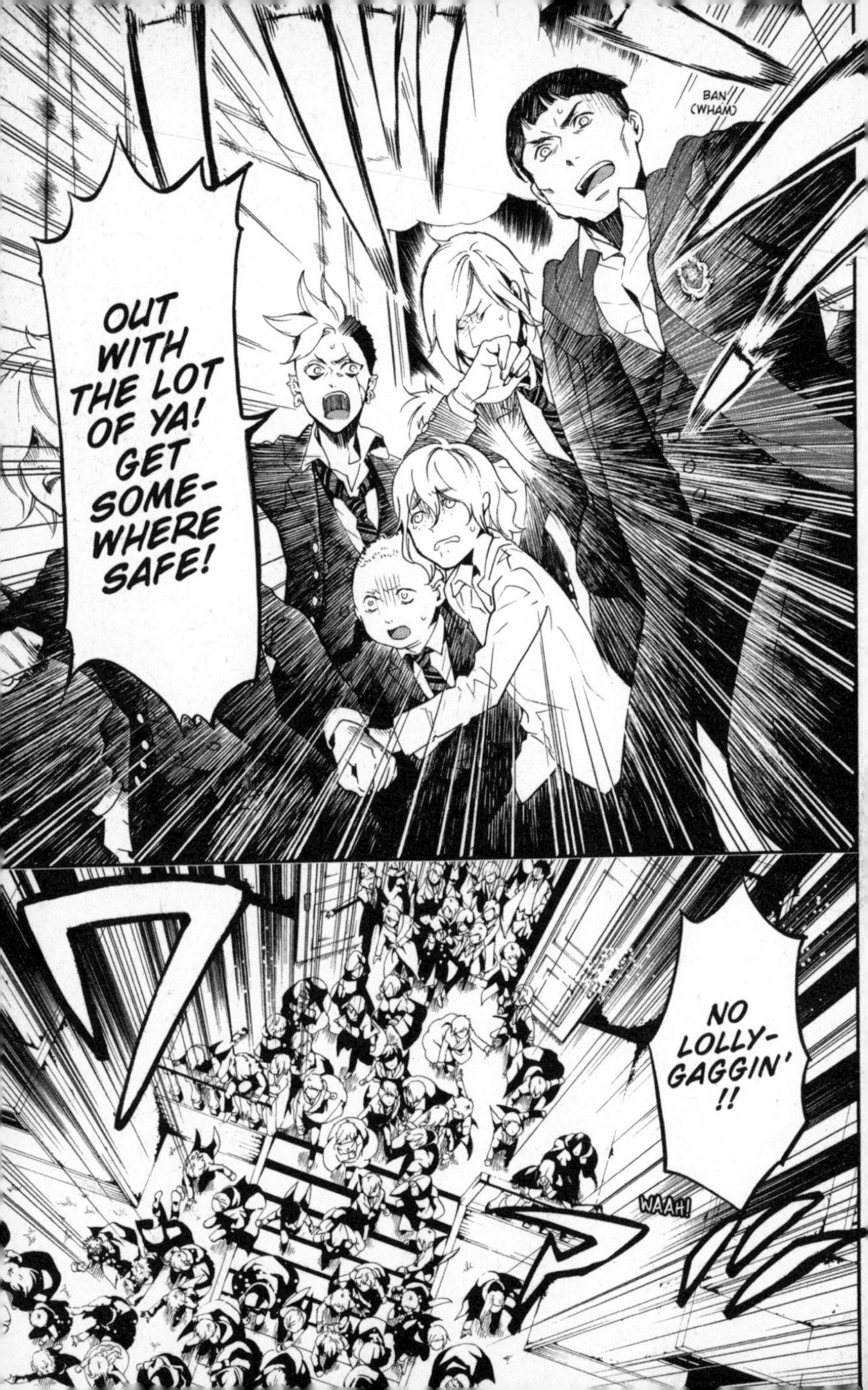
BAN (WHAM)
OUT WITH THE LOT OF YA! GET SOME-WHERE SAFE!
NO LOLLY-GAGGIN' !!
WAAH!

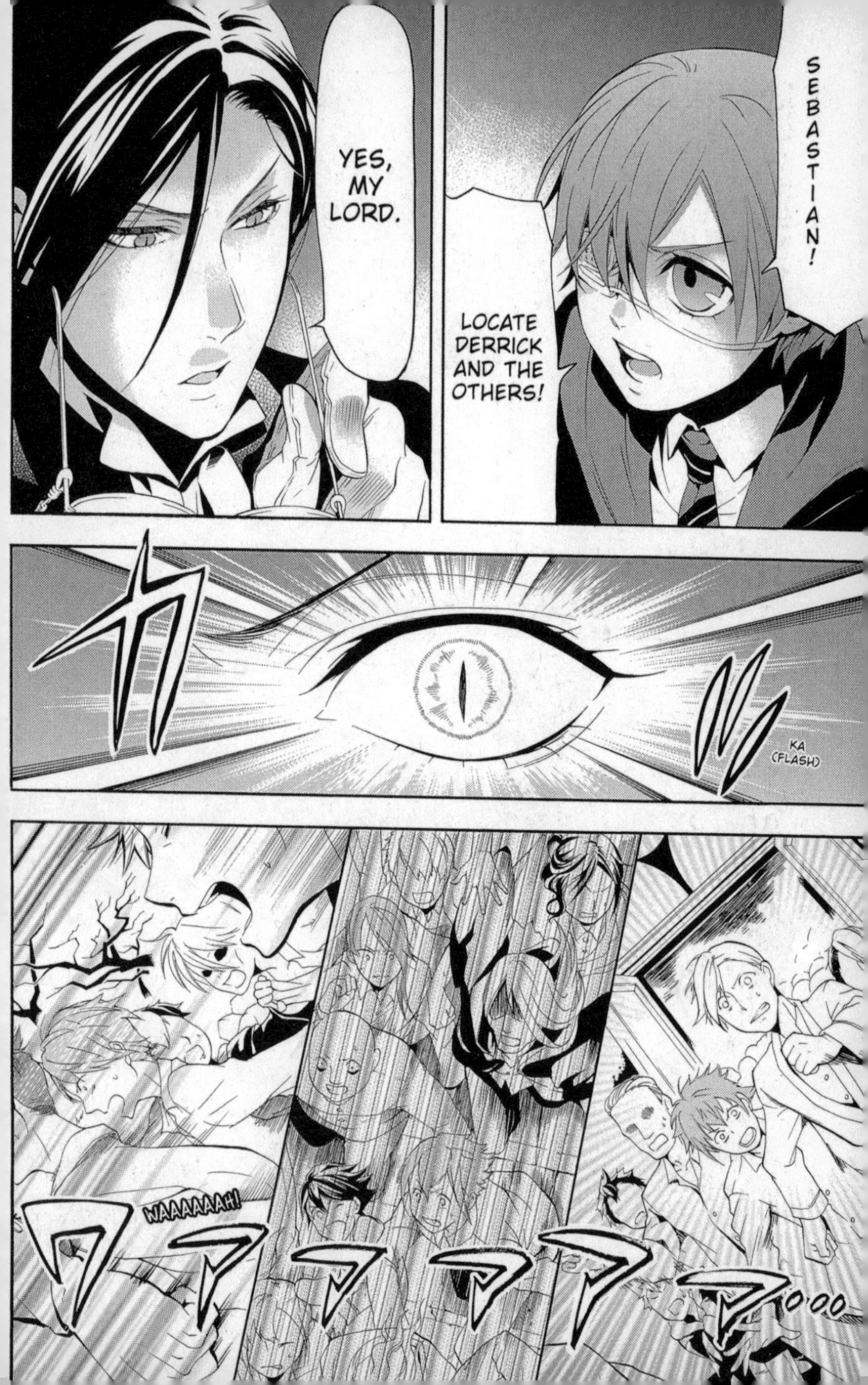
SEBASTIAN!
LOCATE DERRICK AND THE OTHERS!
YES, MY LORD.
KA (FLASH)
WAAAAAAH!

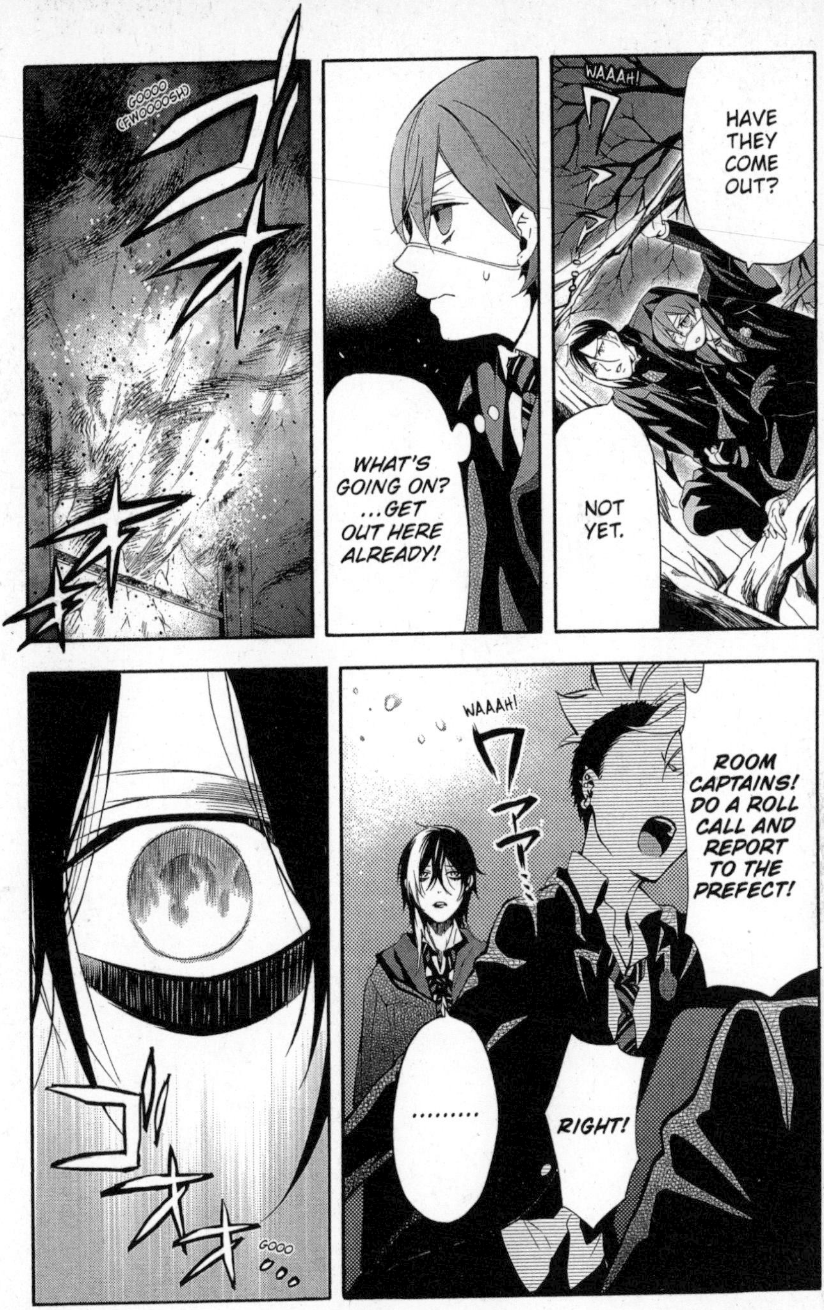
WAAAH!
HAVE THEY COME OUT?
NOT YET.
WHAT'S GOING ON? ...GET OUT HERE ALREADY!
GOOOO (FWOOOOSH)
WAAAH!
ROOM CAPTAINS! DO A ROLL CALL AND REPORT TO THE PREFECT!
RIGHT!
....
GOOOOOO

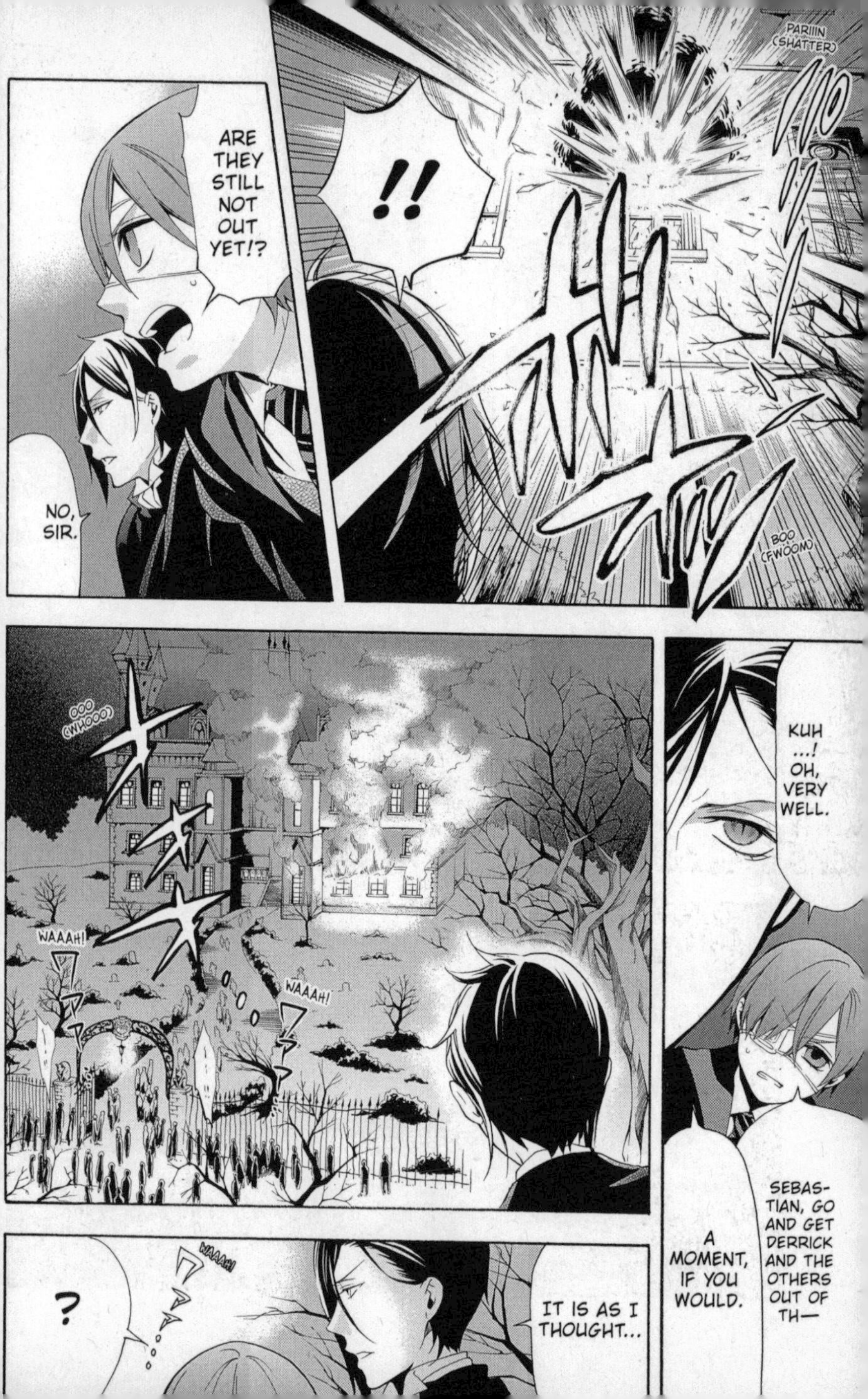
PARIIN (SHATTER)
BOO (FWOOM)
!!
ARE THEY STILL NOT OUT YET!?
NO, SIR.
KUH ...! OH, VERY WELL.
SEBASTIAN, GO AND GET DERRICK AND THE OTHERS OUT OF TH—
A MOMENT, IF YOU WOULD.
OOO (WHOOO)
WAAAH!
WAAAH!
WAAAH!
IT IS AS I THOUGHT...
?

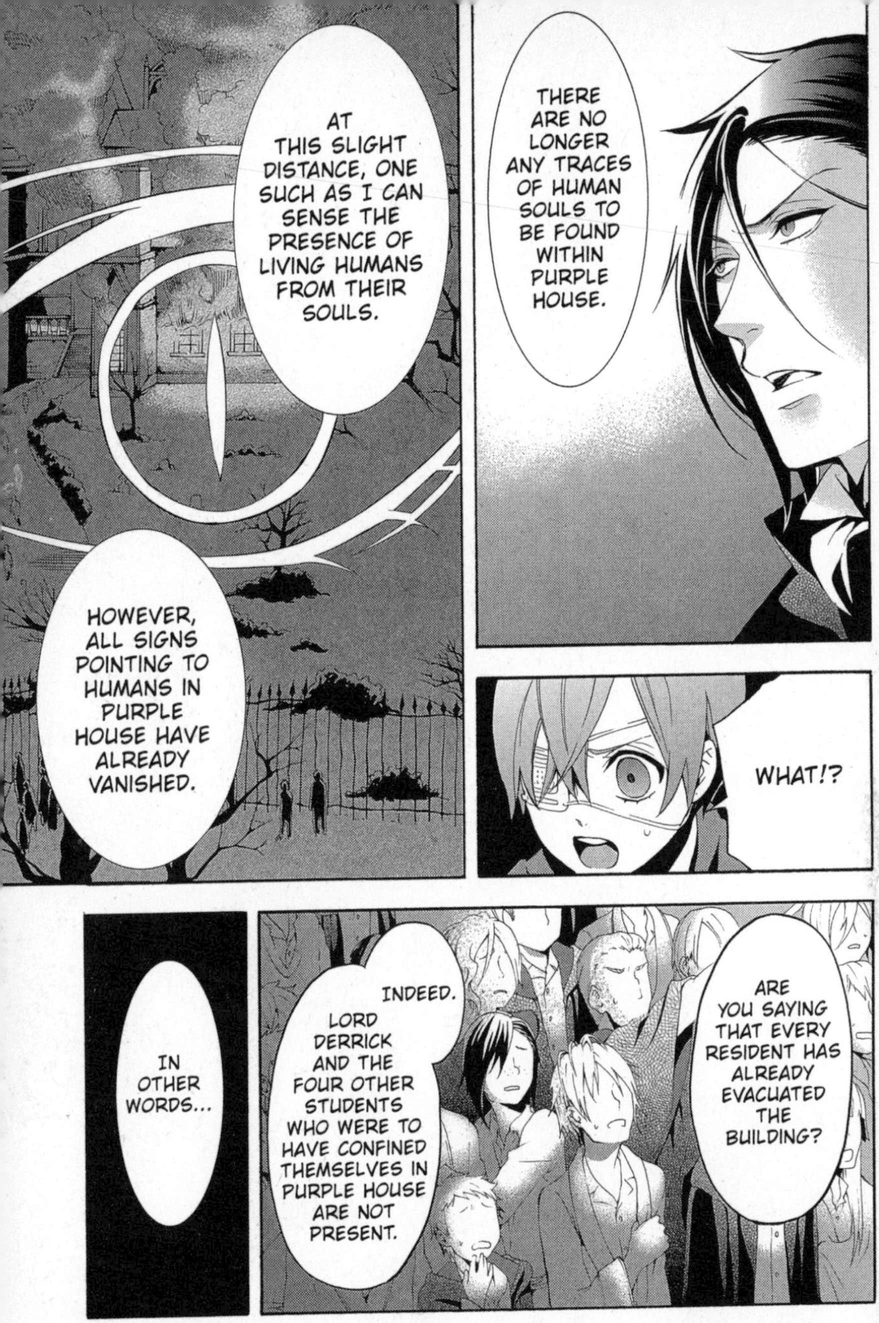
THERE ARE NO LONGER ANY TRACES OF HUMAN SOULS TO BE FOUND WITHIN PURPLE HOUSE.
WHAT!?
AT THIS SLIGHT DISTANCE, ONE SUCH AS I CAN SENSE THE PRESENCE OF LIVING HUMANS FROM THEIR SOULS.
HOWEVER, ALL SIGNS POINTING TO HUMANS IN PURPLE HOUSE HAVE ALREADY VANISHED.
ARE YOU SAYING THAT EVERY RESIDENT HAS ALREADY EVACUATED THE BUILDING?
INDEED.
LORD DERRICK AND THE FOUR OTHER STUDENTS WHO WERE TO HAVE CONFINED THEMSELVES IN PURPLE HOUSE ARE NOT PRESENT.
IN OTHER WORDS...

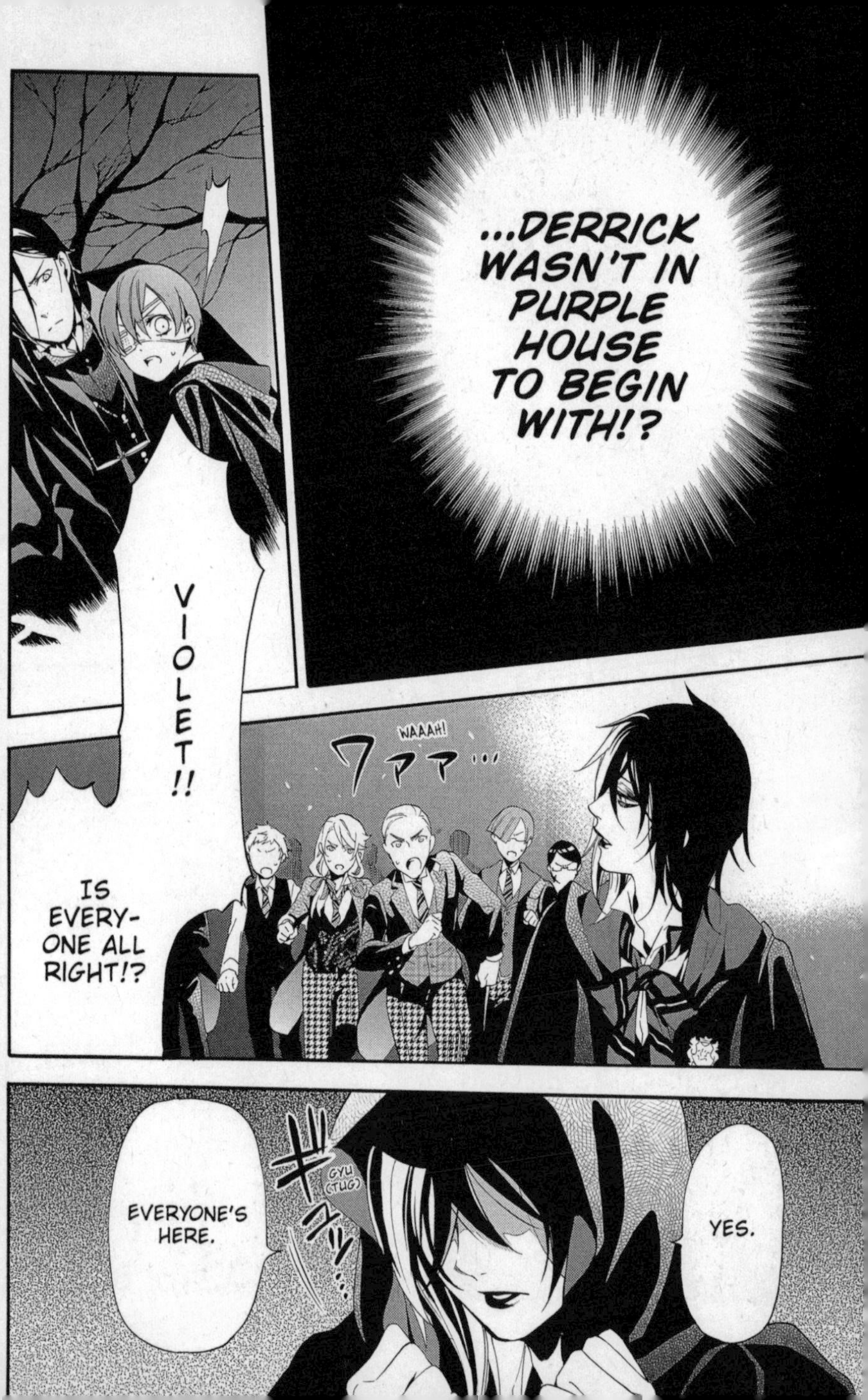

...DERRICK WASN'T IN PURPLE HOUSE TO BEGIN WITH!?
VIOLET!!
WAAAH!
IS EVERY-ONE ALL RIGHT!?
YES.
GYU (TUG)
EVERYONE'S HERE.

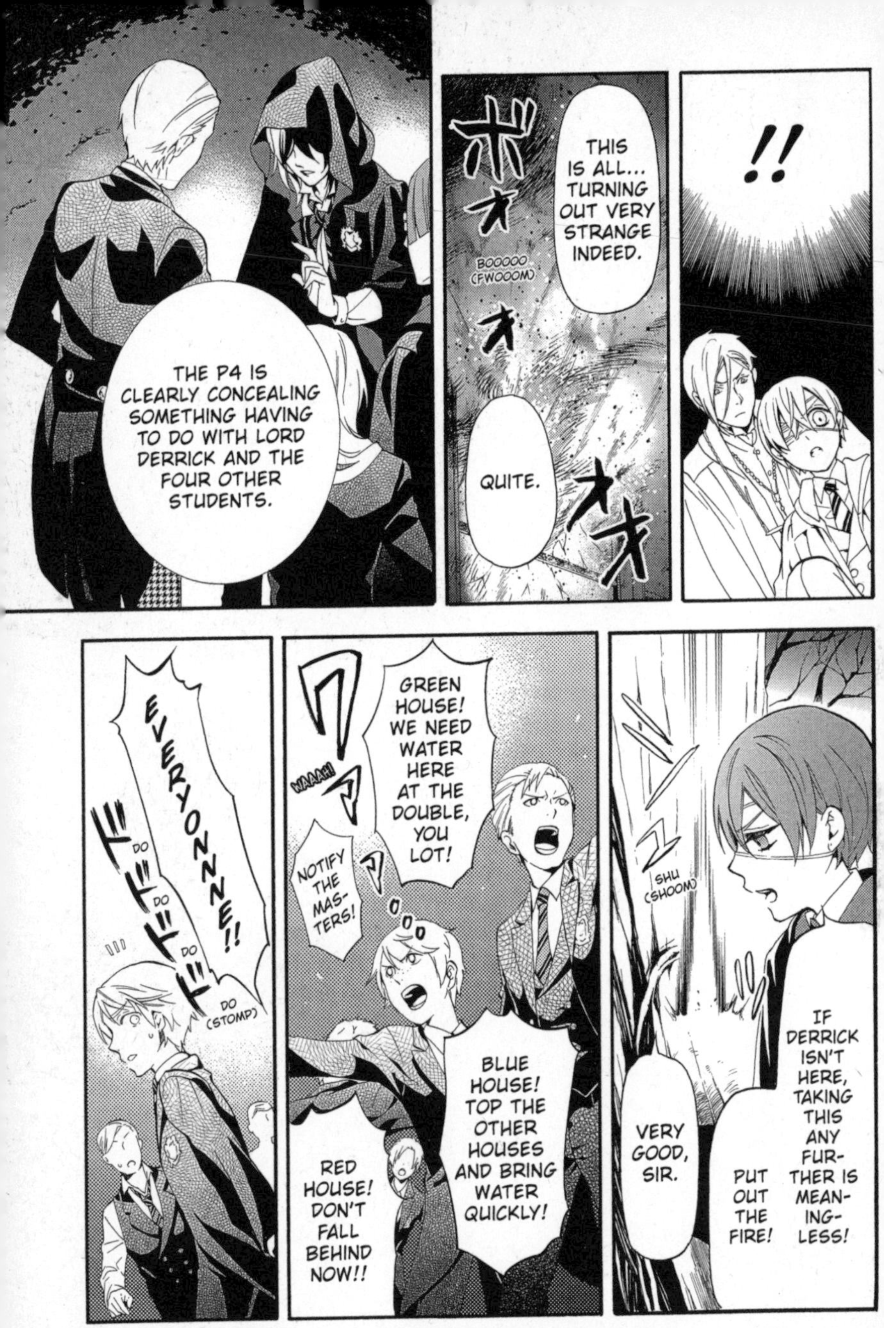
!!
THIS IS ALL... TURNING OUT VERY STRANGE INDEED.
BOOOOO (FWOOOM)
QUITE.
THE P4 IS CLEARLY CONCEALING SOMETHING HAVING TO DO WITH LORD DERRICK AND THE FOUR OTHER STUDENTS.
SHU (SHOOM)
IF DERRICK ISN'T HERE, TAKING THIS ANY FURTHER IS MEANINGLESS!
PUT OUT THE FIRE!
VERY GOOD, SIR.
GREEN HOUSE! WE NEED WATER HERE AT THE DOUBLE, YOU LOT!
WAAAH!
NOTIFY THE MASTERS!
BLUE HOUSE! TOP THE OTHER HOUSES AND BRING WATER QUICKLY!
RED HOUSE! DON'T FALL BEHIND NOW!!
EVERYONNNE!!
DO DO DO DO (STOMP)

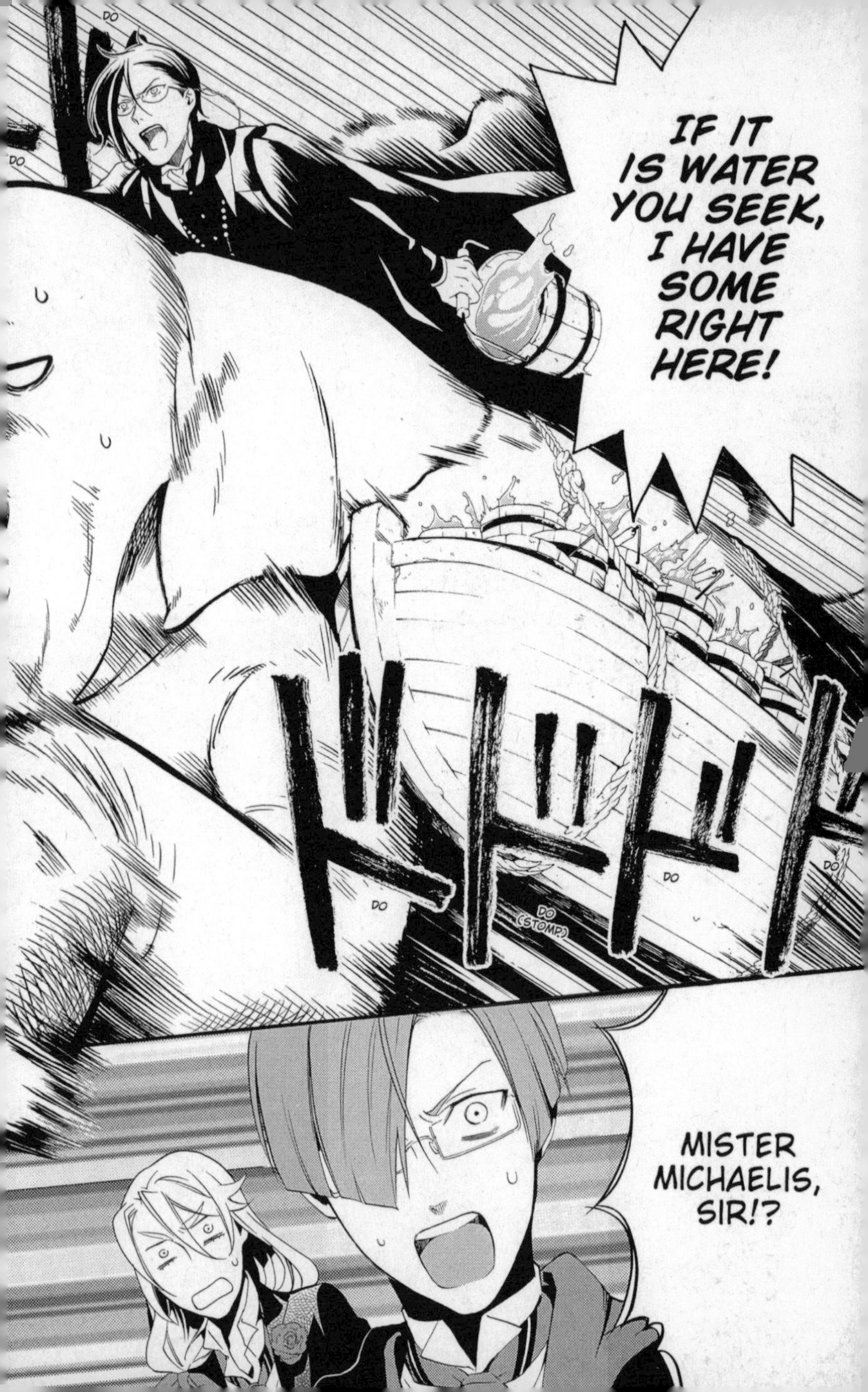
IF IT IS WATER YOU SEEK, I HAVE SOME RIGHT HERE!
DO
DO
DO
DO
DO
DO (STOMP)
MISTER MICHAELIS, SIR!?

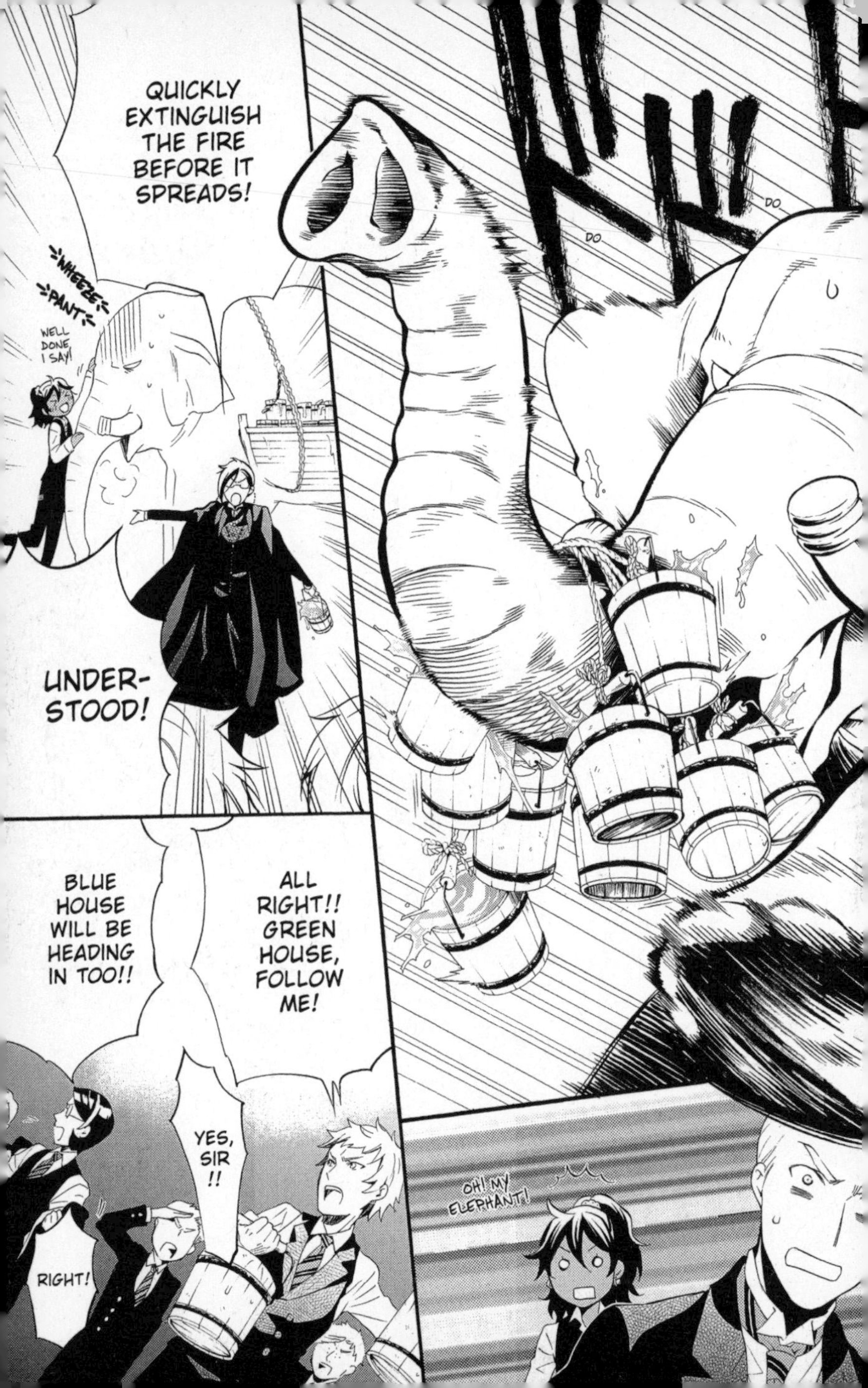

DO
DO
QUICKLY EXTINGUISH THE FIRE BEFORE IT SPREADS!
WHEEZE
PANT
WELL DONE I SAY!
UNDER-STOOD!
OH! MY ELEPHANT!
ALL RIGHT!! GREEN HOUSE, FOLLOW ME!
BLUE HOUSE WILL BE HEADING IN TOO!!
YES, SIR!!
RIGHT!

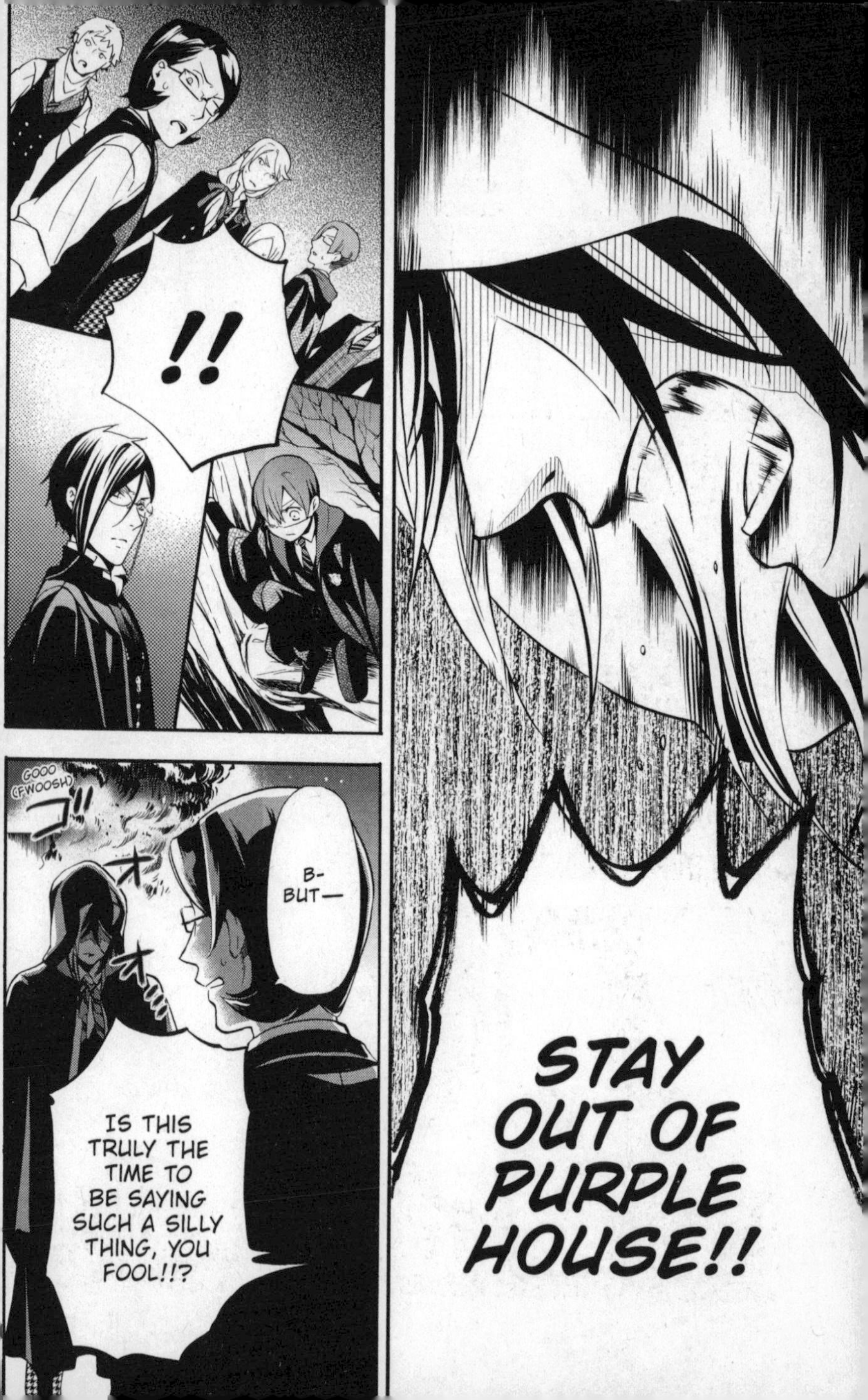
STAY OUT OF PURPLE HOUSE!!
!!
B-BUT—
GOOO (FWOOSH)
IS THIS TRULY THE TIME TO BE SAYING SUCH A SILLY THING, YOU FOOL!!?

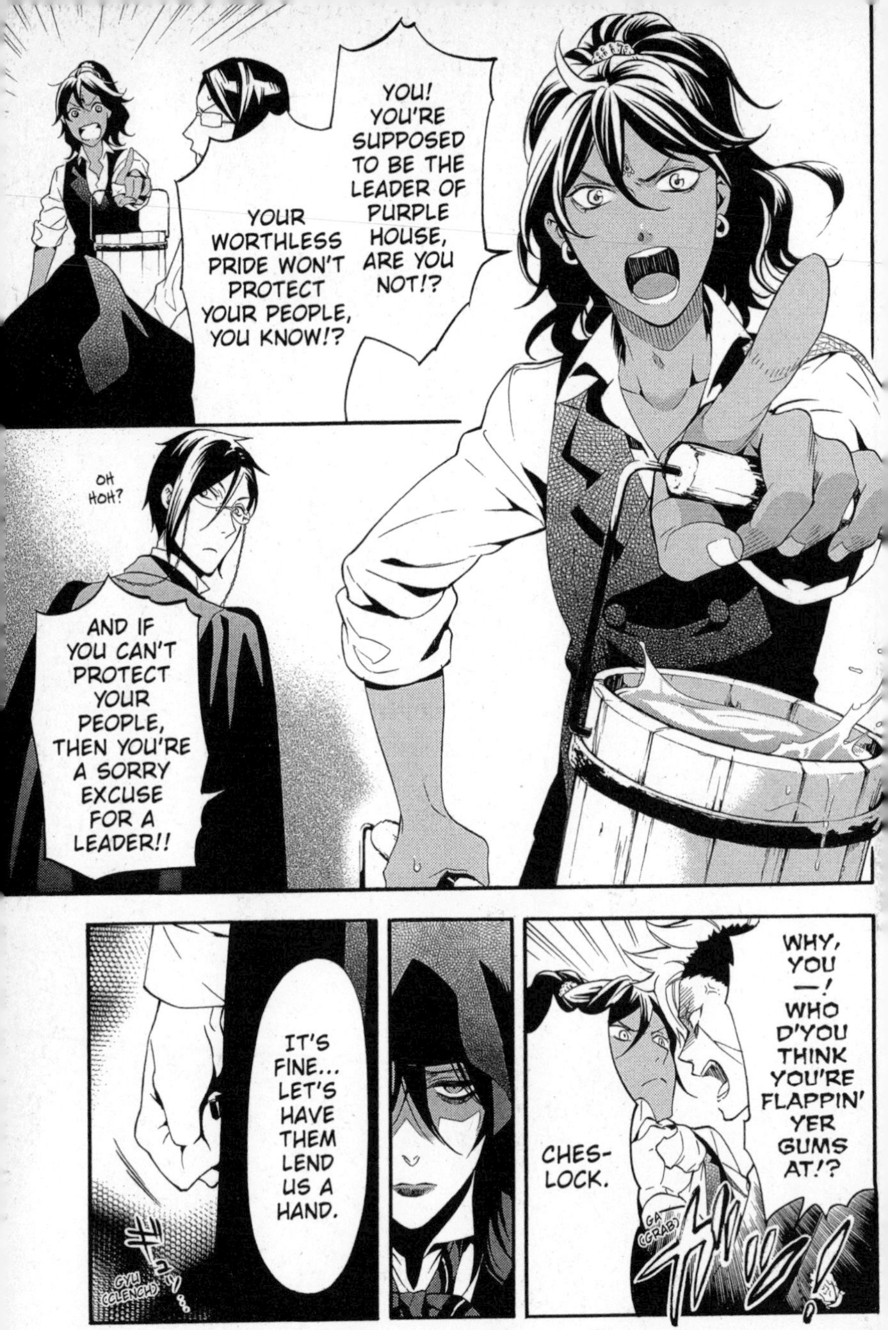
YOU! YOU'RE SUPPOSED TO BE THE LEADER OF PURPLE HOUSE, ARE YOU NOT!?
YOUR WORTHLESS PRIDE WON'T PROTECT YOUR PEOPLE, YOU KNOW!?
OH HOH?
AND IF YOU CAN'T PROTECT YOUR PEOPLE, THEN YOU'RE A SORRY EXCUSE FOR A LEADER!!
WHY, YOU —! WHO D'YOU THINK YOU'RE FLAPPIN' YER GUMS AT!?
CHES-LOCK.
GA (GRAB)
IT'S FINE... LET'S HAVE THEM LEND US A HAND.
GYU (CLENCH)

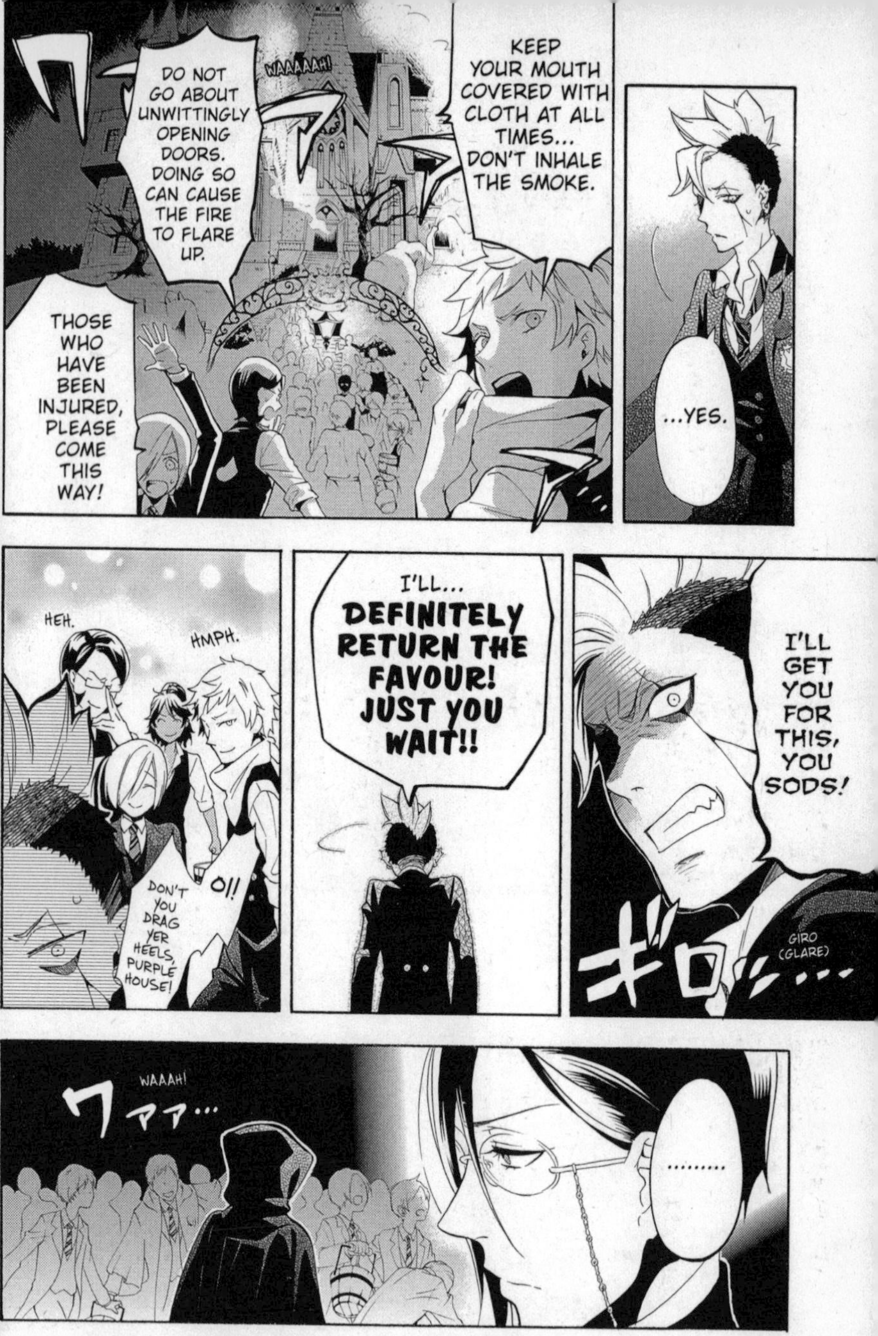
...YES.
KEEP YOUR MOUTH COVERED WITH CLOTH AT ALL TIMES... DON'T INHALE THE SMOKE.
WAAAAAH!
DO NOT GO ABOUT UNWITTINGLY OPENING DOORS. DOING SO CAN CAUSE THE FIRE TO FLARE UP.
THOSE WHO HAVE BEEN INJURED, PLEASE COME THIS WAY!
I'LL GET YOU FOR THIS, YOU SODS!
GIRO (GLARE)
I'LL... DEFINITELY RETURN THE FAVOUR! JUST YOU WAIT!!
HMPH.
HEH.
OI!
DON'T YOU DRAG YER HEELS, PURPLE HOUSE!
....
WAAAH!

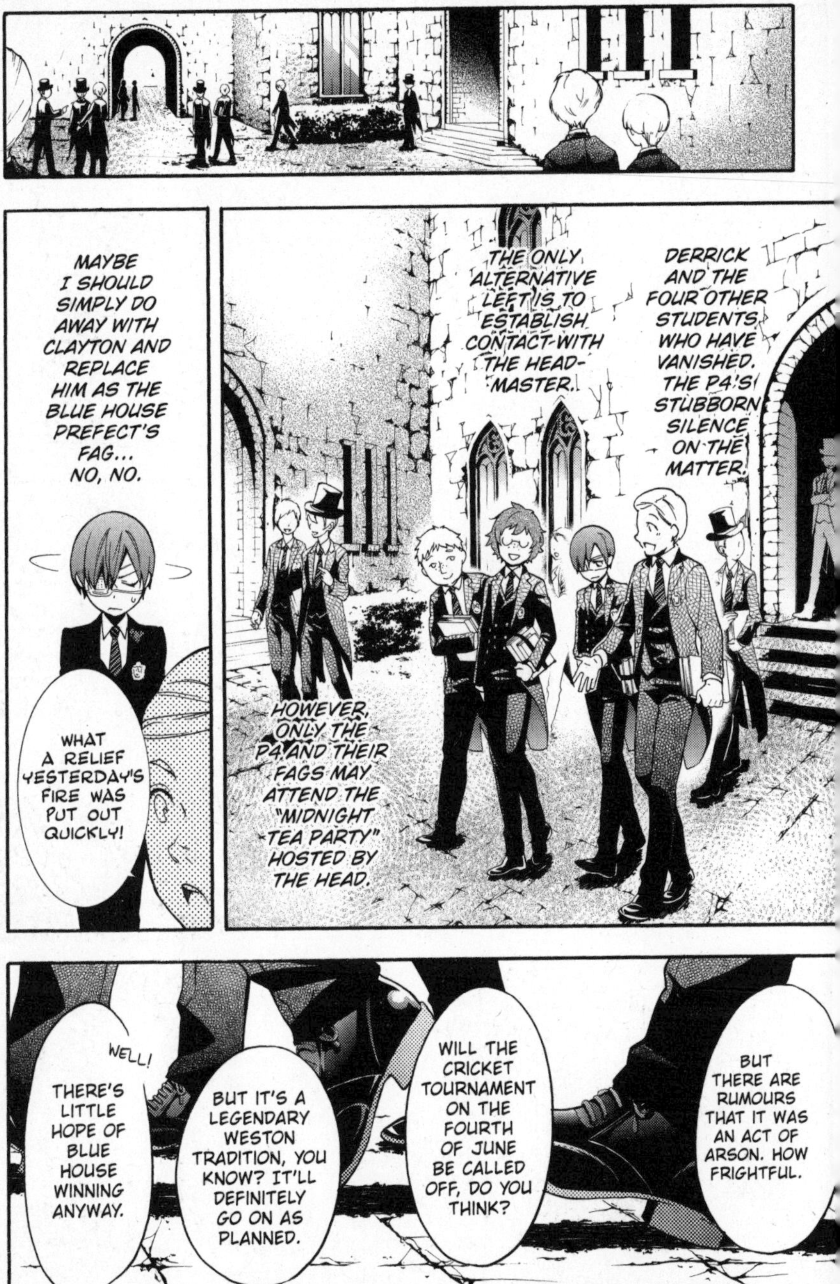
DERRICK AND THE FOUR OTHER STUDENTS WHO HAVE VANISHED. THE P4'S STUBBORN SILENCE ON THE MATTER.
THE ONLY ALTERNATIVE LEFT IS TO ESTABLISH CONTACT WITH THE HEAD-MASTER.
HOWEVER, ONLY THE P4 AND THEIR FAGS MAY ATTEND THE "MIDNIGHT TEA PARTY" HOSTED BY THE HEAD.
MAYBE I SHOULD SIMPLY DO AWAY WITH CLAYTON AND REPLACE HIM AS THE BLUE HOUSE PREFECT'S FAG... NO, NO.
WHAT A RELIEF YESTERDAY'S FIRE WAS PUT OUT QUICKLY!
BUT THERE ARE RUMOURS THAT IT WAS AN ACT OF ARSON. HOW FRIGHTFUL.
WILL THE CRICKET TOURNAMENT ON THE FOURTH OF JUNE BE CALLED OFF, DO YOU THINK?
BUT IT'S A LEGENDARY WESTON TRADITION, YOU KNOW? IT'LL DEFINITELY GO ON AS PLANNED.
WELL!
THERE'S LITTLE HOPE OF BLUE HOUSE WINNING ANYWAY.

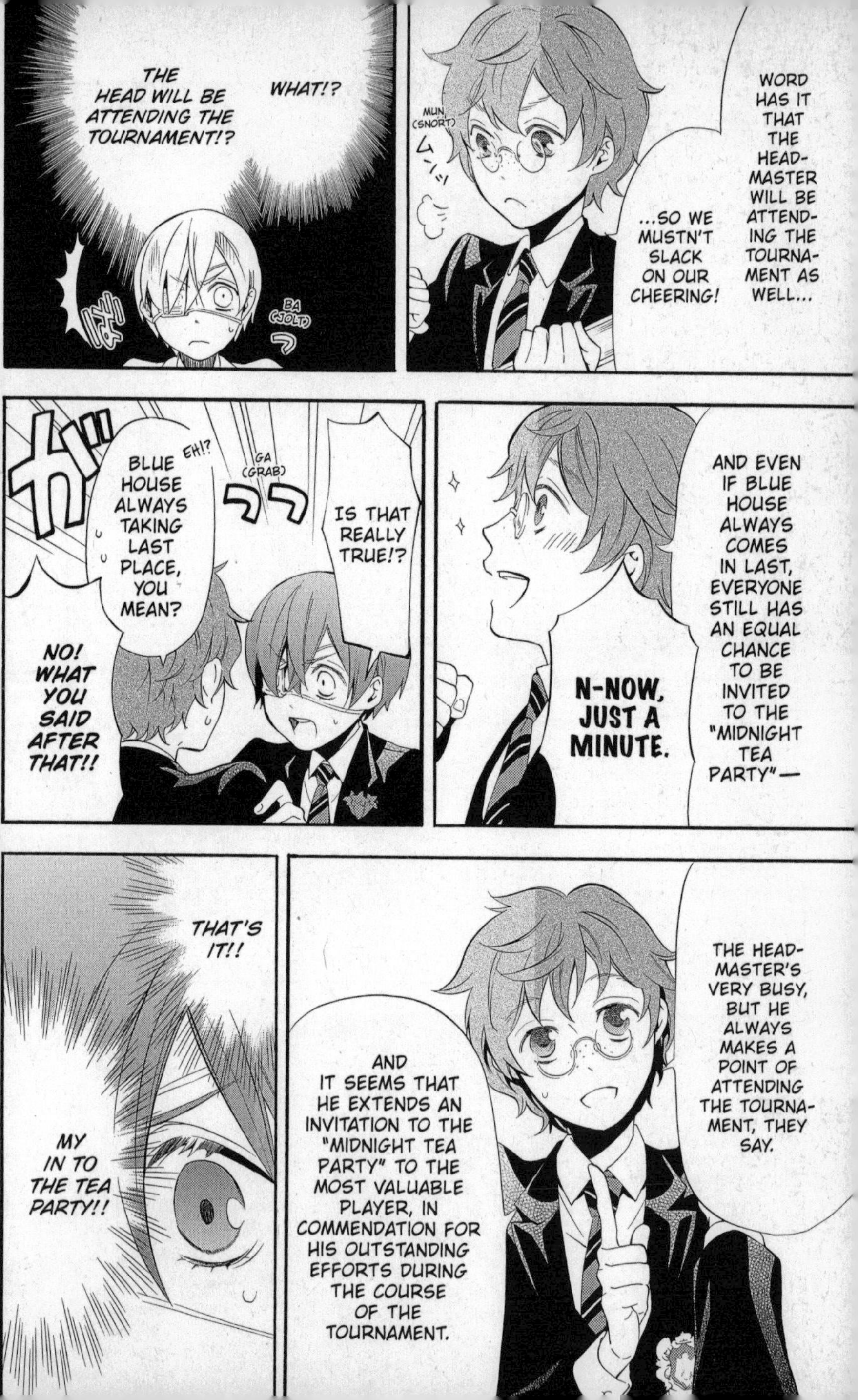
WORD HAS IT THAT THE HEADMASTER WILL BE ATTENDING THE TOURNAMENT AS WELL...
...SO WE MUSTN'T SLACK ON OUR CHEERING!
MUN (SNORT)
WHAT!?
THE HEAD WILL BE ATTENDING THE TOURNAMENT!?
BA (JOLT)
AND EVEN IF BLUE HOUSE ALWAYS COMES IN LAST, EVERYONE STILL HAS AN EQUAL CHANCE TO BE INVITED TO THE "MIDNIGHT TEA PARTY"—
N-NOW, JUST A MINUTE.
IS THAT REALLY TRUE!?
GA (GRAB)
EH!?
BLUE HOUSE ALWAYS TAKING LAST PLACE, YOU MEAN?
NO! WHAT YOU SAID AFTER THAT!!
THE HEADMASTER'S VERY BUSY, BUT HE ALWAYS MAKES A POINT OF ATTENDING THE TOURNAMENT, THEY SAY.
AND IT SEEMS THAT HE EXTENDS AN INVITATION TO THE "MIDNIGHT TEA PARTY" TO THE MOST VALUABLE PLAYER, IN COMMENDATION FOR HIS OUTSTANDING EFFORTS DURING THE COURSE OF THE TOURNAMENT.
THAT'S IT!!
MY IN TO THE TEA PARTY!!

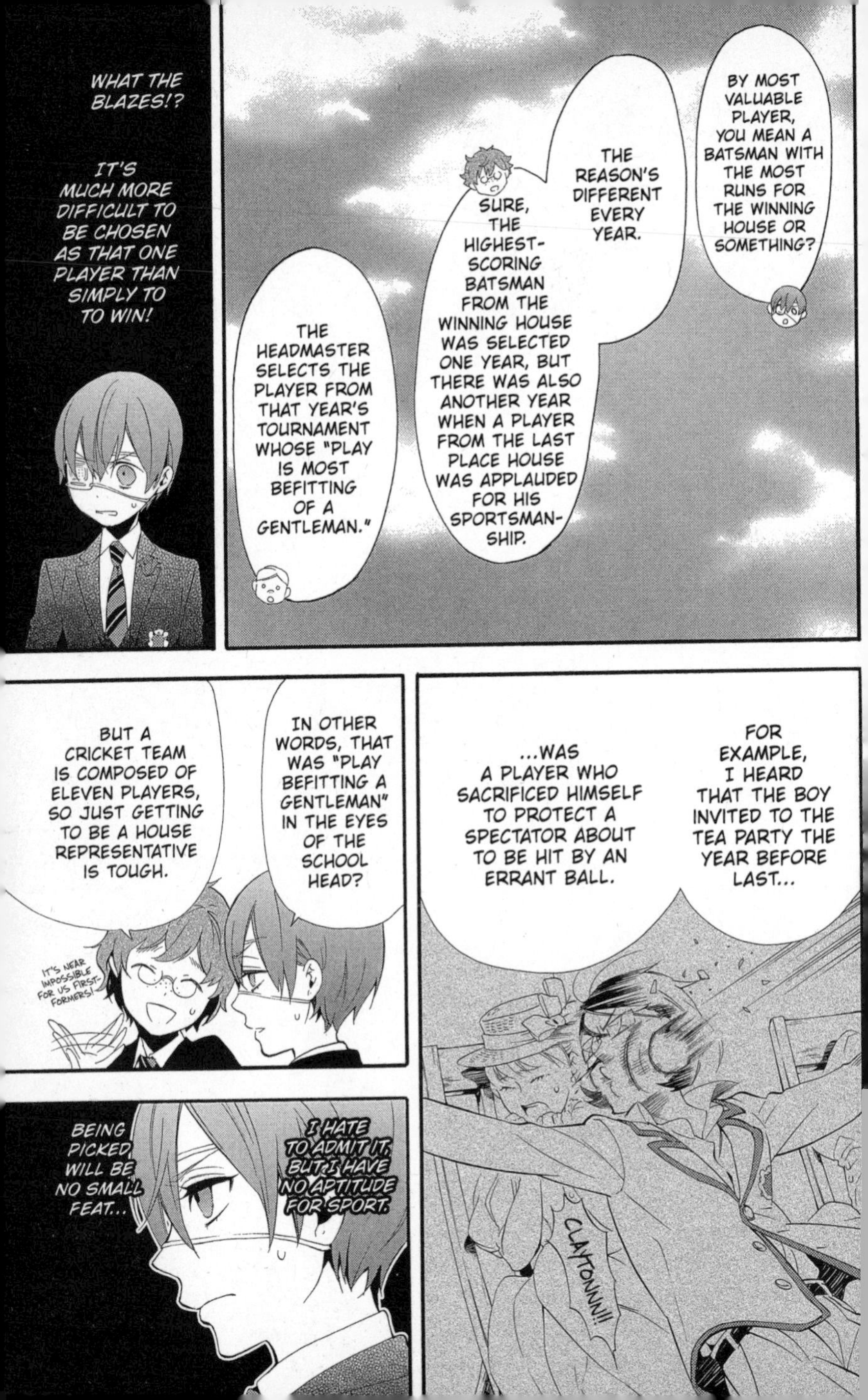

BY MOST VALUABLE PLAYER, YOU MEAN A BATSMAN WITH THE MOST RUNS FOR THE WINNING HOUSE OR SOMETHING?
THE REASON'S DIFFERENT EVERY YEAR.
SURE, THE HIGHEST-SCORING BATSMAN FROM THE WINNING HOUSE WAS SELECTED ONE YEAR, BUT THERE WAS ALSO ANOTHER YEAR WHEN A PLAYER FROM THE LAST PLACE HOUSE WAS APPLAUDED FOR HIS SPORTSMANSHIP.
THE HEADMASTER SELECTS THE PLAYER FROM THAT YEAR'S TOURNAMENT WHOSE "PLAY IS MOST BEFITTING OF A GENTLEMAN."
WHAT THE BLAZES!?
IT'S MUCH MORE DIFFICULT TO BE CHOSEN AS THAT ONE PLAYER THAN SIMPLY TO TO WIN!
FOR EXAMPLE, I HEARD THAT THE BOY INVITED TO THE TEA PARTY THE YEAR BEFORE LAST...
...WAS A PLAYER WHO SACRIFICED HIMSELF TO PROTECT A SPECTATOR ABOUT TO BE HIT BY AN ERRANT BALL.
CLAYTONNN!!
IN OTHER WORDS, THAT WAS "PLAY BEFITTING A GENTLEMAN" IN THE EYES OF THE SCHOOL HEAD?
BUT A CRICKET TEAM IS COMPOSED OF ELEVEN PLAYERS, SO JUST GETTING TO BE A HOUSE REPRESENTATIVE IS TOUGH.
IT'S NEAR IMPOSSIBLE FOR US FIRST-FORMERS!
I HATE TO ADMIT IT, BUT I HAVE NO APTITUDE FOR SPORT.
BEING PICKED WILL BE NO SMALL FEAT...

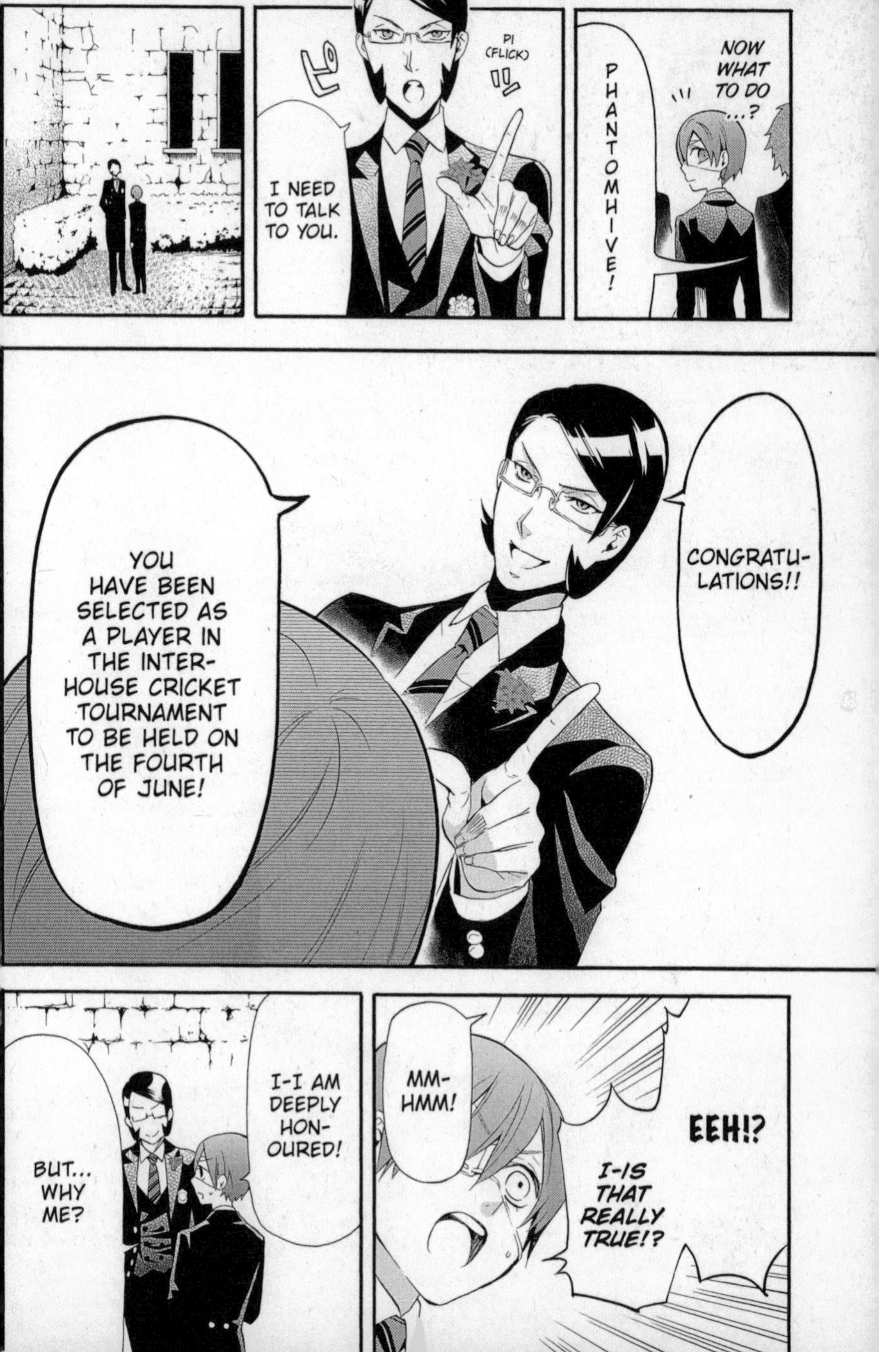
NOW WHAT TO DO...?
PHANTOMHIVE!
PI (FLICK)
I NEED TO TALK TO YOU.
CONGRATULATIONS!!
YOU HAVE BEEN SELECTED AS A PLAYER IN THE INTER-HOUSE CRICKET TOURNAMENT TO BE HELD ON THE FOURTH OF JUNE!
EEH!?
I-IS THAT REALLY TRUE!?
MM-HMM!
I-I AM DEEPLY HON-OURED!
BUT... WHY ME?

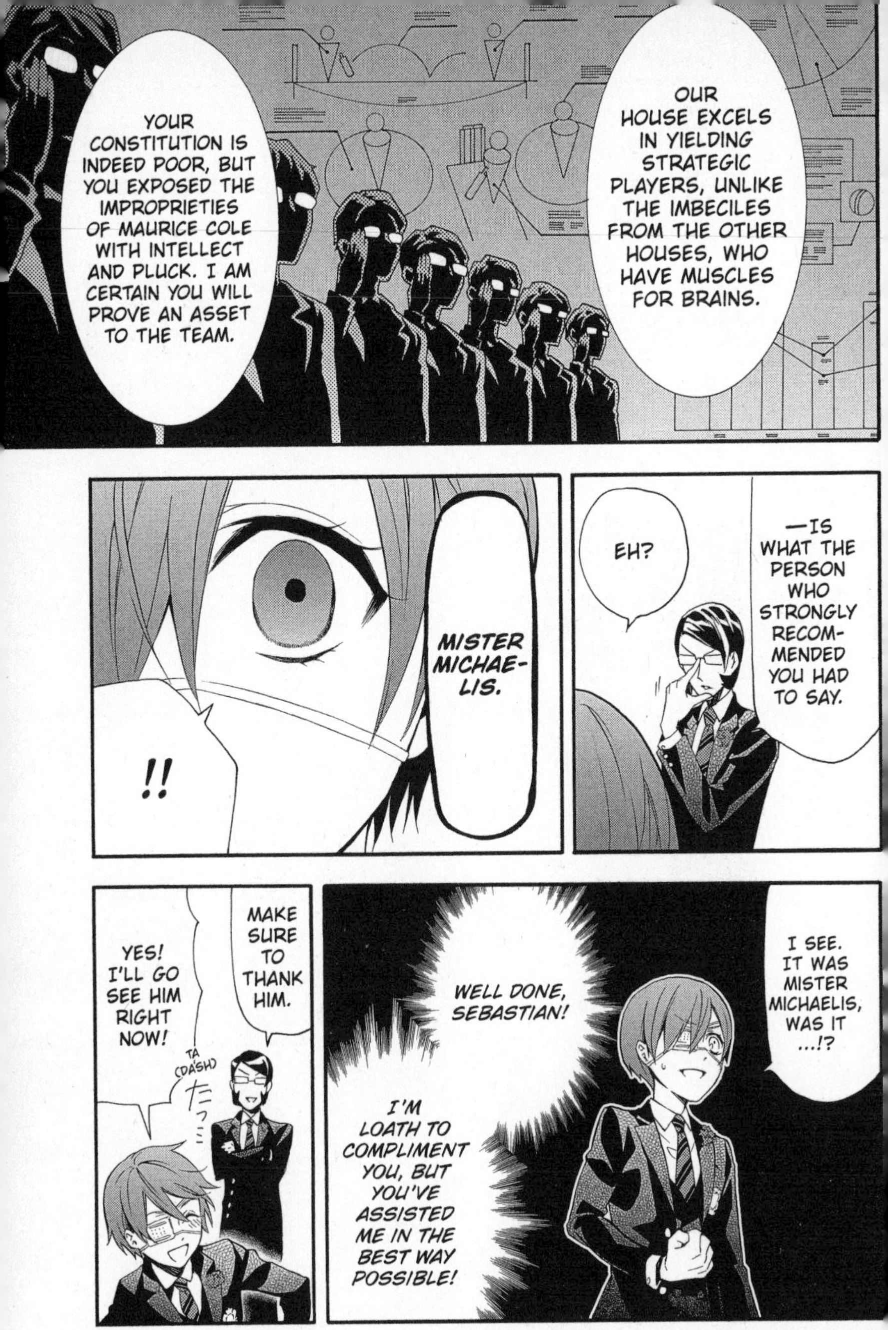
OUR HOUSE EXCELS IN YIELDING STRATEGIC PLAYERS, UNLIKE THE IMBECILES FROM THE OTHER HOUSES, WHO HAVE MUSCLES FOR BRAINS.
YOUR CONSTITUTION IS INDEED POOR, BUT YOU EXPOSED THE IMPROPRIETIES OF MAURICE COLE WITH INTELLECT AND PLUCK. I AM CERTAIN YOU WILL PROVE AN ASSET TO THE TEAM.
—IS WHAT THE PERSON WHO STRONGLY RECOM-MENDED YOU HAD TO SAY.
EH?
MISTER MICHAE-LIS.
!!
I SEE. IT WAS MISTER MICHAELIS, WAS IT ...!?
WELL DONE, SEBASTIAN!
I'M LOATH TO COMPLIMENT YOU, BUT YOU'VE ASSISTED ME IN THE BEST WAY POSSIBLE!
MAKE SURE TO THANK HIM.
YES! I'LL GO SEE HIM RIGHT NOW!
TA (DASH)

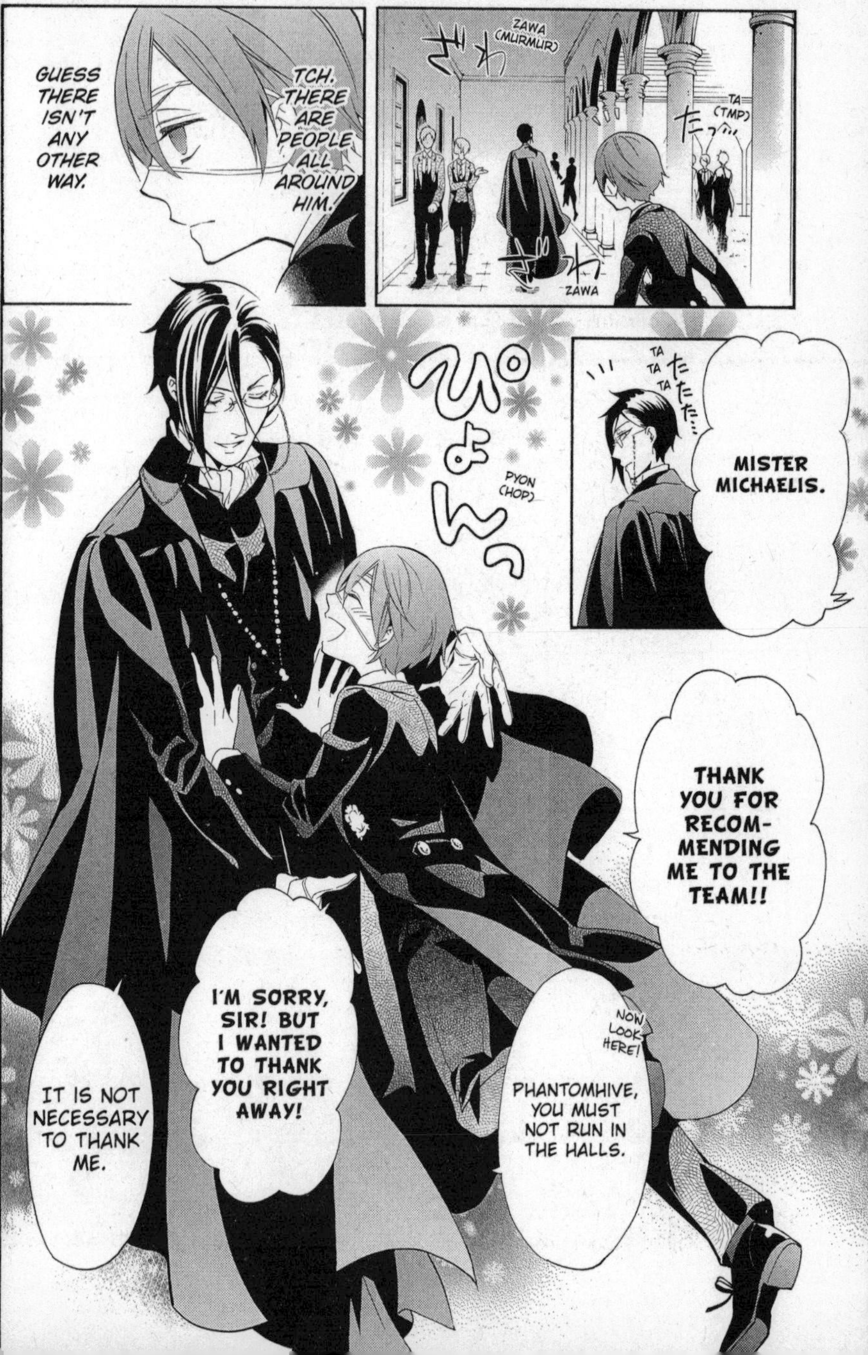
ZAWA (MURMUR)
TA (TMP)
ZAWA
TCH. THERE ARE PEOPLE ALL AROUND HIM!
GUESS THERE ISN'T ANY OTHER WAY.
TA TA TA
MISTER MICHAELIS.
PYON (HOP)
THANK YOU FOR RECOMMENDING ME TO THE TEAM!!
NOW LOOK HERE!
PHANTOMHIVE, YOU MUST NOT RUN IN THE HALLS.
I'M SORRY, SIR! BUT I WANTED TO THANK YOU RIGHT AWAY!
IT IS NOT NECESSARY TO THANK ME.

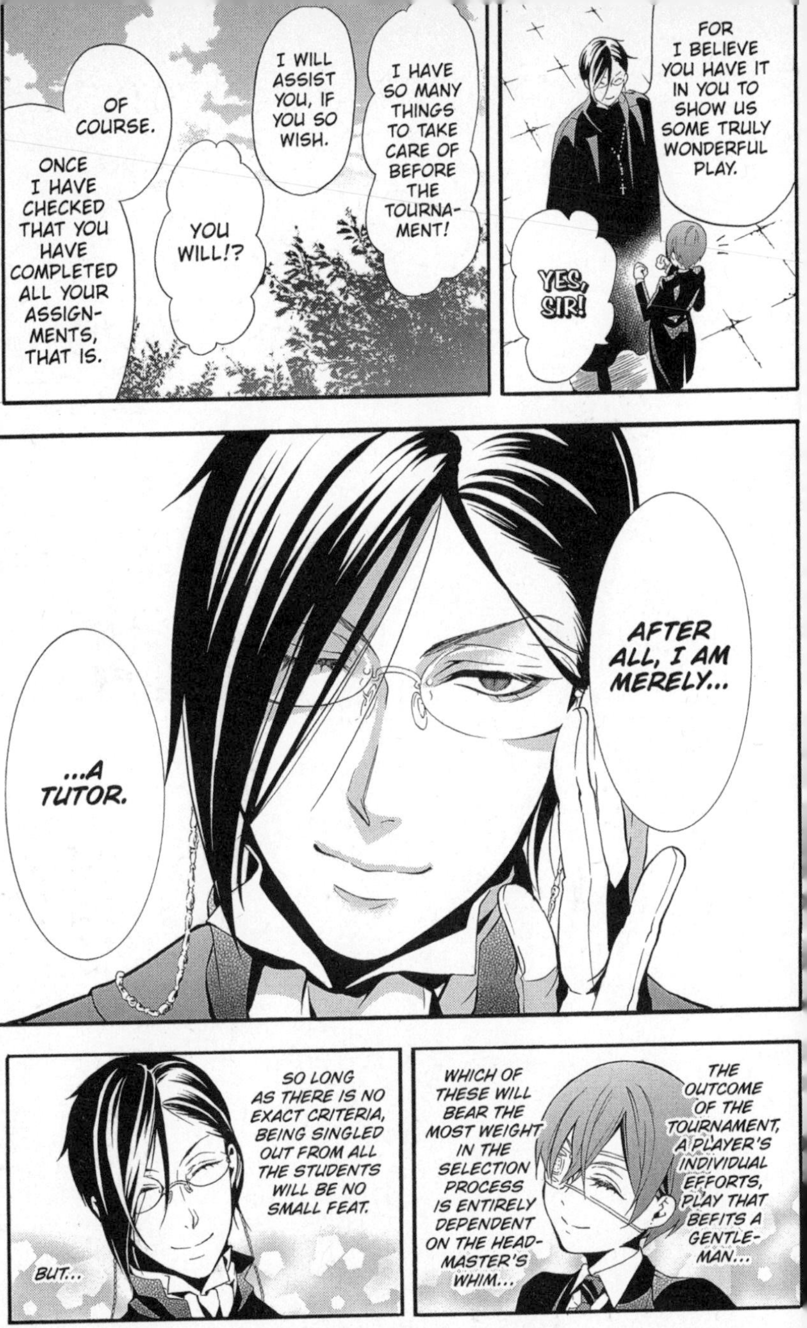
FOR I BELIEVE YOU HAVE IT IN YOU TO SHOW US SOME TRULY WONDERFUL PLAY.
YES, SIR!
I HAVE SO MANY THINGS TO TAKE CARE OF BEFORE THE TOURNAMENT!
I WILL ASSIST YOU, IF YOU SO WISH.
YOU WILL!?
OF COURSE.
ONCE I HAVE CHECKED THAT YOU HAVE COMPLETED ALL YOUR ASSIGNMENTS, THAT IS.
AFTER ALL, I AM MERELY...
...A TUTOR.
THE OUTCOME OF THE TOURNAMENT, A PLAYER'S INDIVIDUAL EFFORTS, PLAY THAT BEFITS A GENTLEMAN...
WHICH OF THESE WILL BEAR THE MOST WEIGHT IN THE SELECTION PROCESS IS ENTIRELY DEPENDENT ON THE HEADMASTER'S WHIM...
SO LONG AS THERE IS NO EXACT CRITERIA, BEING SINGLED OUT FROM ALL THE STUDENTS WILL BE NO SMALL FEAT.
BUT...

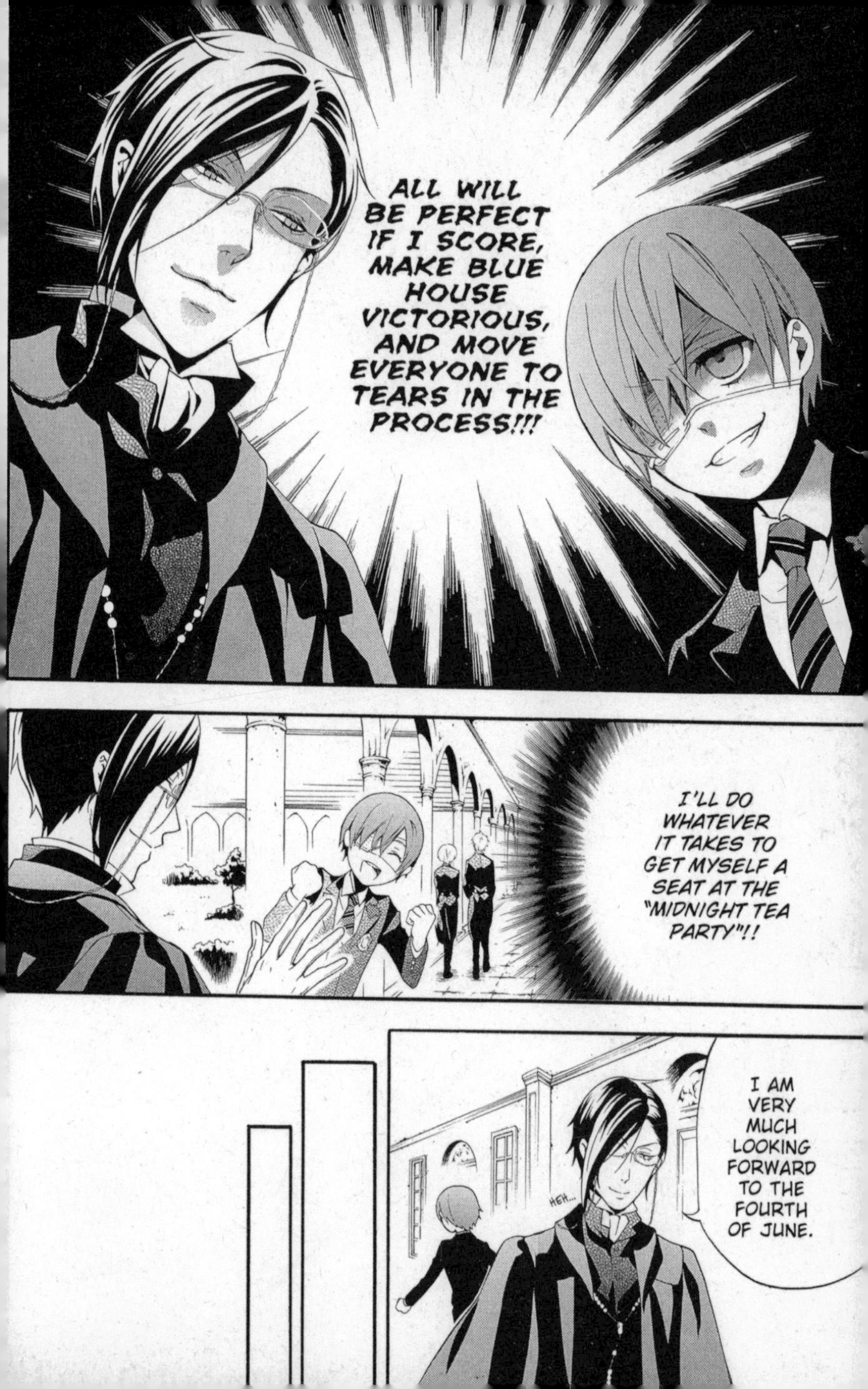
ALL WILL BE PERFECT IF I SCORE, MAKE BLUE HOUSE VICTORIOUS, AND MOVE EVERYONE TO TEARS IN THE PROCESS!!!
I'LL DO WHATEVER IT TAKES TO GET MYSELF A SEAT AT THE "MIDNIGHT TEA PARTY"!!
I AM VERY MUCH LOOKING FORWARD TO THE FOURTH OF JUNE.
HEH...

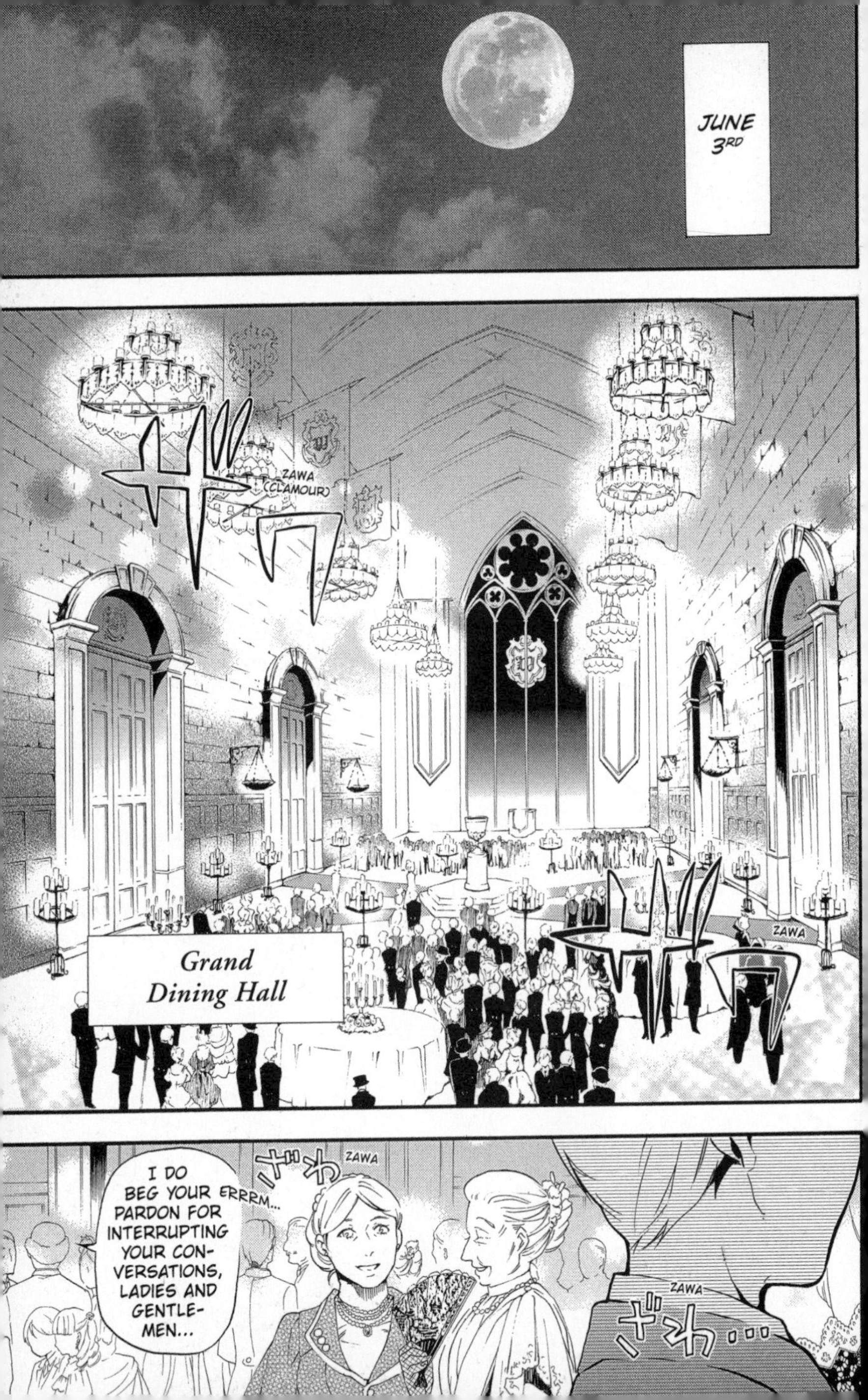

JUNE 3RD
ザワ
ZAWA (CLAMOUR)
ザワ
ZAWA
Grand Dining Hall
ざわ
ZAWA
ERRRM...
I DO BEG YOUR PARDON FOR INTERRUPTING YOUR CONVERSATIONS, LADIES AND GENTLEMEN...
ZAWA
ざわ...

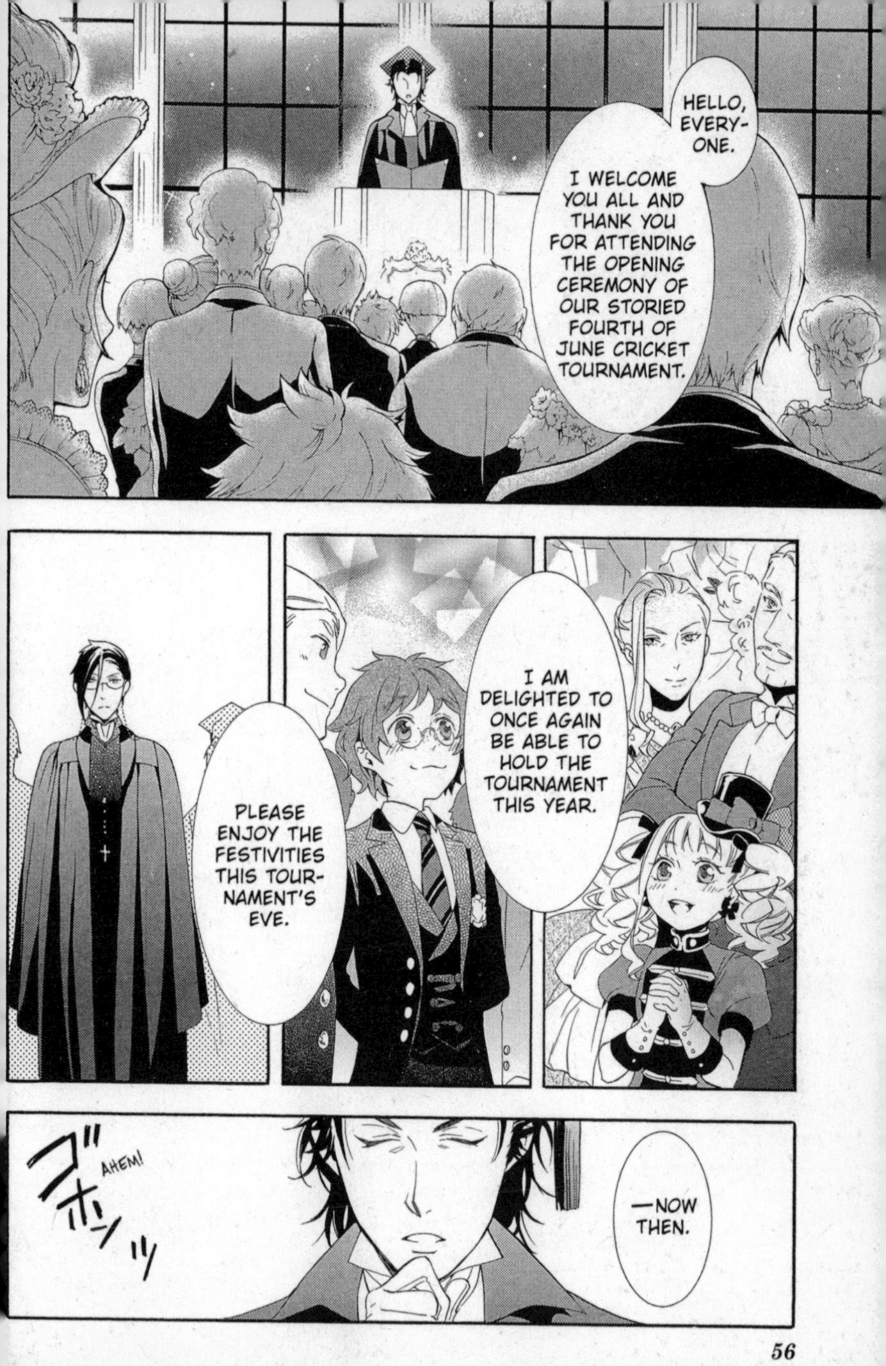
HELLO, EVERY-ONE.
I WELCOME YOU ALL AND THANK YOU FOR ATTENDING THE OPENING CEREMONY OF OUR STORIED FOURTH OF JUNE CRICKET TOURNAMENT.
I AM DELIGHTED TO ONCE AGAIN BE ABLE TO HOLD THE TOURNAMENT THIS YEAR.
PLEASE ENJOY THE FESTIVITIES THIS TOUR-NAMENT'S EVE.
—NOW THEN.
ゴホンッ
AHEM!

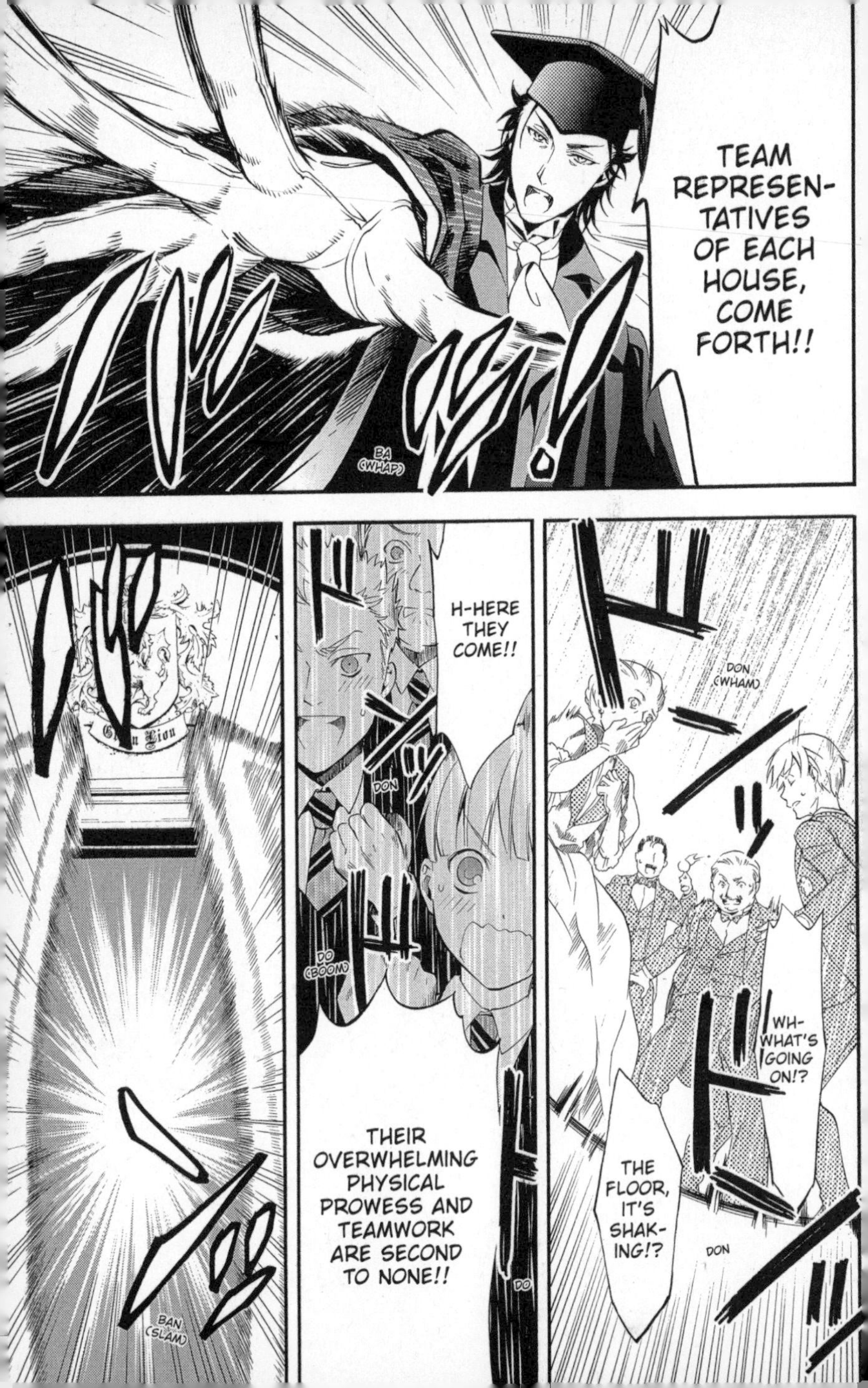
TEAM REPRESEN-TATIVES OF EACH HOUSE, COME FORTH!!
BA (WHAP)
DON (WHAM)
WH-WHAT'S GOING ON!?
THE FLOOR, IT'S SHAK-ING!?
DON
H-HERE THEY COME!!
DON
DO (BOOM)
THEIR OVERWHELMING PHYSICAL PROWESS AND TEAMWORK ARE SECOND TO NONE!!
DO
BAN (SLAM)

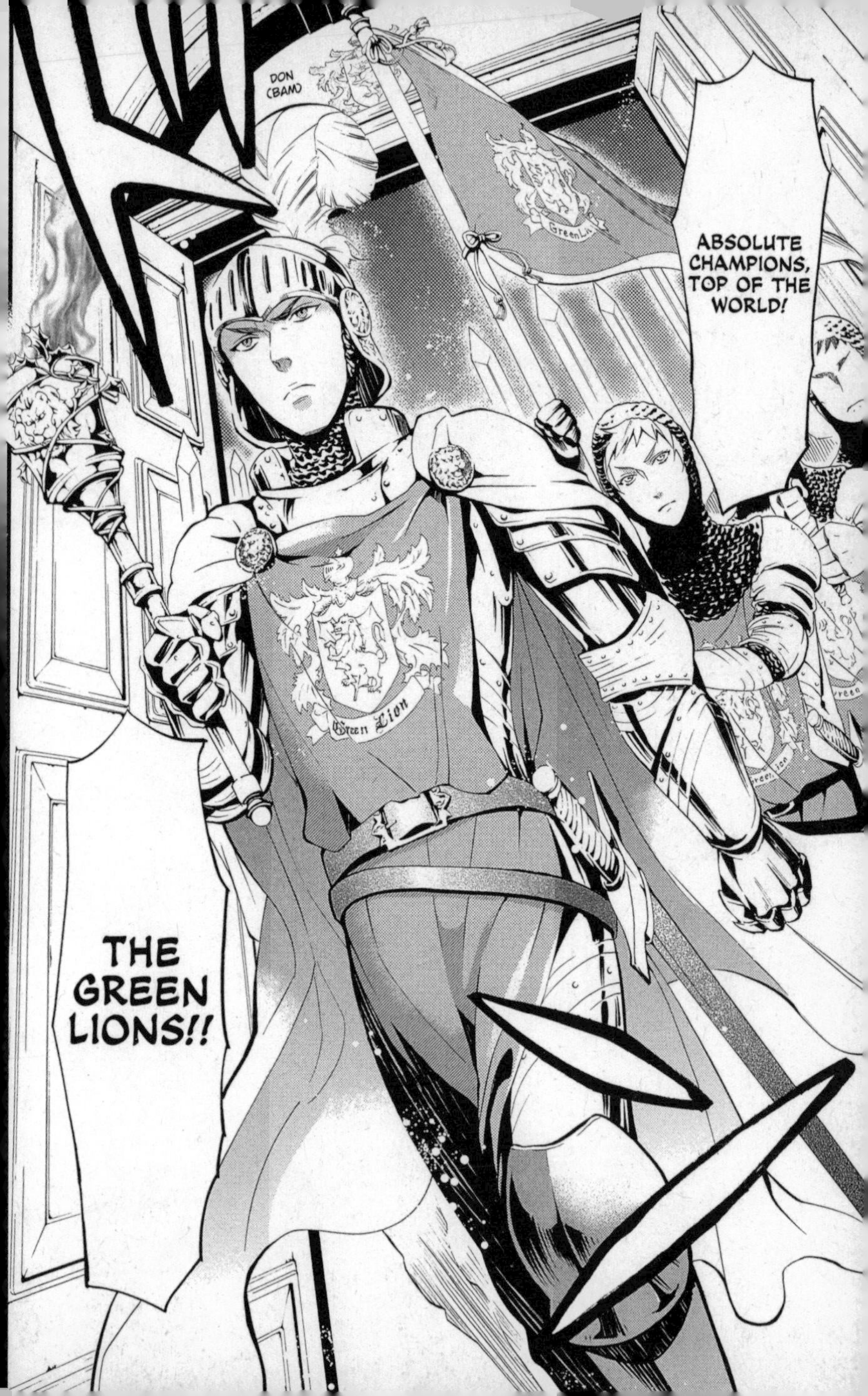
ABSOLUTE CHAMPIONS, TOP OF THE WORLD!
DON (BAM)
Green Lion
THE GREEN LIONS!!

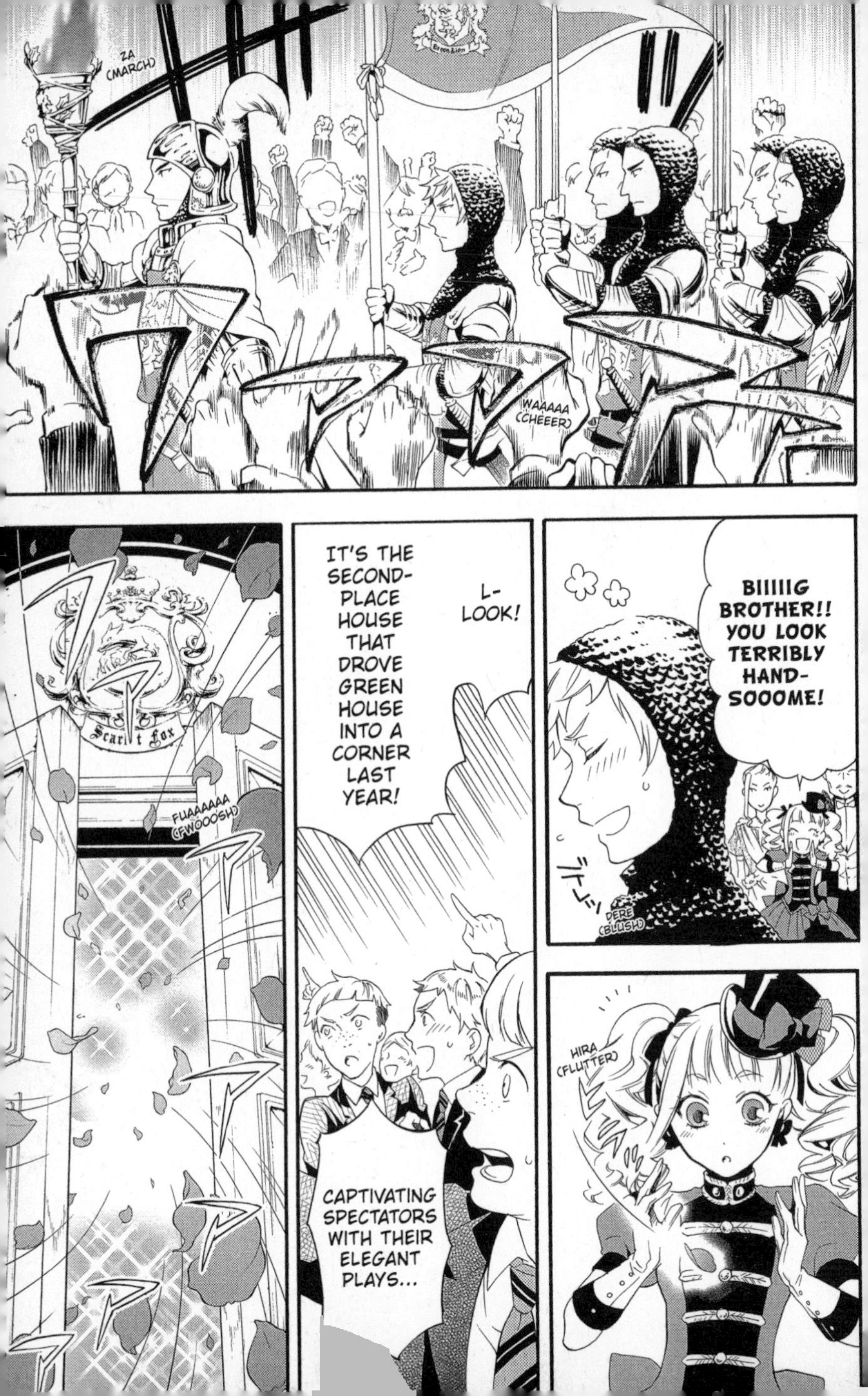
ZA (MARCH)
WAAAAA (CHEEER)
BIIIIIG BROTHER!! YOU LOOK TERRIBLY HAND-SOOOME!
DERE (BLUSH)
HIRA (FLUTTER)
L- LOOK!
IT'S THE SECOND-PLACE HOUSE THAT DROVE GREEN HOUSE INTO A CORNER LAST YEAR!
CAPTIVATING SPECTATORS WITH THEIR ELEGANT PLAYS...
FUAAAAAA (FWOOOSH)

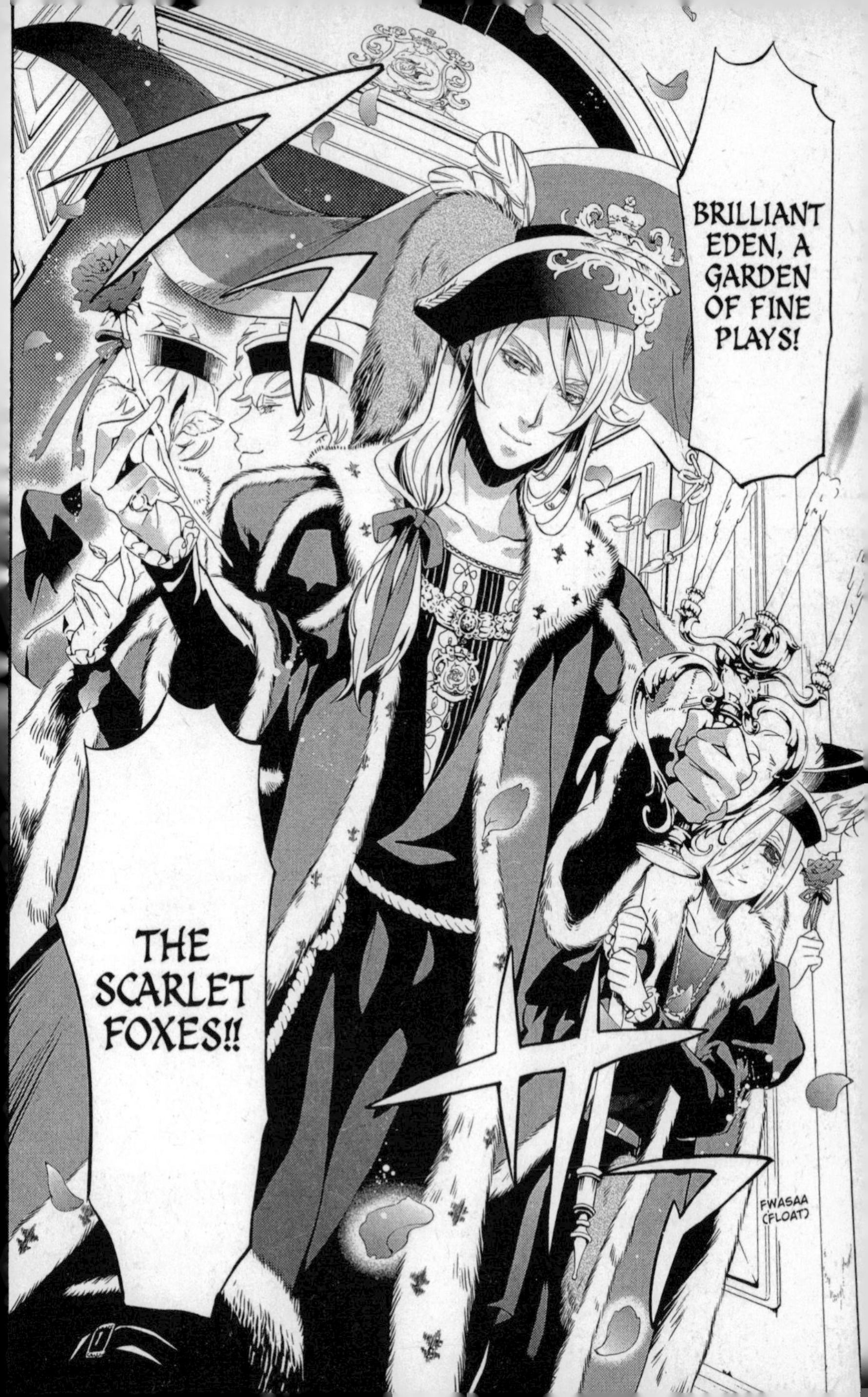
BRILLIANT EDEN, A GARDEN OF FINE PLAYS!
THE SCARLET FOXES!!
FWASAA (FLOAT)

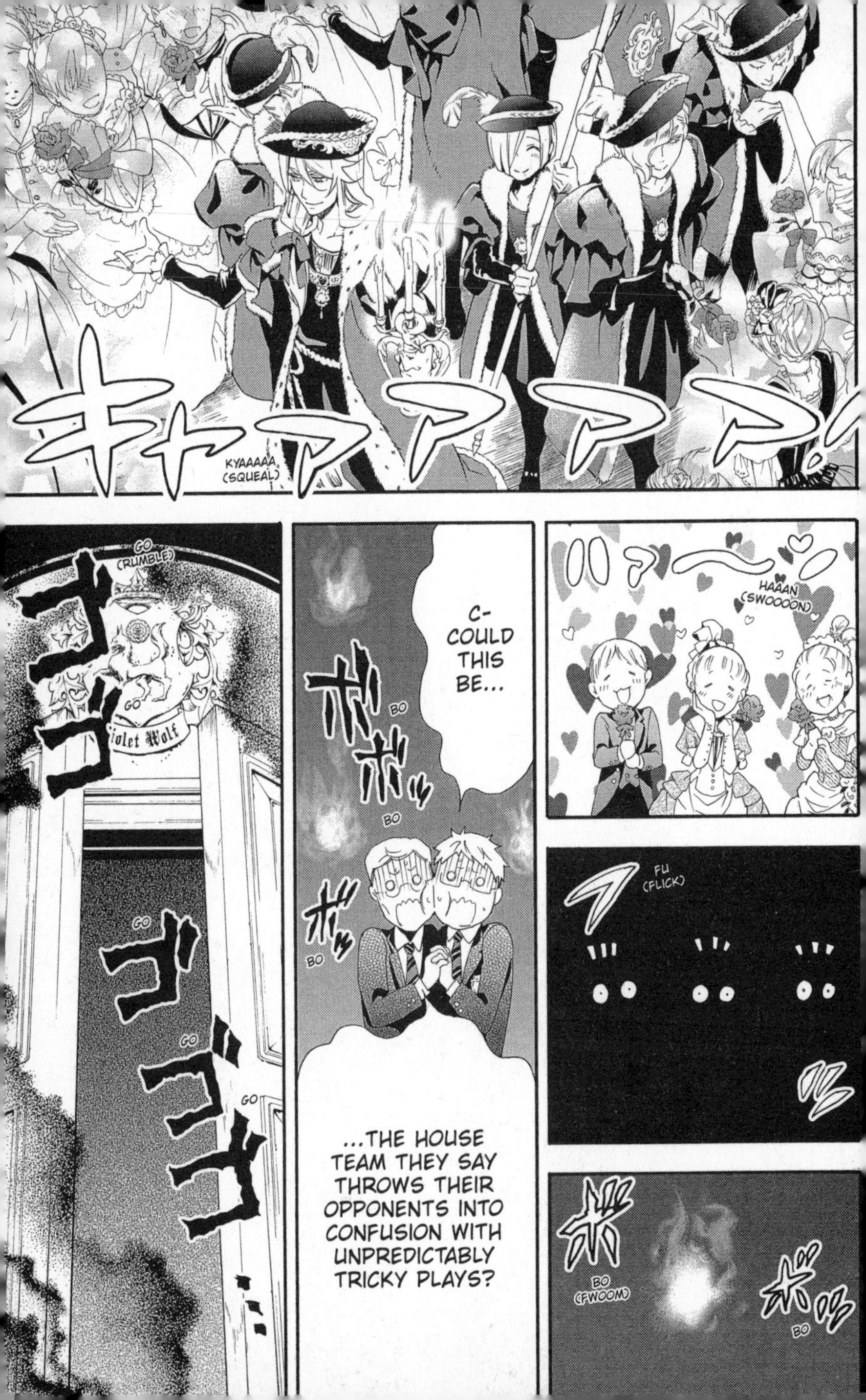
KYAAAAA (SQUEAL)
HAAAN (SWOOOON)
FU (FLICK)
BO (FWOOM)
BO
BO
C-COULD THIS BE...
BO
BO
...THE HOUSE TEAM THEY SAY THROWS THEIR OPPONENTS INTO CONFUSION WITH UNPREDICTABLY TRICKY PLAYS?
GO (RUMBLE)
GO
iolet Wolf
GO
GO
GO

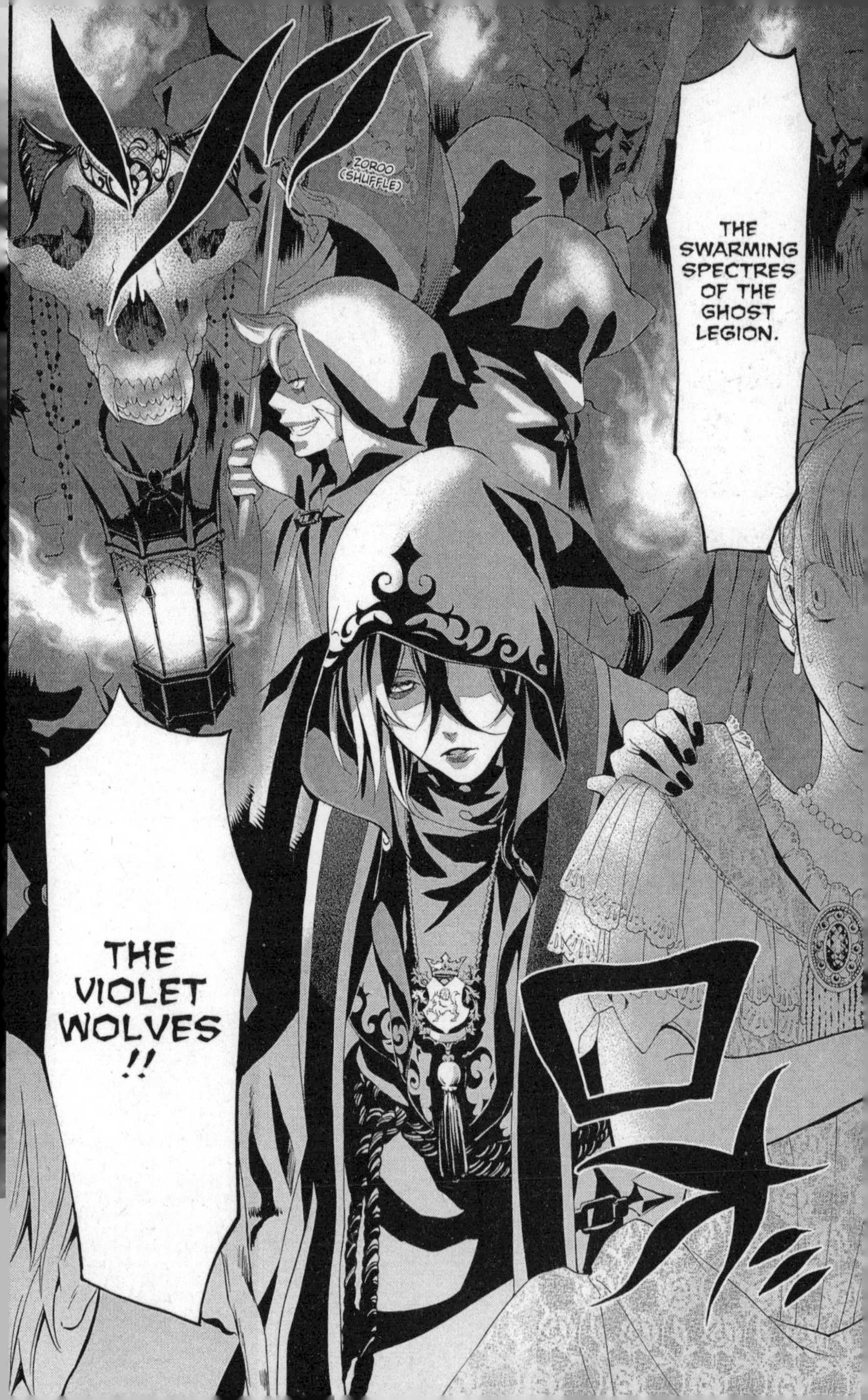
THE SWARMING SPECTRES OF THE GHOST LEGION.
ZOROO (SHUFFLE)
THE VIOLET WOLVES!!

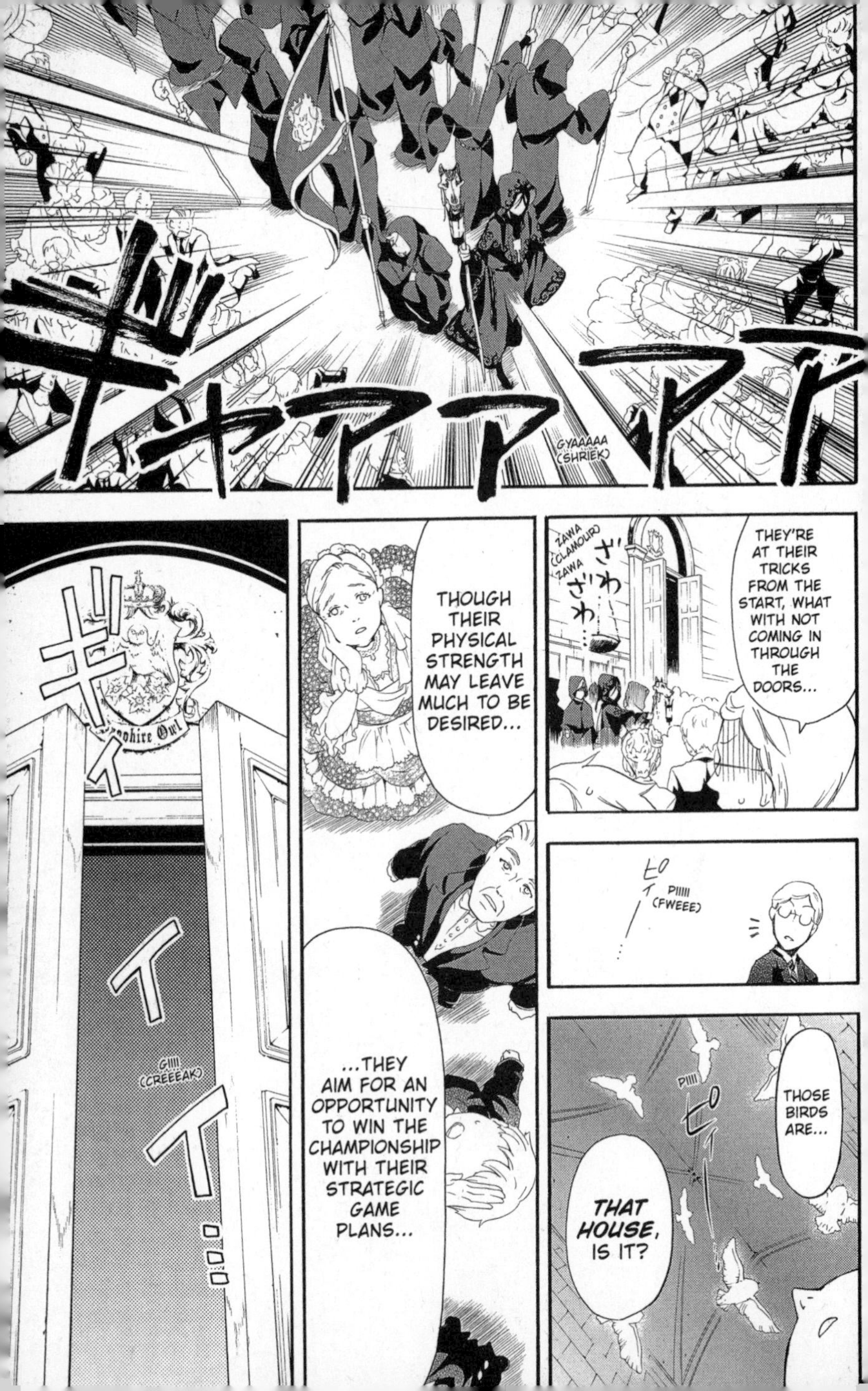
ギャアアア
GYAAAAA (SHRIEK)
ZAWA (CLAMOUR) ZAWA
ざわざわ...
THEY'RE AT THEIR TRICKS FROM THE START, WHAT WITH NOT COMING IN THROUGH THE DOORS...
ピイ...
PIIII (FWEEE)
PIIII
ピイー
THOSE BIRDS ARE...
THAT HOUSE, IS IT?
THOUGH THEIR PHYSICAL STRENGTH MAY LEAVE MUCH TO BE DESIRED...
...THEY AIM FOR AN OPPORTUNITY TO WIN THE CHAMPIONSHIP WITH THEIR STRATEGIC GAME PLANS...
ギイイイ...
GIIII (CREEEAK)

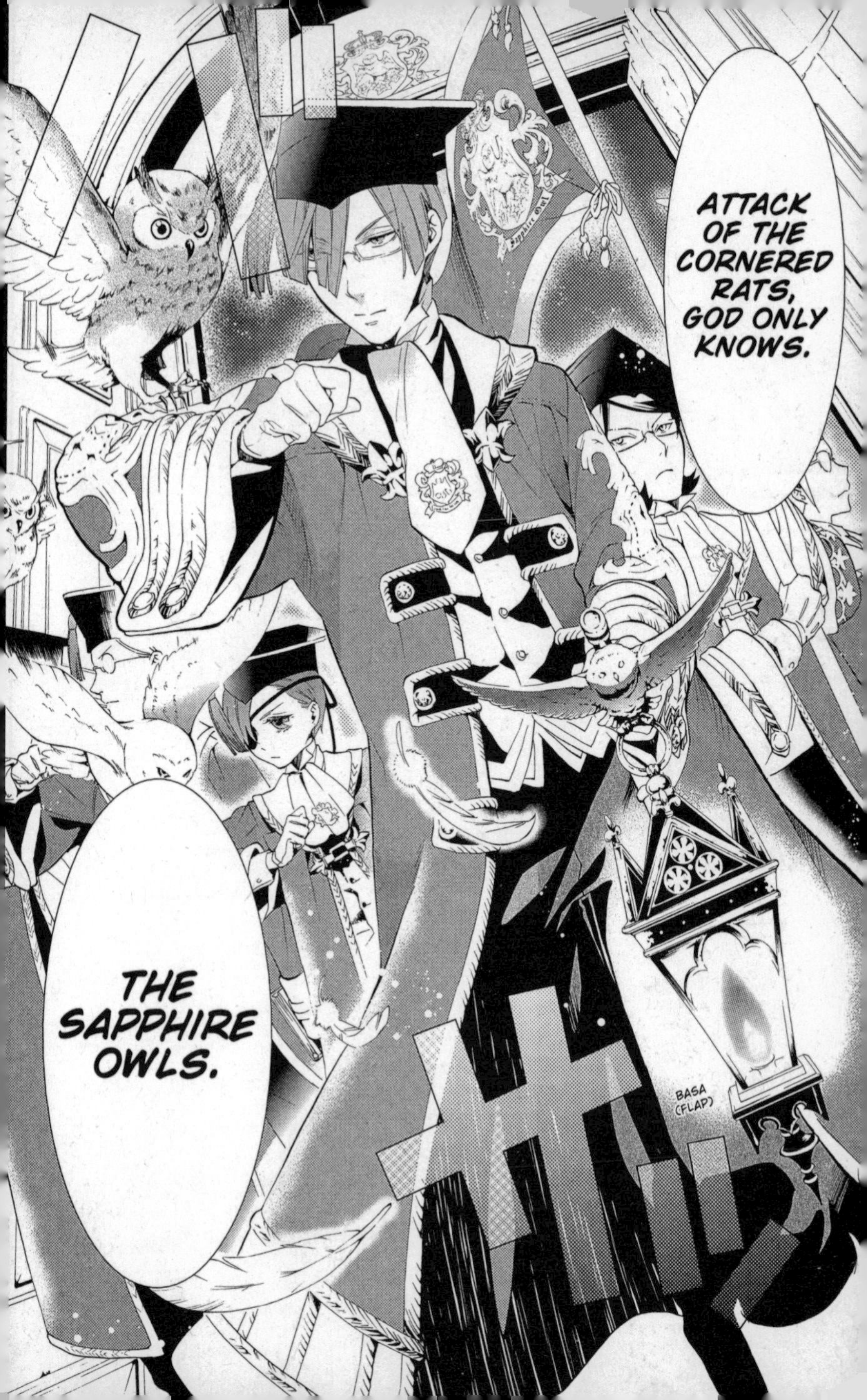
ATTACK OF THE CORNERED RATS, GOD ONLY KNOWS.
BASA (FLAP)
THE SAPPHIRE OWLS.

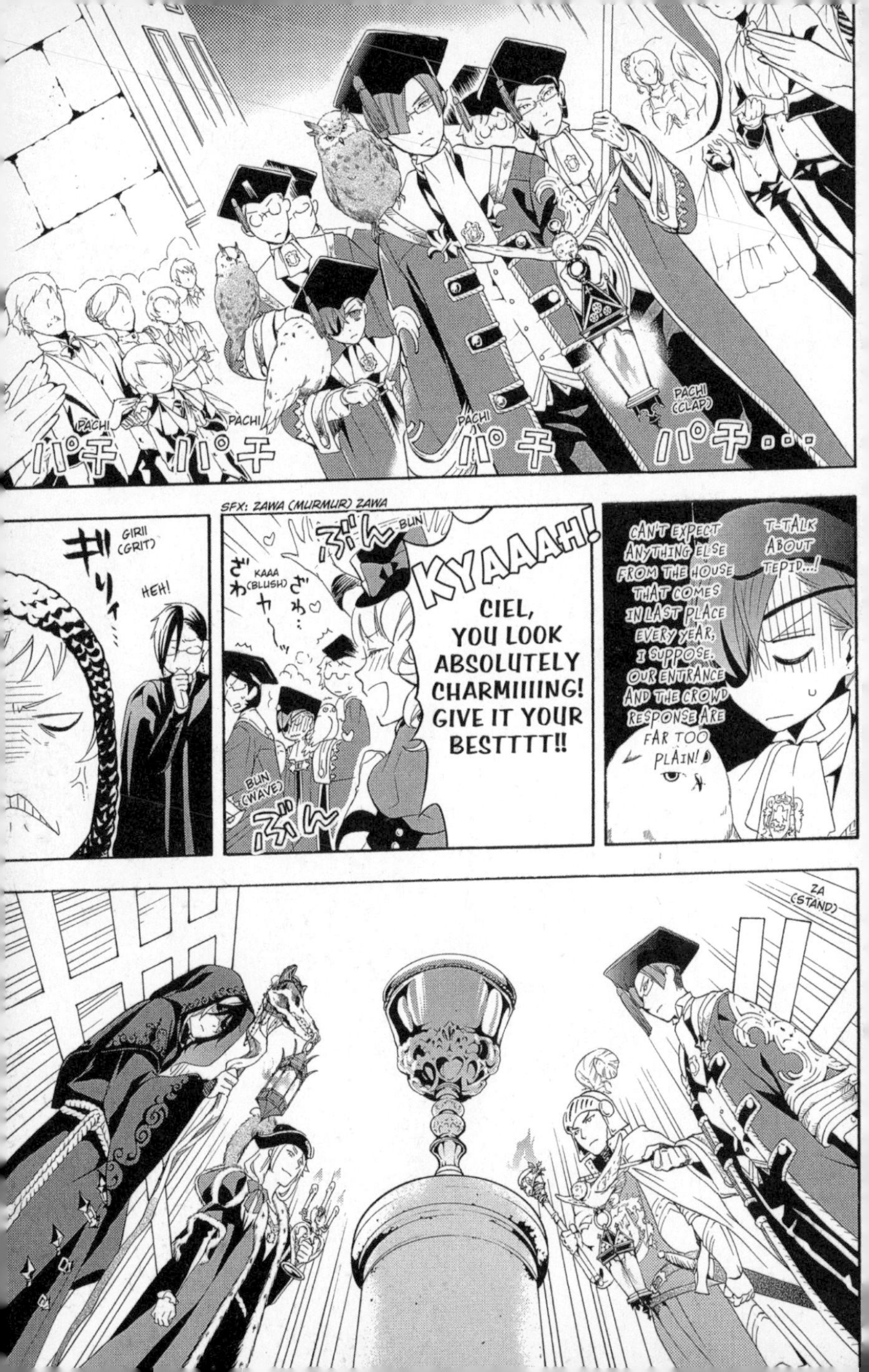
PACHI (CLAP)
パチ…
PACHI
パチ
PACHI
パチ
PACHI
パチ
T-TALK ABOUT TEPID...!
CAN'T EXPECT ANYTHING ELSE FROM THE HOUSE THAT COMES IN LAST PLACE EVERY YEAR, I SUPPOSE. OUR ENTRANCE AND THE CROWD RESPONSE ARE FAR TOO PLAIN!
SFX: ZAWA (MURMUR) ZAWA
BUN
ぶん
KYAAAH!
CIEL, YOU LOOK ABSOLUTELY CHARMIIIING! GIVE IT YOUR BESTTTT!!
KAAA (BLUSH)
BUN (WAVE)
ぶん
GIRII (GRIT)
ギリィ
HEH!
ZA (STAND)

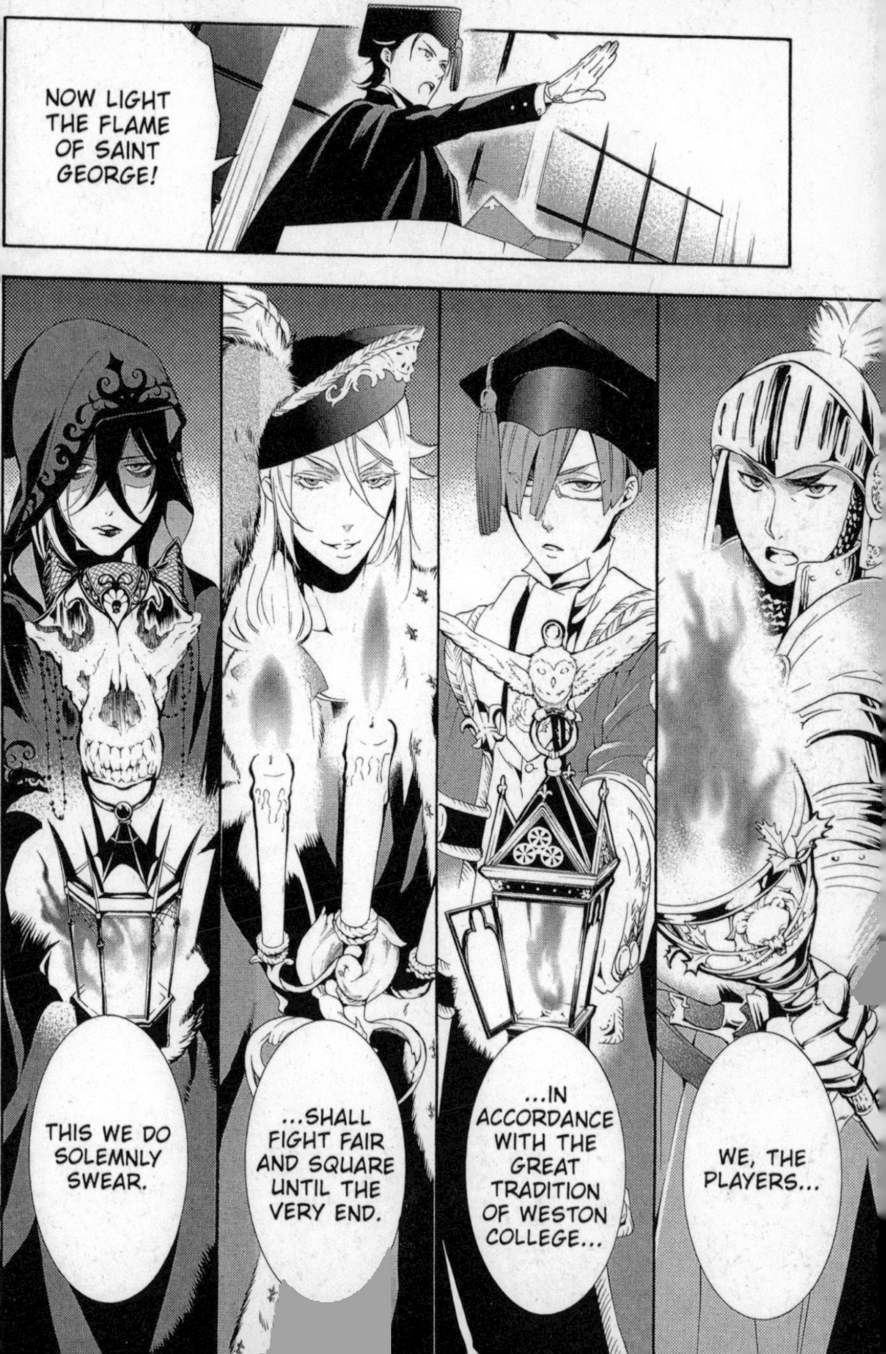
NOW LIGHT THE FLAME OF SAINT GEORGE!
WE, THE PLAYERS...
...IN ACCORDANCE WITH THE GREAT TRADITION OF WESTON COLLEGE...
...SHALL FIGHT FAIR AND SQUARE UNTIL THE VERY END.
THIS WE DO SOLEMNLY SWEAR.

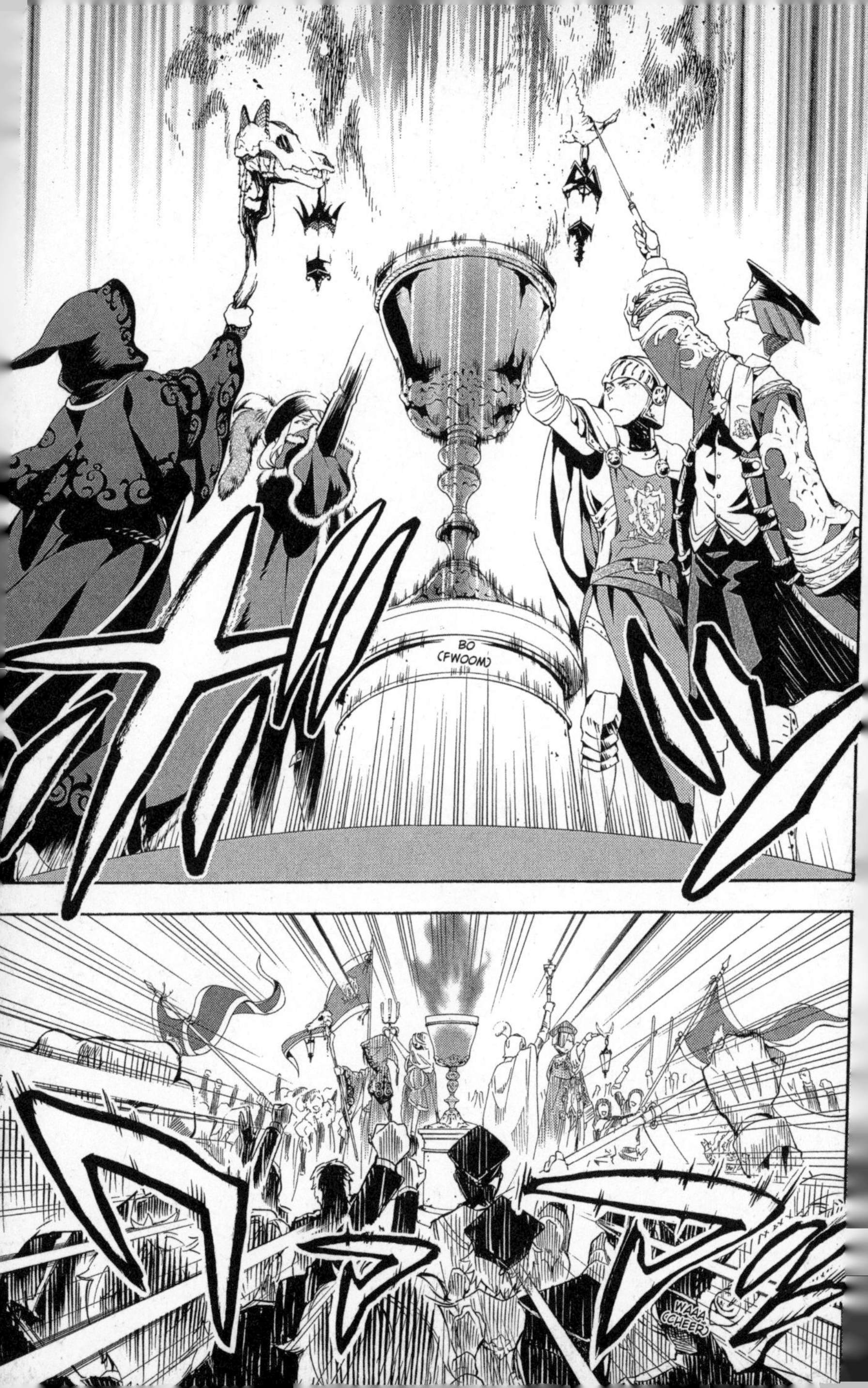
BO
(FWOOM)
WAAA
(CHEER)

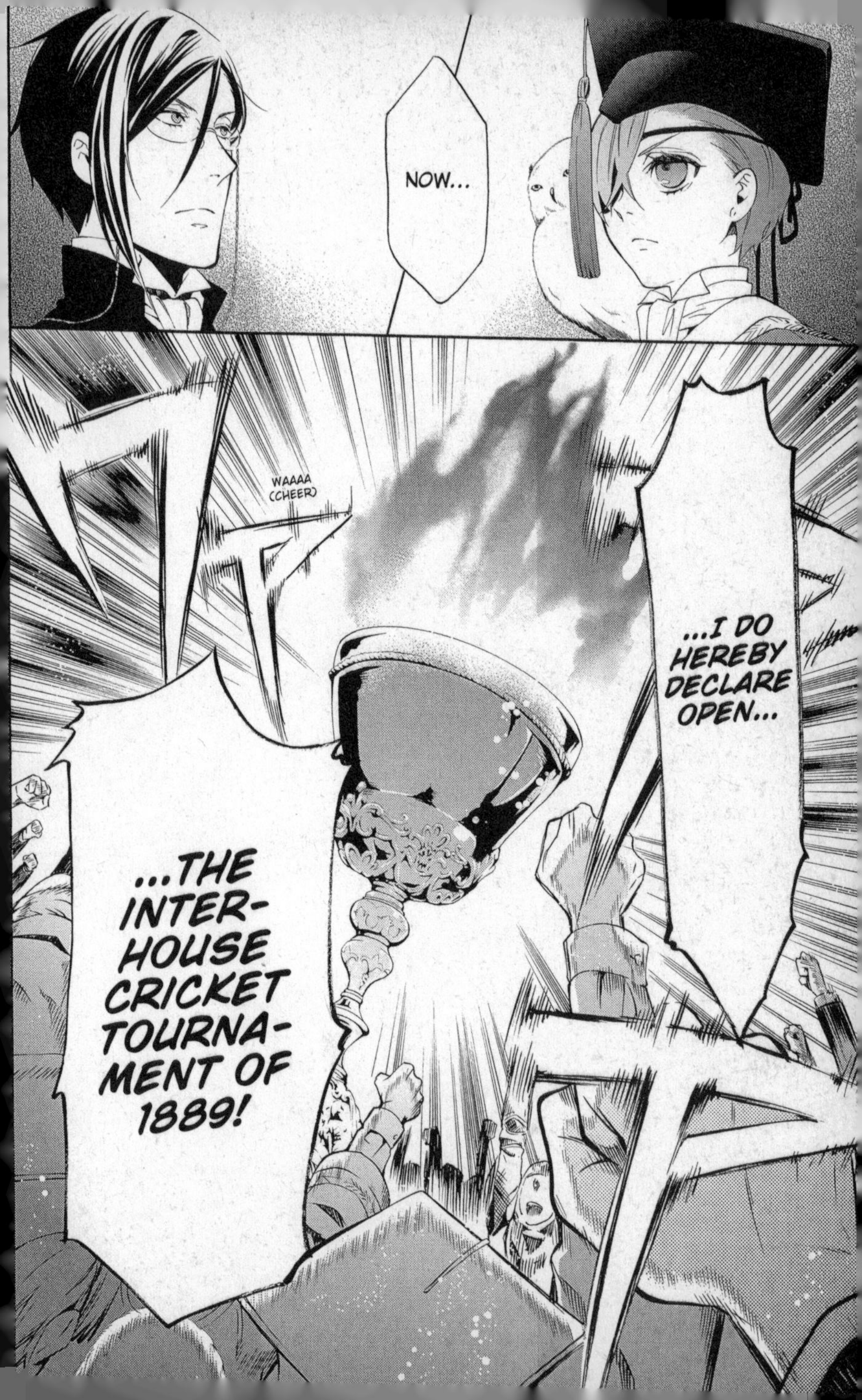
NOW...
...I DO HEREBY DECLARE OPEN...
WAAAA (CHEER)
...THE INTER-HOUSE CRICKET TOURNA-MENT OF 1889!

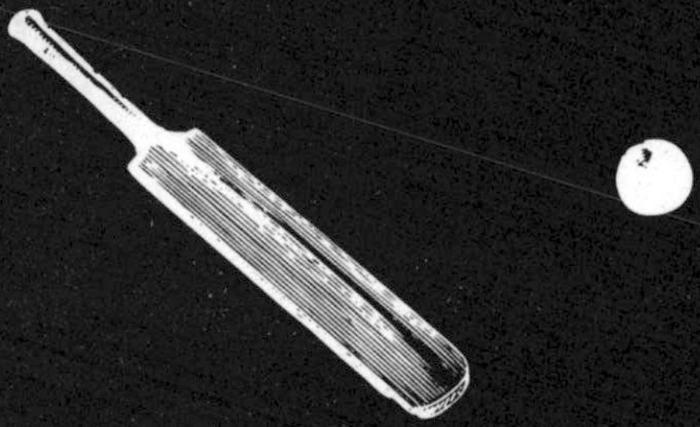

Black Butler

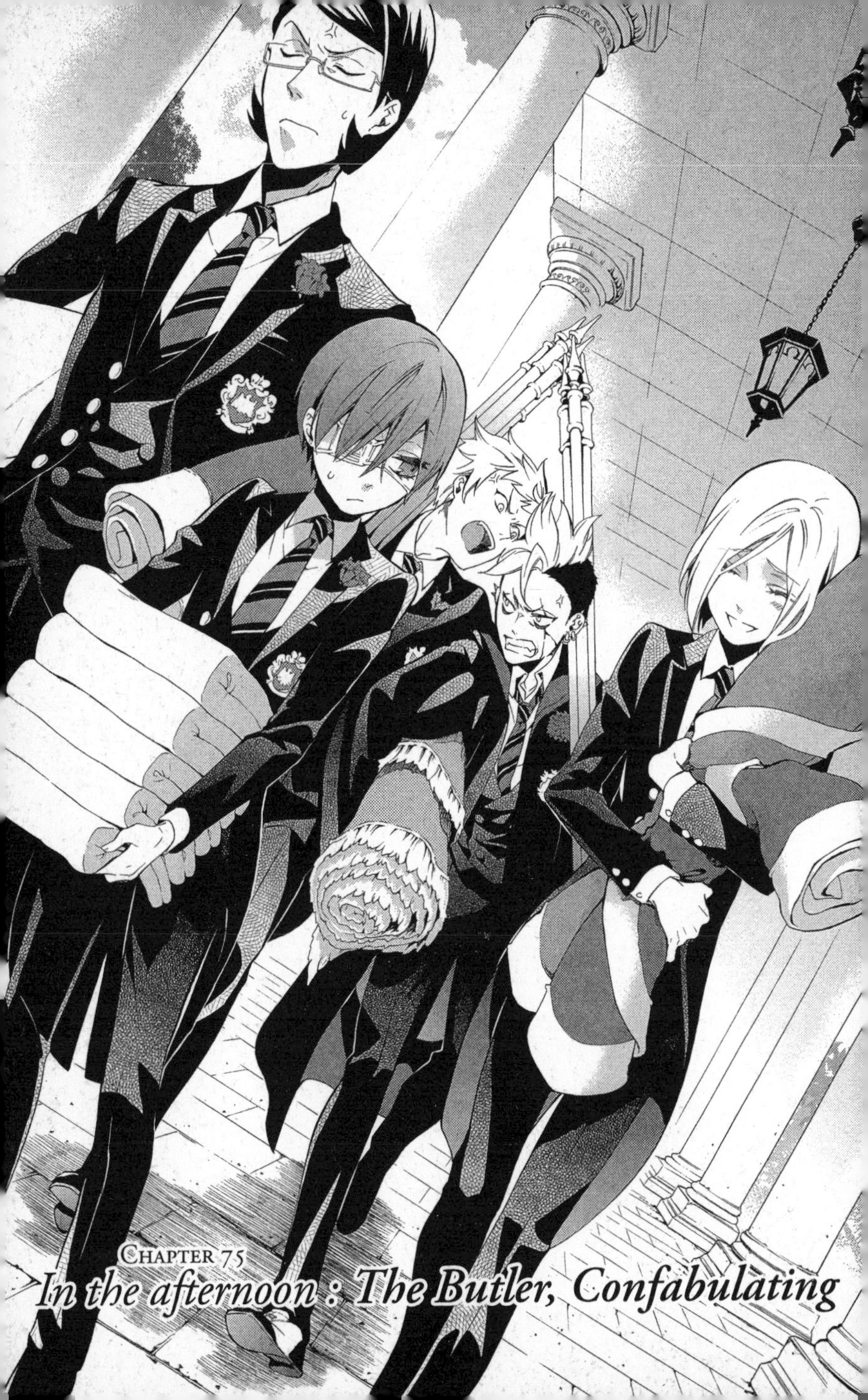

Chapter 75
In the afternoon : The Butler, Confabulating

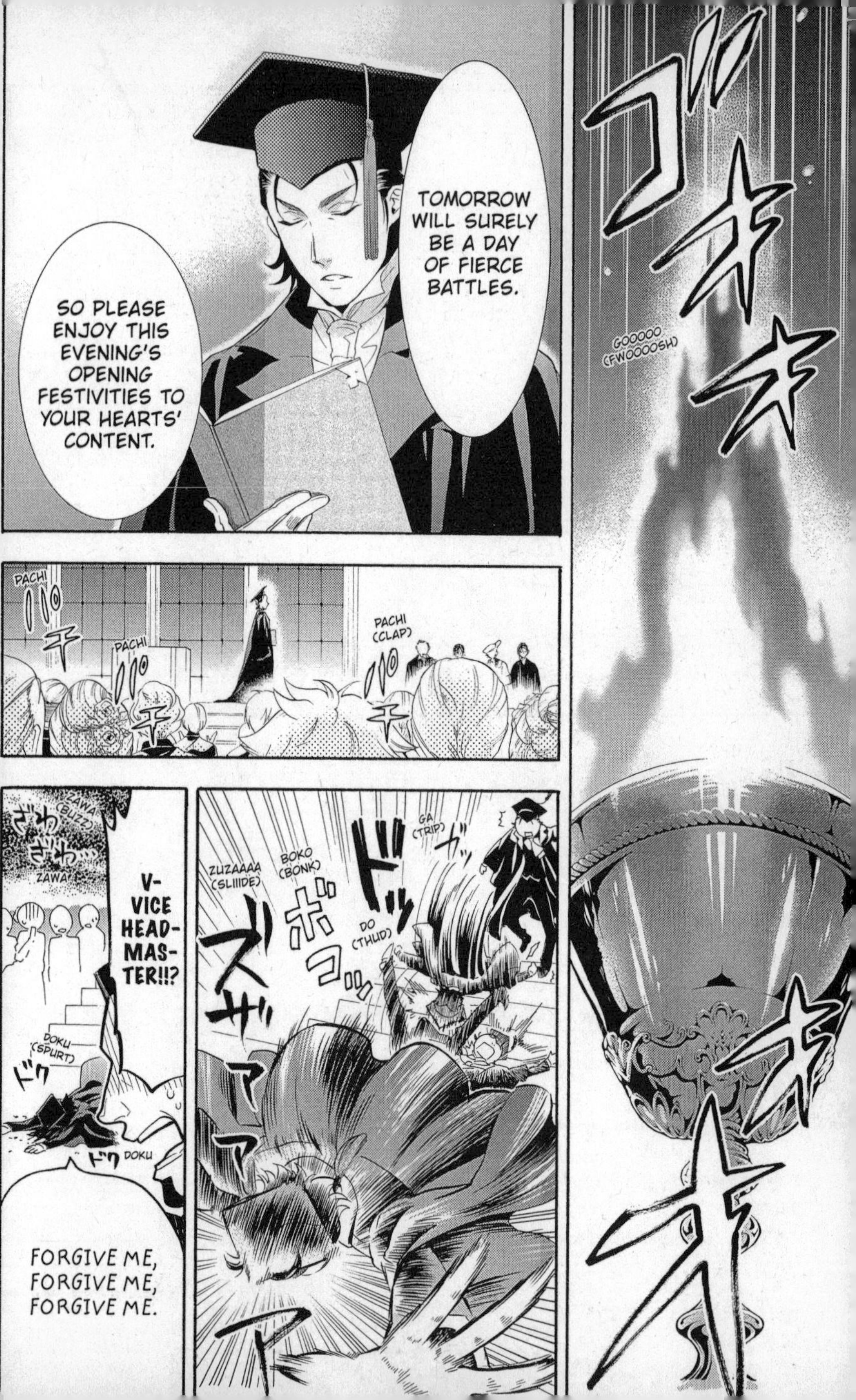
GOOOOO (FWOOOOSH)
TOMORROW WILL SURELY BE A DAY OF FIERCE BATTLES.
SO PLEASE ENJOY THIS EVENING'S OPENING FESTIVITIES TO YOUR HEARTS' CONTENT.
PACHI (CLAP)
PACHI
PACHI
GA (TRIP)
DO (THUD)
BOKO (BONK)
ZUZAAAA (SLIIIDE)
ZAWA (BUZZ)
ZAWA
V-VICE HEAD-MASTER!!?
DOKU (SPURT)
DOKU
FORGIVE ME, FORGIVE ME, FORGIVE ME.

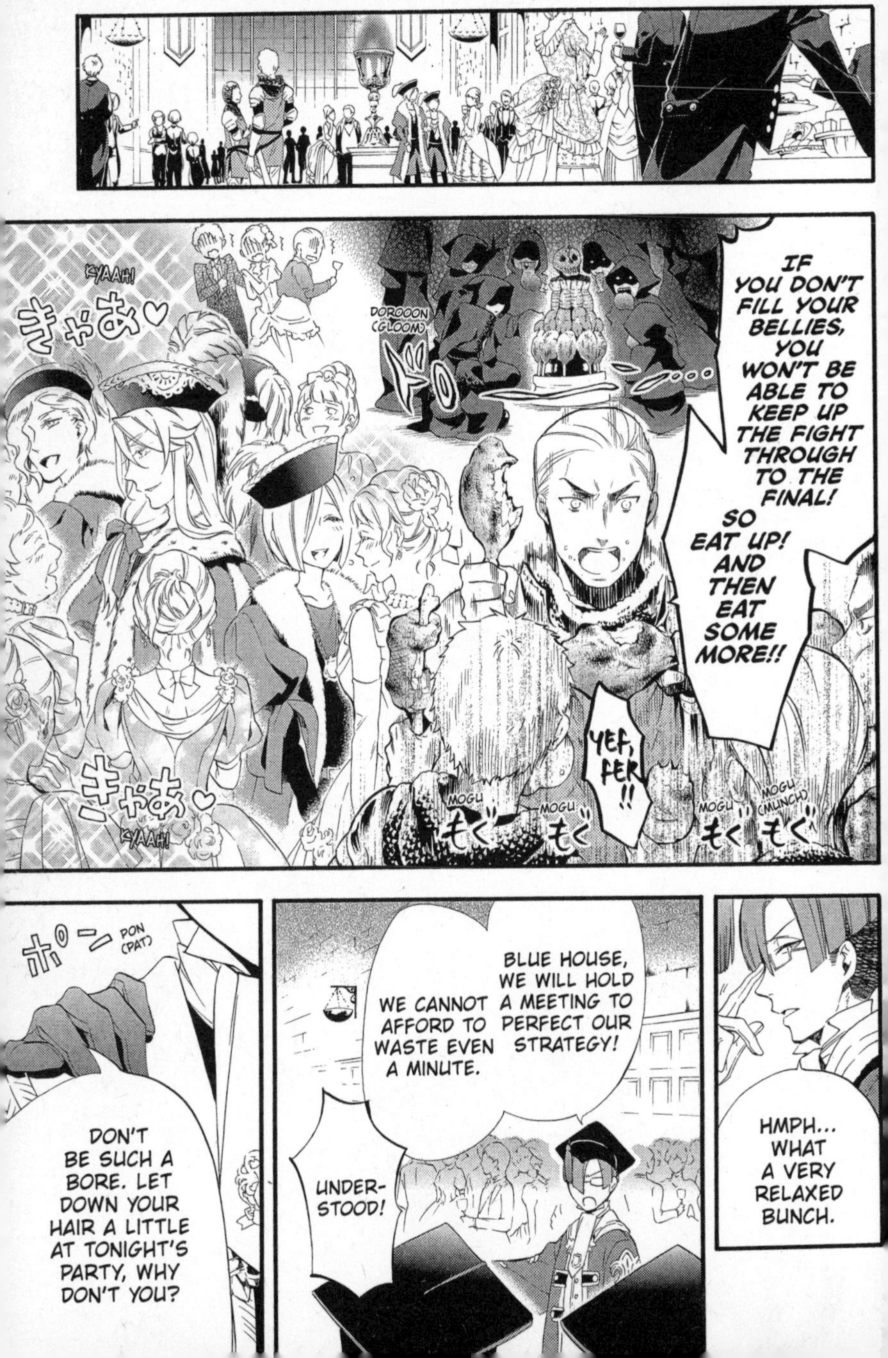
IF YOU DON'T FILL YOUR BELLIES, YOU WON'T BE ABLE TO KEEP UP THE FIGHT THROUGH TO THE FINAL! SO EAT UP! AND THEN EAT SOME MORE!!
DOROOON (GLOOM)
ドロ〜ン…
KYAAH!
きゃあ♡
YEF, FER!!
MOGU (MUNCH)
もぐ
MOGU
もぐ
MOGU
もぐ
MOGU
もぐ
きゃあ♡
KYAAH!
HMPH... WHAT A VERY RELAXED BUNCH.
BLUE HOUSE, WE WILL HOLD A MEETING TO PERFECT OUR STRATEGY!
WE CANNOT AFFORD TO WASTE EVEN A MINUTE.
UNDER-STOOD!
PON (PAT)
ポーン
DON'T BE SUCH A BORE. LET DOWN YOUR HAIR A LITTLE AT TONIGHT'S PARTY, WHY DON'T YOU?

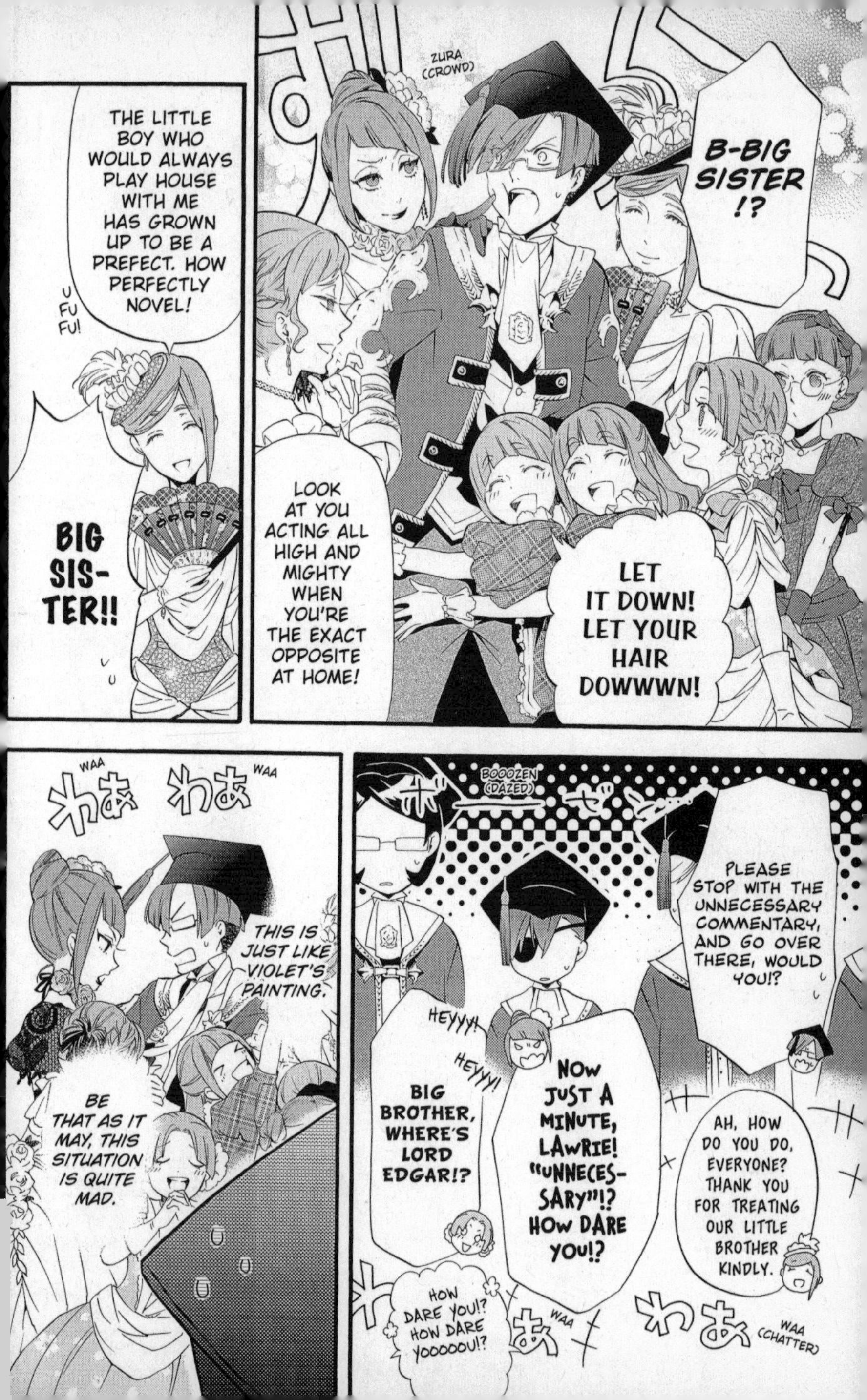
ZURA (CROWD)
B-BIG SISTER!?
LET IT DOWN! LET YOUR HAIR DOWWWN!
LOOK AT YOU ACTING ALL HIGH AND MIGHTY WHEN YOU'RE THE EXACT OPPOSITE AT HOME!
THE LITTLE BOY WHO WOULD ALWAYS PLAY HOUSE WITH ME HAS GROWN UP TO BE A PREFECT. HOW PERFECTLY NOVEL!
U FU FU!
BIG SIS-TER!!
BOOOZEN (DAZED)
PLEASE STOP WITH THE UNNECESSARY COMMENTARY, AND GO OVER THERE, WOULD YOU!?
AH, HOW DO YOU DO, EVERYONE? THANK YOU FOR TREATING OUR LITTLE BROTHER KINDLY.
NOW JUST A MINUTE, LAWRIE! "UNNECES-SARY"!? HOW DARE YOU!?
HEYYY!
HEYYY!
BIG BROTHER, WHERE'S LORD EDGAR!?
WAA (CHATTER)
WAA
HOW DARE YOU!? HOW DARE YOOOOOU!?
WAA
WAA
THIS IS JUST LIKE VIOLET'S PAINTING.
BE THAT AS IT MAY, THIS SITUATION IS QUITE MAD.

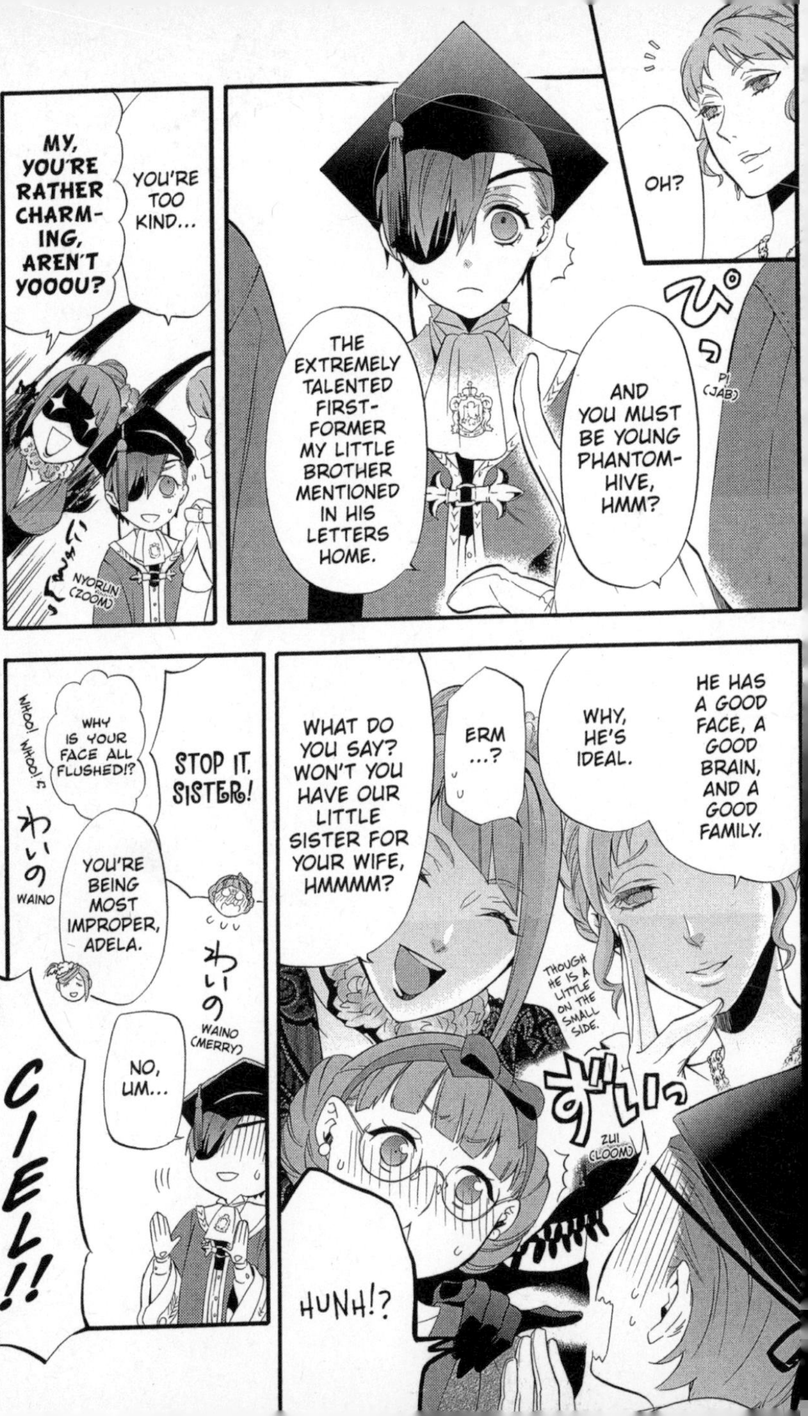
OH?
ぴっ
PI (JAB)
AND YOU MUST BE YOUNG PHANTOM-HIVE, HMM?
THE EXTREMELY TALENTED FIRST-FORMER MY LITTLE BROTHER MENTIONED IN HIS LETTERS HOME.
YOU'RE TOO KIND...
MY, YOU'RE RATHER CHARM-ING, AREN'T YOOOU?
NYORUN (ZOOM)
HE HAS A GOOD FACE, A GOOD BRAIN, AND A GOOD FAMILY.
WHY, HE'S IDEAL.
ERM ...?
WHAT DO YOU SAY? WON'T YOU HAVE OUR LITTLE SISTER FOR YOUR WIFE, HMMMM?
THOUGH HE IS A LITTLE ON THE SMALL SIDE.
ずいっ
ZUI (LOOM)
HUNH!?
STOP IT, SISTER!
WHY IS YOUR FACE ALL FLUSHED!?
WHOO! WHOO! ♫
わいの
WAINO
YOU'RE BEING MOST IMPROPER, ADELA.
わいの
WAINO (MERRY)
NO, UM...
CIEL!!

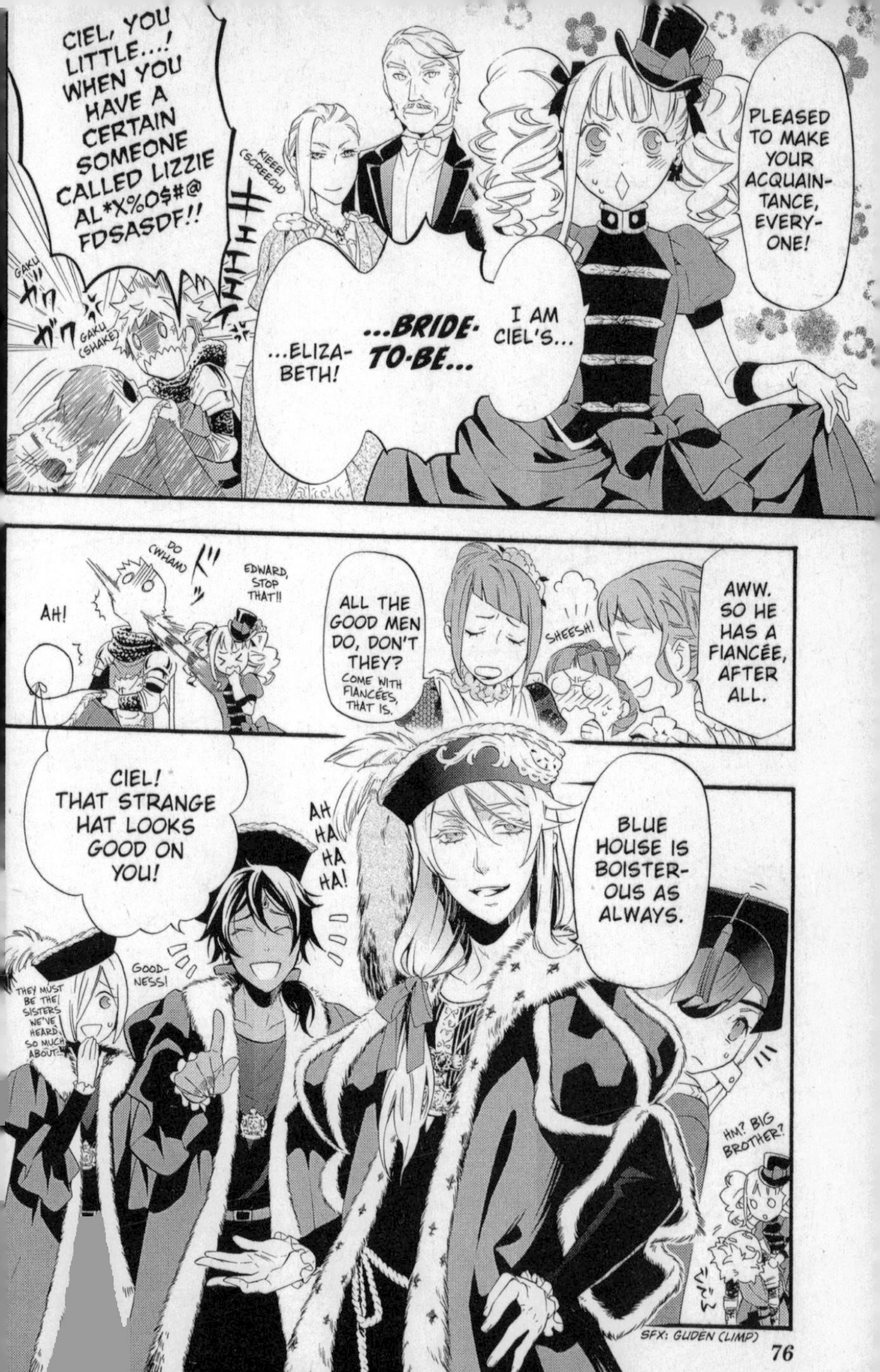
PLEASED TO MAKE YOUR ACQUAINTANCE, EVERYONE!
I AM CIEL'S...
...BRIDE-TO-BE...
...ELIZABETH!
KIEEE! (SCREECH)
CIEL, YOU LITTLE...! WHEN YOU HAVE A CERTAIN SOMEONE CALLED LIZZIE AL*X%O$#@ FDSASDF!!
GAKU
GAKU (SHAKE)
AWW. SO HE HAS A FIANCÉE, AFTER ALL.
SHEESH!
ALL THE GOOD MEN DO, DON'T THEY?
COME WITH FIANCÉES, THAT IS.
EDWARD, STOP THAT!!
DO (WHAM)
AH!
BLUE HOUSE IS BOISTEROUS AS ALWAYS.
AH HA HA HA!
CIEL! THAT STRANGE HAT LOOKS GOOD ON YOU!
GOODNESS!
THEY MUST BE THE SISTERS WE'VE HEARD SO MUCH ABOUT...!
HM? BIG BROTHER?
SFX: GUDEN (LIMP)

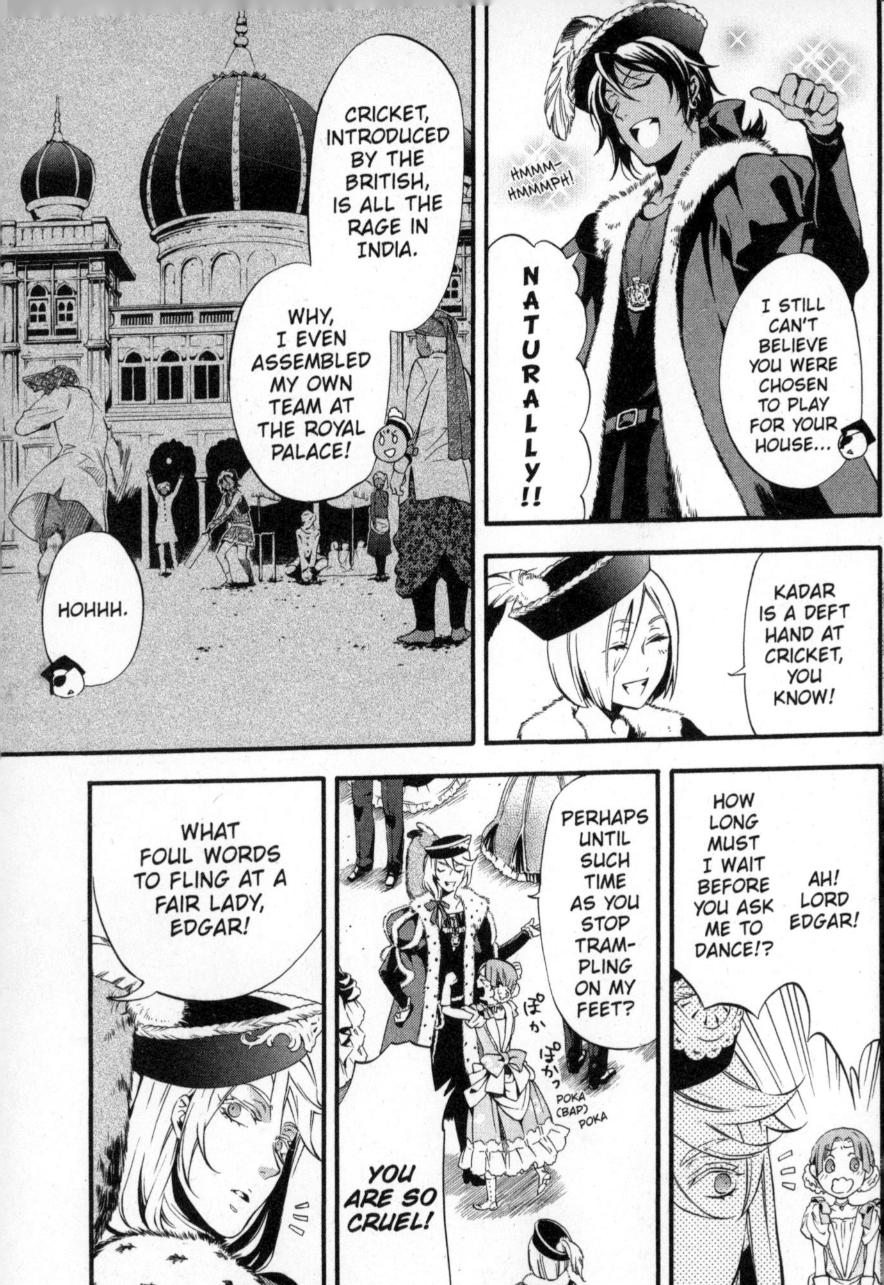
I STILL CAN'T BELIEVE YOU WERE CHOSEN TO PLAY FOR YOUR HOUSE...
NATURALLY!!
HMMMM-HMMMPH!
KADAR IS A DEFT HAND AT CRICKET, YOU KNOW!
CRICKET, INTRODUCED BY THE BRITISH, IS ALL THE RAGE IN INDIA.
WHY, I EVEN ASSEMBLED MY OWN TEAM AT THE ROYAL PALACE!
HOHHH.
AH! LORD EDGAR!
HOW LONG MUST I WAIT BEFORE YOU ASK ME TO DANCE!?
PERHAPS UNTIL SUCH TIME AS YOU STOP TRAMPLING ON MY FEET?
ぽか ぽかっ
POKA (BAP) POKA
YOU ARE SO CRUEL!
WHAT FOUL WORDS TO FLING AT A FAIR LADY, EDGAR!

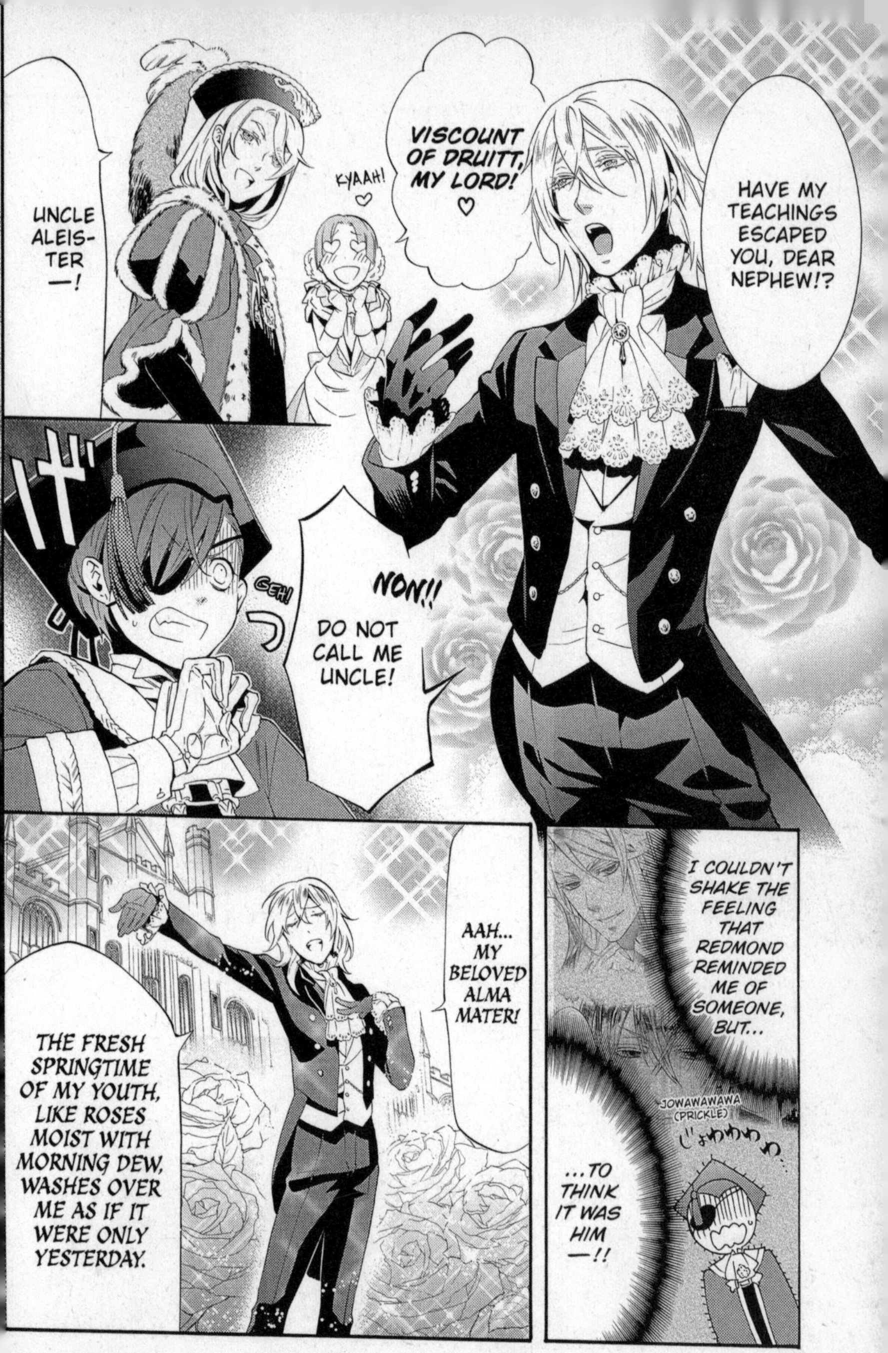
HAVE MY TEACHINGS ESCAPED YOU, DEAR NEPHEW!?
VISCOUNT OF DRUITT, MY LORD! ♡
KYAAH! ♡
UNCLE ALEISTER—!
NON!!
DO NOT CALL ME UNCLE!
GEH!
I COULDN'T SHAKE THE FEELING THAT REDMOND REMINDED ME OF SOMEONE, BUT...
...TO THINK IT WAS HIM—!!
JOWAWAWAWA (PRICKLE)
AAH... MY BELOVED ALMA MATER!
THE FRESH SPRINGTIME OF MY YOUTH, LIKE ROSES MOIST WITH MORNING DEW, WASHES OVER ME AS IF IT WERE ONLY YESTERDAY.

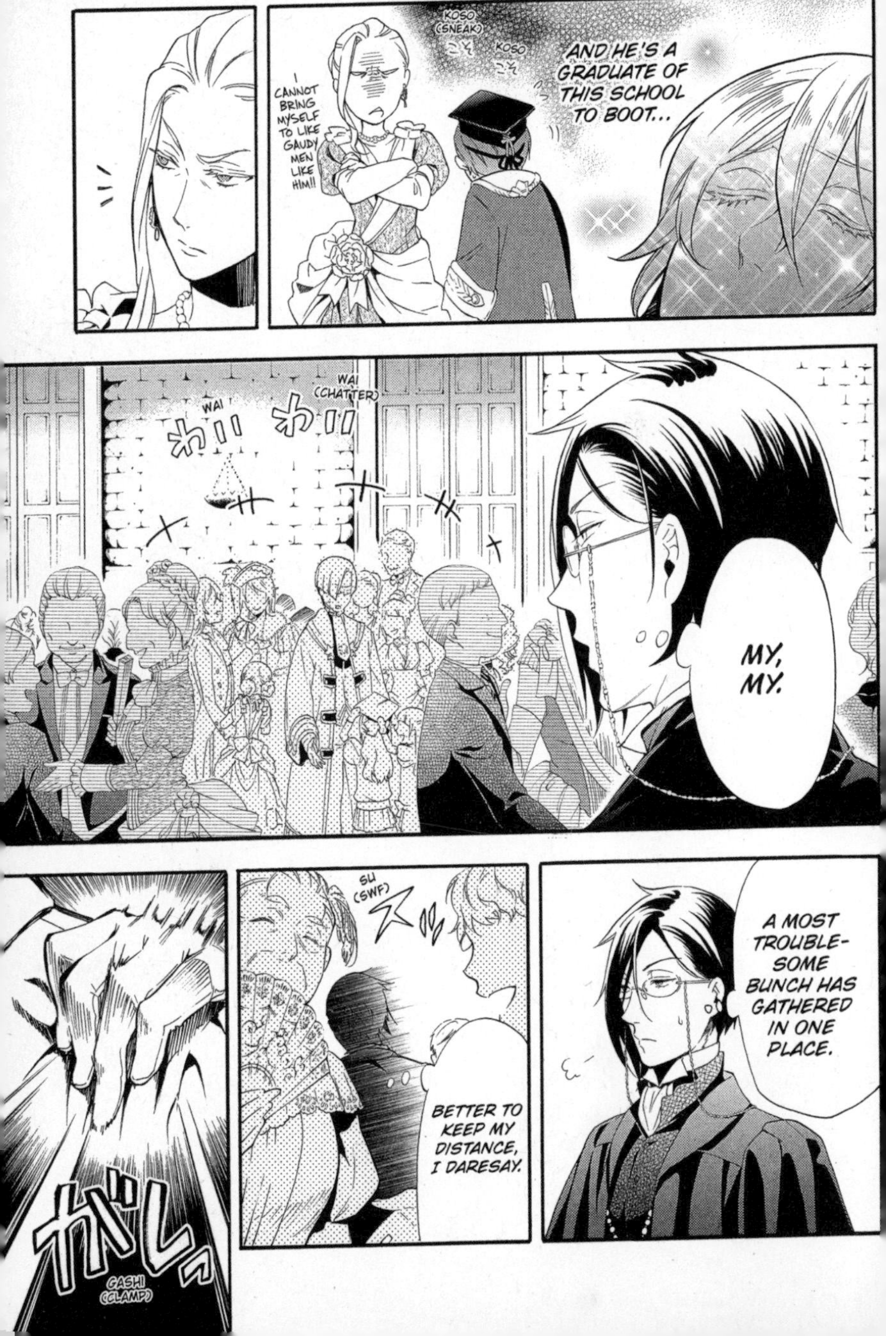
AND HE'S A GRADUATE OF THIS SCHOOL TO BOOT...
KOSO (SNEAK)
こそ
KOSO
こそ
I CANNOT BRING MYSELF TO LIKE GAUDY MEN LIKE HIM!!
MY, MY.
WAI (CHATTER)
わぃ
WAI
わぃ
A MOST TROUBLE-SOME BUNCH HAS GATHERED IN ONE PLACE.
SU (SWF)
ス
BETTER TO KEEP MY DISTANCE, I DARESAY.
がしっ
GASHI (CLAMP)

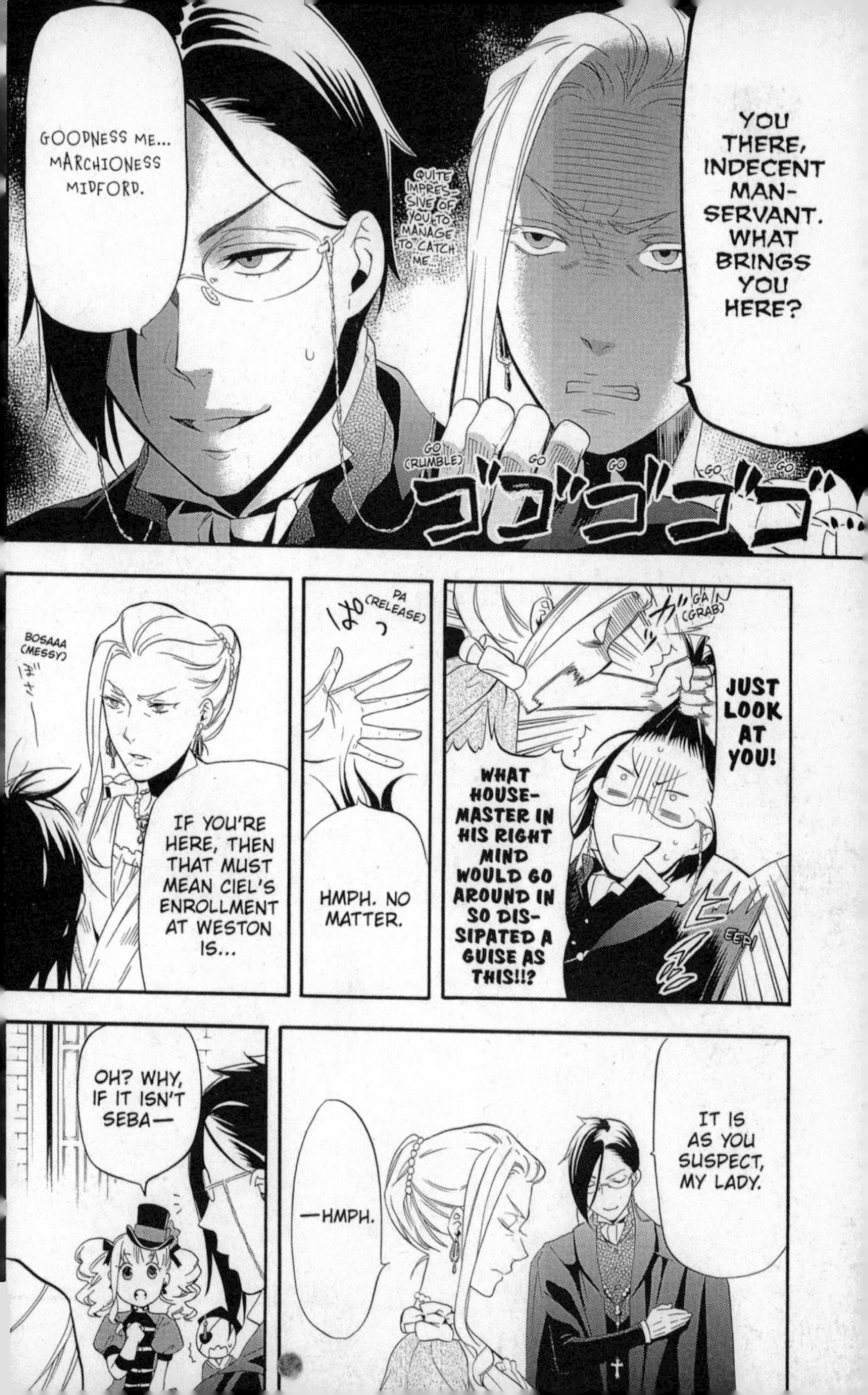
YOU THERE, INDECENT MAN-SERVANT. WHAT BRINGS YOU HERE?
QUITE IMPRESSIVE OF YOU TO MANAGE TO CATCH ME...
GOODNESS ME... MARCHIONESS MIDFORD.
GO GO GO GO GO (RUMBLE)
GA (GRAB)
JUST LOOK AT YOU!
WHAT HOUSE-MASTER IN HIS RIGHT MIND WOULD GO AROUND IN SO DIS-SIPATED A GUISE AS THIS!!?
EEP!
PA (RELEASE)
HMPH. NO MATTER.
BOSAAA (MESSY)
IF YOU'RE HERE, THEN THAT MUST MEAN CIEL'S ENROLLMENT AT WESTON IS...
IT IS AS YOU SUSPECT, MY LADY.
—HMPH.
OH? WHY, IF IT ISN'T SEBA—

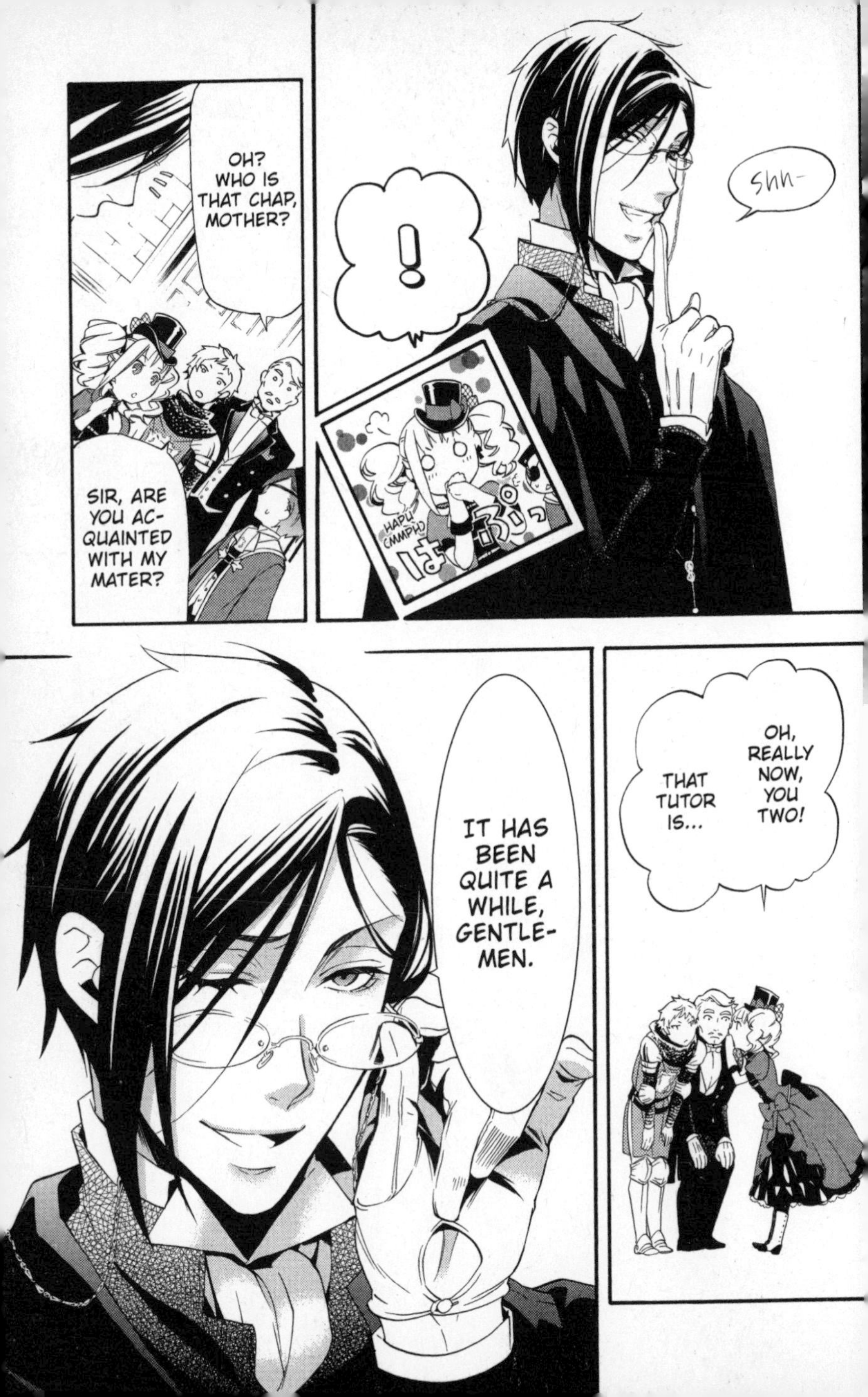
Shh-
!
HAPU (MMPH)
はぷっ
OH? WHO IS THAT CHAP, MOTHER?
SIR, ARE YOU AC-QUAINTED WITH MY MATER?
OH, REALLY NOW, YOU TWO!
THAT TUTOR IS...
IT HAS BEEN QUITE A WHILE, GENTLE-MEN.

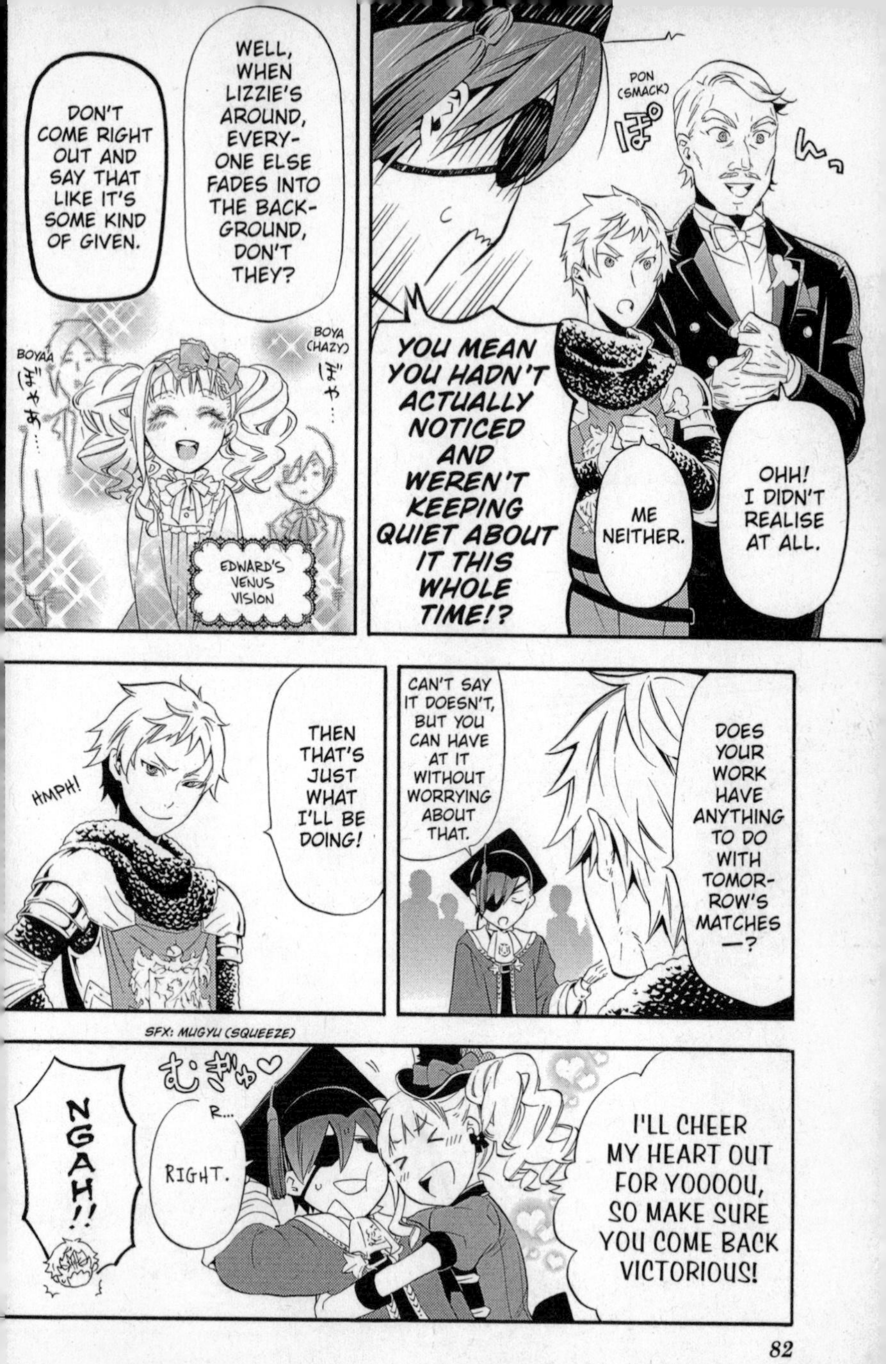
PON (SMACK)
ぽん
OHH! I DIDN'T REALISE AT ALL.
ME NEITHER.
YOU MEAN YOU HADN'T ACTUALLY NOTICED AND WEREN'T KEEPING QUIET ABOUT IT THIS WHOLE TIME!?
BOYA (HAZY)
ぼや…
WELL, WHEN LIZZIE'S AROUND, EVERY-ONE ELSE FADES INTO THE BACK-GROUND, DON'T THEY?
DON'T COME RIGHT OUT AND SAY THAT LIKE IT'S SOME KIND OF GIVEN.
BOYAA
ぼやあ…
EDWARD'S VENUS VISION
DOES YOUR WORK HAVE ANYTHING TO DO WITH TOMOR-ROW'S MATCHES —?
CAN'T SAY IT DOESN'T, BUT YOU CAN HAVE AT IT WITHOUT WORRYING ABOUT THAT.
THEN THAT'S JUST WHAT I'LL BE DOING!
HMPH!
SFX: MUGYU (SQUEEZE)
I'LL CHEER MY HEART OUT FOR YOOOOU, SO MAKE SURE YOU COME BACK VICTORIOUS!
むぎゅ♡
R...
RIGHT.
NGAH!!

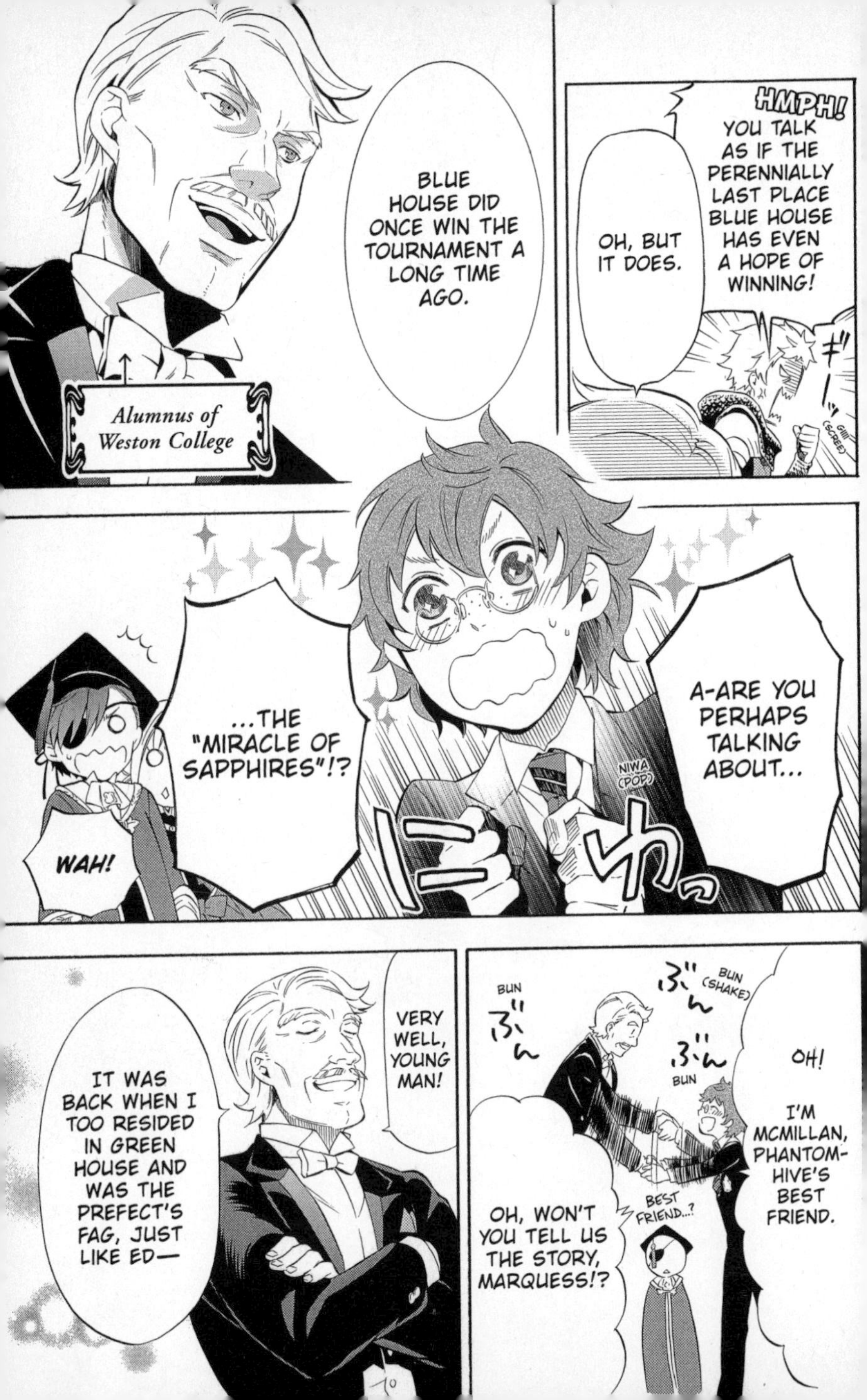
HMPH!
YOU TALK AS IF THE PERENNIALLY LAST PLACE BLUE HOUSE HAS EVEN A HOPE OF WINNING!
GIII (SCREE)
OH, BUT IT DOES.
BLUE HOUSE DID ONCE WIN THE TOURNAMENT A LONG TIME AGO.
Alumnus of Weston College
A-ARE YOU PERHAPS TALKING ABOUT...
NIWA (POP)
...THE "MIRACLE OF SAPPHIRES"!?
WAH!
BUN (SHAKE)
OH!
I'M MCMILLAN, PHANTOMHIVE'S BEST FRIEND.
BUN
BUN
BEST FRIEND...?
OH, WON'T YOU TELL US THE STORY, MARQUESS!?
VERY WELL, YOUNG MAN!
IT WAS BACK WHEN I TOO RESIDED IN GREEN HOUSE AND WAS THE PREFECT'S FAG, JUST LIKE ED—

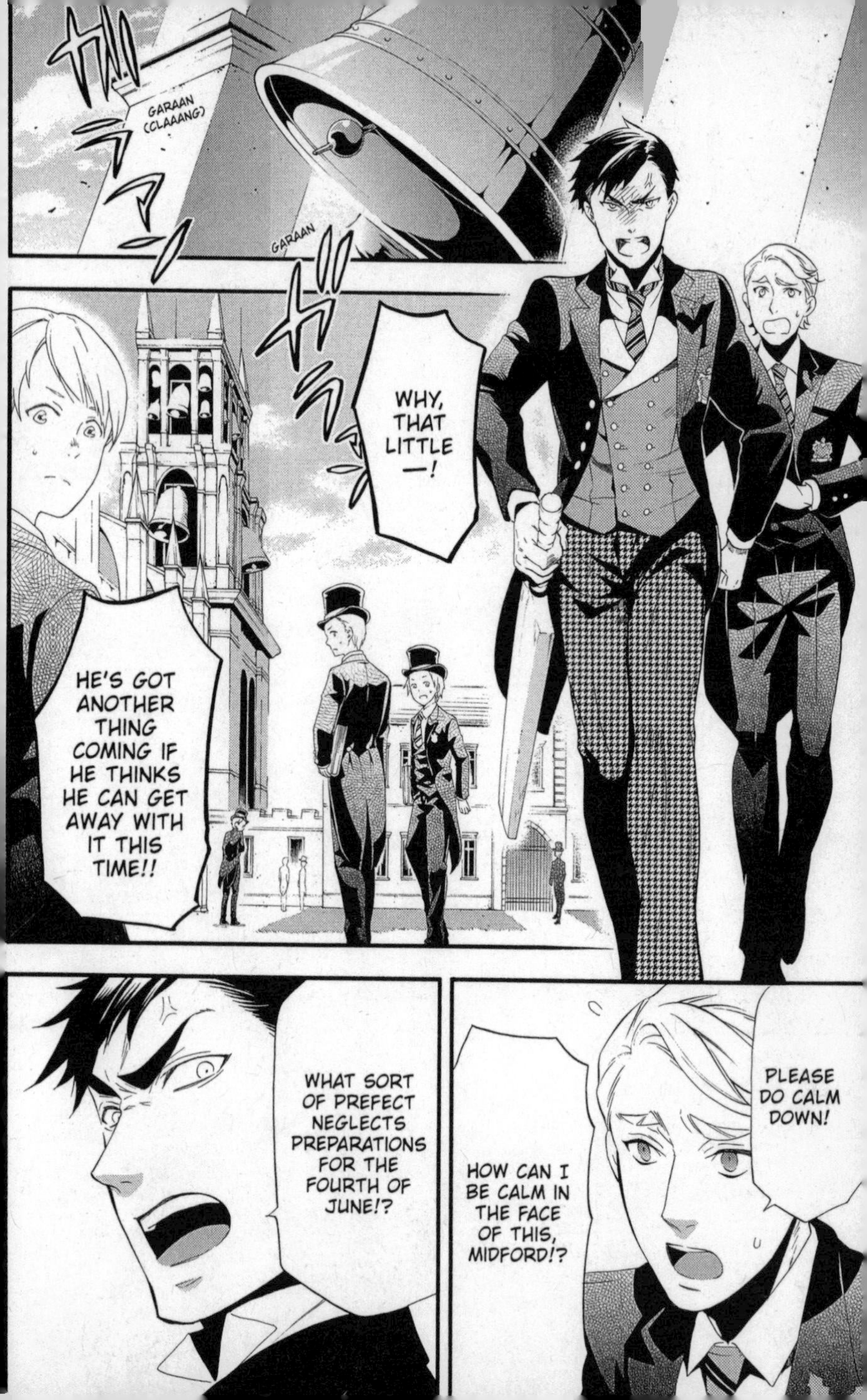
GARAAN (CLAAANG)
GARAAN
WHY, THAT LITTLE—!
HE'S GOT ANOTHER THING COMING IF HE THINKS HE CAN GET AWAY WITH IT THIS TIME!!
PLEASE DO CALM DOWN!
HOW CAN I BE CALM IN THE FACE OF THIS, MIDFORD!?
WHAT SORT OF PREFECT NEGLECTS PREPARATIONS FOR THE FOURTH OF JUNE!?

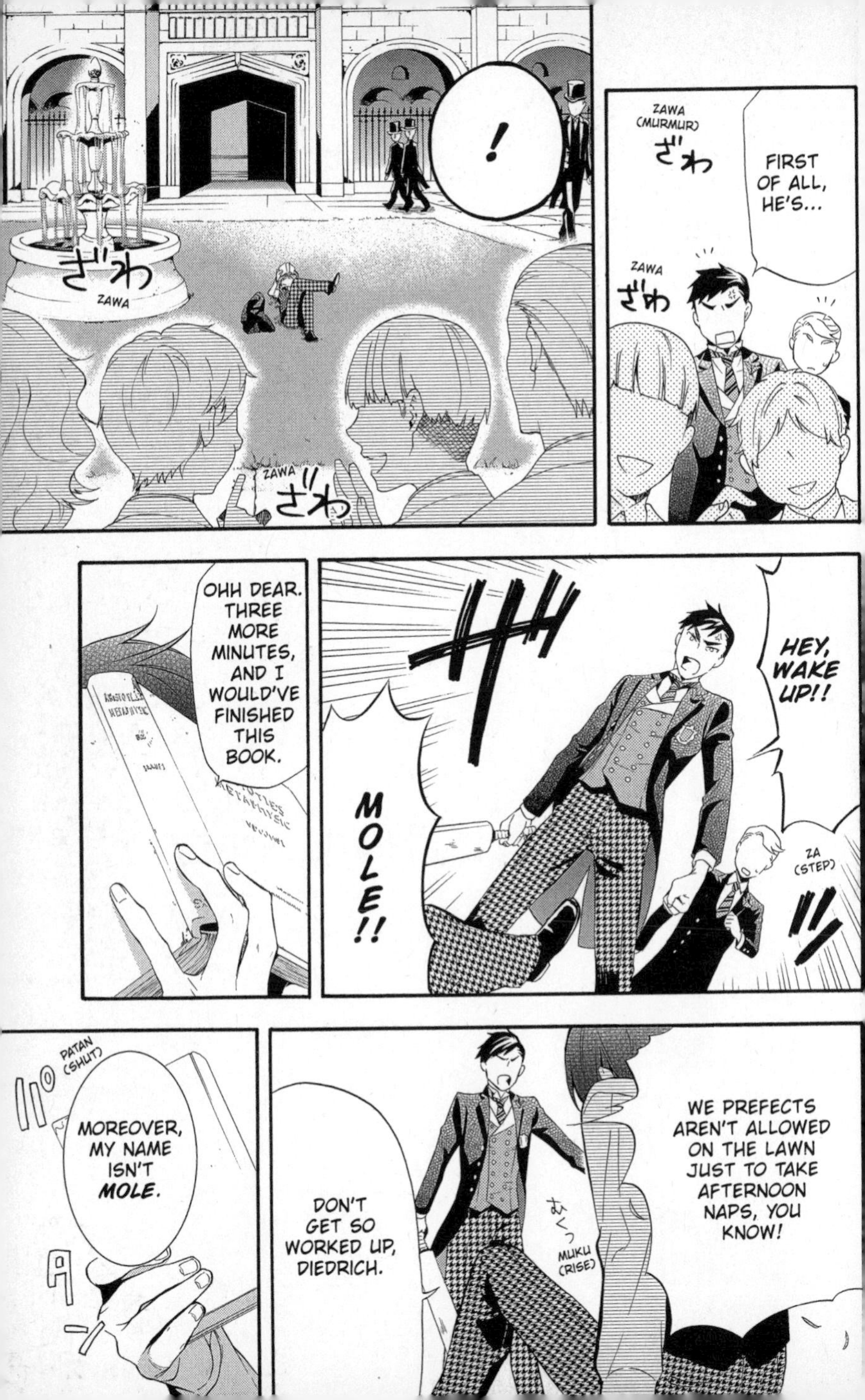
ZAWA (MURMUR)
ざわ
FIRST OF ALL, HE'S...
ZAWA
ざわ
!
ざわ
ZAWA
ZAWA
ざわ
HEY, WAKE UP!!
MOLE!!
ZA (STEP)
OHH DEAR. THREE MORE MINUTES, AND I WOULD'VE FINISHED THIS BOOK.
WE PREFECTS AREN'T ALLOWED ON THE LAWN JUST TO TAKE AFTERNOON NAPS, YOU KNOW!
むくっ
MUKU (RISE)
DON'T GET SO WORKED UP, DIEDRICH.
PATAN (SHUT)
MOREOVER, MY NAME ISN'T MOLE.

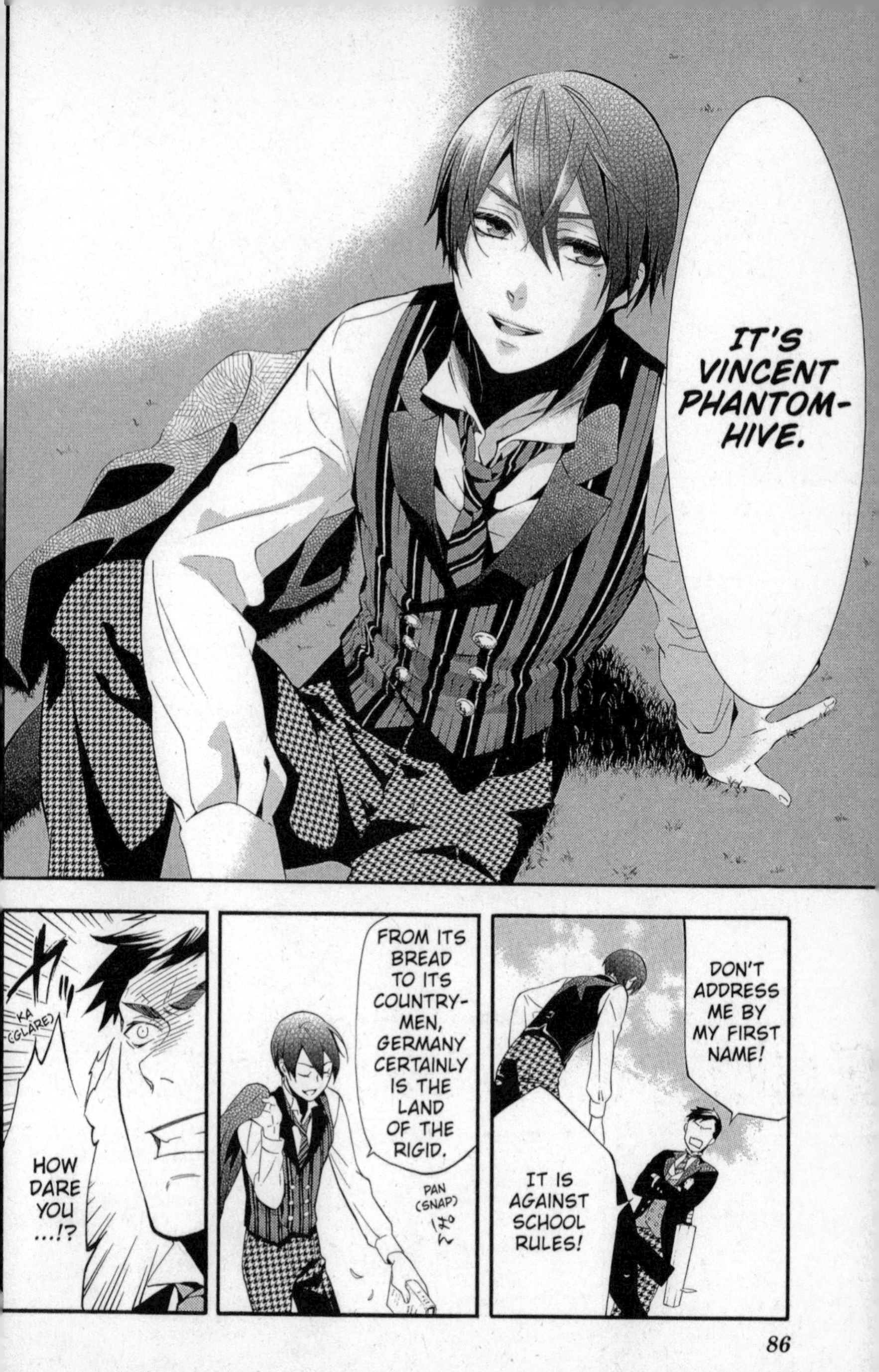
IT'S VINCENT PHANTOM-HIVE.
DON'T ADDRESS ME BY MY FIRST NAME!
IT IS AGAINST SCHOOL RULES!
FROM ITS BREAD TO ITS COUNTRY-MEN, GERMANY CERTAINLY IS THE LAND OF THE RIGID.
PAN (SNAP)
ぱん
KA (GLARE)
HOW DARE YOU ...!?

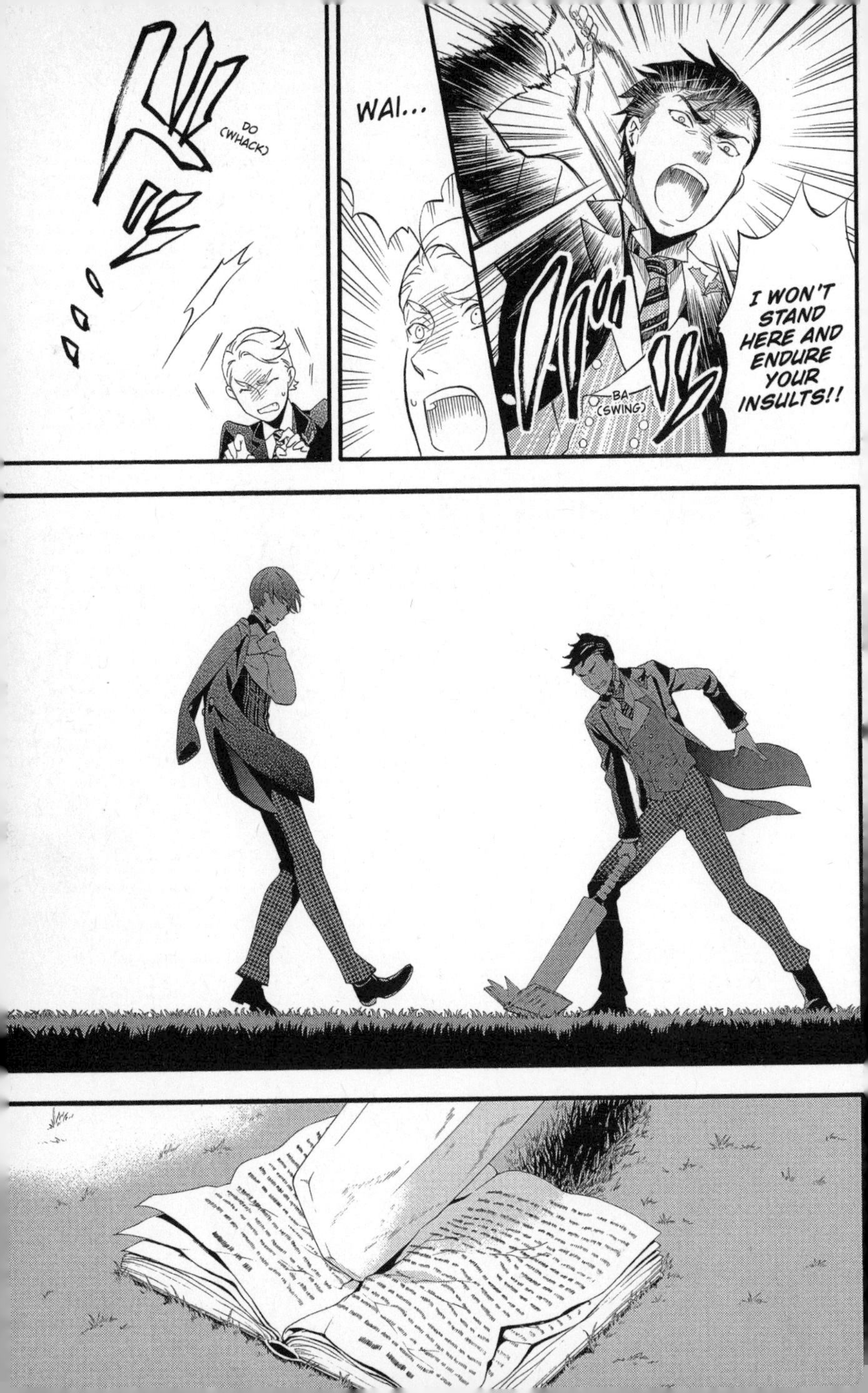
I WON'T STAND HERE AND ENDURE YOUR INSULTS!!
BA (SWING)
WAI...
DO (WHACK)

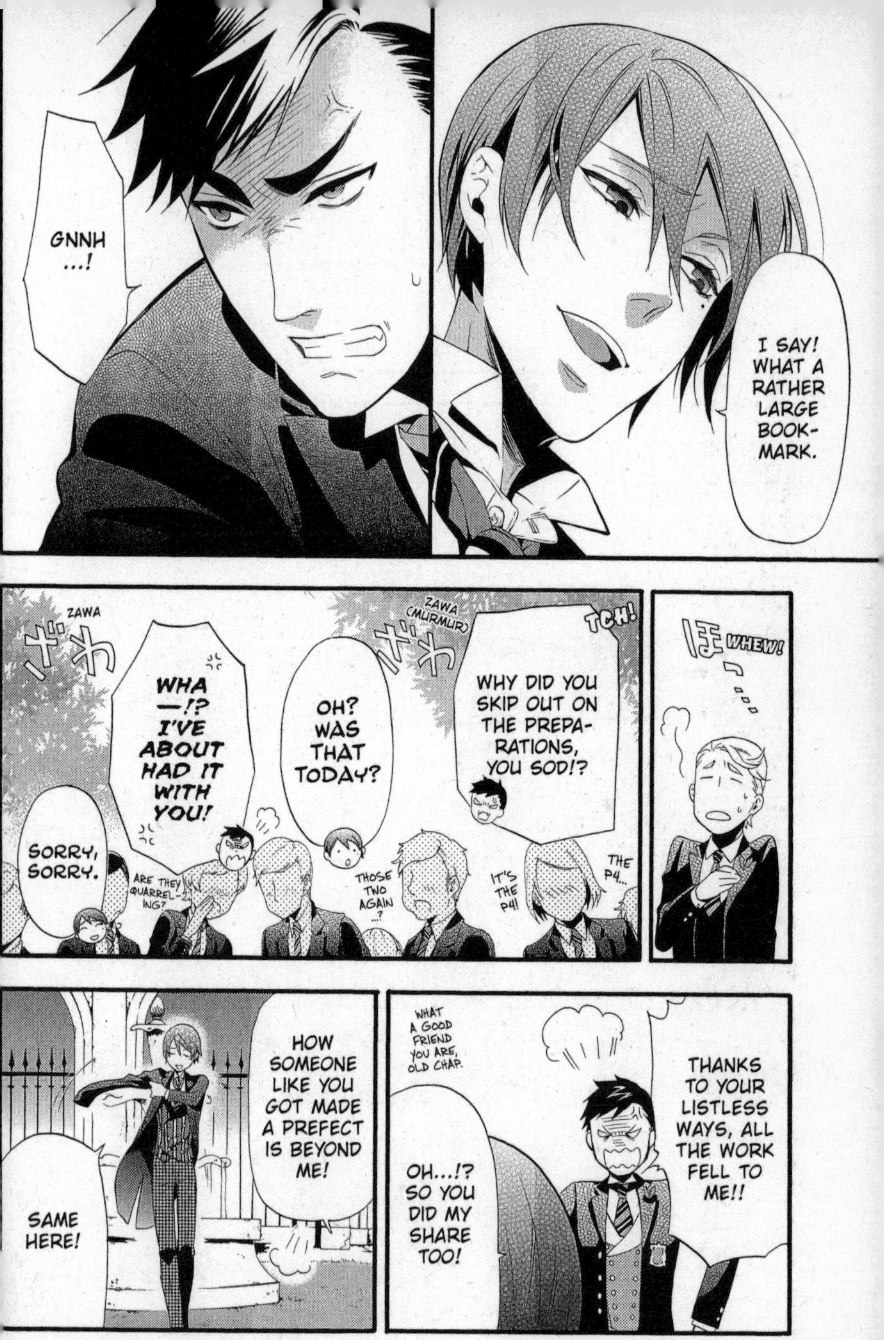
I SAY! WHAT A RATHER LARGE BOOK-MARK.
GNNH ...!
ほっ
WHEW!
TCH!
ざわ
ZAWA (MURMUR)
WHY DID YOU SKIP OUT ON THE PREPA-RATIONS, YOU SOD!?
OH? WAS THAT TODAY?
WHA—!? I'VE ABOUT HAD IT WITH YOU!
ざわ
ZAWA
THE P4...
IT'S THE P4!
THOSE TWO AGAIN ...?
ARE THEY QUARREL-ING?
SORRY, SORRY.
THANKS TO YOUR LISTLESS WAYS, ALL THE WORK FELL TO ME!!
WHAT A GOOD FRIEND YOU ARE, OLD CHAP.
OH...!? SO YOU DID MY SHARE TOO!
HOW SOMEONE LIKE YOU GOT MADE A PREFECT IS BEYOND ME!
SAME HERE!

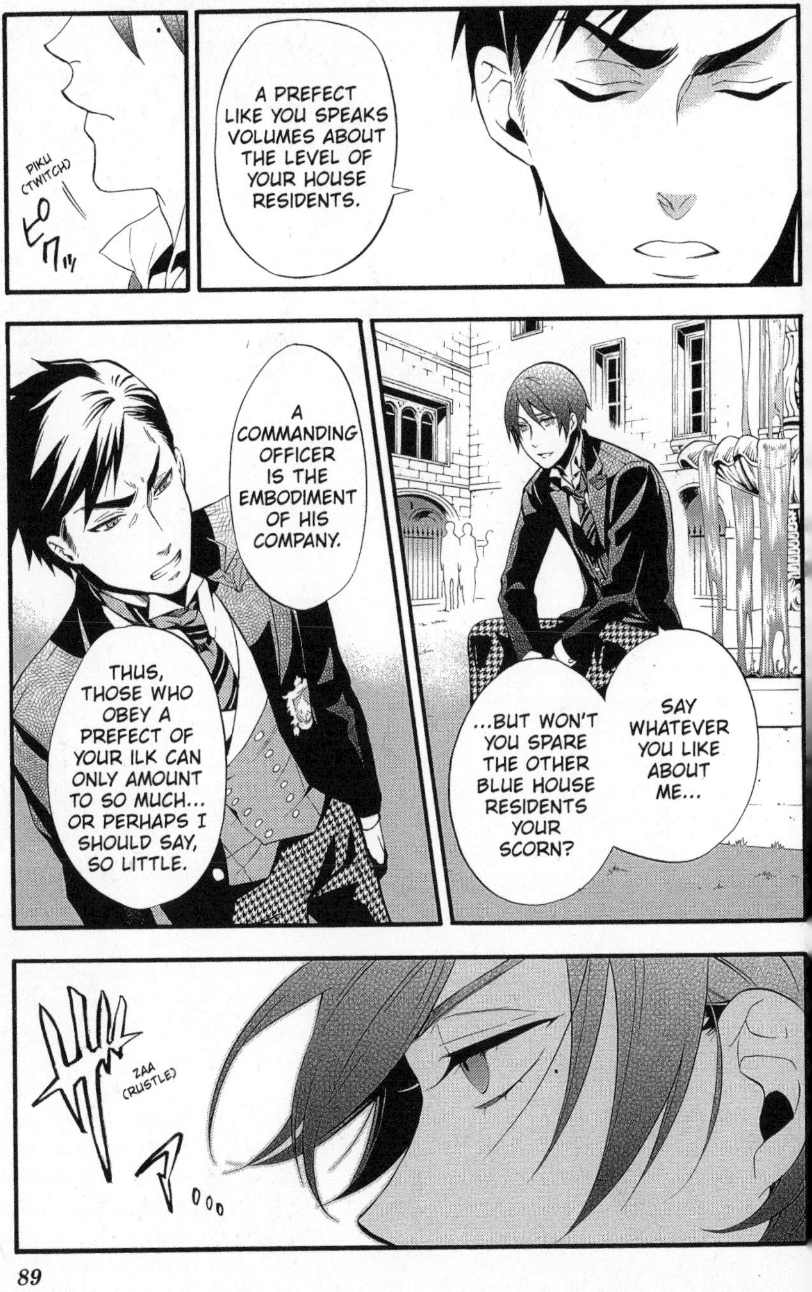
A PREFECT LIKE YOU SPEAKS VOLUMES ABOUT THE LEVEL OF YOUR HOUSE RESIDENTS.
PIKU (TWITCH)
SAY WHATEVER YOU LIKE ABOUT ME...
...BUT WON'T YOU SPARE THE OTHER BLUE HOUSE RESIDENTS YOUR SCORN?
A COMMANDING OFFICER IS THE EMBODIMENT OF HIS COMPANY.
THUS, THOSE WHO OBEY A PREFECT OF YOUR ILK CAN ONLY AMOUNT TO SO MUCH... OR PERHAPS I SHOULD SAY, SO LITTLE.
ZAA (RUSTLE)

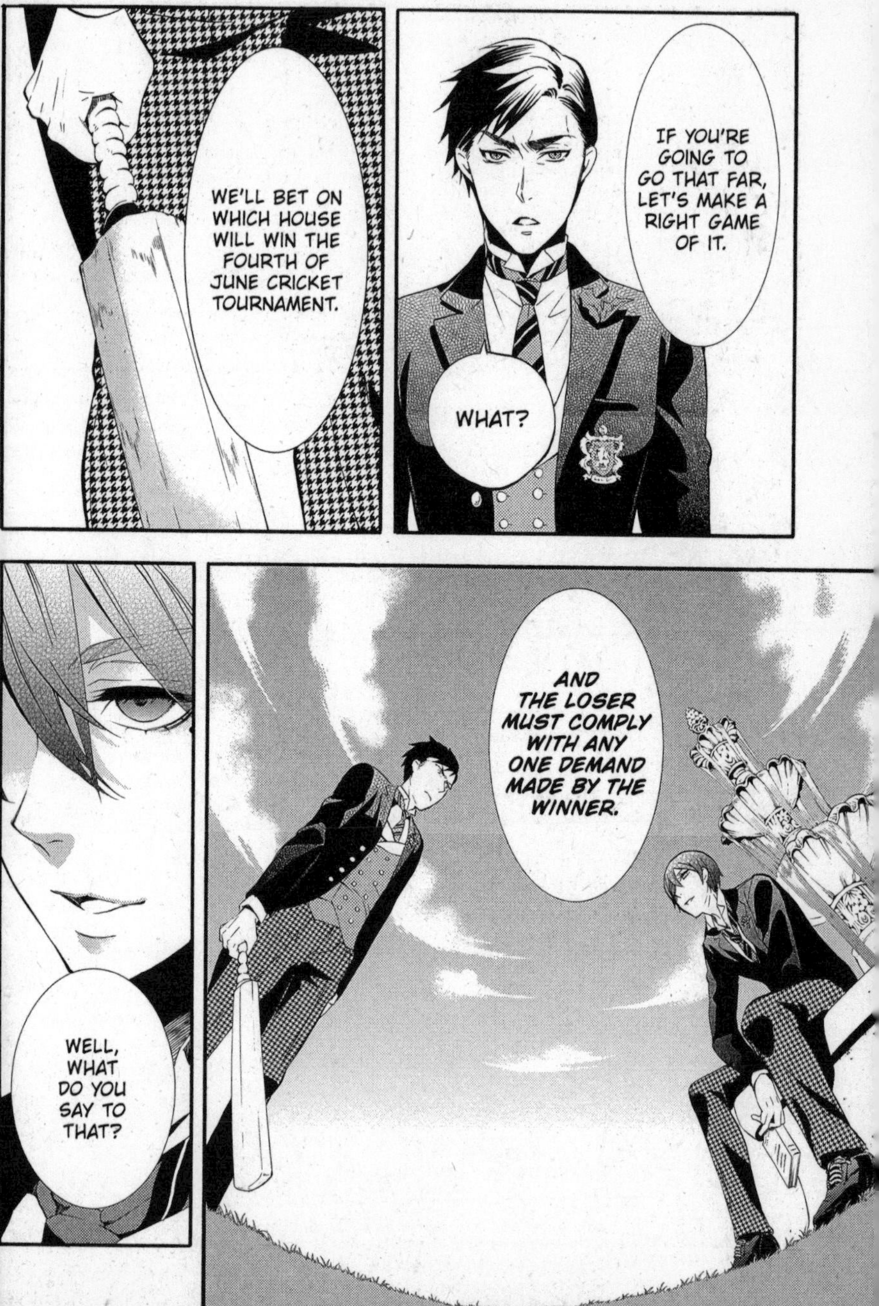
IF YOU'RE GOING TO GO THAT FAR, LET'S MAKE A RIGHT GAME OF IT.
WHAT?
WE'LL BET ON WHICH HOUSE WILL WIN THE FOURTH OF JUNE CRICKET TOURNAMENT.
AND THE LOSER MUST COMPLY WITH ANY ONE DEMAND MADE BY THE WINNER.
WELL, WHAT DO YOU SAY TO THAT?

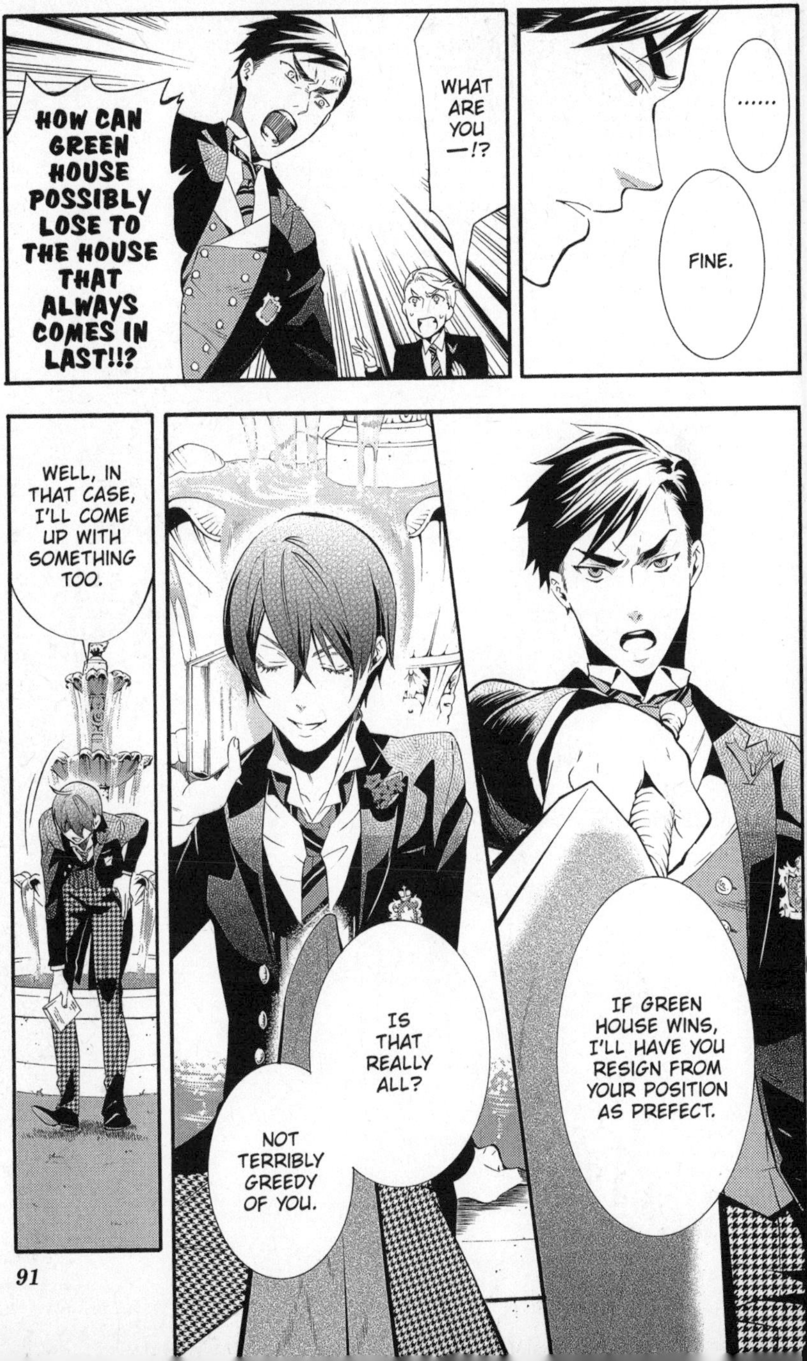
......
FINE.
WHAT ARE YOU—!?
HOW CAN GREEN HOUSE POSSIBLY LOSE TO THE HOUSE THAT ALWAYS COMES IN LAST!!?
IF GREEN HOUSE WINS, I'LL HAVE YOU RESIGN FROM YOUR POSITION AS PREFECT.
IS THAT REALLY ALL?
NOT TERRIBLY GREEDY OF YOU.
WELL, IN THAT CASE, I'LL COME UP WITH SOMETHING TOO.

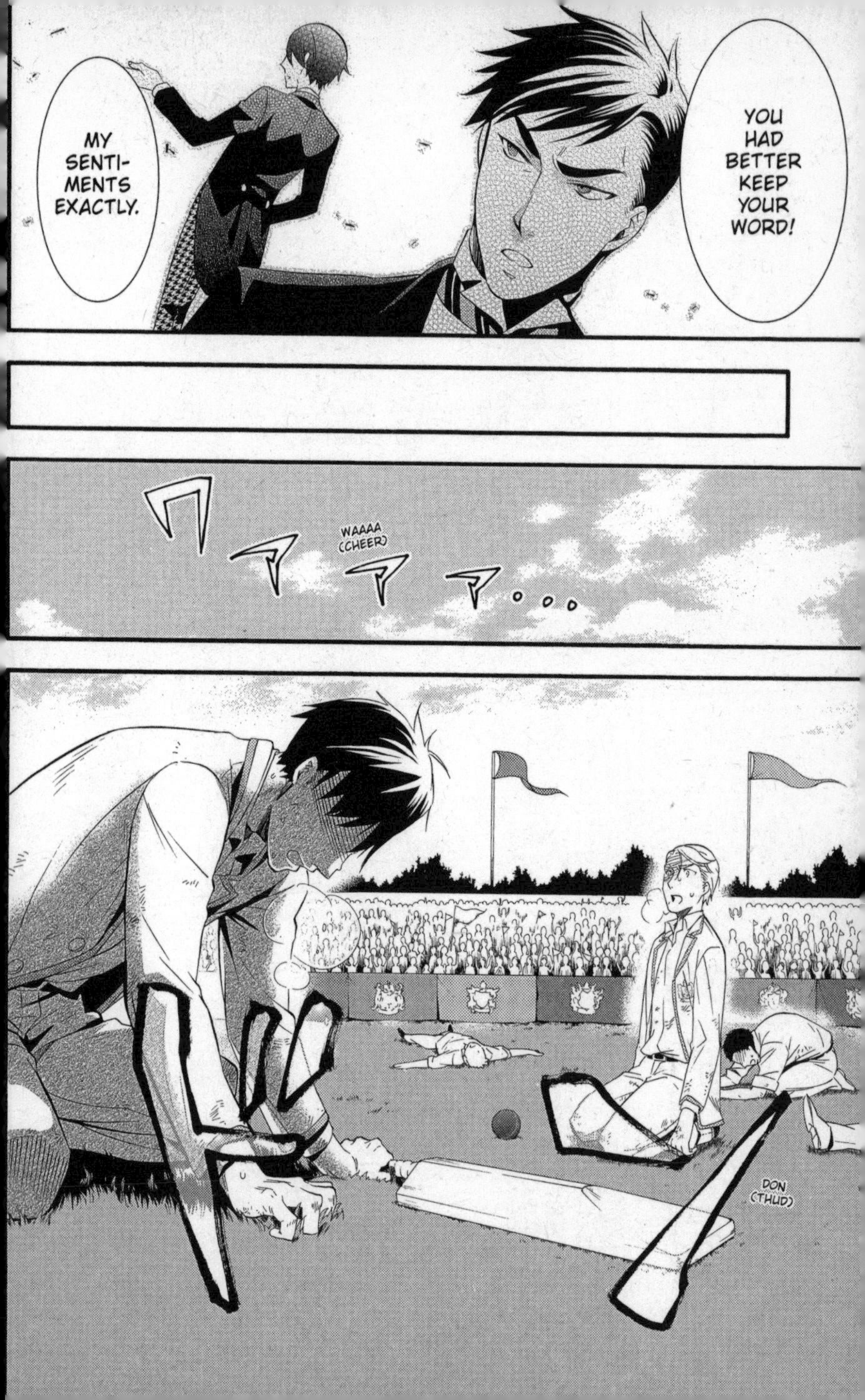
YOU HAD BETTER KEEP YOUR WORD!
MY SENTI-MENTS EXACTLY.
WAAAA (CHEER)
DON (THUD)

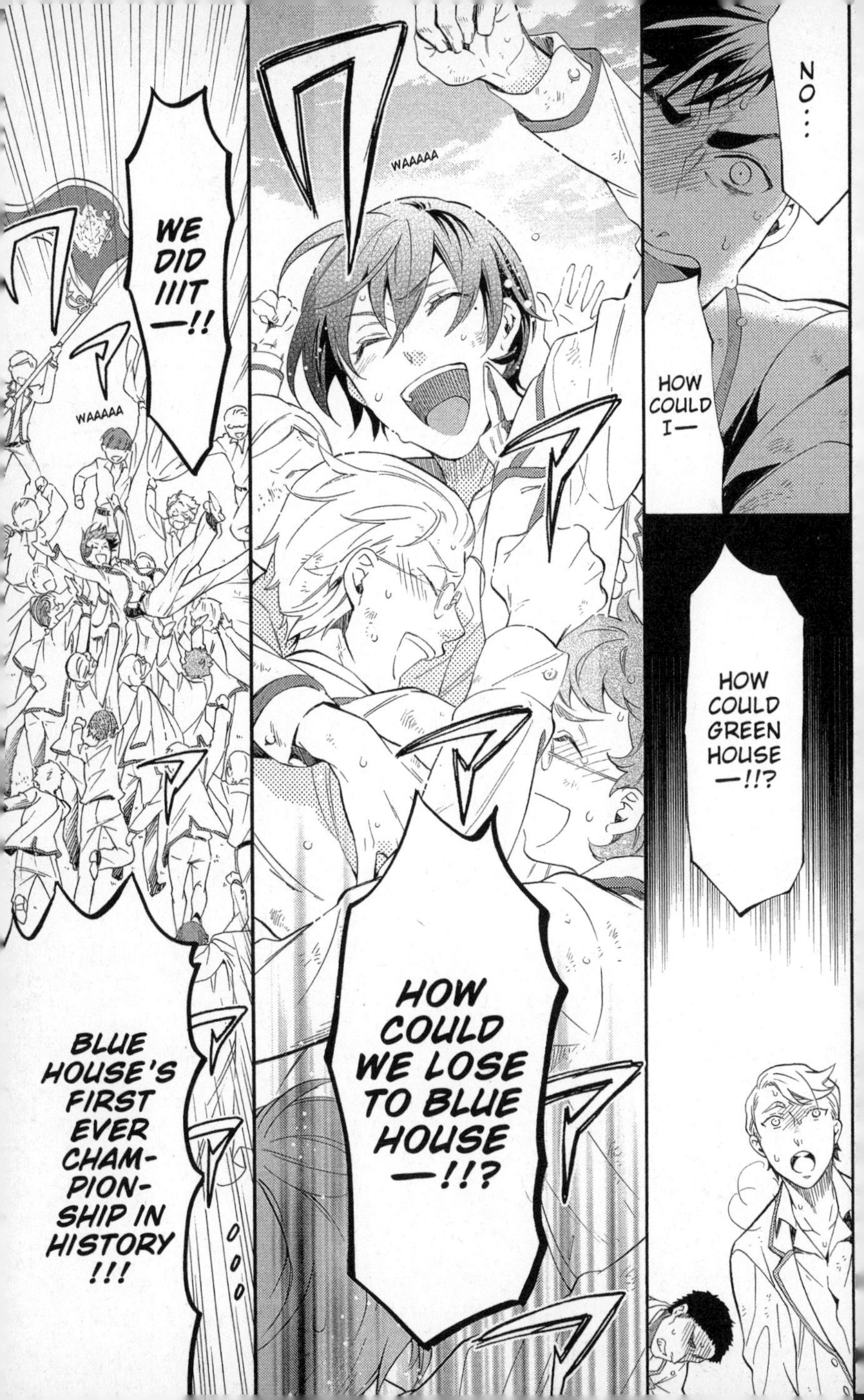
NO...
HOW COULD I—
HOW COULD GREEN HOUSE—!!?
WAAAAA
HOW COULD WE LOSE TO BLUE HOUSE—!!?
WE DID IIIT—!!
WAAAAA
BLUE HOUSE'S FIRST EVER CHAMPIONSHIP IN HISTORY!!!

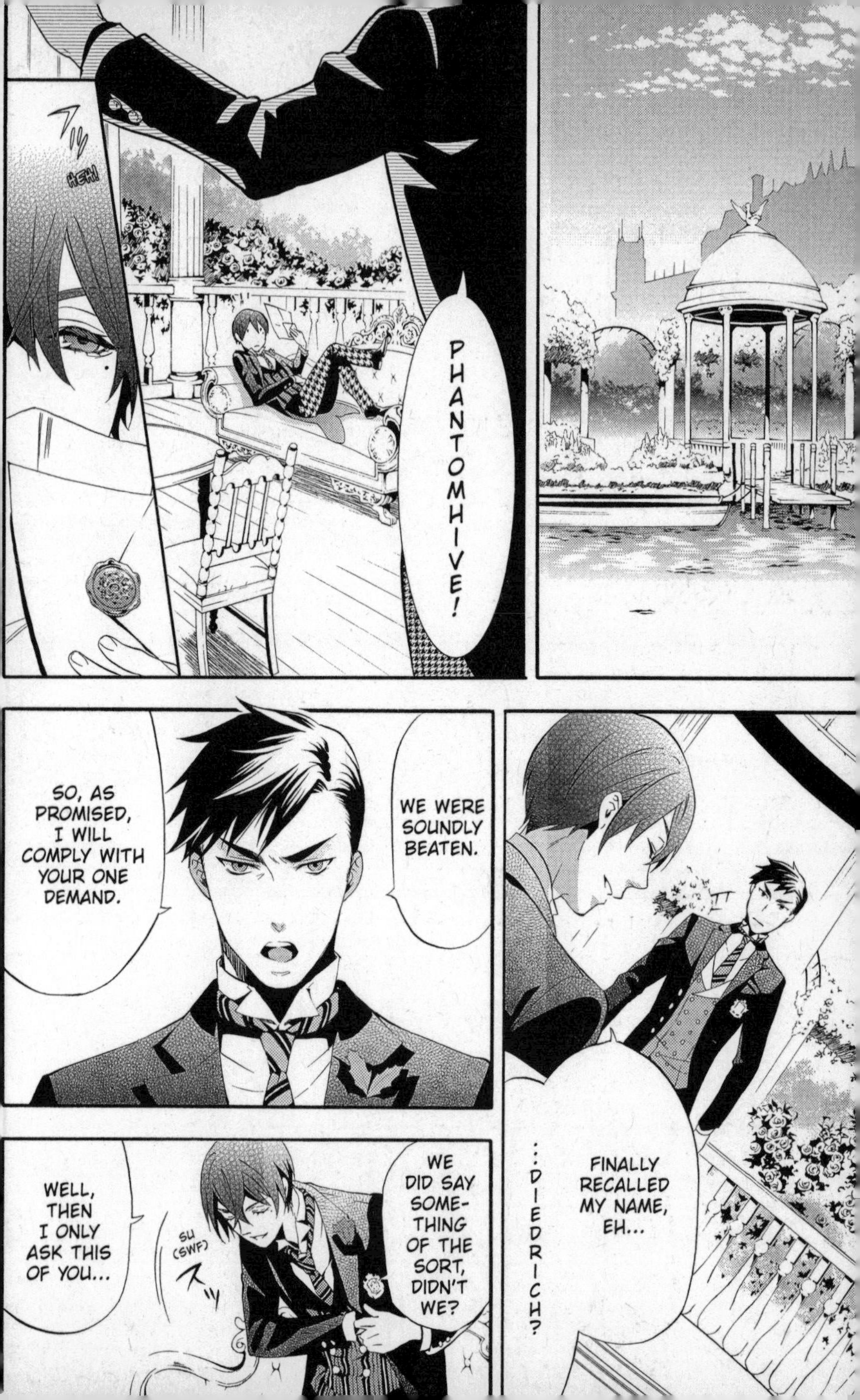
PHANTOMHIVE!
HEH!
FINALLY RECALLED MY NAME, EH...
...DIEDRICH?
WE WERE SOUNDLY BEATEN.
SO, AS PROMISED, I WILL COMPLY WITH YOUR ONE DEMAND.
WE DID SAY SOMETHING OF THE SORT, DIDN'T WE?
SU (SWF)
WELL, THEN I ONLY ASK THIS OF YOU...

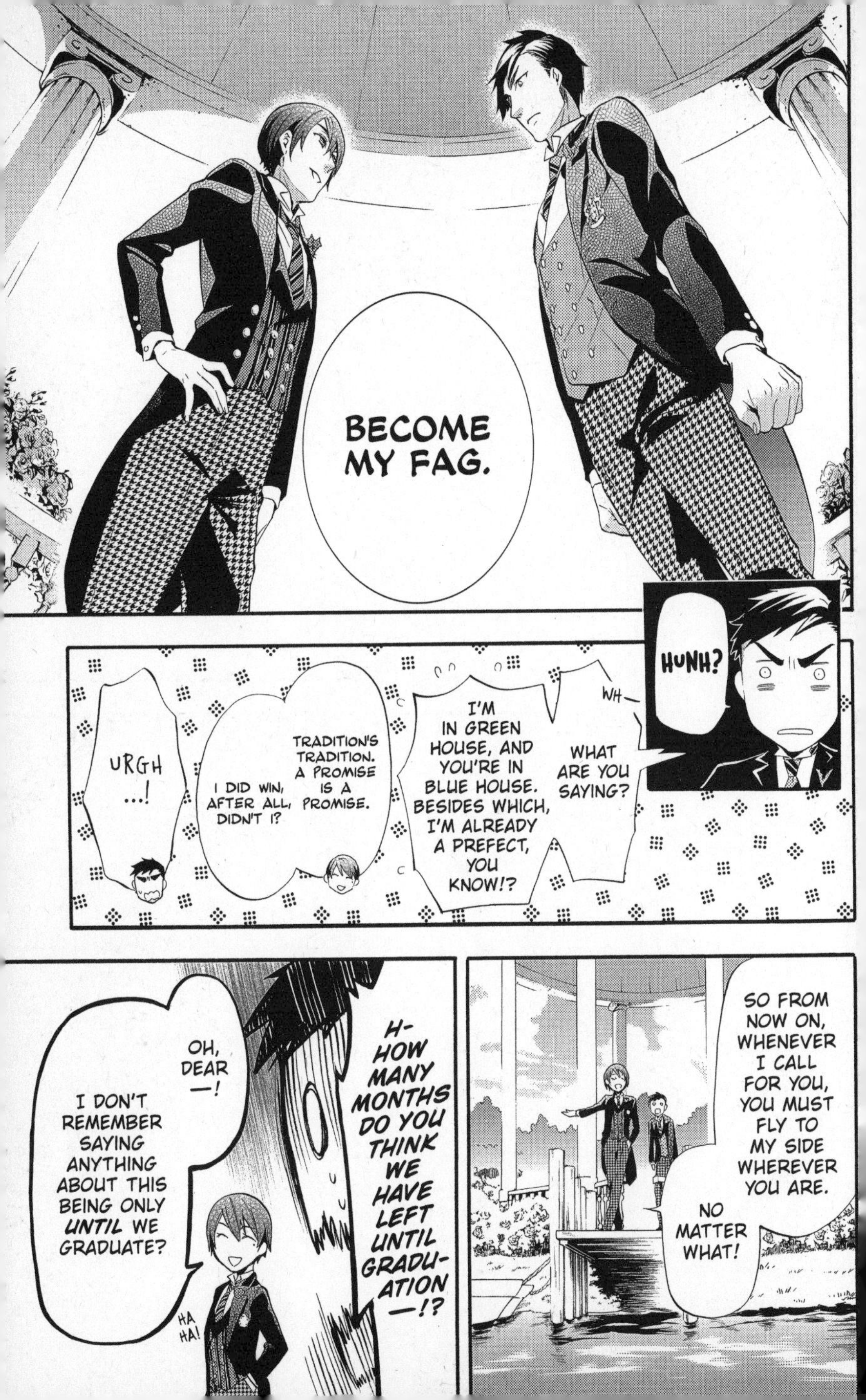
BECOME MY FAG.
HUNH?
WH—
WHAT ARE YOU SAYING?
I'M IN GREEN HOUSE, AND YOU'RE IN BLUE HOUSE. BESIDES WHICH, I'M ALREADY A PREFECT, YOU KNOW!?
TRADITION'S TRADITION. A PROMISE IS A PROMISE.
I DID WIN, AFTER ALL, DIDN'T I?
URGH ...!
SO FROM NOW ON, WHENEVER I CALL FOR YOU, YOU MUST FLY TO MY SIDE WHEREVER YOU ARE.
NO MATTER WHAT!
H-HOW MANY MONTHS DO YOU THINK WE HAVE LEFT UNTIL GRADU-ATION—!?
OH, DEAR—!
I DON'T REMEMBER SAYING ANYTHING ABOUT THIS BEING ONLY *UNTIL* WE GRADUATE?
HA HA!

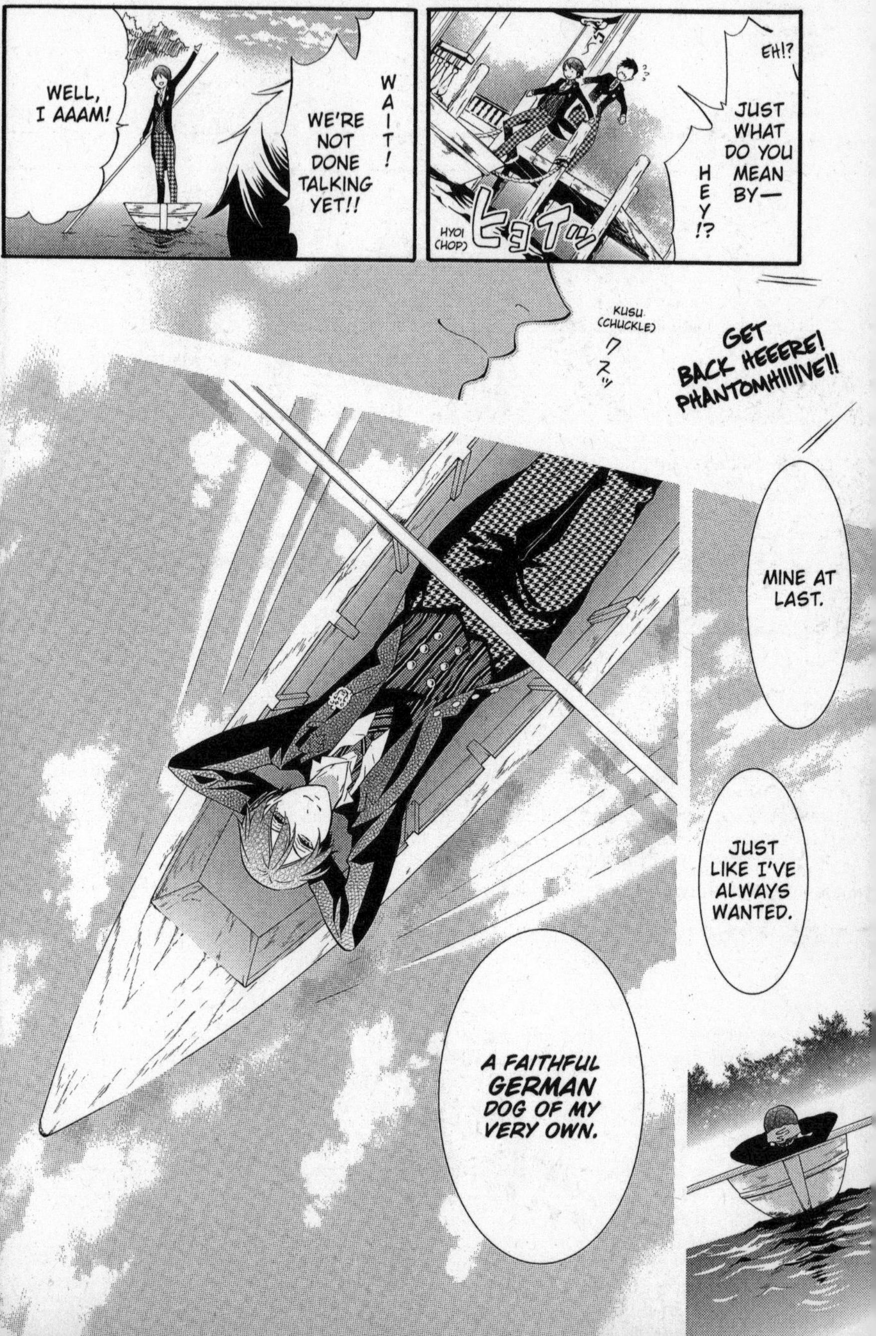
EH!?
JUST WHAT DO YOU MEAN BY—
HEY!?
HYOI (HOP)
ヒョイッ
WAIT!
WE'RE NOT DONE TALKING YET!!
WELL, I AAAM!
KUSU (CHUCKLE)
クスッ
GET BACK HEEERE! PHANTOMHIIIIVE!!
MINE AT LAST.
JUST LIKE I'VE ALWAYS WANTED.
A FAITHFUL GERMAN DOG OF MY VERY OWN.

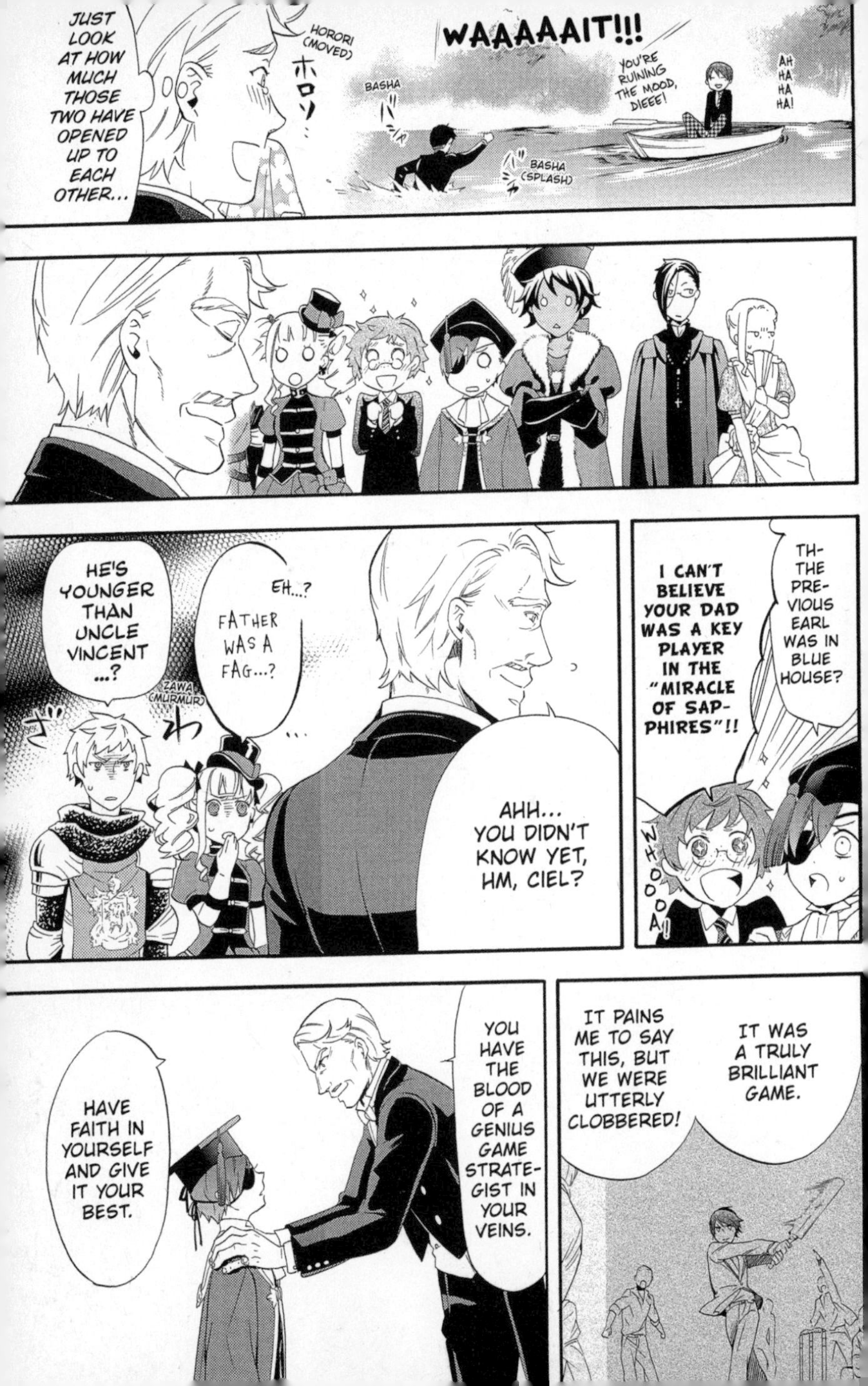
AH HA HA HA!
YOU'RE RUINING THE MOOD, DIEEE!
WAAAAAIT!!!
BASHA
BASHA (SPLASH)
HORORI (MOVED)
JUST LOOK AT HOW MUCH THOSE TWO HAVE OPENED UP TO EACH OTHER...
TH-THE PRE-VIOUS EARL WAS IN BLUE HOUSE?
I CAN'T BELIEVE YOUR DAD WAS A KEY PLAYER IN THE "MIRACLE OF SAP-PHIRES"!!
WHOOOA!
AHH... YOU DIDN'T KNOW YET, HM, CIEL?
EH...?
FATHER WAS A FAG...?
HE'S YOUNGER THAN UNCLE VINCENT ...?
ZAWA (MURMUR)
IT WAS A TRULY BRILLIANT GAME.
IT PAINS ME TO SAY THIS, BUT WE WERE UTTERLY CLOBBERED!
YOU HAVE THE BLOOD OF A GENIUS GAME STRATE-GIST IN YOUR VEINS.
HAVE FAITH IN YOURSELF AND GIVE IT YOUR BEST.

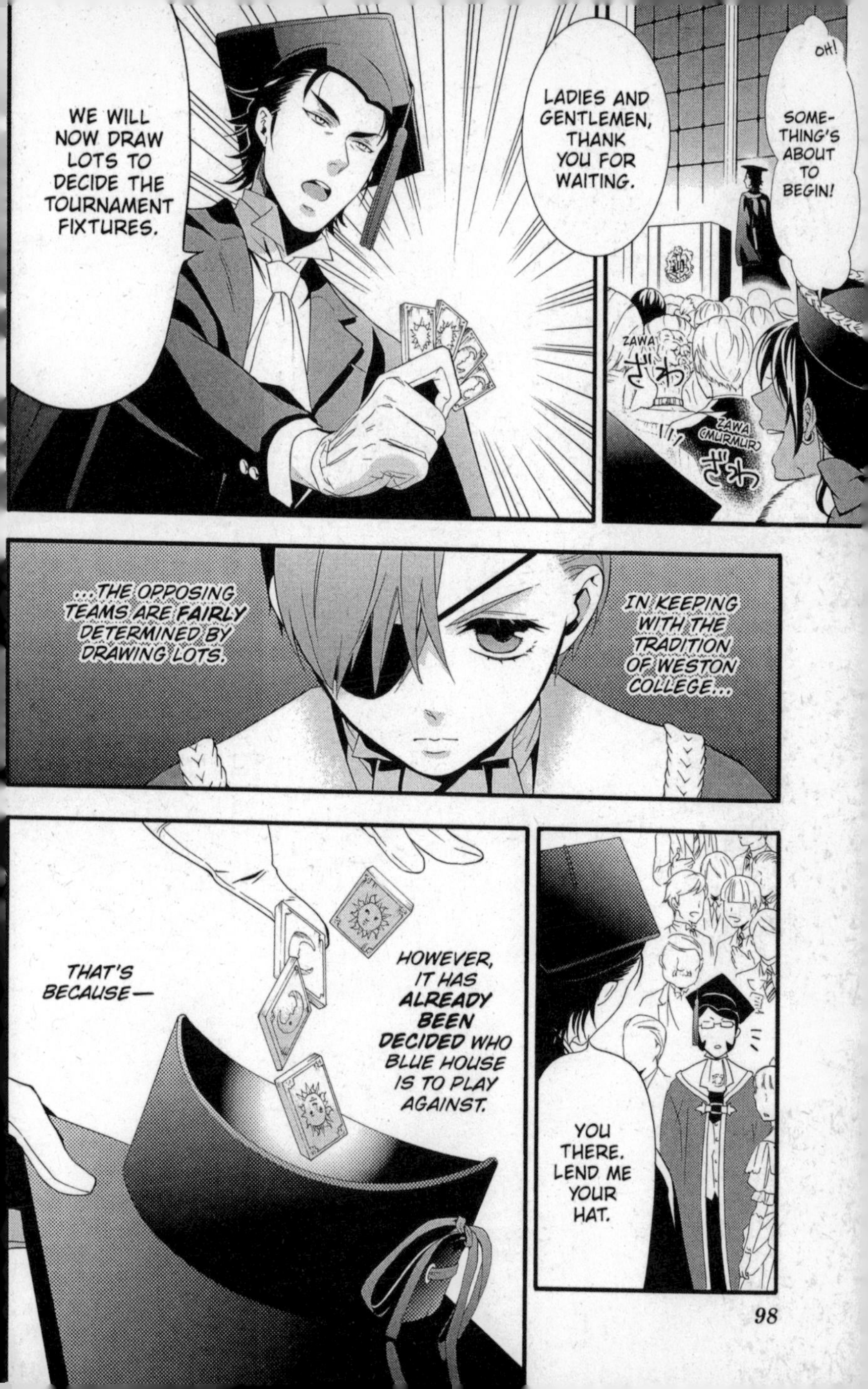
OH!
SOMETHING'S ABOUT TO BEGIN!
LADIES AND GENTLEMEN, THANK YOU FOR WAITING.
ZAWA ざわ
ZAWA (MURMUR) ざわ
WE WILL NOW DRAW LOTS TO DECIDE THE TOURNAMENT FIXTURES.
IN KEEPING WITH THE TRADITION OF WESTON COLLEGE...
...THE OPPOSING TEAMS ARE FAIRLY DETERMINED BY DRAWING LOTS.
YOU THERE. LEND ME YOUR HAT.
HOWEVER, IT HAS ALREADY BEEN DECIDED WHO BLUE HOUSE IS TO PLAY AGAINST.
THAT'S BECAUSE—

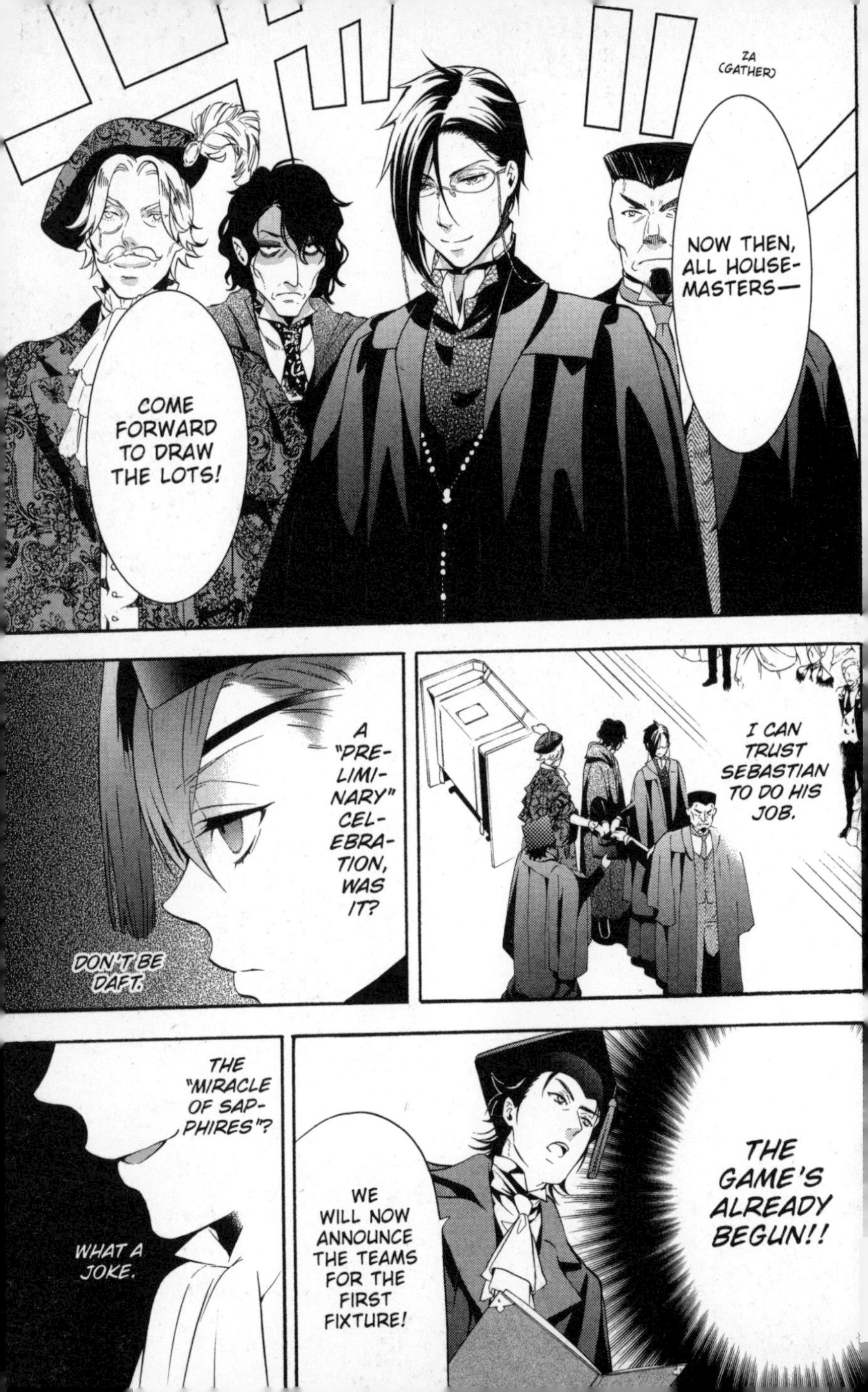
ZA (GATHER)
NOW THEN, ALL HOUSE-MASTERS—
COME FORWARD TO DRAW THE LOTS!
I CAN TRUST SEBASTIAN TO DO HIS JOB.
A "PRELIMINARY" CELEBRATION, WAS IT?
DON'T BE DAFT.
THE GAME'S ALREADY BEGUN!!
WE WILL NOW ANNOUNCE THE TEAMS FOR THE FIRST FIXTURE!
THE "MIRACLE OF SAPPHIRES"?
WHAT A JOKE.

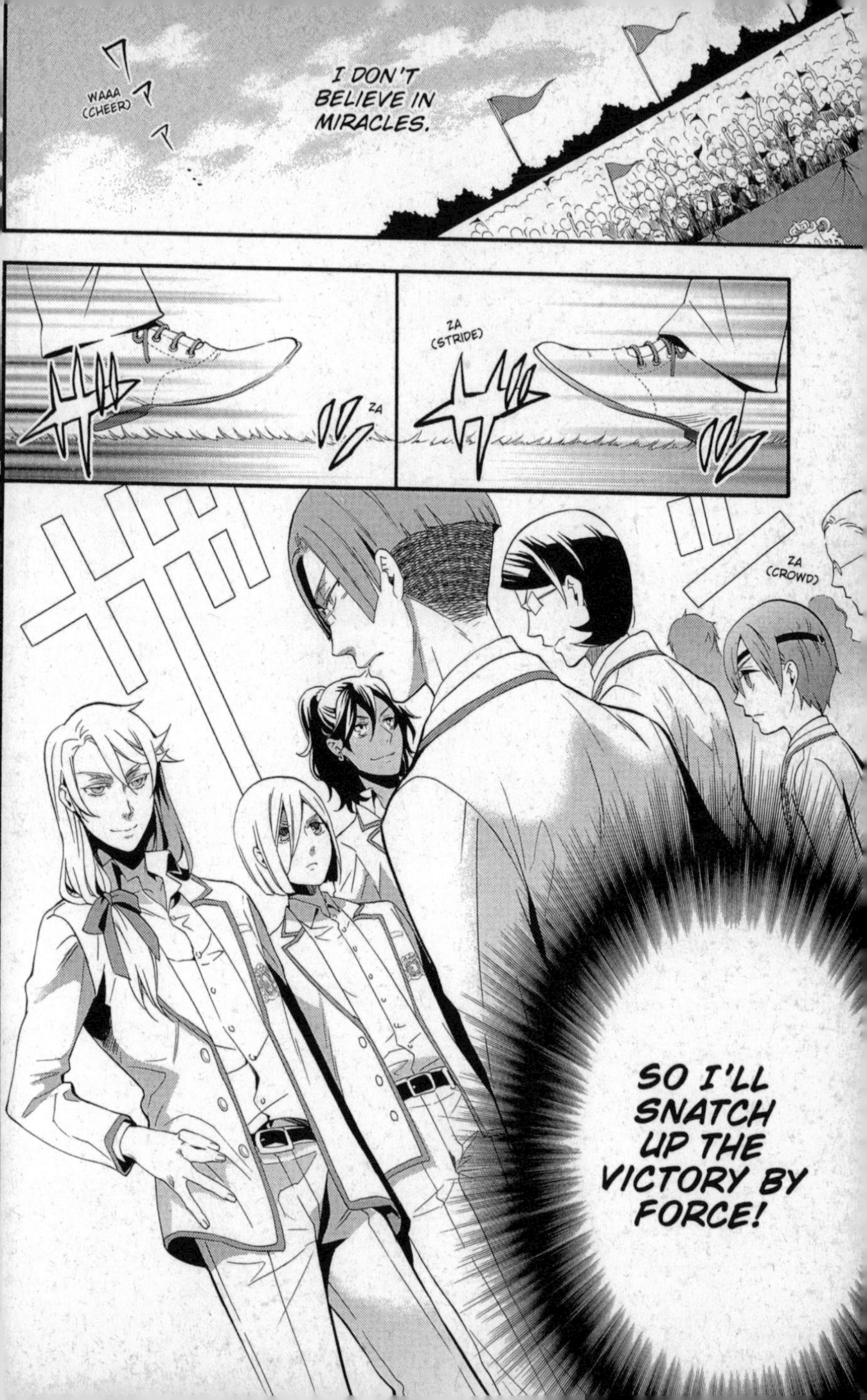
I DON'T BELIEVE IN MIRACLES.
WAAA (CHEER)
ZA (STRIDE)
ZA
ZA (CROWD)
SO I'LL SNATCH UP THE VICTORY BY FORCE!

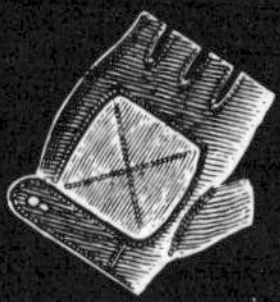

Black Butler

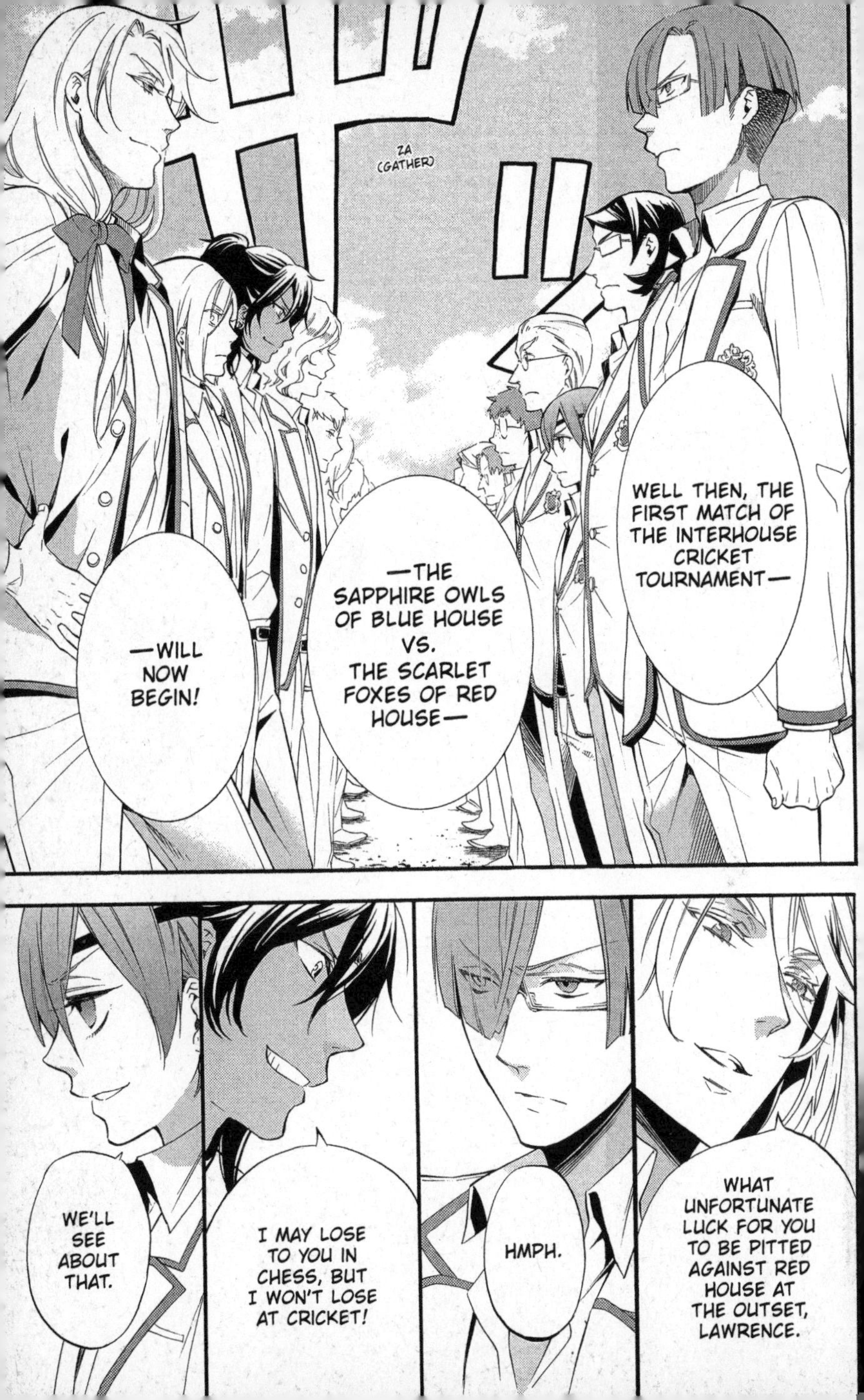
ZA (GATHER)
WELL THEN, THE FIRST MATCH OF THE INTERHOUSE CRICKET TOURNAMENT—
—THE SAPPHIRE OWLS OF BLUE HOUSE VS. THE SCARLET FOXES OF RED HOUSE—
—WILL NOW BEGIN!
WHAT UNFORTUNATE LUCK FOR YOU TO BE PITTED AGAINST RED HOUSE AT THE OUTSET, LAWRENCE.
HMPH.
I MAY LOSE TO YOU IN CHESS, BUT I WON'T LOSE AT CRICKET!
WE'LL SEE ABOUT THAT.

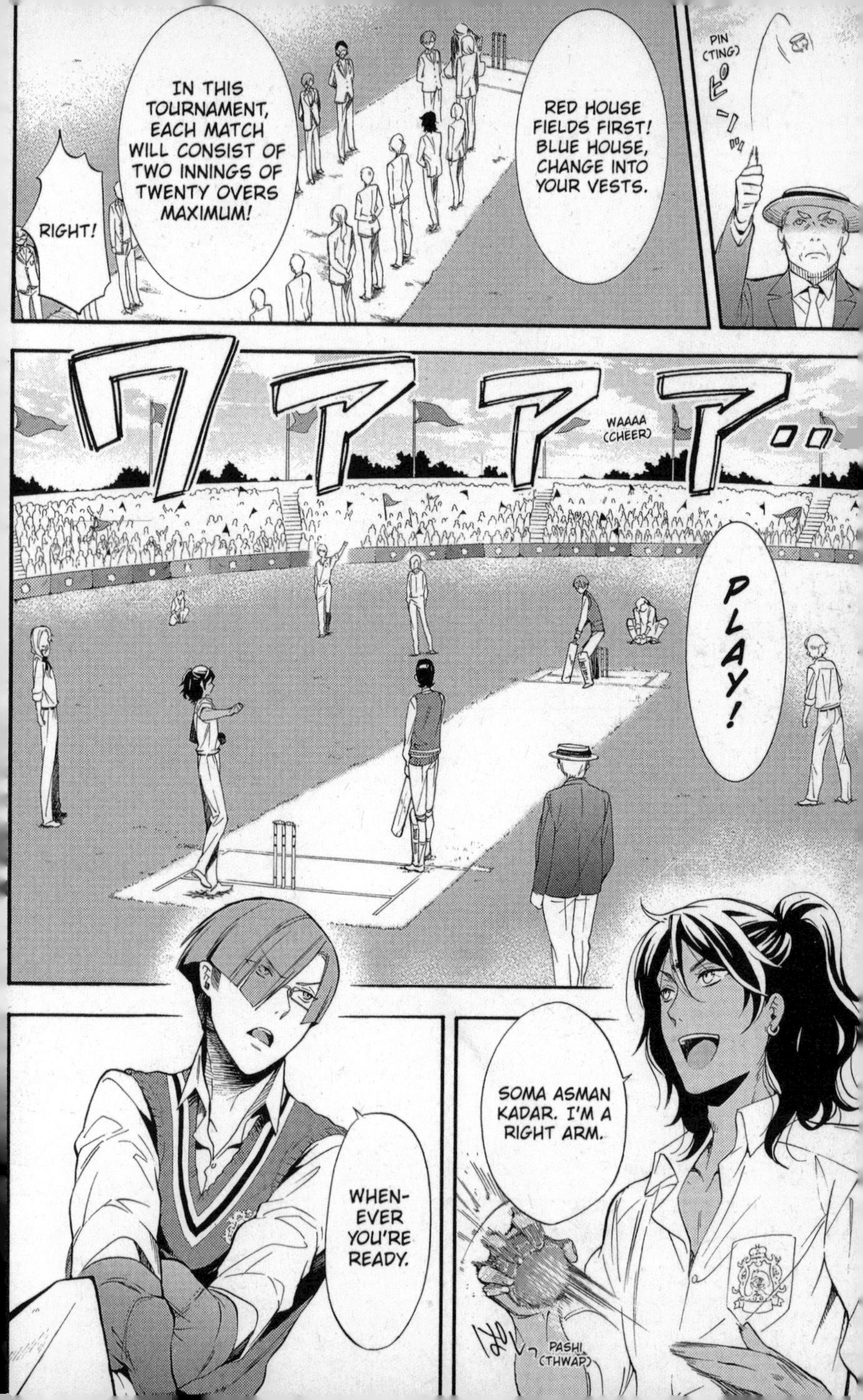

PIN (TING)
ピーッ
RED HOUSE FIELDS FIRST! BLUE HOUSE, CHANGE INTO YOUR VESTS.
IN THIS TOURNAMENT, EACH MATCH WILL CONSIST OF TWO INNINGS OF TWENTY OVERS MAXIMUM!
RIGHT!
ワアアア
WAAAA (CHEER)
PLAY!
SOMA ASMAN KADAR. I'M A RIGHT ARM.
ぱしっ
PASHI (THWAP)
WHEN-EVER YOU'RE READY.

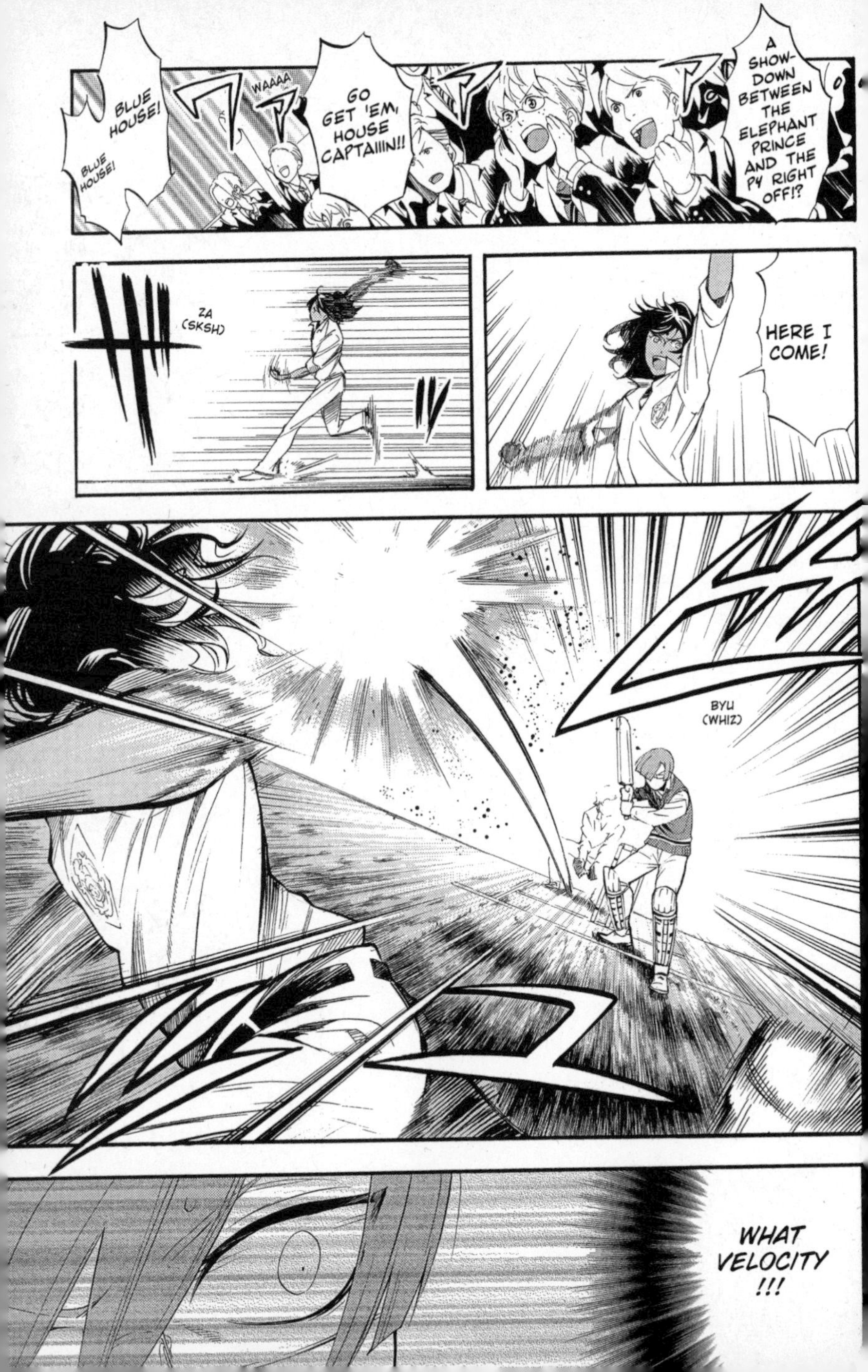
A SHOWDOWN BETWEEN THE ELEPHANT PRINCE AND THE P4 RIGHT OFF!?
GO GET 'EM, HOUSE CAPTAIIIN!!
WAAAA
BLUE HOUSE!
BLUE HOUSE!
HERE I COME!
ZA (SKSH)
BYU (WHIZ)
WHAT VELOCITY !!!

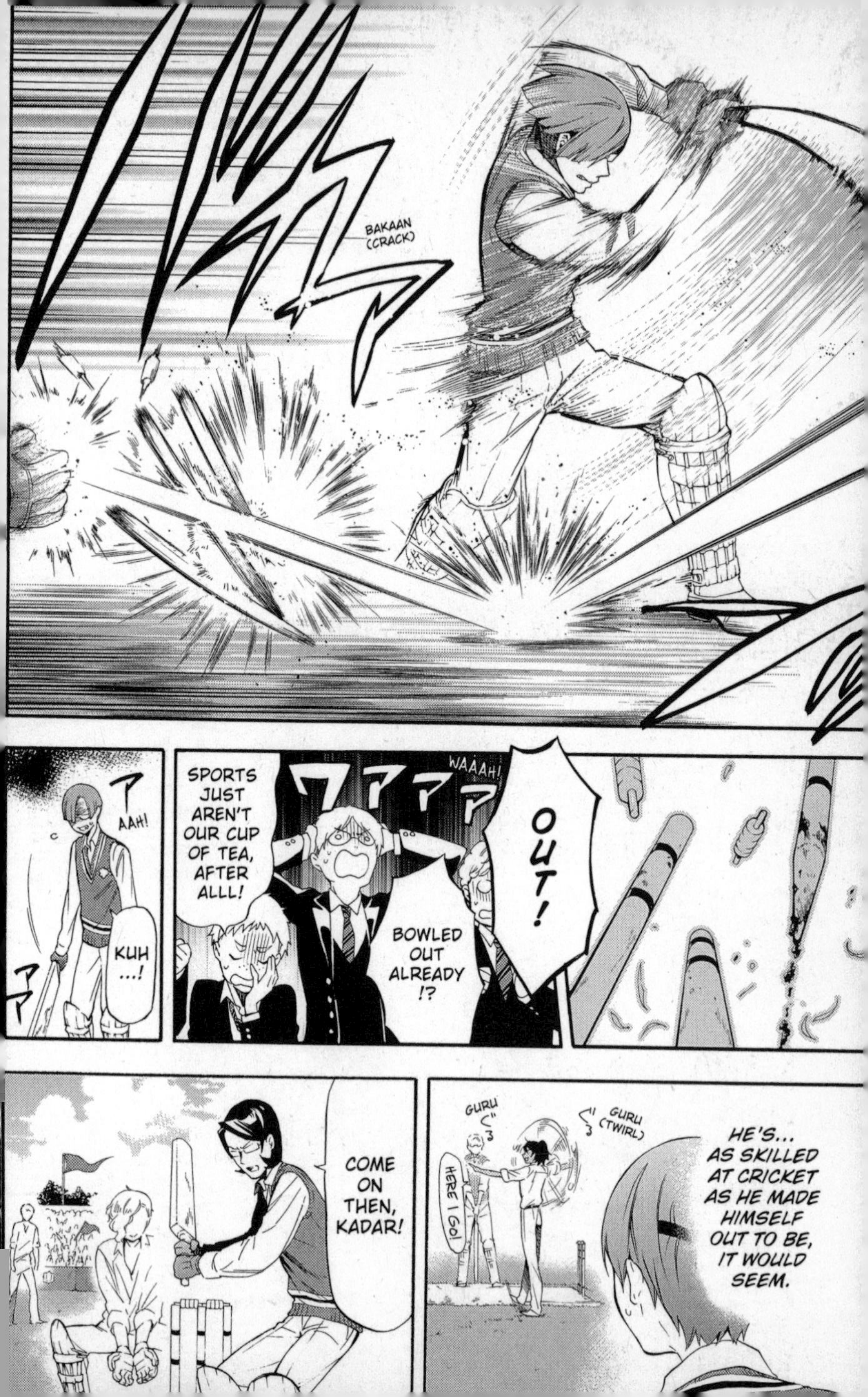
BAKAAN (CRACK)
OUT!
WAAAH!
SPORTS JUST AREN'T OUR CUP OF TEA, AFTER ALLL!
BOWLED OUT ALREADY!?
AAH!
KUH...!
HE'S... AS SKILLED AT CRICKET AS HE MADE HIMSELF OUT TO BE, IT WOULD SEEM.
GURU (TWIRL)
GURU
HERE I GO!
COME ON THEN, KADAR!

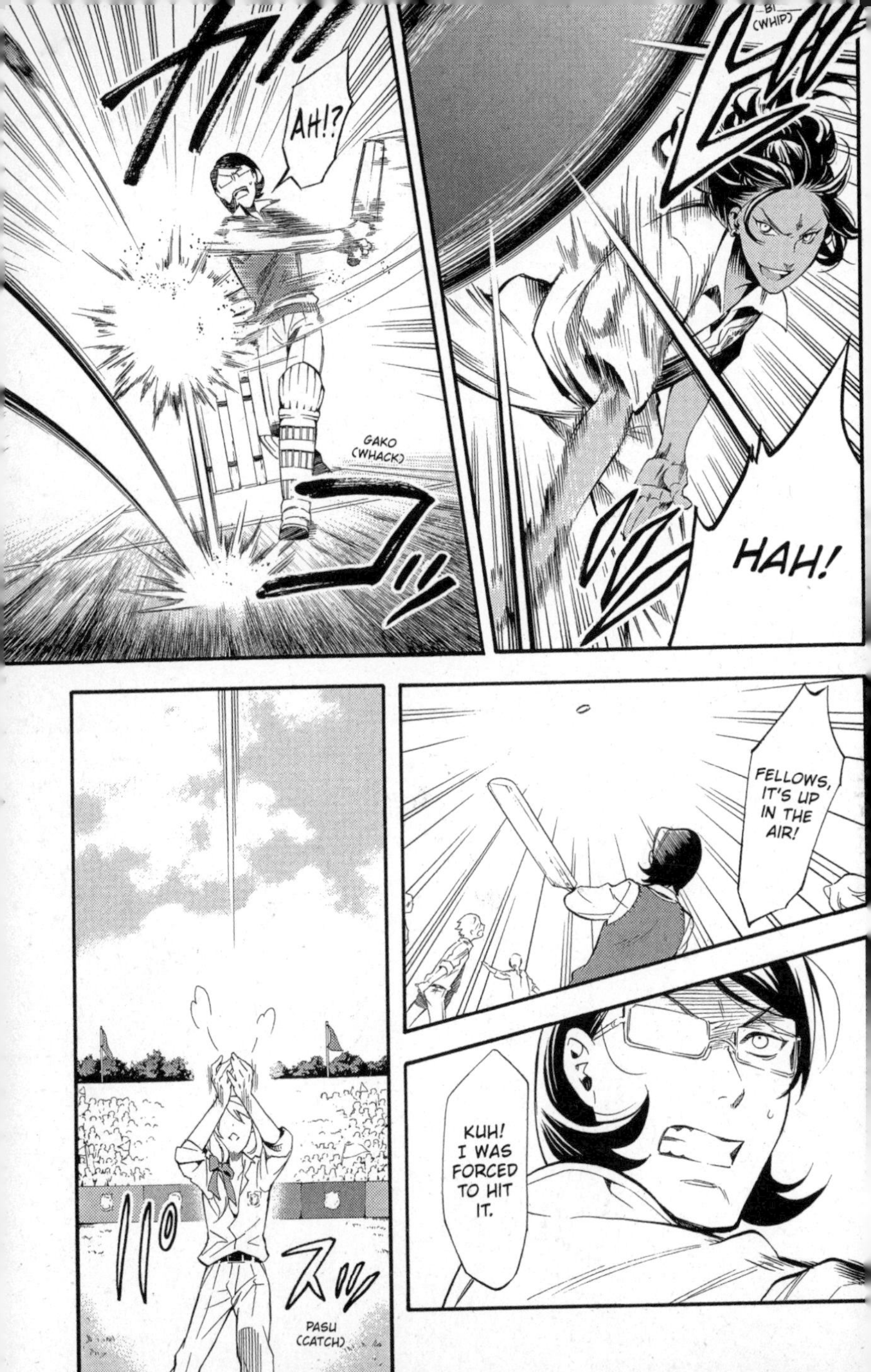
BI (WHIP)
HAH!
AH!?
GAKO (WHACK)
FELLOWS, IT'S UP IN THE AIR!
KUH! I WAS FORCED TO HIT IT.
PASU (CATCH)

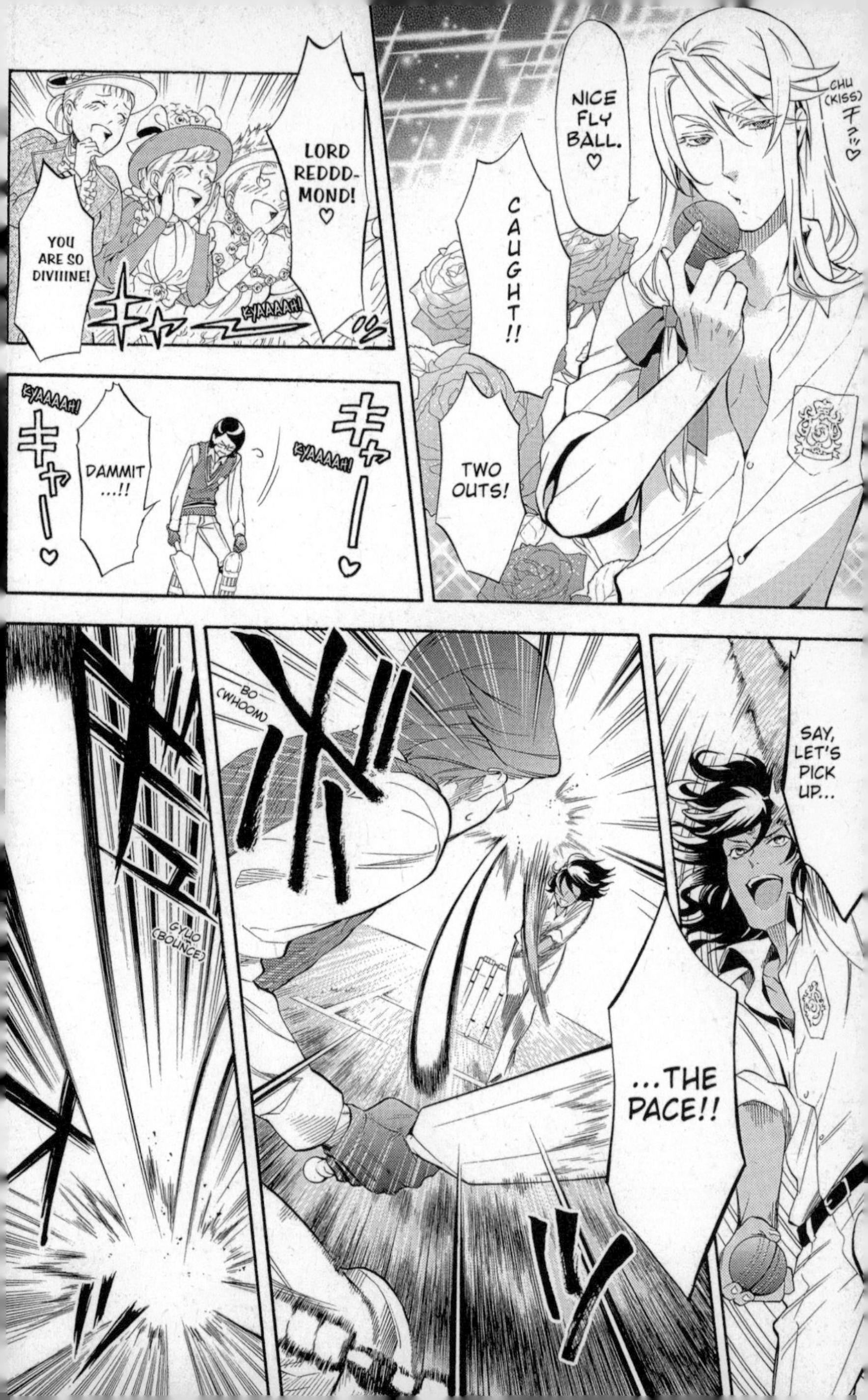
CHU (KISS)
NICE FLY BALL. ♡
CAUGHT!!
TWO OUTS!
LORD REDDD-MOND! ♡
YOU ARE SO DIVIIINE!
KYAAAAH!
KYAAAAH!
DAMMIT ...!!
KYAAAAH!
SAY, LET'S PICK UP...
...THE PACE!!
BO (WHOOM)
GYUO (BOUNCE)

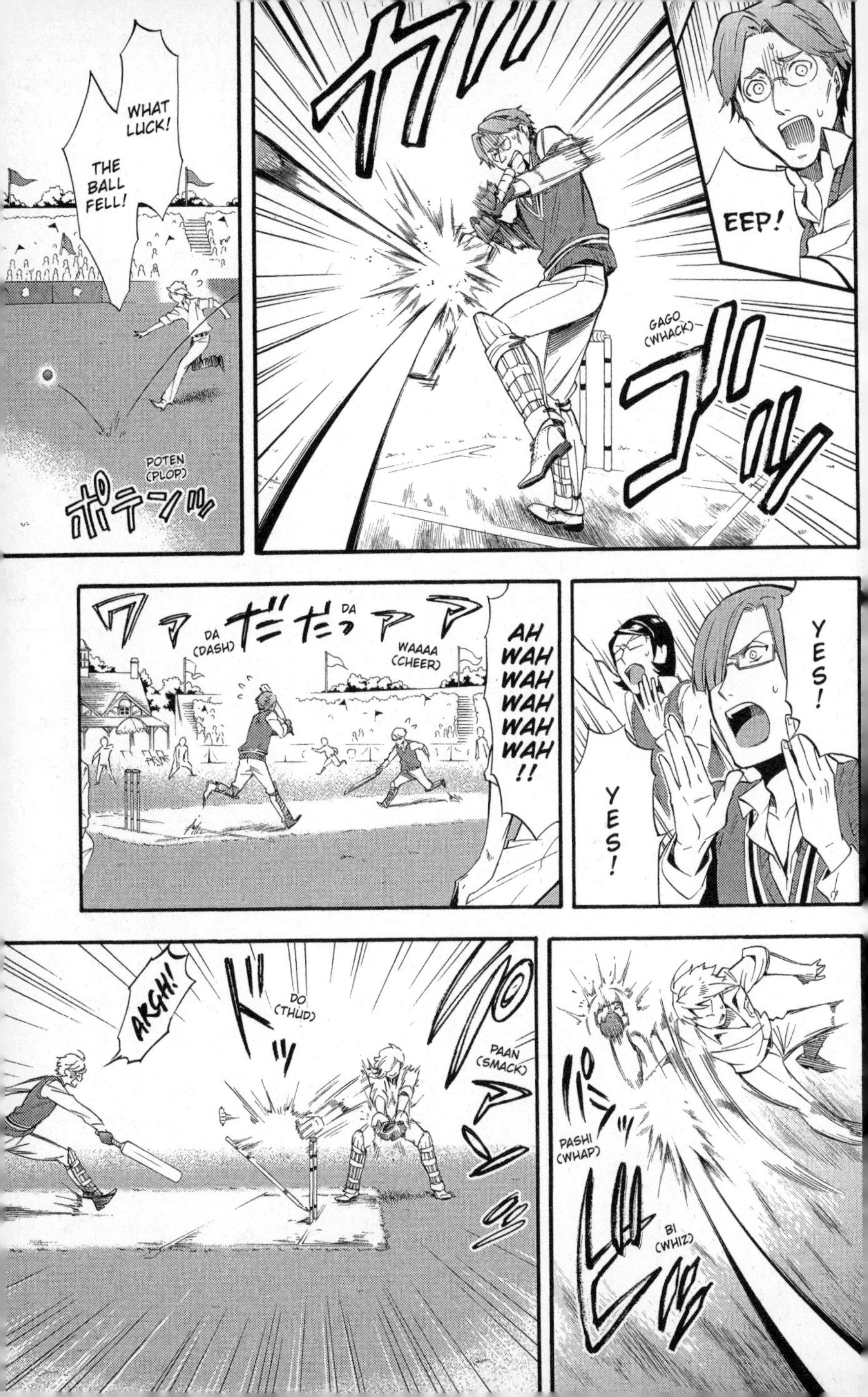
EEP!
GAGO (WHACK)
WHAT LUCK!
THE BALL FELL!
POTEN (PLOP)
ポテンッ
YES!
YES!
AH WAH WAH WAH WAH WAH!!
WAAAA (CHEER)
DA
DA (DASH)
PASHI (WHAP)
BI (WHIZ)
PAAN (SMACK)
DO (THUD)
ARGH!

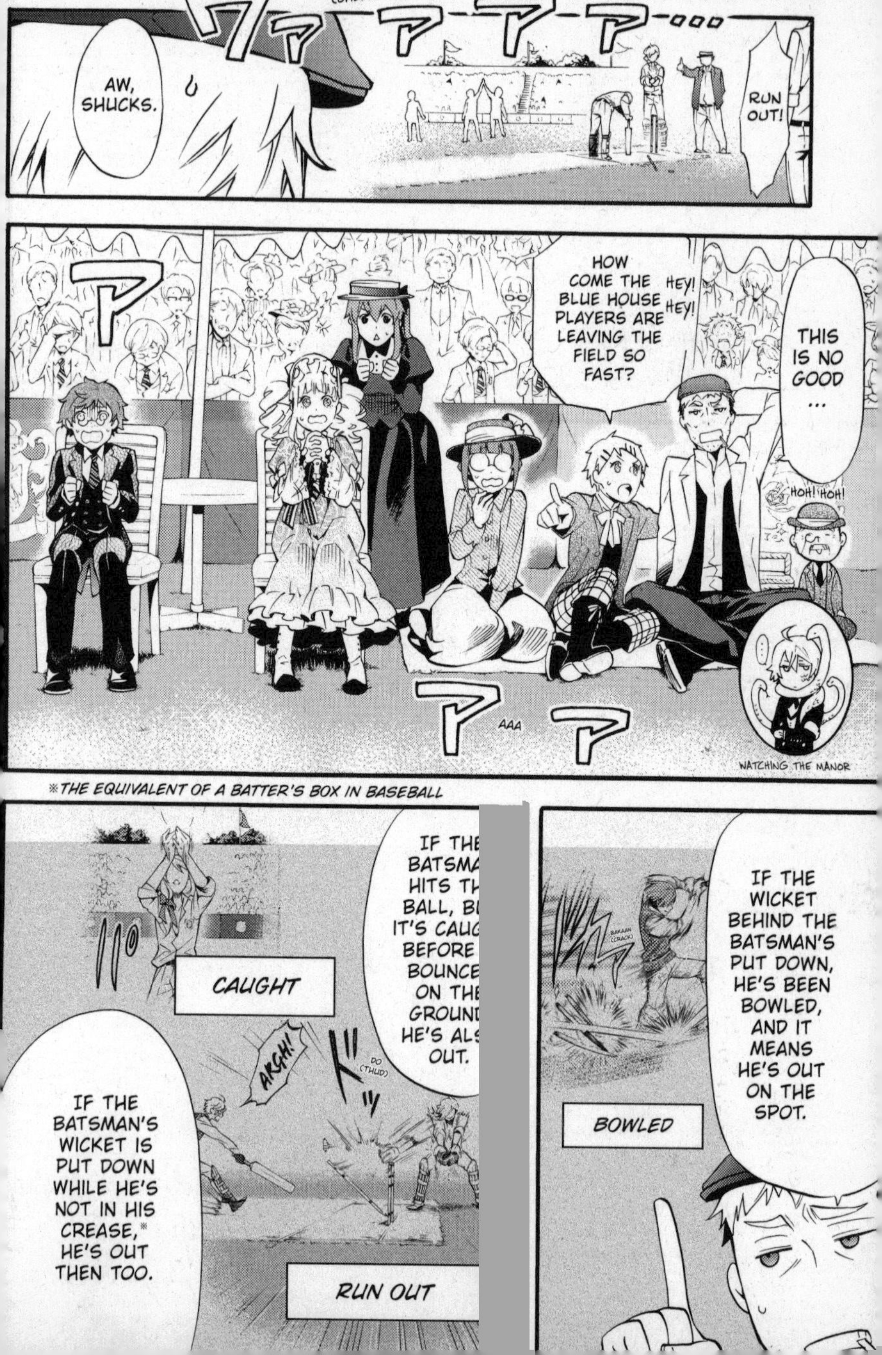
RUN OUT!
WAAAAA (CHEER)
AW, SHUCKS.
THIS IS NO GOOD...
HOH! HOH!
HEY! HEY!
HOW COME THE BLUE HOUSE PLAYERS ARE LEAVING THE FIELD SO FAST?
AAA
WATCHING THE MANOR
※THE EQUIVALENT OF A BATTER'S BOX IN BASEBALL
IF THE WICKET BEHIND THE BATSMAN'S PUT DOWN, HE'S BEEN BOWLED, AND IT MEANS HE'S OUT ON THE SPOT.
BAKAAN (CRACK)
BOWLED
IF THE BATSMA HITS TH BALL, B IT'S CAUG BEFORE BOUNCE ON THE GROUND HE'S ALS OUT.
CAUGHT
ARGH!
DO (THUD)
IF THE BATSMAN'S WICKET IS PUT DOWN WHILE HE'S NOT IN HIS CREASE,※ HE'S OUT THEN TOO.
RUN OUT

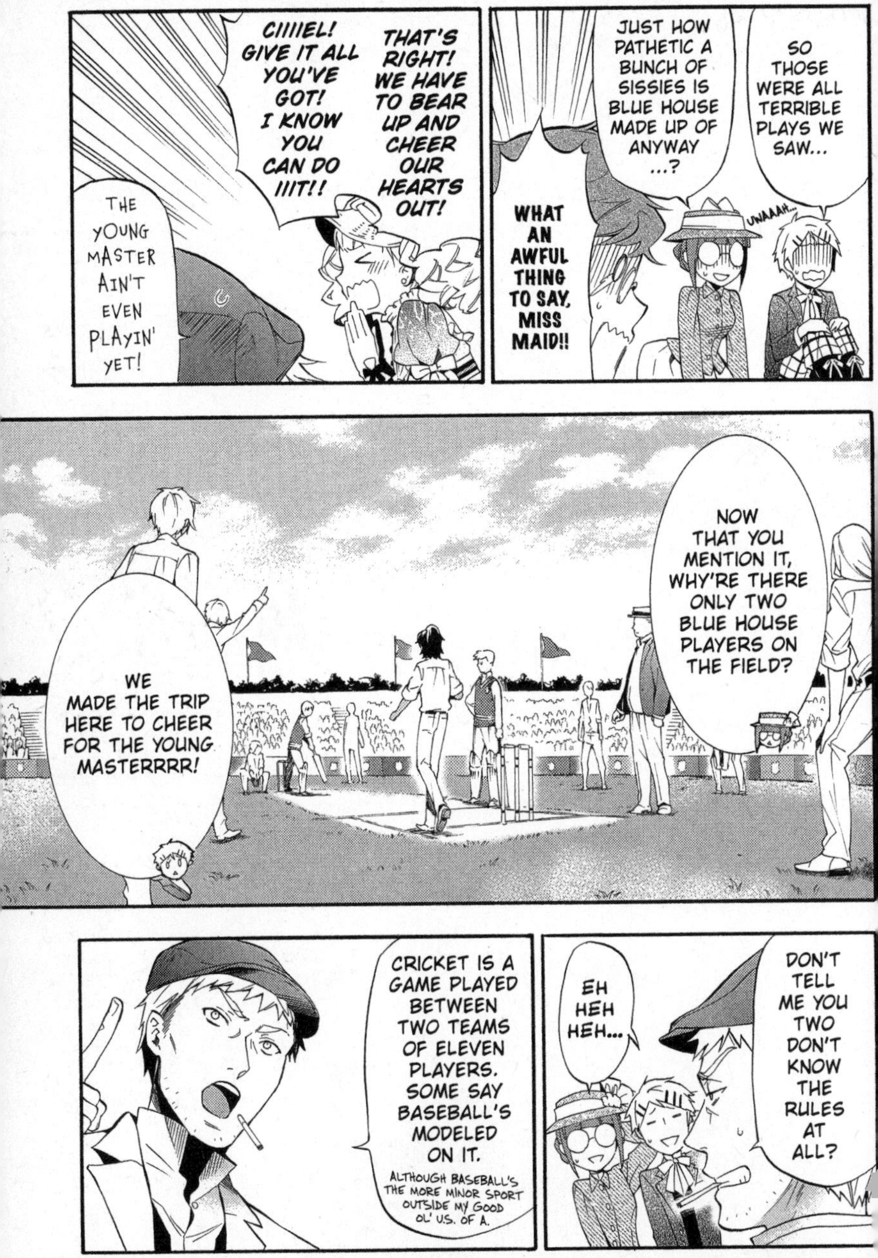
SO THOSE WERE ALL TERRIBLE PLAYS WE SAW...
UNAAAH...
JUST HOW PATHETIC A BUNCH OF SISSIES IS BLUE HOUSE MADE UP OF ANYWAY ...?
WHAT AN AWFUL THING TO SAY, MISS MAID!!
THAT'S RIGHT! WE HAVE TO BEAR UP AND CHEER OUR HEARTS OUT!
CIIIIEL! GIVE IT ALL YOU'VE GOT! I KNOW YOU CAN DO IIIT!!
THE YOUNG MASTER AIN'T EVEN PLAYIN' YET!
NOW THAT YOU MENTION IT, WHY'RE THERE ONLY TWO BLUE HOUSE PLAYERS ON THE FIELD?
WE MADE THE TRIP HERE TO CHEER FOR THE YOUNG MASTERRRR!
DON'T TELL ME YOU TWO DON'T KNOW THE RULES AT ALL?
EH HEH HEH...
CRICKET IS A GAME PLAYED BETWEEN TWO TEAMS OF ELEVEN PLAYERS. SOME SAY BASEBALL'S MODELED ON IT.
ALTHOUGH BASEBALL'S THE MORE MINOR SPORT OUTSIDE MY GOOD OL' U.S. OF A.

How to Play Cricket

BOUNDARY
IN CRICKET, THE TEAMS ATTACK AND DEFEND THE WICKETS.
BOWLER
ITS MOST DISTIN-GUISHING FEATURES ARE THE "WICKETS," WHICH CONSIST OF THREE STUMPS, AND TWO BATSMEN ON THE FIELD OF PLAY.
BATSMAN
WICKET-KEEPER
THE BATSMAN PROTECTS HIS WICKET WHILE BATTING, AND THE BOWLER ATTACKS TO PUT DOWN THE OPPONENT'S WICKET.

TO SCORE, THE TWO BATSMEN MUST RUN BETWEEN THE WICKETS TO THEIR OPPOSITE CREASES AFTER THE BALL'S BEEN HIT, EARNING THEIR TEAM ONE RUN.

WICKET
CREASE

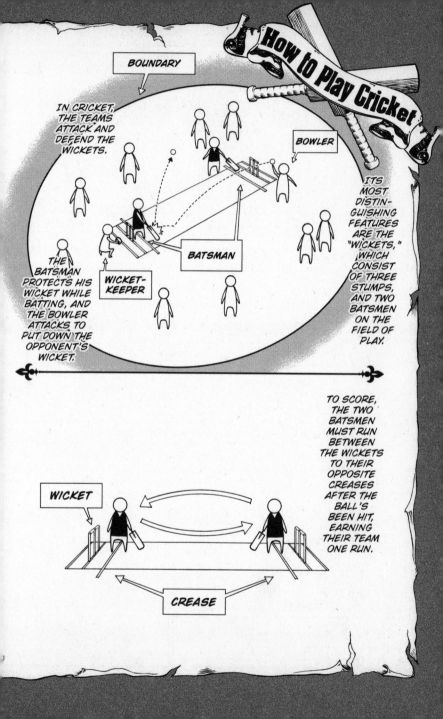

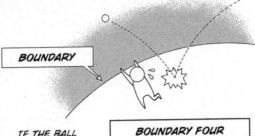

ON TOP OF THAT, IF THE BATTED BALL TOUCHES OR CROSSES THE BOUNDARY AFTER BOUNCING, THE BATTING TEAM SCORES FOUR RUNS.

BOUNDARY
BOUNDARY FOUR

IF THE BALL PASSES OVER THE BOUNDARY WITHOUT BOUNCING, THE BATTING TEAM SCORES SIX RUNS.

BOUNDARY SIX

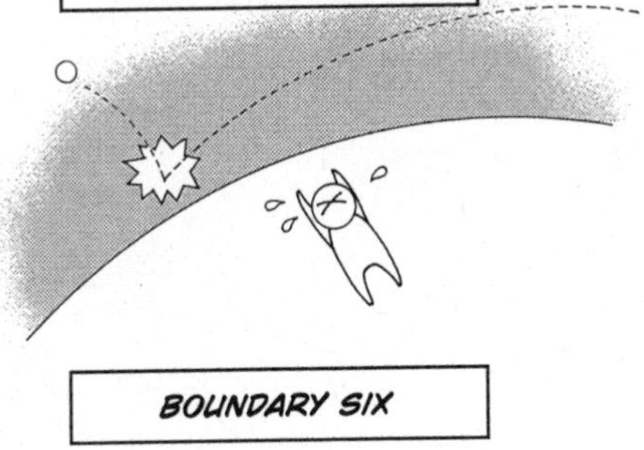

WHAT YOU MIGHT CALL A HOME RUN.

WHEN A BOWLER HAS BOWLED SIX TIMES, ANOTHER BOWLER TAKES OVER. THIS IS CALLED AN "OVER."

ON THE OTHER HAND, A BATSMAN CAN CONTINUE HITTING UNTIL HE IS OUT.

ONE OVER
× SIX BOWLS

ONE INNINGS
× TEN OUTS

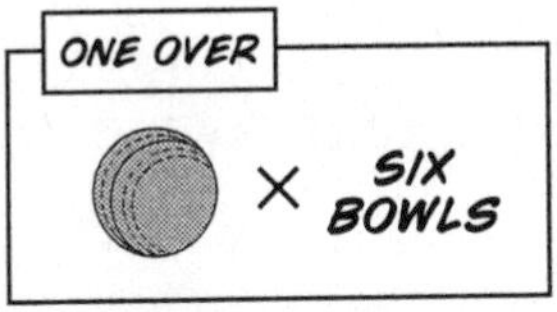

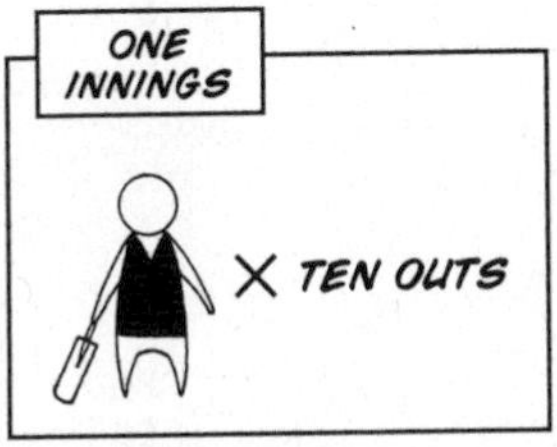

ONE INNINGS EQUALS TEN OUTS, OR DISMISSALS. THEN THE BATTING AND FIELDING TEAMS SWITCH.

UNLIKE BASEBALL, ONE INNINGS TAKES A LONG TIME TO PLAY. IN TRADITIONAL CRICKET, A MATCH CONSISTS OF TWO INNINGS EACH AND TAKES ABOUT FIVE DAYS TO FINISH.

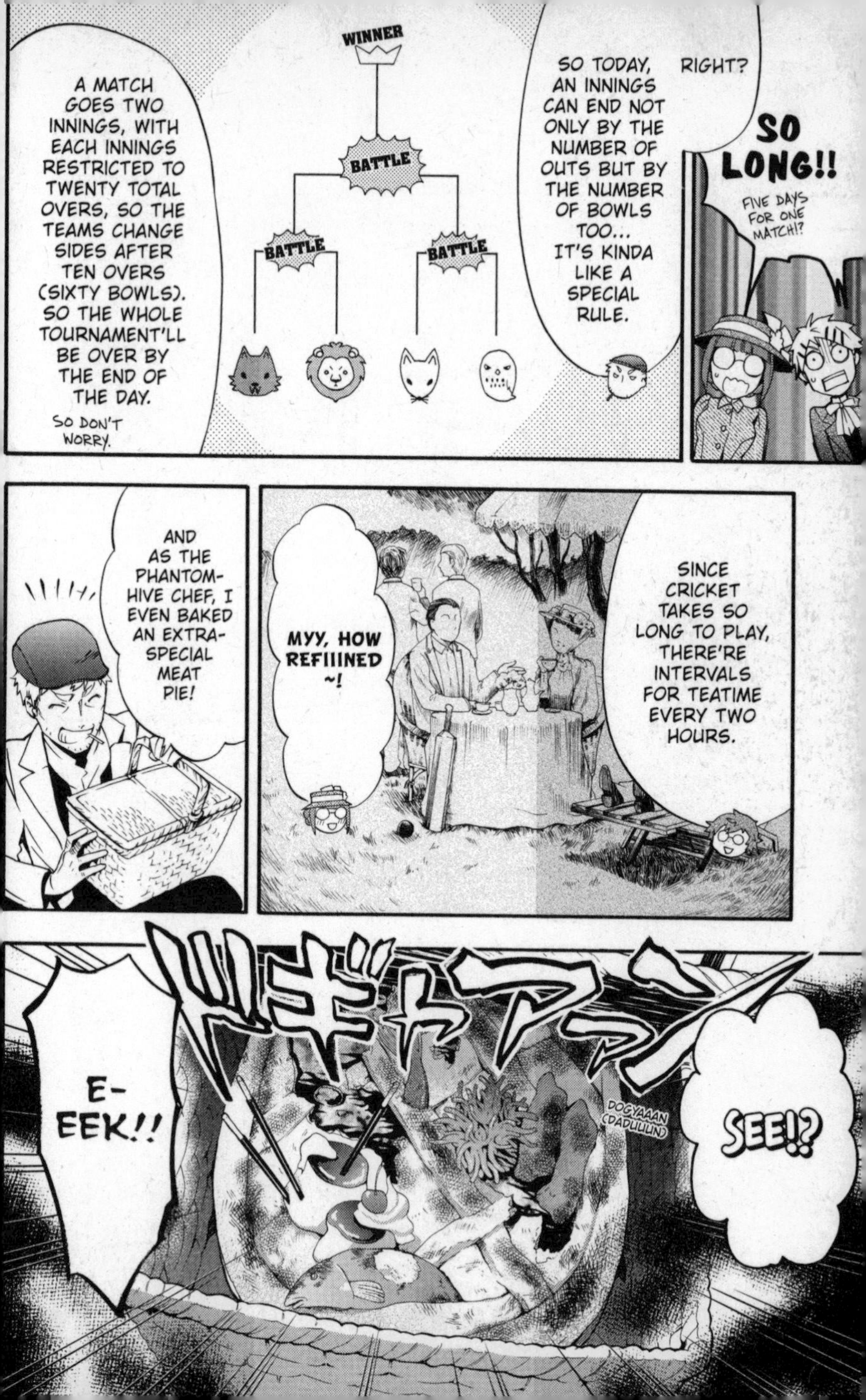

SO LONG!!
FIVE DAYS FOR ONE MATCH!?
RIGHT?
SO TODAY, AN INNINGS CAN END NOT ONLY BY THE NUMBER OF OUTS BUT BY THE NUMBER OF BOWLS TOO... IT'S KINDA LIKE A SPECIAL RULE.
WINNER
BATTLE
BATTLE
BATTLE
A MATCH GOES TWO INNINGS, WITH EACH INNINGS RESTRICTED TO TWENTY TOTAL OVERS, SO THE TEAMS CHANGE SIDES AFTER TEN OVERS (SIXTY BOWLS). SO THE WHOLE TOURNAMENT'LL BE OVER BY THE END OF THE DAY.
SO DON'T WORRY.
SINCE CRICKET TAKES SO LONG TO PLAY, THERE'RE INTERVALS FOR TEATIME EVERY TWO HOURS.
MYY, HOW REFIIIINED ~!
AND AS THE PHANTOM-HIVE CHEF, I EVEN BAKED AN EXTRA-SPECIAL MEAT PIE!
SEE!?
DOGYAAAN (DADUUUN)
E-EEK!!

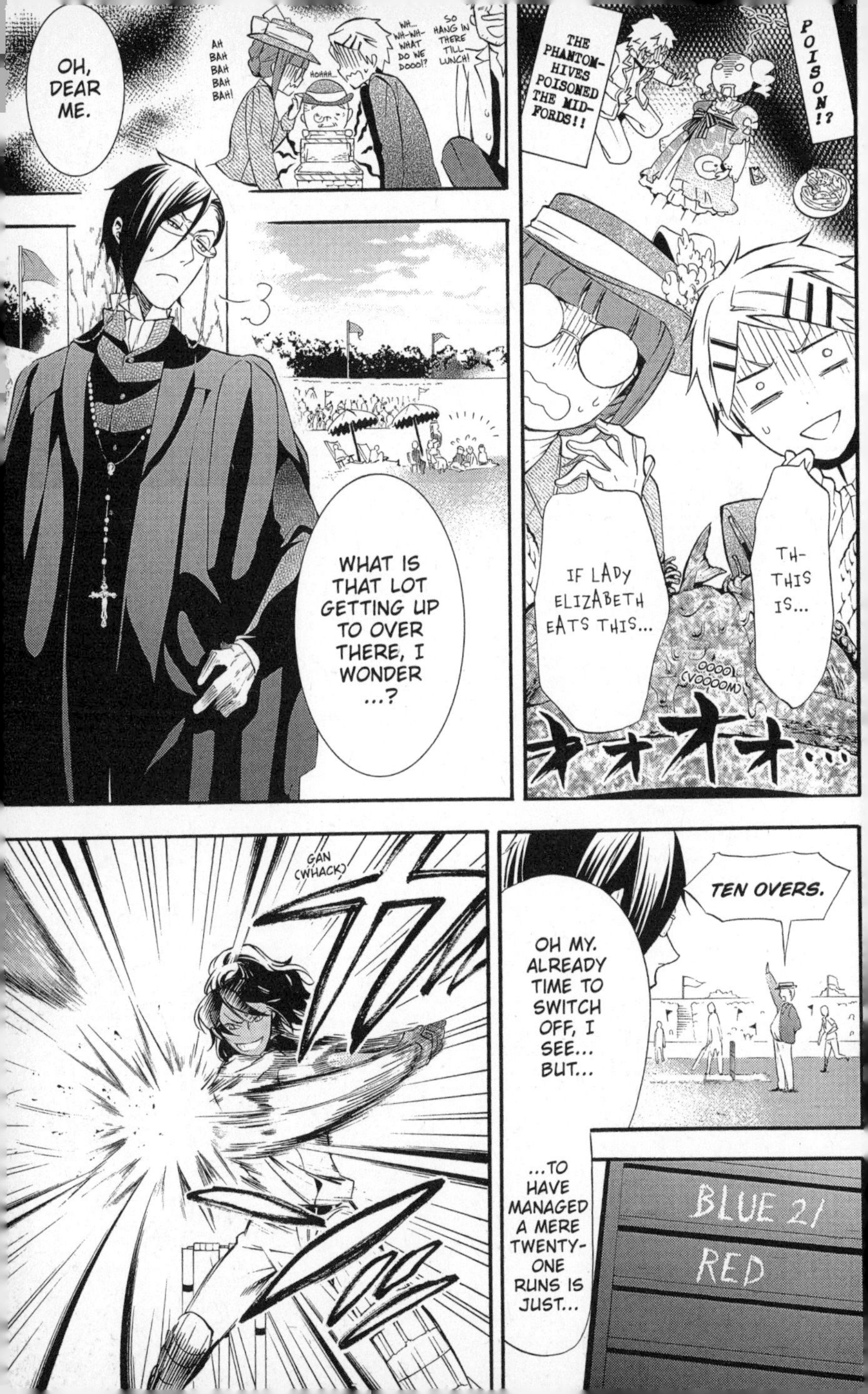
POISON!?
THE PHANTOMHIVES POISONED THE MIDFORDS!!
SO HANG IN THERE TILL LUNCH!
WH... WH-WH-WHAT DO WE DOOO!?
AH BAH BAH BAH BAH!
HOHHH...
OH, DEAR ME.
TH-THIS IS...
IF LADY ELIZABETH EATS THIS...
OOOO (VOOOOM)
WHAT IS THAT LOT GETTING UP TO OVER THERE, I WONDER...?
TEN OVERS.
OH MY. ALREADY TIME TO SWITCH OFF, I SEE... BUT...
...TO HAVE MANAGED A MERE TWENTY-ONE RUNS IS JUST...
BLUE 21
RED
GAN (WHACK)

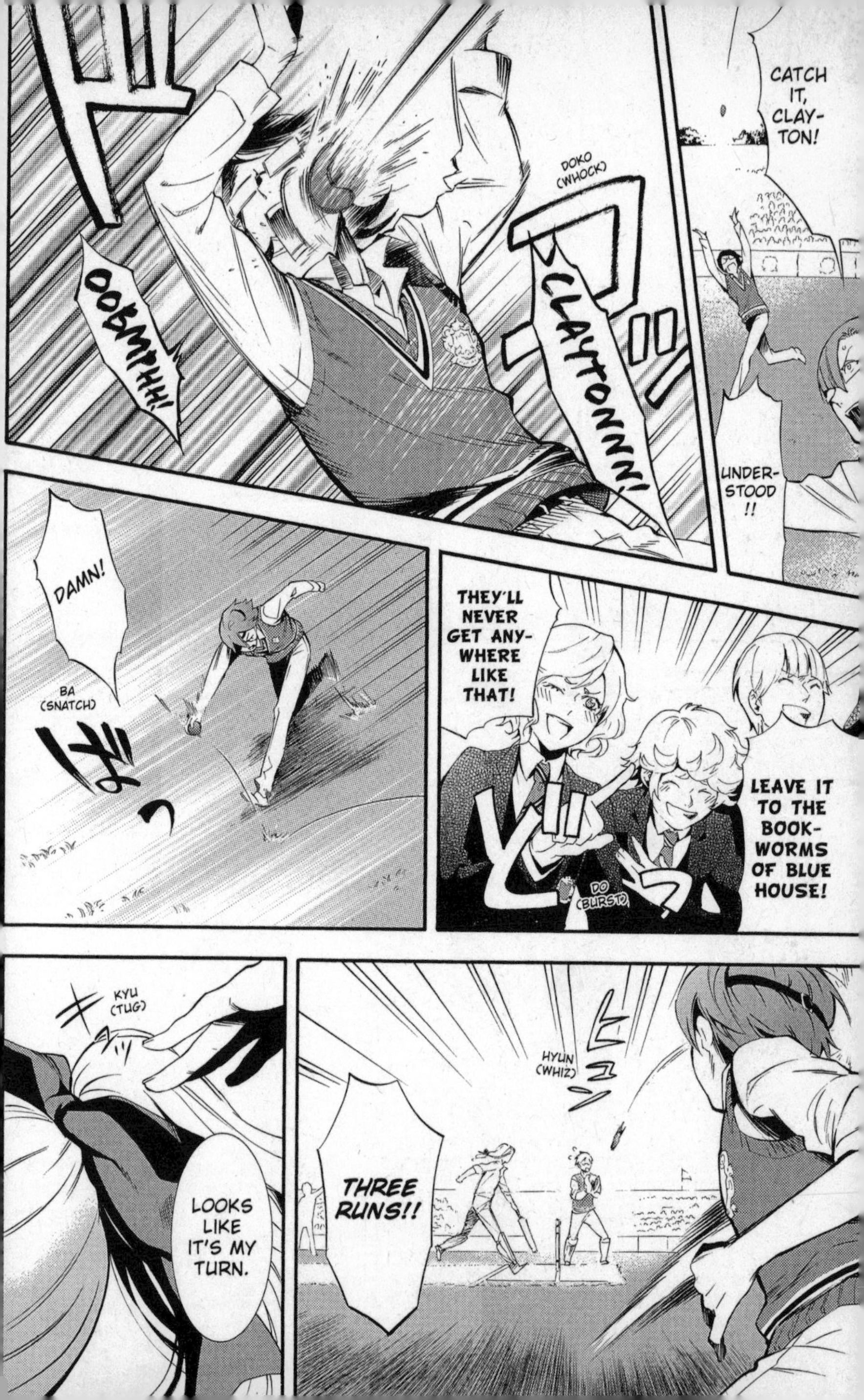
CATCH IT, CLAY-TON!
UNDER-STOOD!!
DOKO (WHOCK)
CLAYTONNN!
OOMPHH!
THEY'LL NEVER GET ANY-WHERE LIKE THAT!
LEAVE IT TO THE BOOK-WORMS OF BLUE HOUSE!
DO (BURST)
DAMN!
BA (SNATCH)
HYUN (WHIZ)
THREE RUNS!!
KYU (TUG)
LOOKS LIKE IT'S MY TURN.

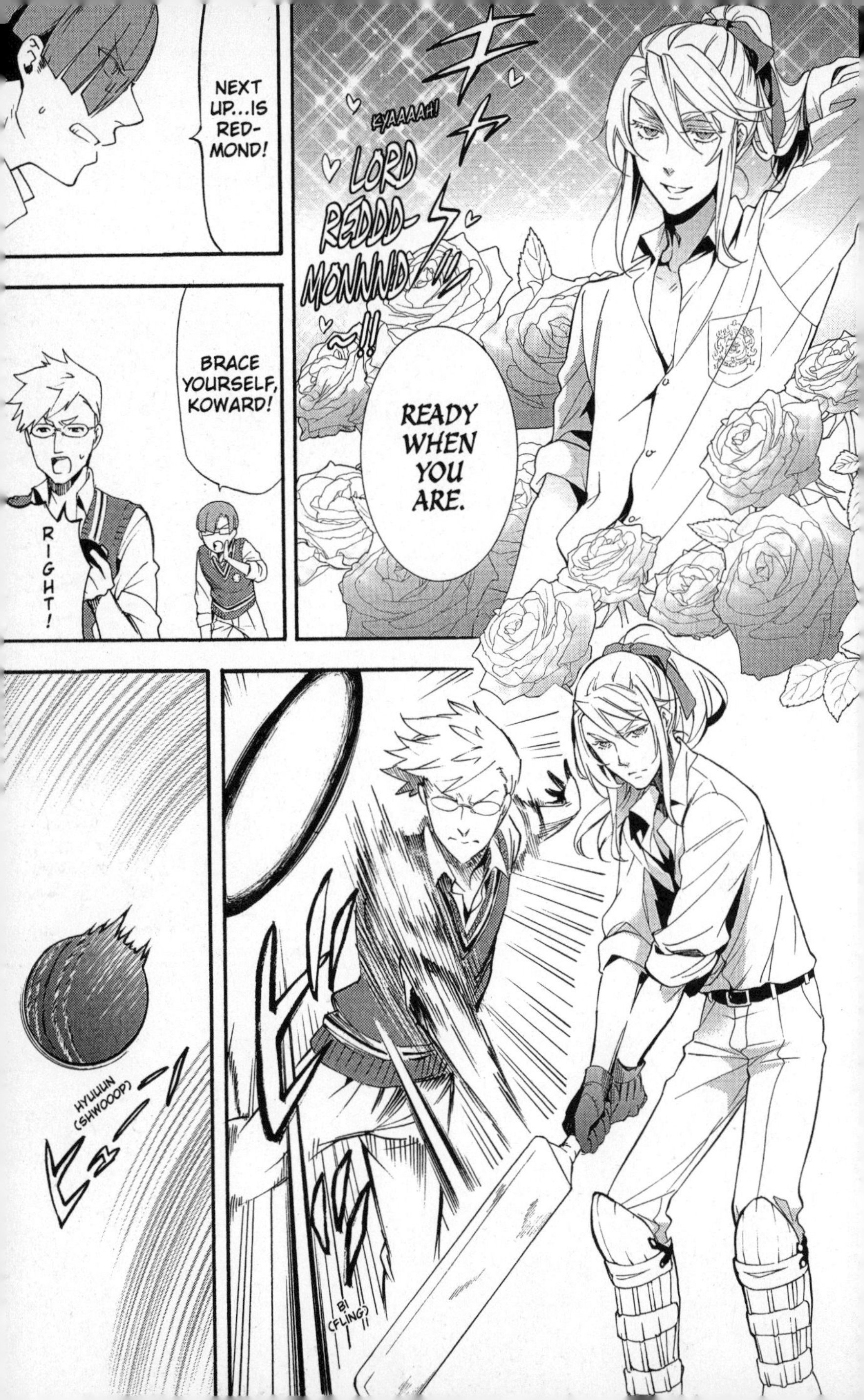
KYAAAAH!
LORD REDDD-MONNND~!!
READY WHEN YOU ARE.
NEXT UP...IS RED-MOND!
BRACE YOURSELF, KOWARD!
RIGHT!
BI (FLING)
HYUUUN (SHWOOOP)

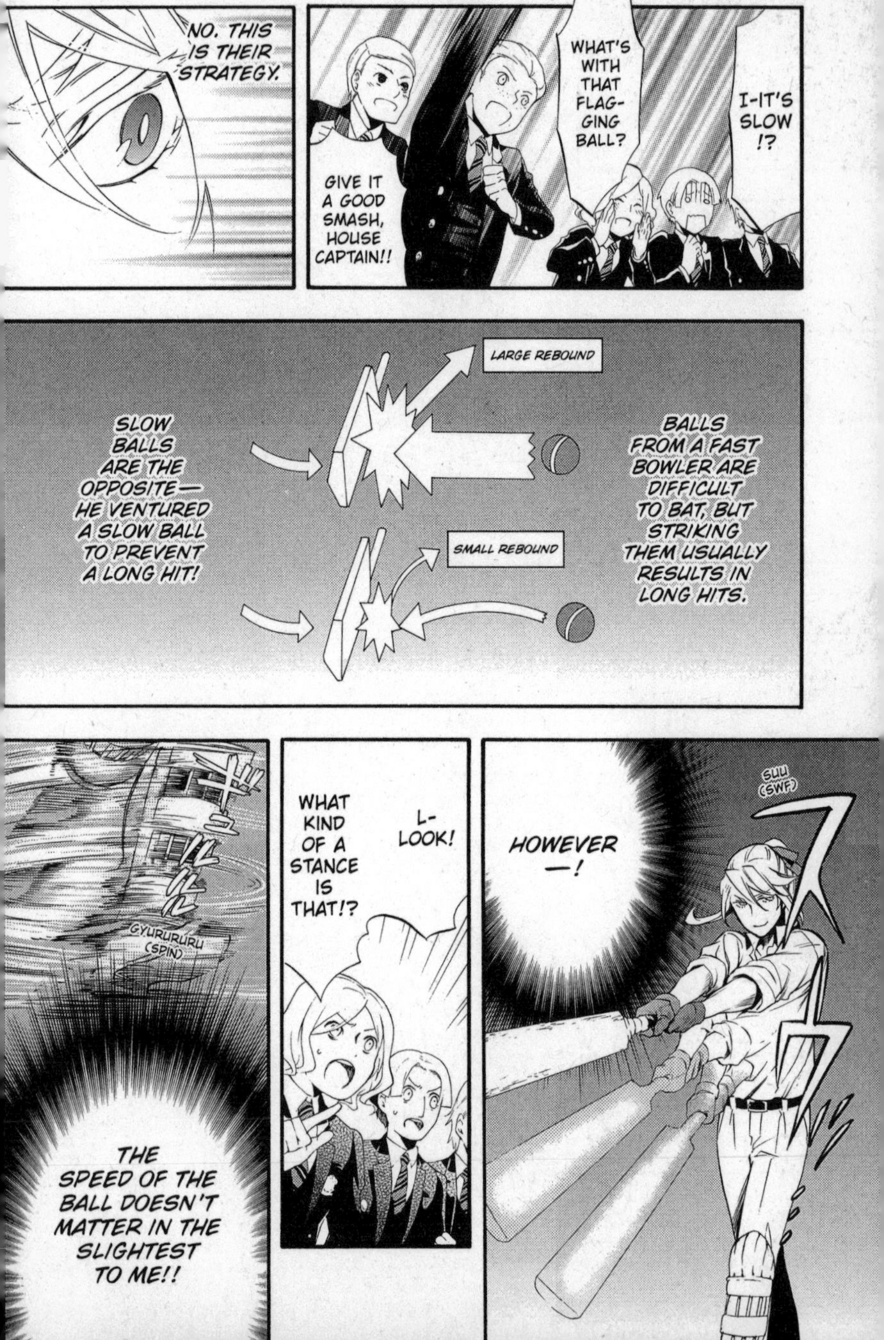
I-IT'S SLOW!?
WHAT'S WITH THAT FLAGGING BALL?
GIVE IT A GOOD SMASH, HOUSE CAPTAIN!!
NO. THIS IS THEIR STRATEGY.
BALLS FROM A FAST BOWLER ARE DIFFICULT TO BAT, BUT STRIKING THEM USUALLY RESULTS IN LONG HITS.
LARGE REBOUND
SMALL REBOUND
SLOW BALLS ARE THE OPPOSITE—HE VENTURED A SLOW BALL TO PREVENT A LONG HIT!
SUU (SWF)
HOWEVER—!
L-LOOK!
WHAT KIND OF A STANCE IS THAT!?
GYURURURU (SPIN)
THE SPEED OF THE BALL DOESN'T MATTER IN THE SLIGHTEST TO ME!!

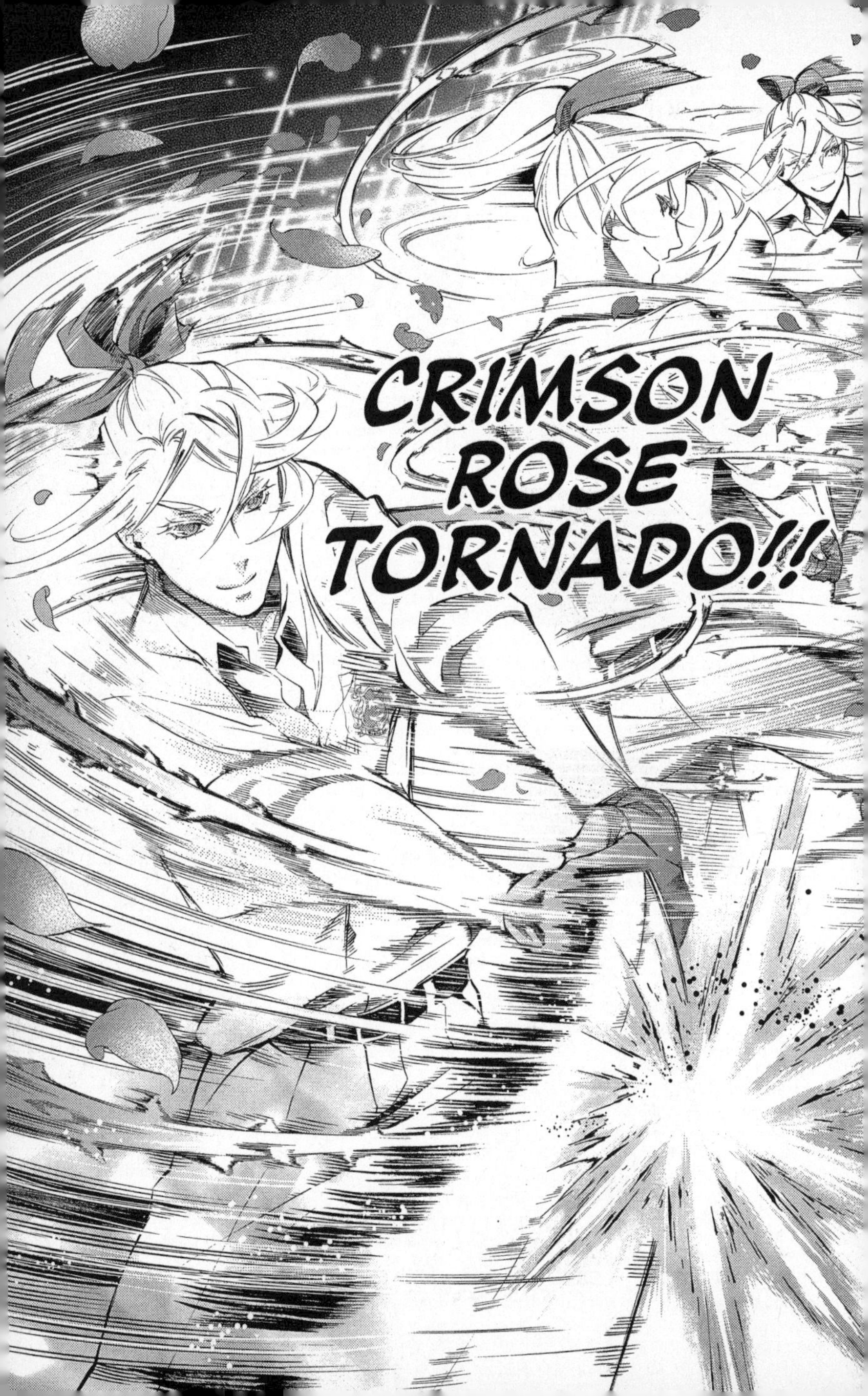
CRIMSON ROSE TORNADO!!!

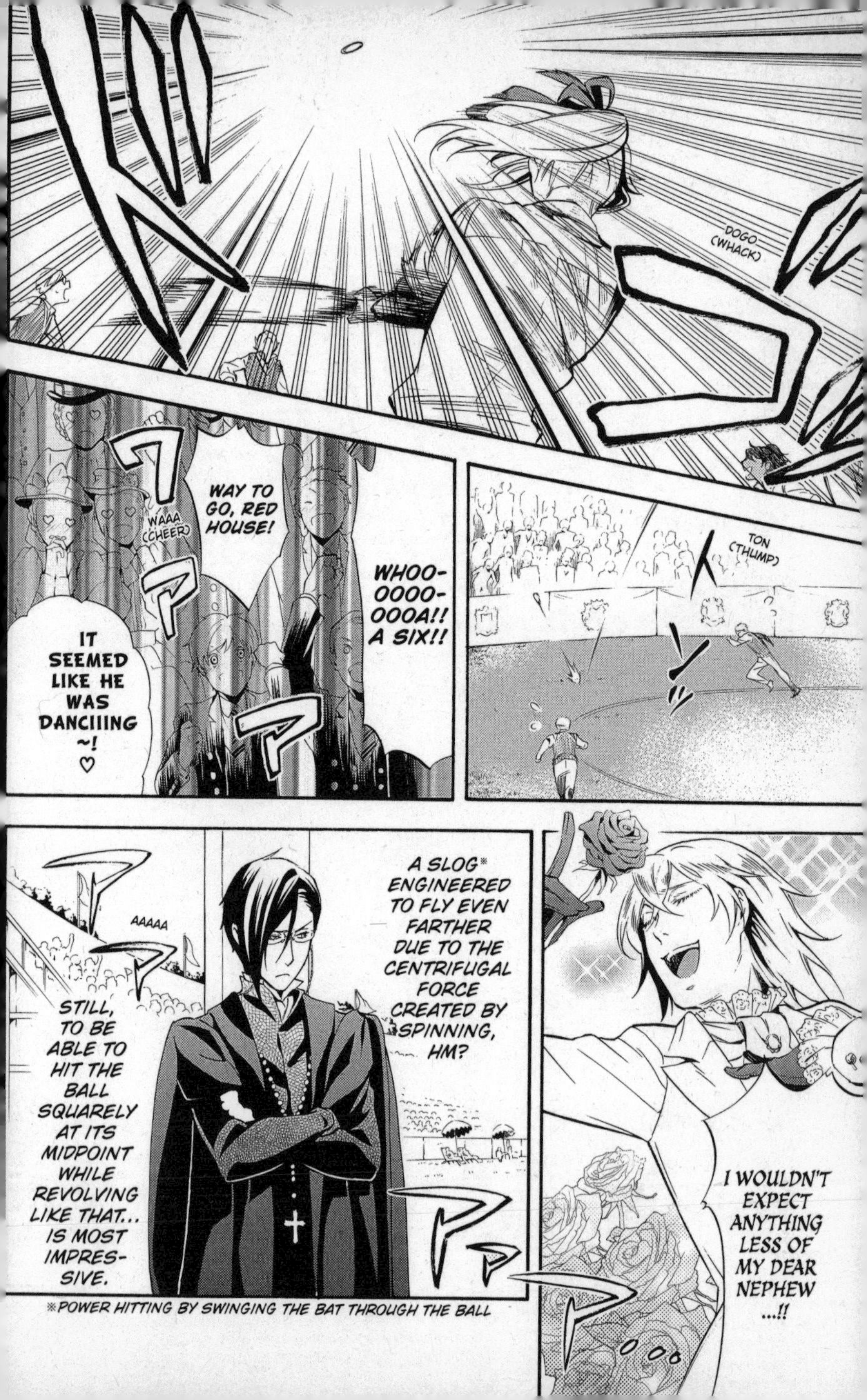
DOGO (WHACK)
TON (THUMP)
WHOO-OOOO-OOOA!! A SIX!!
WAY TO GO, RED HOUSE!
WAAA (CHEER)
IT SEEMED LIKE HE WAS DANCIIING ~! ♡
I WOULDN'T EXPECT ANYTHING LESS OF MY DEAR NEPHEW ...!!
A SLOG* ENGINEERED TO FLY EVEN FARTHER DUE TO THE CENTRIFUGAL FORCE CREATED BY SPINNING, HM?
AAAAA
STILL, TO BE ABLE TO HIT THE BALL SQUARELY AT ITS MIDPOINT WHILE REVOLVING LIKE THAT... IS MOST IMPRES-SIVE.
※POWER HITTING BY SWINGING THE BAT THROUGH THE BALL

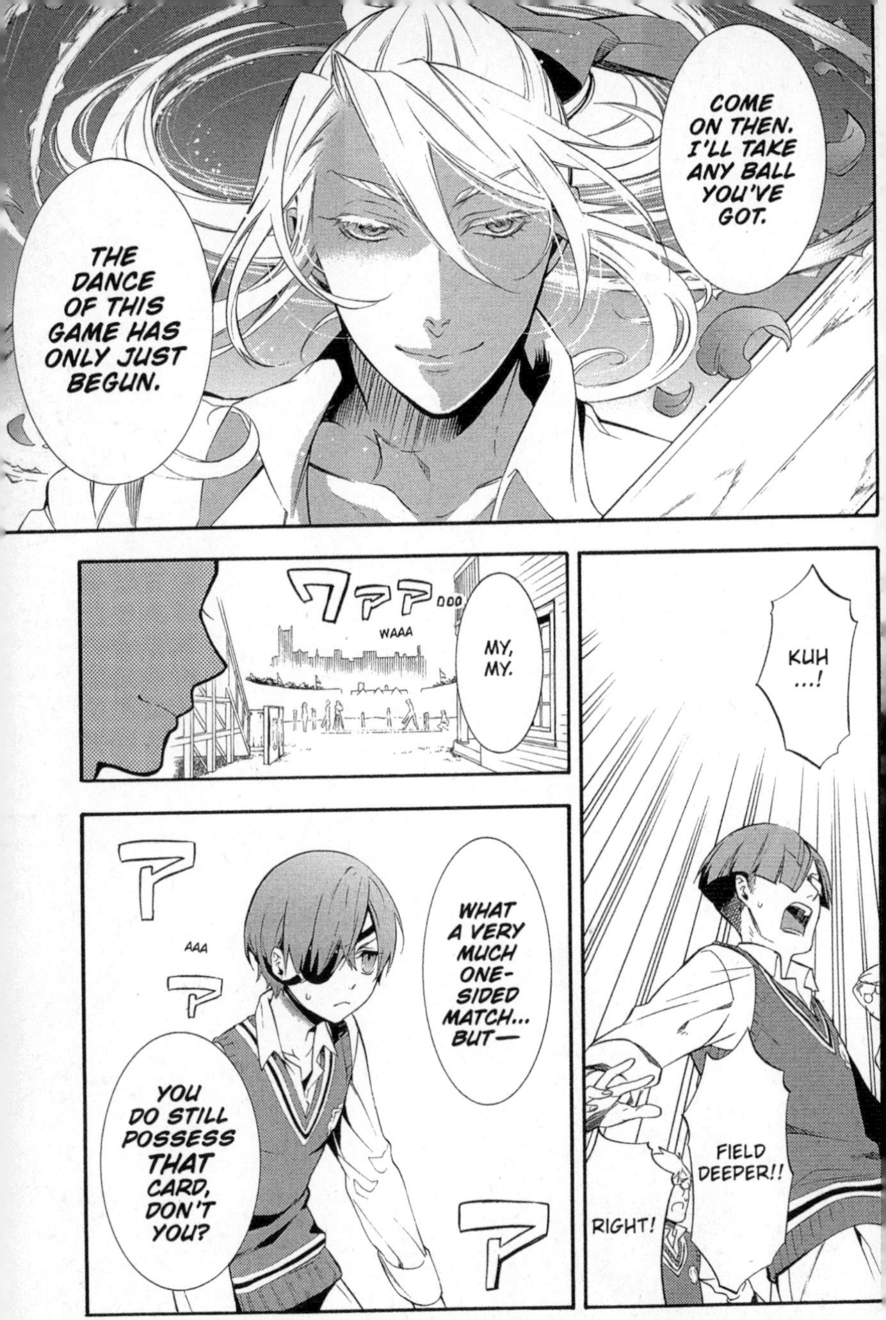
COME ON THEN. I'LL TAKE ANY BALL YOU'VE GOT.
THE DANCE OF THIS GAME HAS ONLY JUST BEGUN.
KUH ...!
FIELD DEEPER!!
RIGHT!
ワァァ...
WAAA
MY, MY.
ァ
AAA
ァ
ァ
WHAT A VERY MUCH ONE-SIDED MATCH... BUT—
YOU DO STILL POSSESS THAT CARD, DON'T YOU?

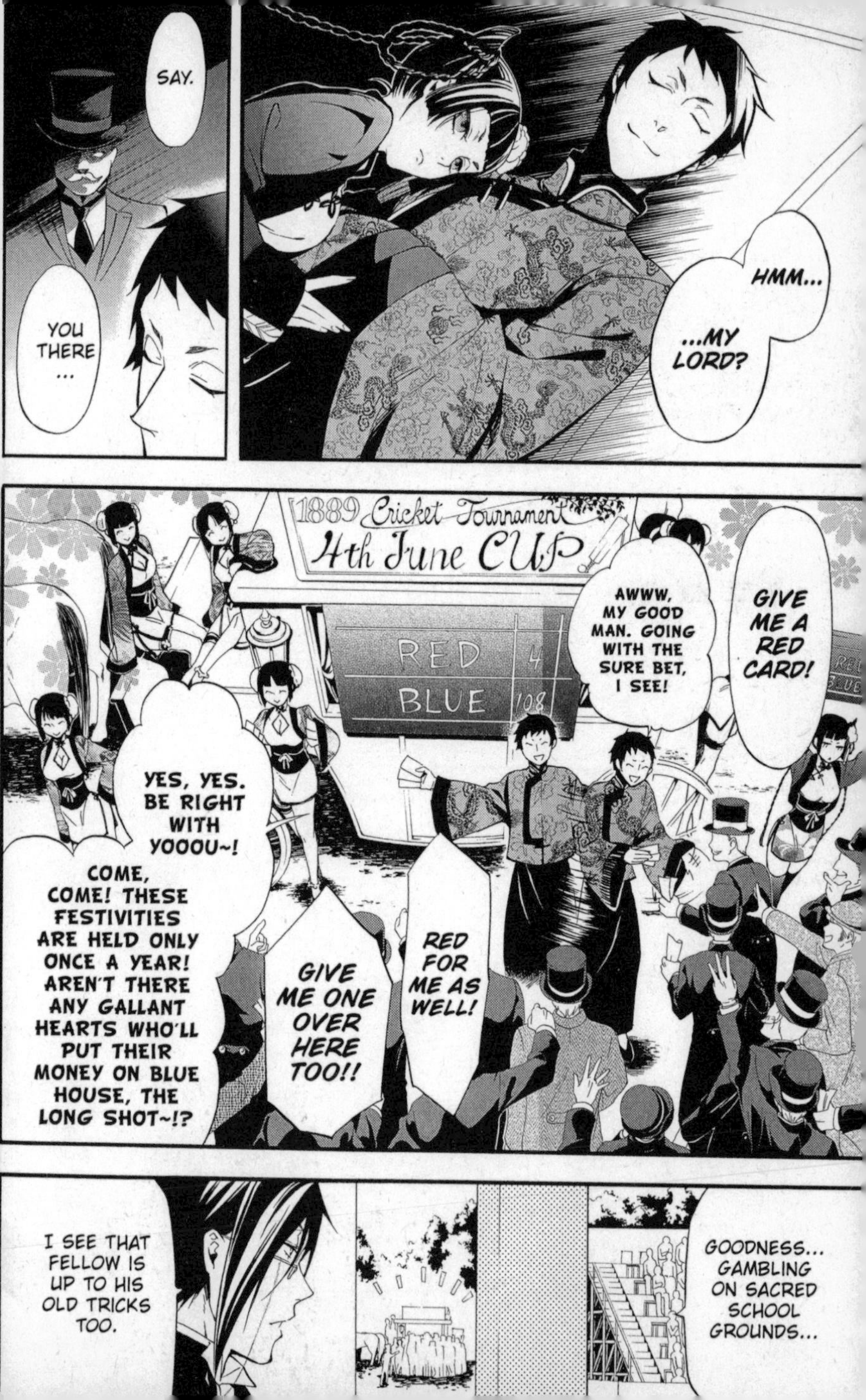
HMM...
...MY LORD?
SAY.
YOU THERE ...
1889 Cricket Tournament
4th June CUP
RED 4
BLUE 108
GIVE ME A RED CARD!
AWWW, MY GOOD MAN. GOING WITH THE SURE BET, I SEE!
RED FOR ME AS WELL!
GIVE ME ONE OVER HERE TOO!!
YES, YES. BE RIGHT WITH YOOOU~!
COME, COME! THESE FESTIVITIES ARE HELD ONLY ONCE A YEAR! AREN'T THERE ANY GALLANT HEARTS WHO'LL PUT THEIR MONEY ON BLUE HOUSE, THE LONG SHOT~!?
GOODNESS... GAMBLING ON SACRED SCHOOL GROUNDS...
I SEE THAT FELLOW IS UP TO HIS OLD TRICKS TOO.

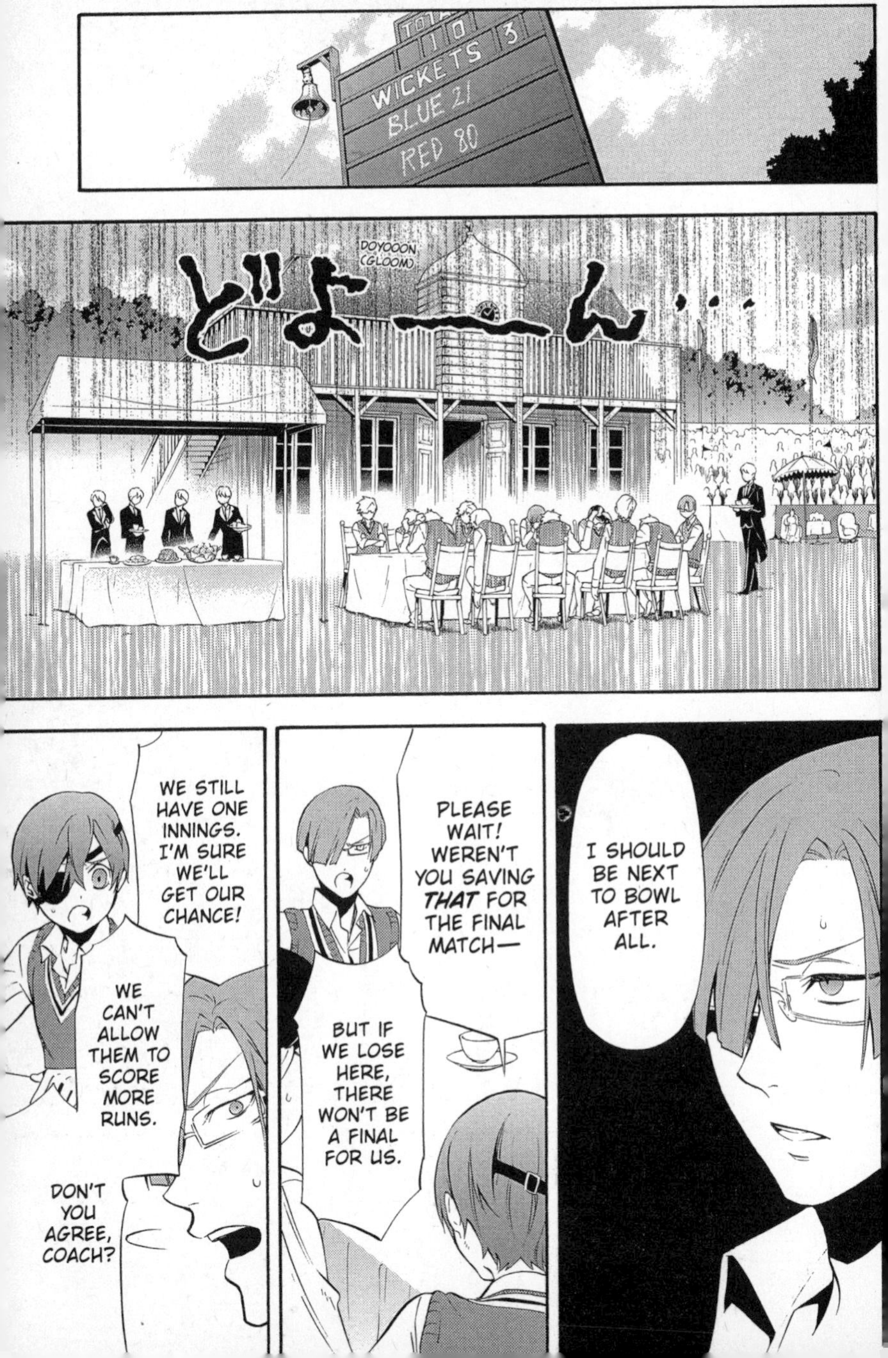
WICKETS 3
BLUE 21
RED 80
どよーん…
DOYOOON (GLOOM)
I SHOULD BE NEXT TO BOWL AFTER ALL.
PLEASE WAIT! WEREN'T YOU SAVING *THAT* FOR THE FINAL MATCH—
BUT IF WE LOSE HERE, THERE WON'T BE A FINAL FOR US.
WE STILL HAVE ONE INNINGS. I'M SURE WE'LL GET OUR CHANCE!
WE CAN'T ALLOW THEM TO SCORE MORE RUNS.
DON'T YOU AGREE, COACH?

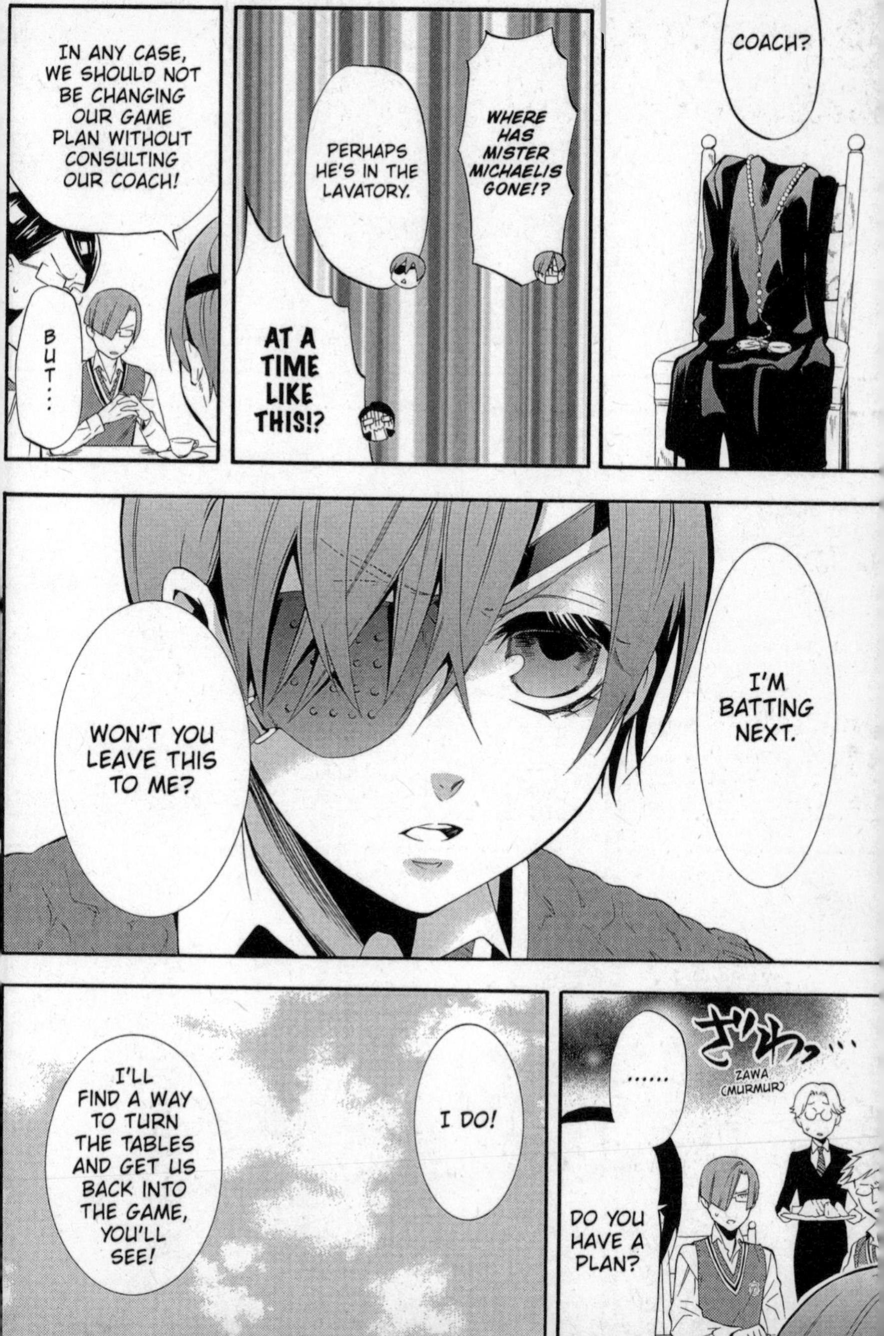
COACH?
WHERE HAS MISTER MICHAELIS GONE!?
PERHAPS HE'S IN THE LAVATORY.
AT A TIME LIKE THIS!?
IN ANY CASE, WE SHOULD NOT BE CHANGING OUR GAME PLAN WITHOUT CONSULTING OUR COACH!
BUT...
I'M BATTING NEXT.
WON'T YOU LEAVE THIS TO ME?
ZAWA (MURMUR)
......
DO YOU HAVE A PLAN?
I DO!
I'LL FIND A WAY TO TURN THE TABLES AND GET US BACK INTO THE GAME, YOU'LL SEE!

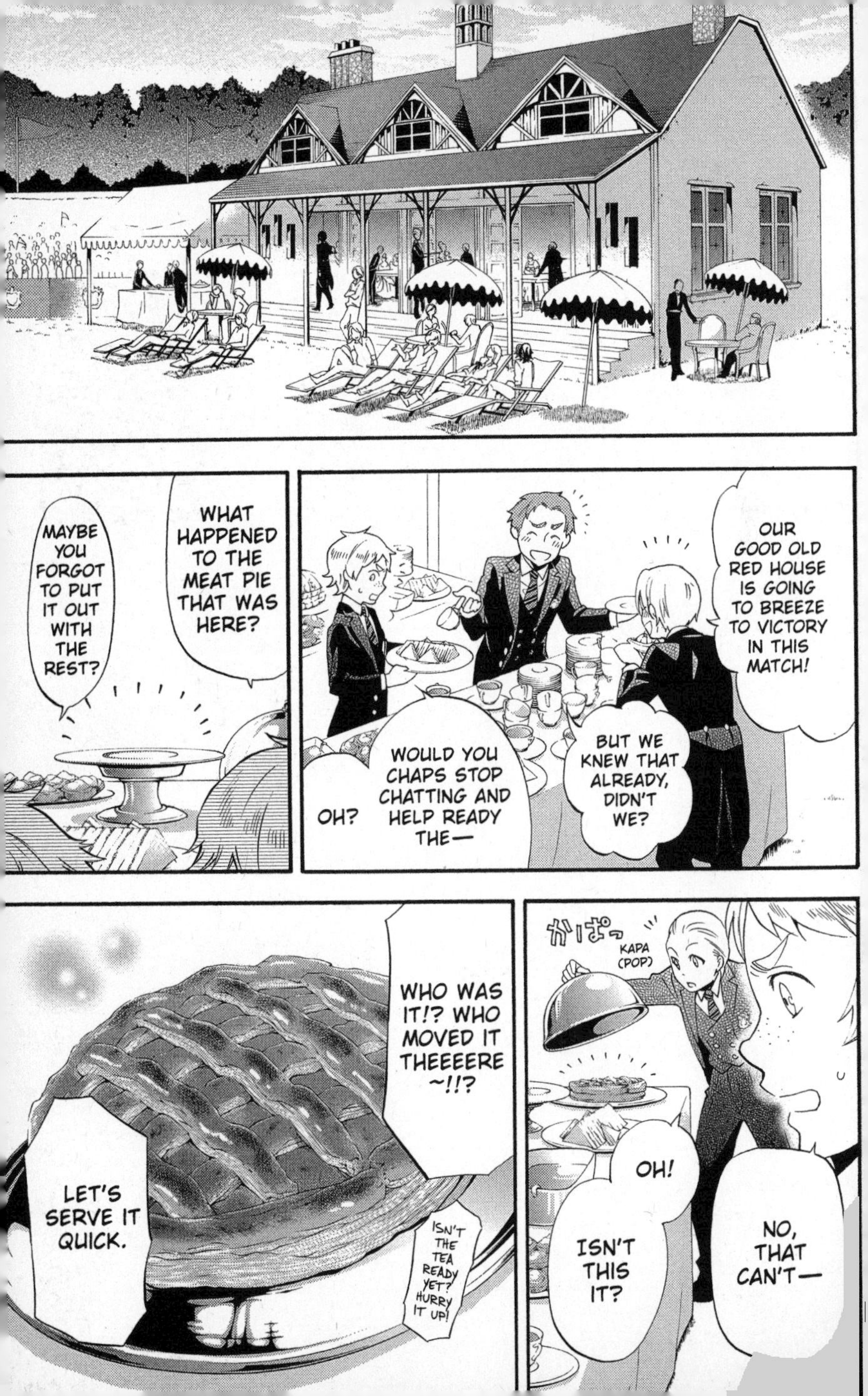
OUR GOOD OLD RED HOUSE IS GOING TO BREEZE TO VICTORY IN THIS MATCH!
BUT WE KNEW THAT ALREADY, DIDN'T WE?
WOULD YOU CHAPS STOP CHATTING AND HELP READY THE—
OH?
WHAT HAPPENED TO THE MEAT PIE THAT WAS HERE?
MAYBE YOU FORGOT TO PUT IT OUT WITH THE REST?
かぱっ
KAPA (POP)
NO, THAT CAN'T—
OH!
ISN'T THIS IT?
WHO WAS IT!? WHO MOVED IT THEEEERE~!!?
ISN'T THE TEA READY YET? HURRY IT UP!
LET'S SERVE IT QUICK.

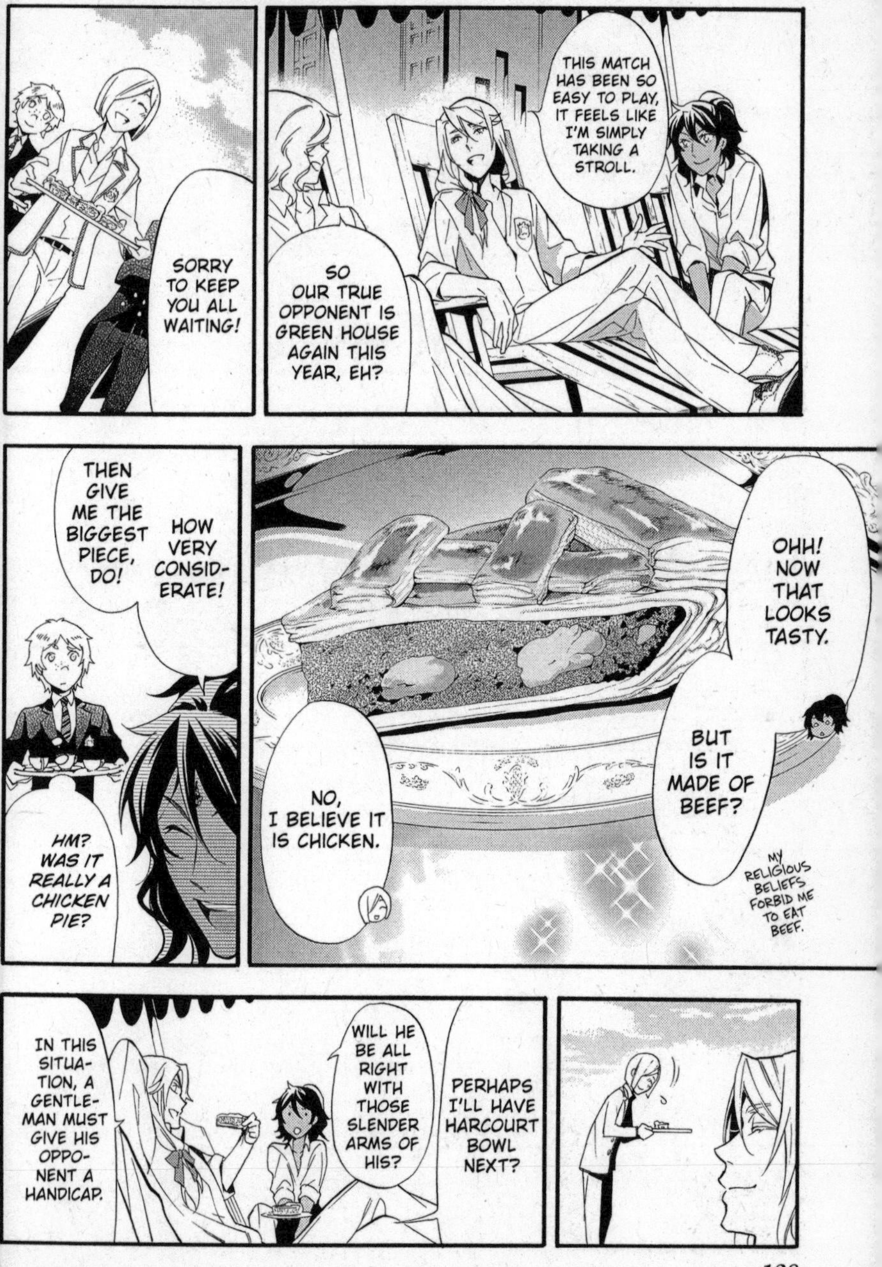
THIS MATCH HAS BEEN SO EASY TO PLAY, IT FEELS LIKE I'M SIMPLY TAKING A STROLL.
SO OUR TRUE OPPONENT IS GREEN HOUSE AGAIN THIS YEAR, EH?
SORRY TO KEEP YOU ALL WAITING!
OHH! NOW THAT LOOKS TASTY.
BUT IS IT MADE OF BEEF?
MY RELIGIOUS BELIEFS FORBID ME TO EAT BEEF.
NO, I BELIEVE IT IS CHICKEN.
HOW VERY CONSID-ERATE!
THEN GIVE ME THE BIGGEST PIECE, DO!
HM? WAS IT REALLY A CHICKEN PIE?
PERHAPS I'LL HAVE HARCOURT BOWL NEXT?
WILL HE BE ALL RIGHT WITH THOSE SLENDER ARMS OF HIS?
IN THIS SITUA-TION, A GENTLE-MAN MUST GIVE HIS OPPO-NENT A HANDICAP.

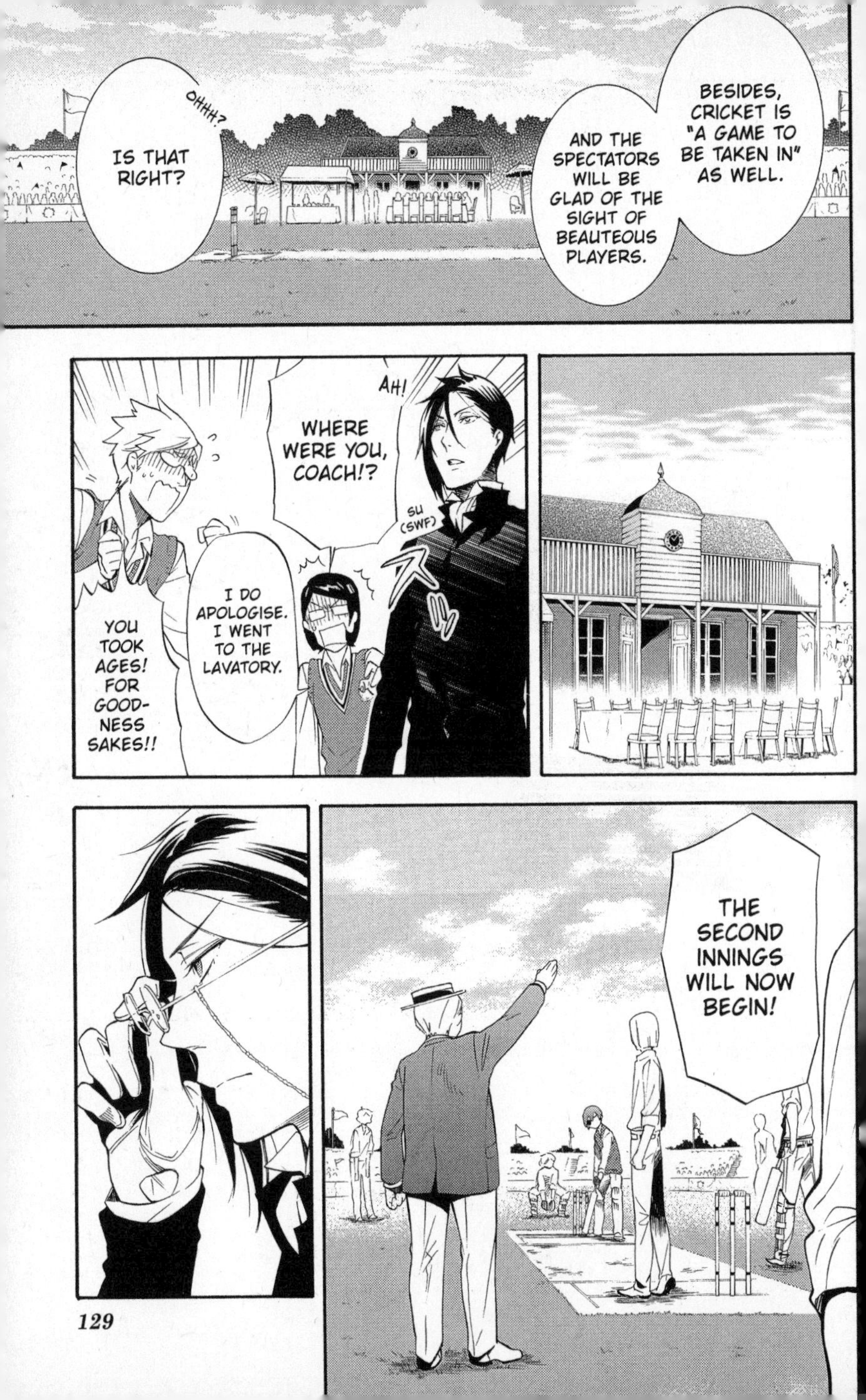
BESIDES, CRICKET IS "A GAME TO BE TAKEN IN" AS WELL.
AND THE SPECTATORS WILL BE GLAD OF THE SIGHT OF BEAUTEOUS PLAYERS.
OHHH?
IS THAT RIGHT?
AH!
WHERE WERE YOU, COACH!?
SU (SWF)
I DO APOLOGISE. I WENT TO THE LAVATORY.
YOU TOOK AGES! FOR GOODNESS SAKES!!
THE SECOND INNINGS WILL NOW BEGIN!

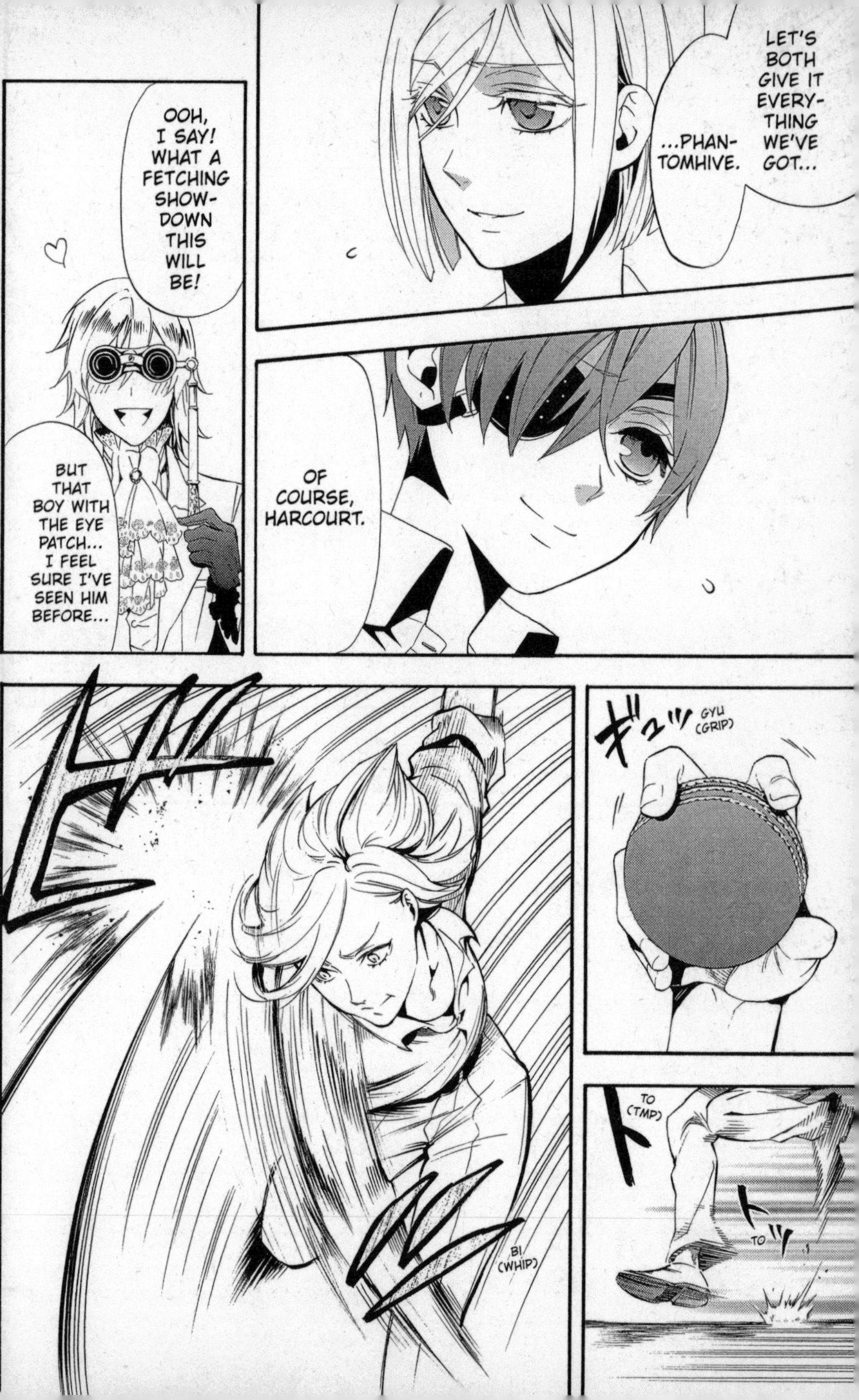
LET'S BOTH GIVE IT EVERYTHING WE'VE GOT...
...PHAN-TOMHIVE.
OF COURSE, HARCOURT.
OOH, I SAY! WHAT A FETCHING SHOW-DOWN THIS WILL BE!
BUT THAT BOY WITH THE EYE PATCH... I FEEL SURE I'VE SEEN HIM BEFORE...
GYU (GRIP)
TO (TMP)
TO
BI (WHIP)

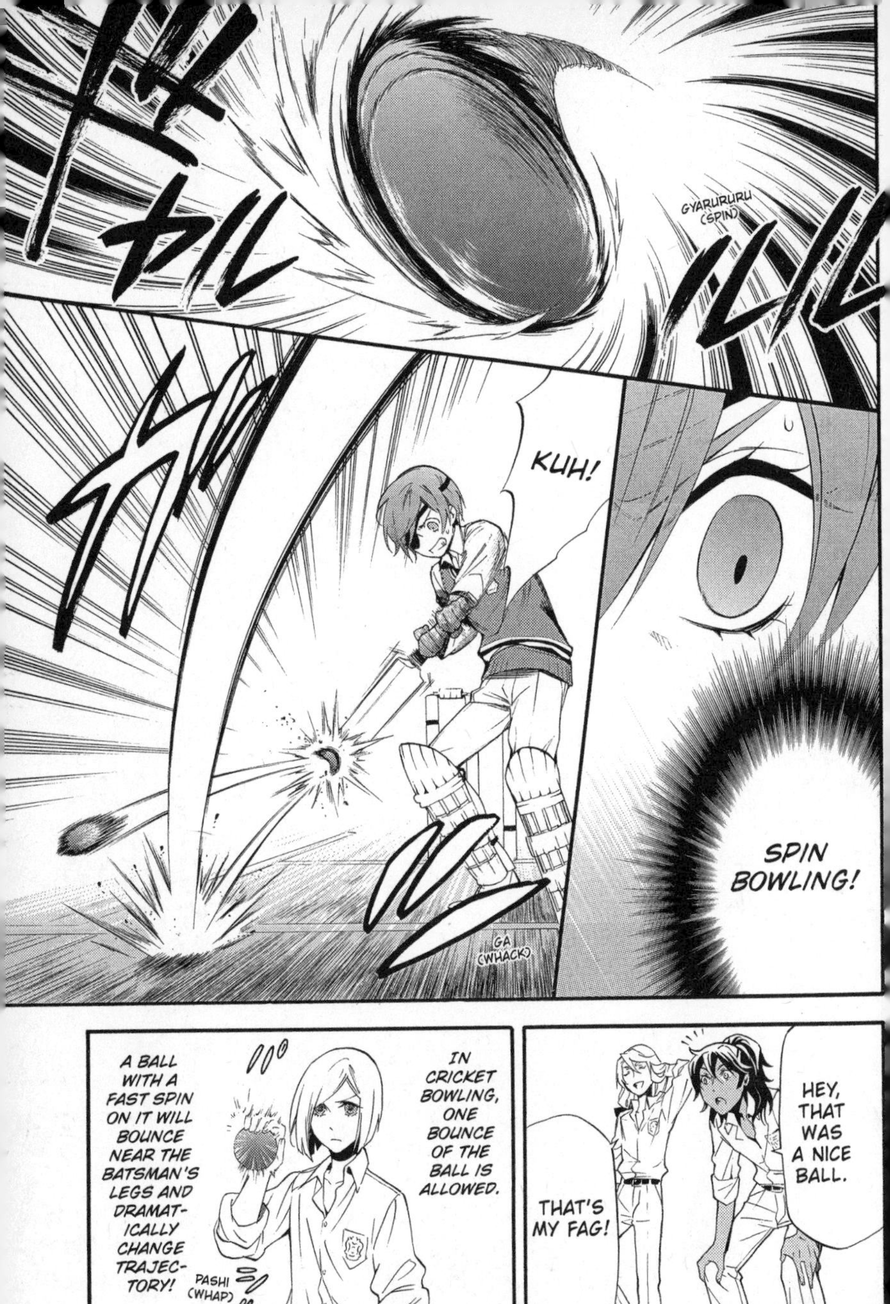
GYARURURU (SPIN)
SPIN BOWLING!
KUH!
GA (WHACK)
HEY, THAT WAS A NICE BALL.
THAT'S MY FAG!
IN CRICKET BOWLING, ONE BOUNCE OF THE BALL IS ALLOWED.
A BALL WITH A FAST SPIN ON IT WILL BOUNCE NEAR THE BATSMAN'S LEGS AND DRAMATICALLY CHANGE TRAJECTORY!
PASHI (WHAP)

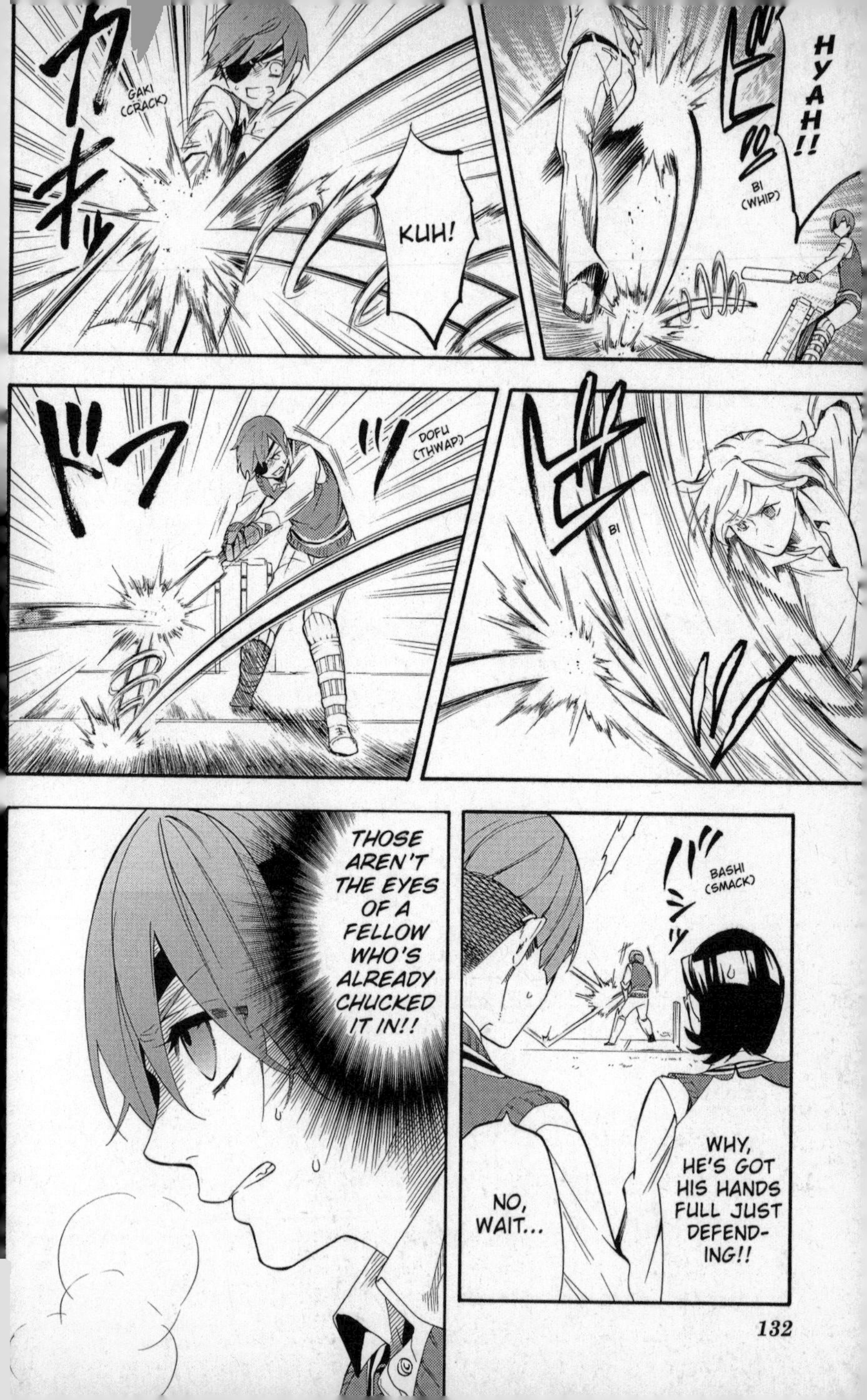
HYAH!!
BI (WHIP)
GAKI (CRACK)
KUH!
BI
DOFU (THWAP)
BASHI (SMACK)
WHY, HE'S GOT HIS HANDS FULL JUST DEFENDING!!
NO, WAIT...
THOSE AREN'T THE EYES OF A FELLOW WHO'S ALREADY CHUCKED IT IN!!

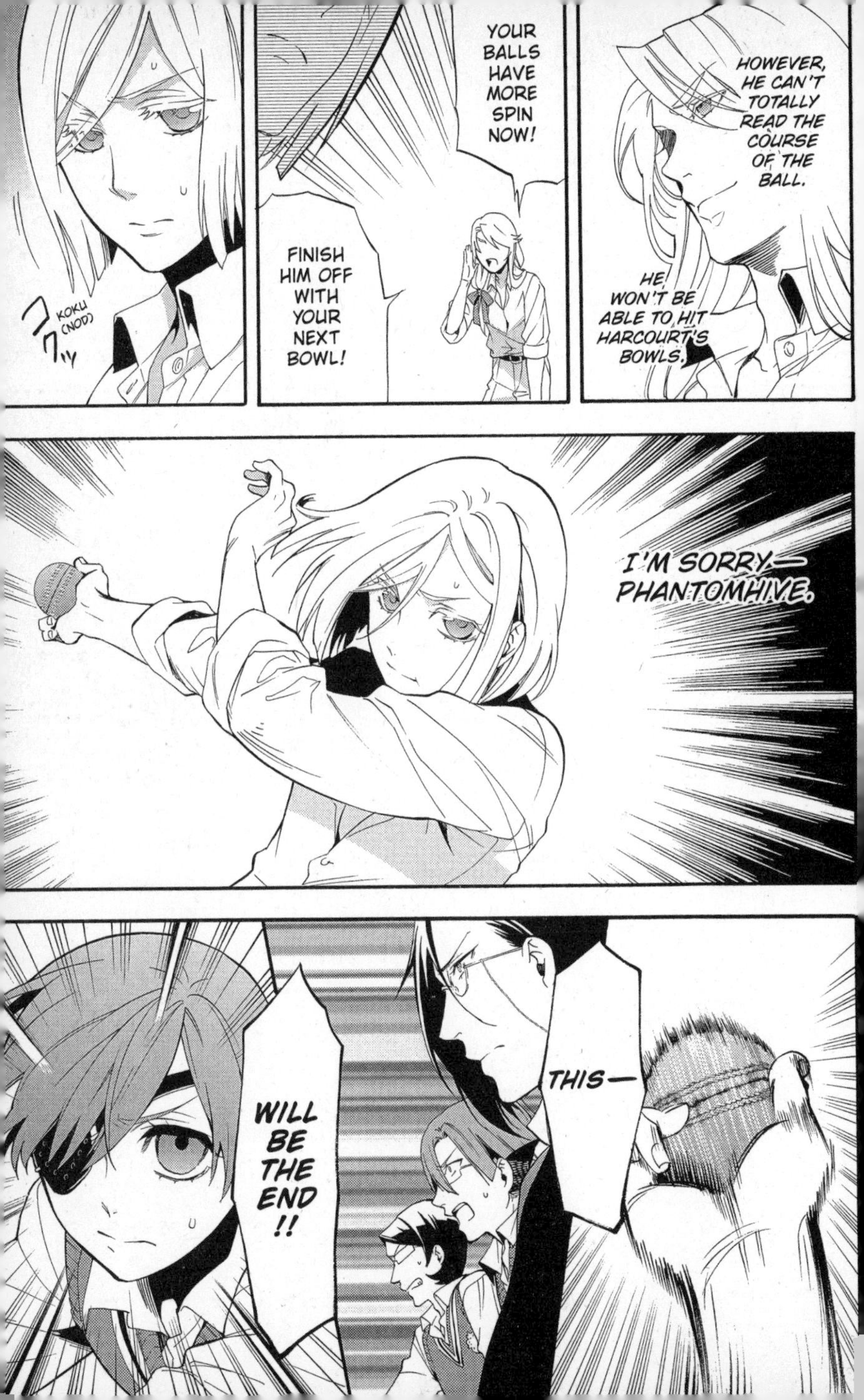
HOWEVER, HE CAN'T TOTALLY READ THE COURSE OF THE BALL.
HE WON'T BE ABLE TO HIT HARCOURT'S BOWLS.
YOUR BALLS HAVE MORE SPIN NOW!
FINISH HIM OFF WITH YOUR NEXT BOWL!
KOKU (NOD)
I'M SORRY— PHANTOMHIVE.
THIS—
WILL BE THE END!!

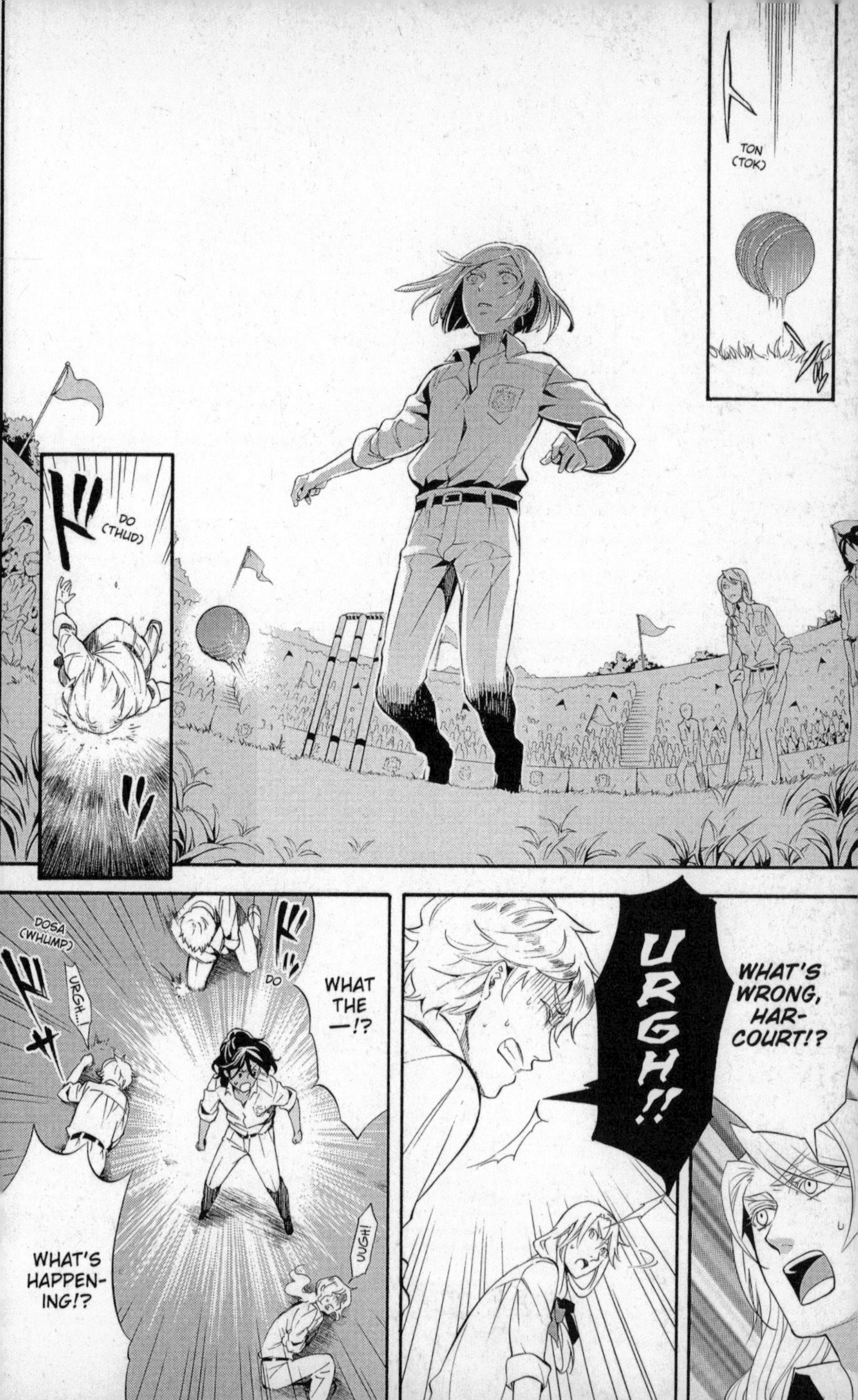

TON (TOK)
DO (THUD)
WHAT'S WRONG, HAR-COURT!?
URGH!!
DO
WHAT THE—!?
DOSA (WHUMP)
URGH...
UUGH!
WHAT'S HAPPEN-ING!?

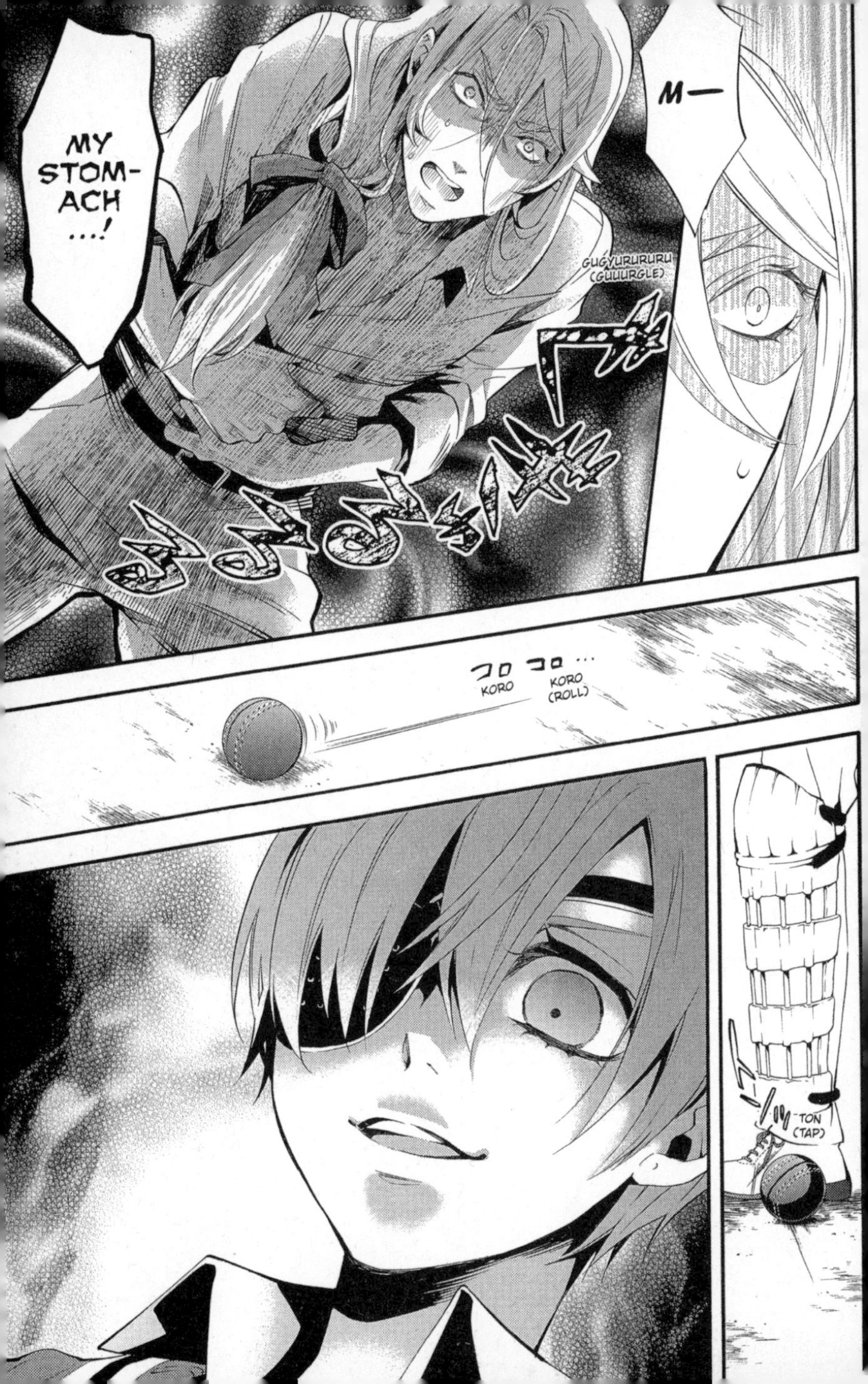
M—
MY STOMACH....!
GUGYURURURU (GUUURGLE)
コロ コロ…
KORO KORO (ROLL)
TON (TAP)

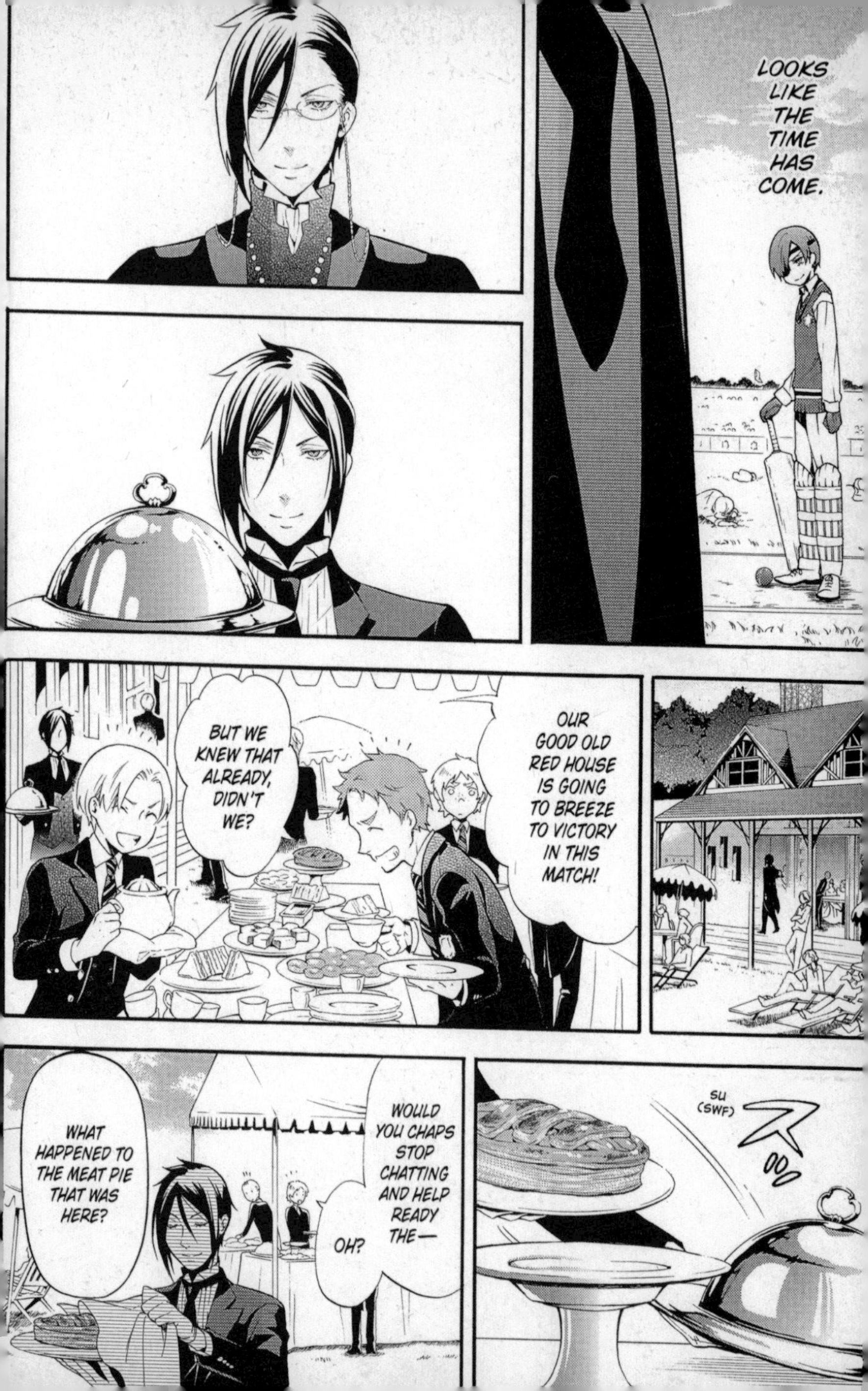
LOOKS LIKE THE TIME HAS COME.
OUR GOOD OLD RED HOUSE IS GOING TO BREEZE TO VICTORY IN THIS MATCH!
BUT WE KNEW THAT ALREADY, DIDN'T WE?
SU (SWF)
WOULD YOU CHAPS STOP CHATTING AND HELP READY THE—
OH?
WHAT HAPPENED TO THE MEAT PIE THAT WAS HERE?

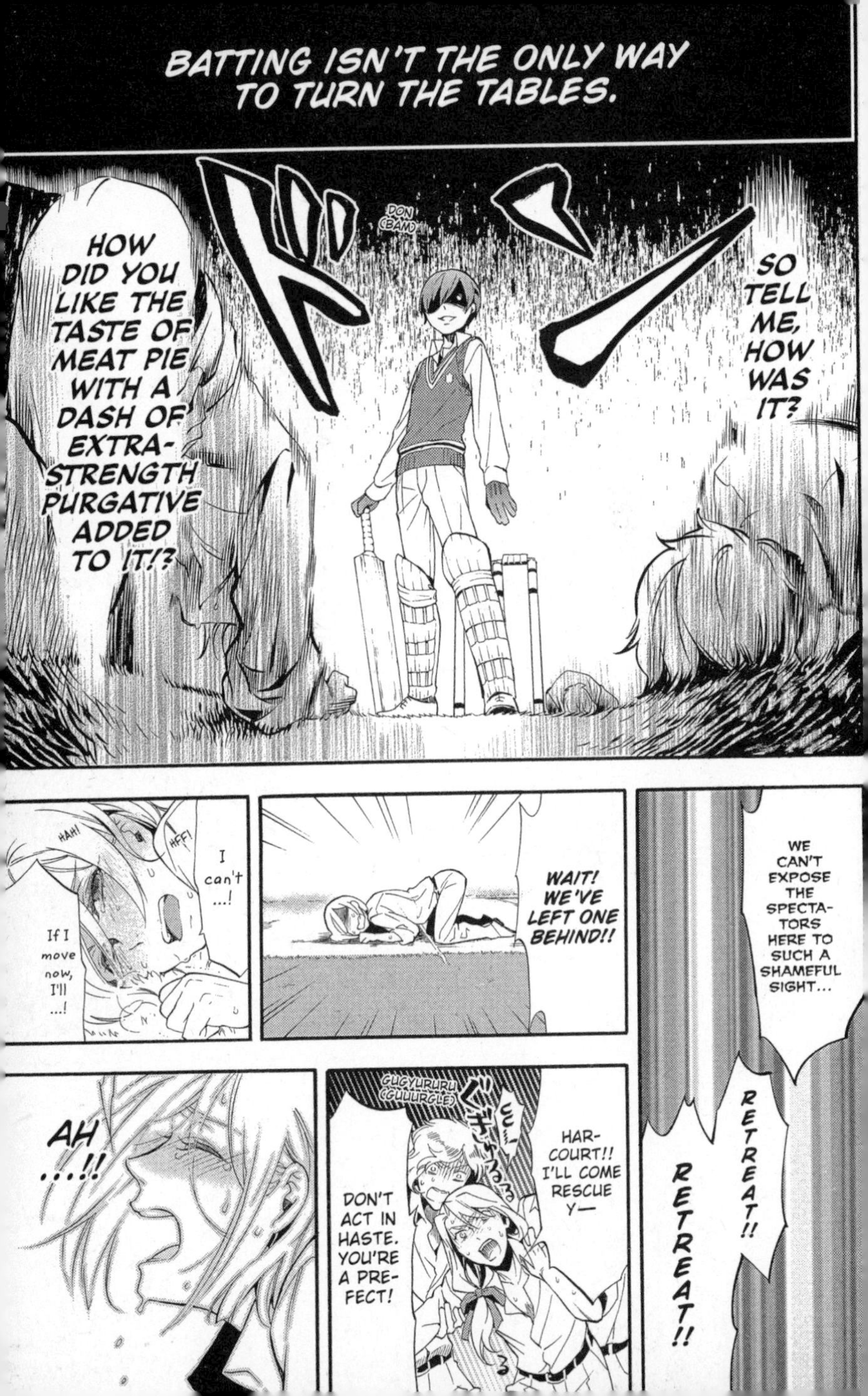
BATTING ISN'T THE ONLY WAY TO TURN THE TABLES.
SO TELL ME, HOW WAS IT?
DON (BAM)
HOW DID YOU LIKE THE TASTE OF MEAT PIE WITH A DASH OF EXTRA-STRENGTH PURGATIVE ADDED TO IT!?
WE CAN'T EXPOSE THE SPECTATORS HERE TO SUCH A SHAMEFUL SIGHT...
RETREAT!!
RETREAT!!
WAIT! WE'VE LEFT ONE BEHIND!!
HFF!
HAH!
I can't ...!
If I move now, I'll ...!
GUGYURURU (GUUURGLE)
HAR-COURT!! I'LL COME RESCUE Y—
DON'T ACT IN HASTE. YOU'RE A PRE-FECT!
AH ...!!

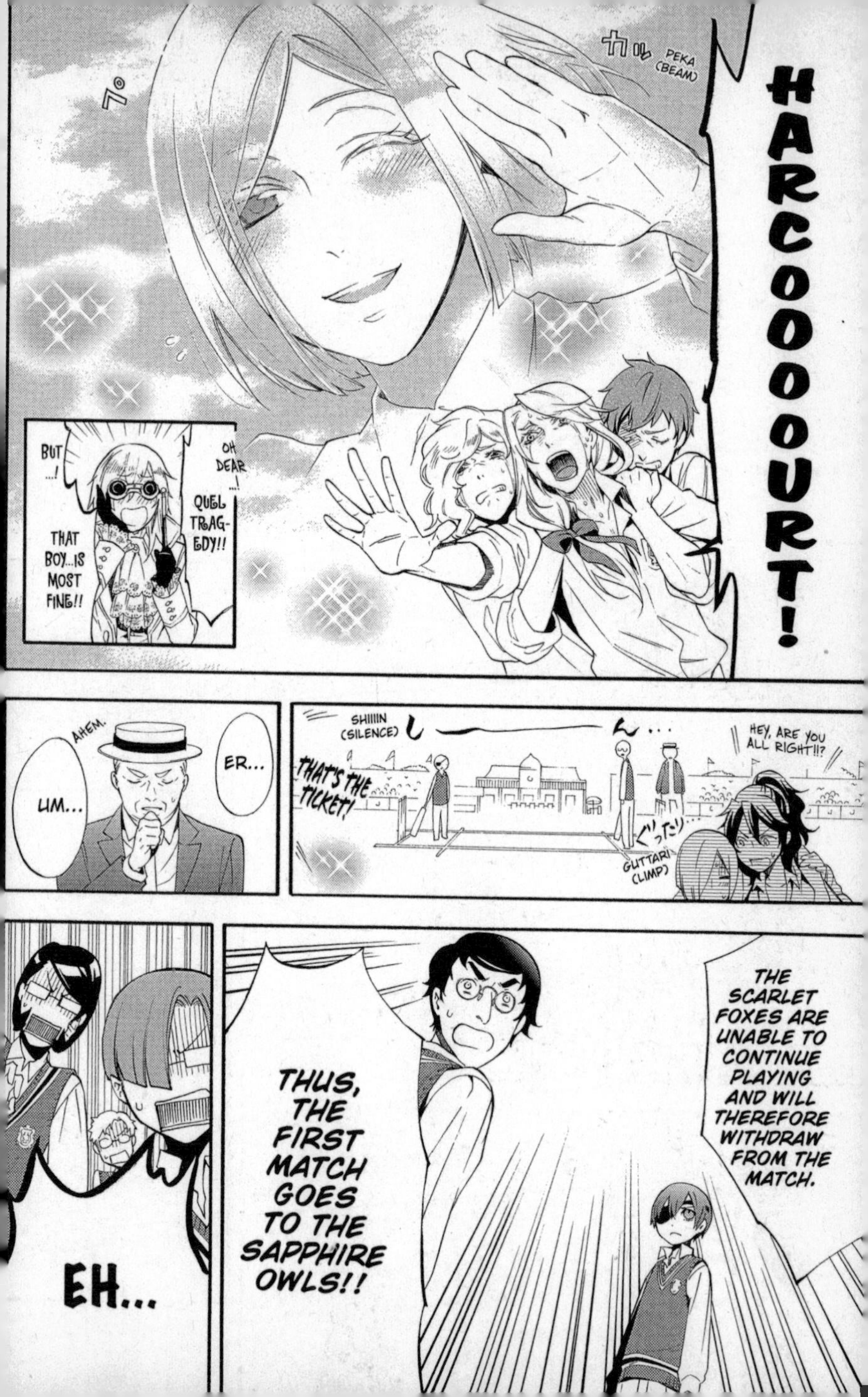
PEKA (BEAM)
HARCOOOOOURT!
OH DEAR...! QUEL TRAG-EDY!!
BUT...! THAT BOY...IS MOST FINE!!
HEY, ARE YOU ALL RIGHT!!?
ぐったり…
GUTTARI (LIMP)
しーん…
SHIIIIN (SILENCE)
THAT'S THE TICKET!
ER...
AHEM.
UM...
THE SCARLET FOXES ARE UNABLE TO CONTINUE PLAYING AND WILL THEREFORE WITHDRAW FROM THE MATCH.
THUS, THE FIRST MATCH GOES TO THE SAPPHIRE OWLS!!
EH...

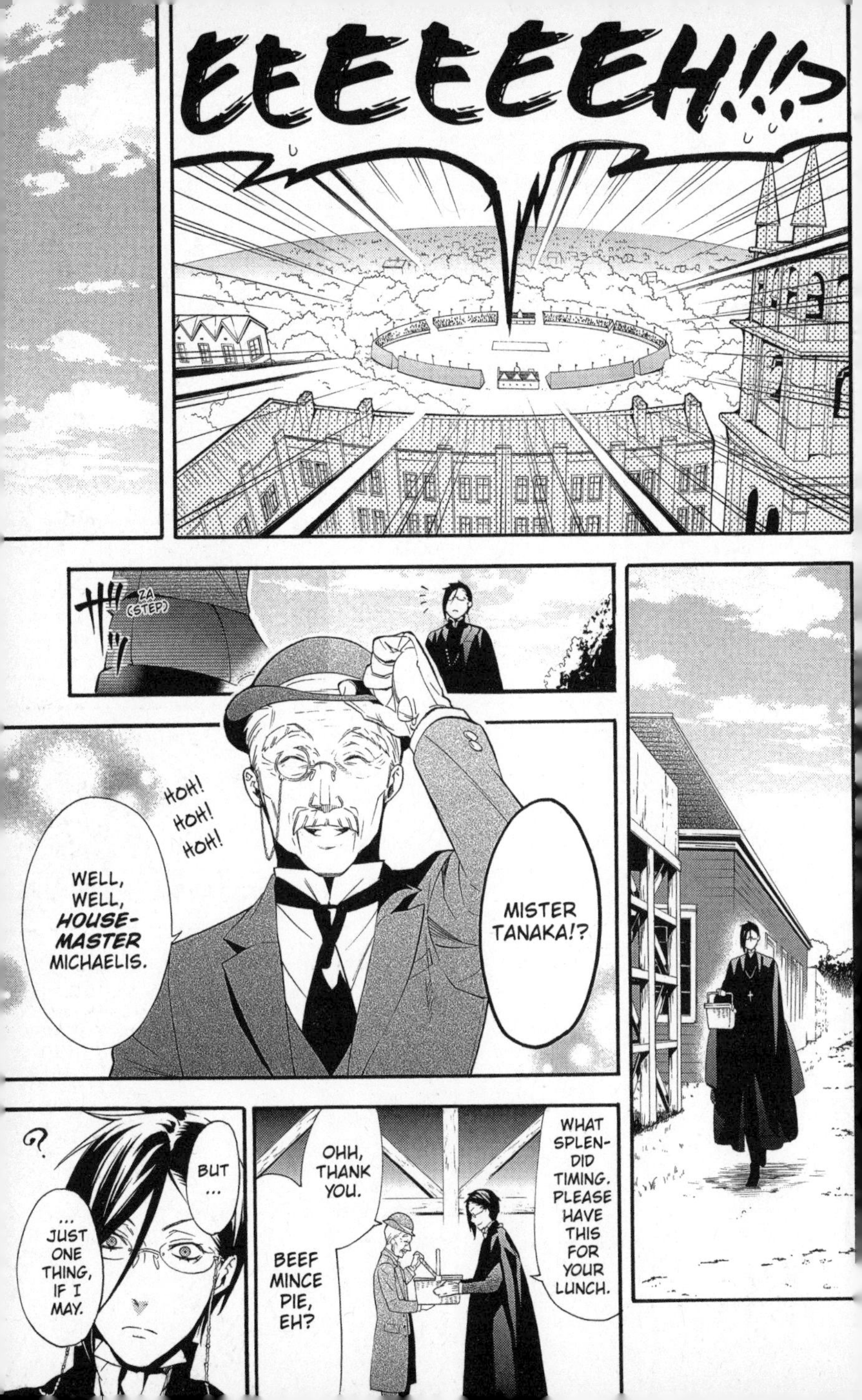
EEEEEEEH!!?
ZA (STEP)
MISTER TANAKA!?
HOH! HOH! HOH!
WELL, WELL, *HOUSE-MASTER* MICHAELIS.
WHAT SPLEN-DID TIMING. PLEASE HAVE THIS FOR YOUR LUNCH.
OHH, THANK YOU.
BEEF MINCE PIE, EH?
BUT ...
... JUST ONE THING, IF I MAY.

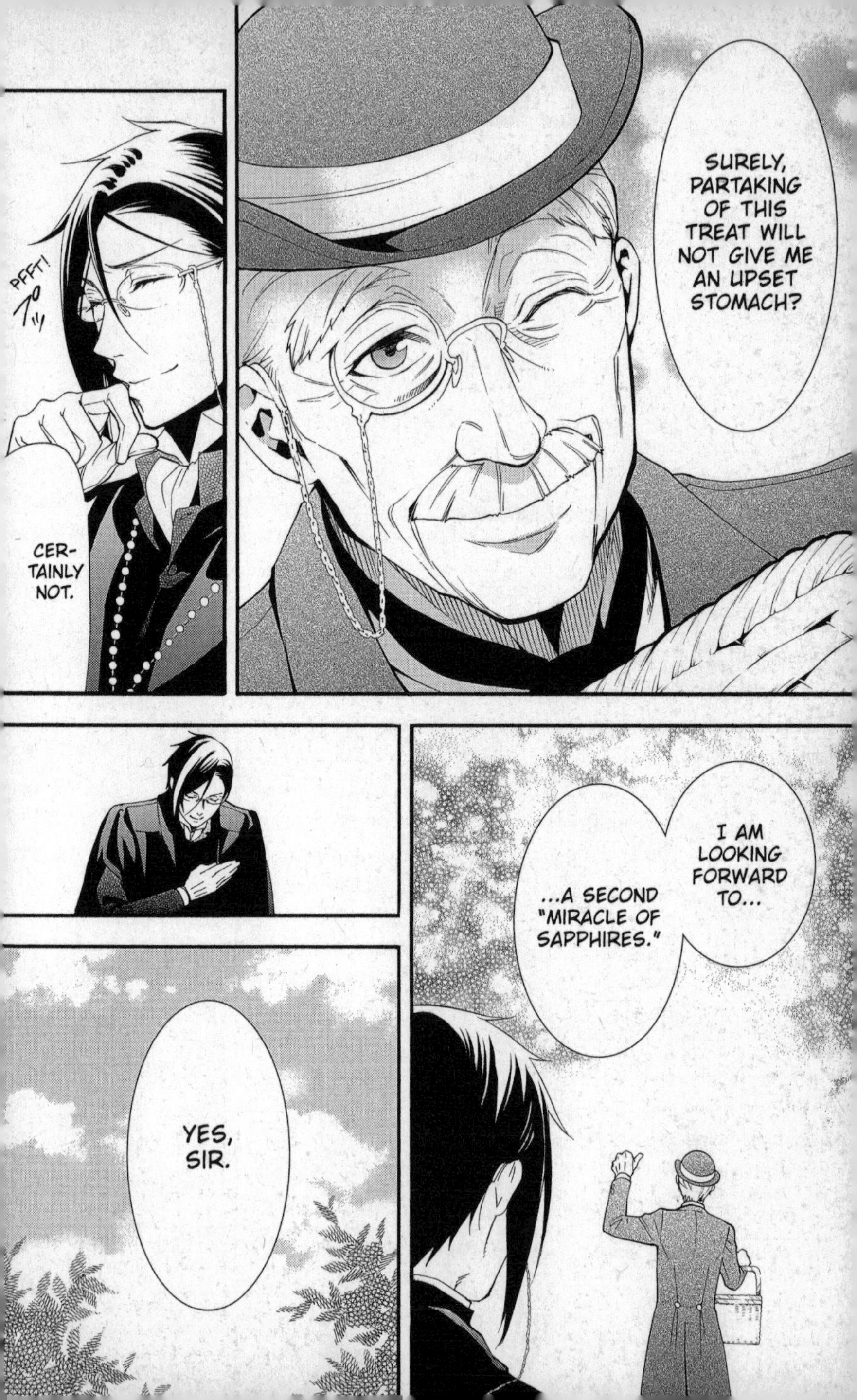
SURELY, PARTAKING OF THIS TREAT WILL NOT GIVE ME AN UPSET STOMACH?
PFFT!
CER-TAINLY NOT.
I AM LOOKING FORWARD TO...
...A SECOND "MIRACLE OF SAPPHIRES."
YES, SIR.

Black Butler

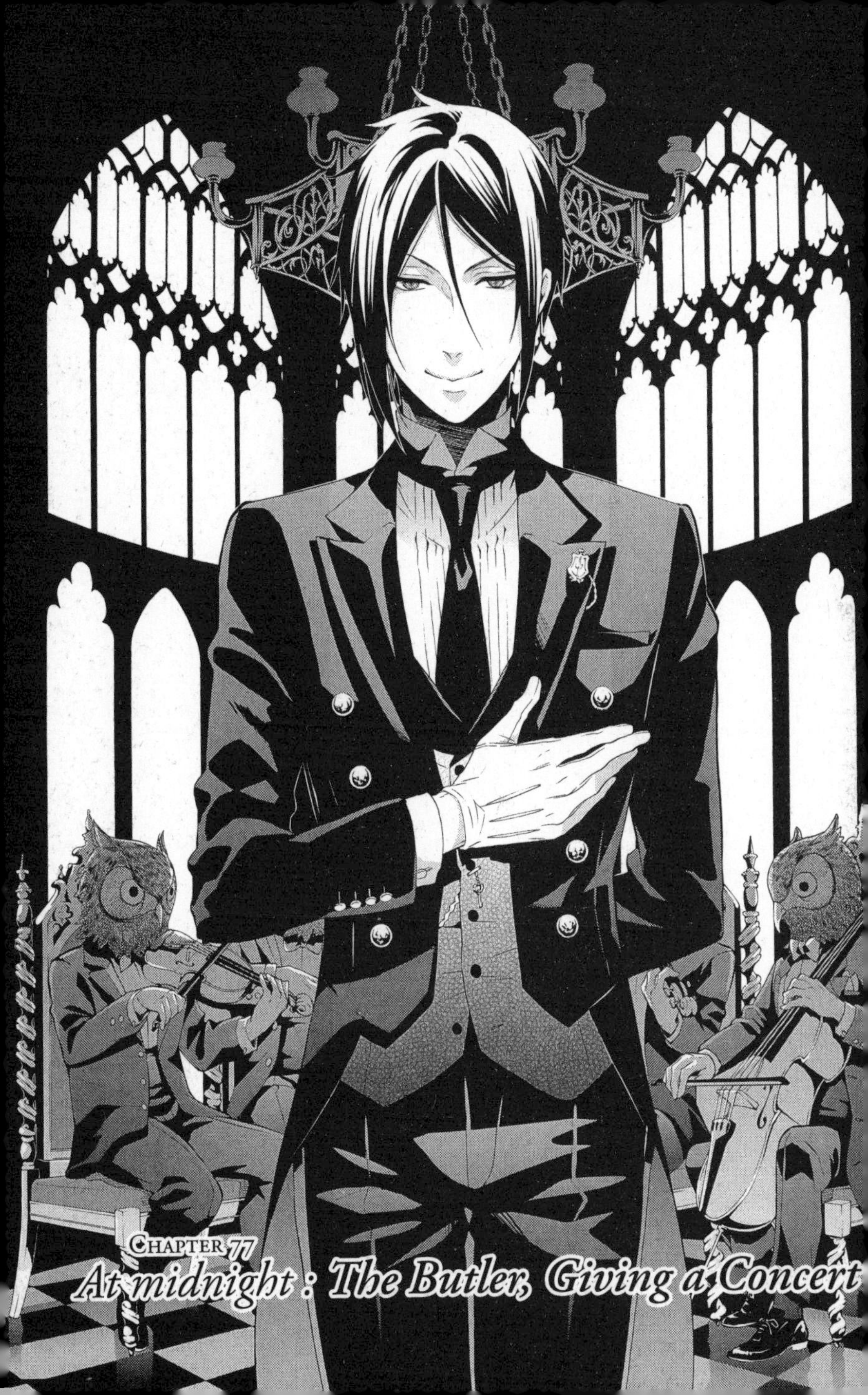
Chapter 77
At midnight : The Butler, Giving a Concert

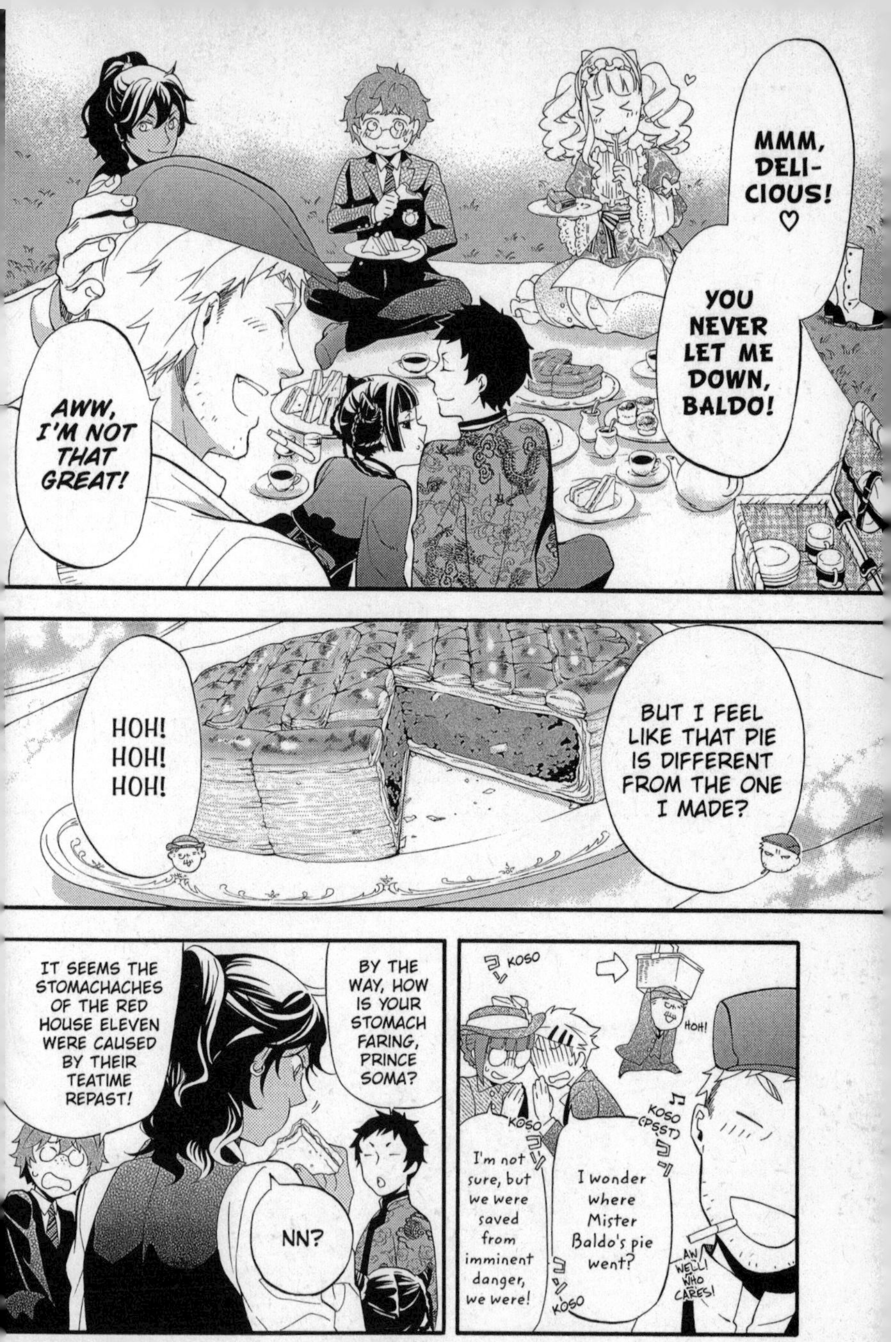
MMM, DELICIOUS! ♡
YOU NEVER LET ME DOWN, BALDO!
AWW, I'M NOT THAT GREAT!
BUT I FEEL LIKE THAT PIE IS DIFFERENT FROM THE ONE I MADE?
HOH! HOH! HOH!
KOSO
HOH!
KOSO (PSST)
I wonder where Mister Baldo's pie went?
KOSO
I'm not sure, but we were saved from imminent danger, we were!
KOSO
AW WELL! WHO CARES!
BY THE WAY, HOW IS YOUR STOMACH FARING, PRINCE SOMA?
IT SEEMS THE STOMACHACHES OF THE RED HOUSE ELEVEN WERE CAUSED BY THEIR TEATIME REPAST!
NN?

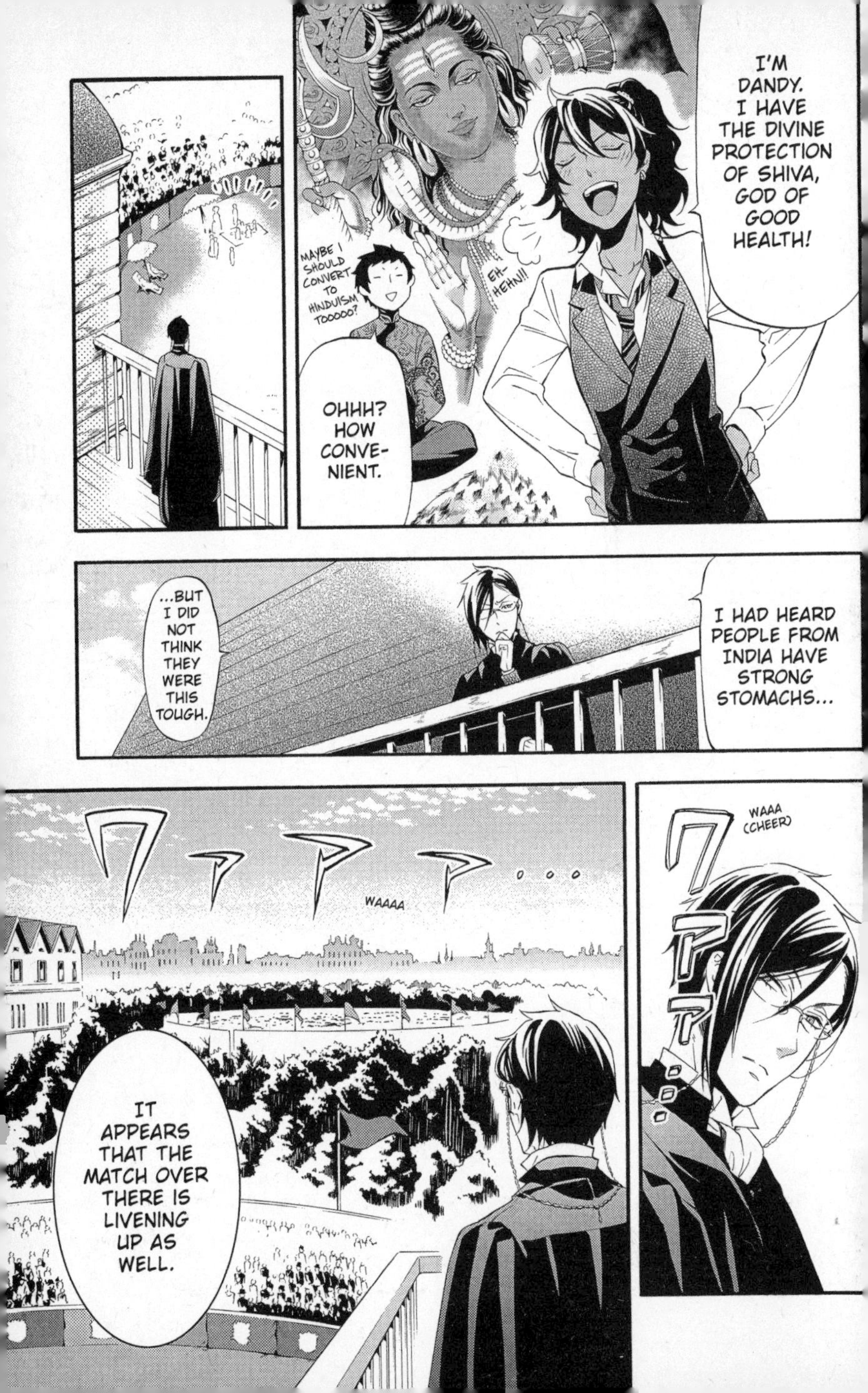
I'M DANDY. I HAVE THE DIVINE PROTECTION OF SHIVA, GOD OF GOOD HEALTH!
EH-HEHN!!
MAYBE I SHOULD CONVERT TO HINDUISM TOOOOO?
OHHH? HOW CONVE-NIENT.
I HAD HEARD PEOPLE FROM INDIA HAVE STRONG STOMACHS...
...BUT I DID NOT THINK THEY WERE THIS TOUGH.
WAAA (CHEER)
WAAAA
IT APPEARS THAT THE MATCH OVER THERE IS LIVENING UP AS WELL.

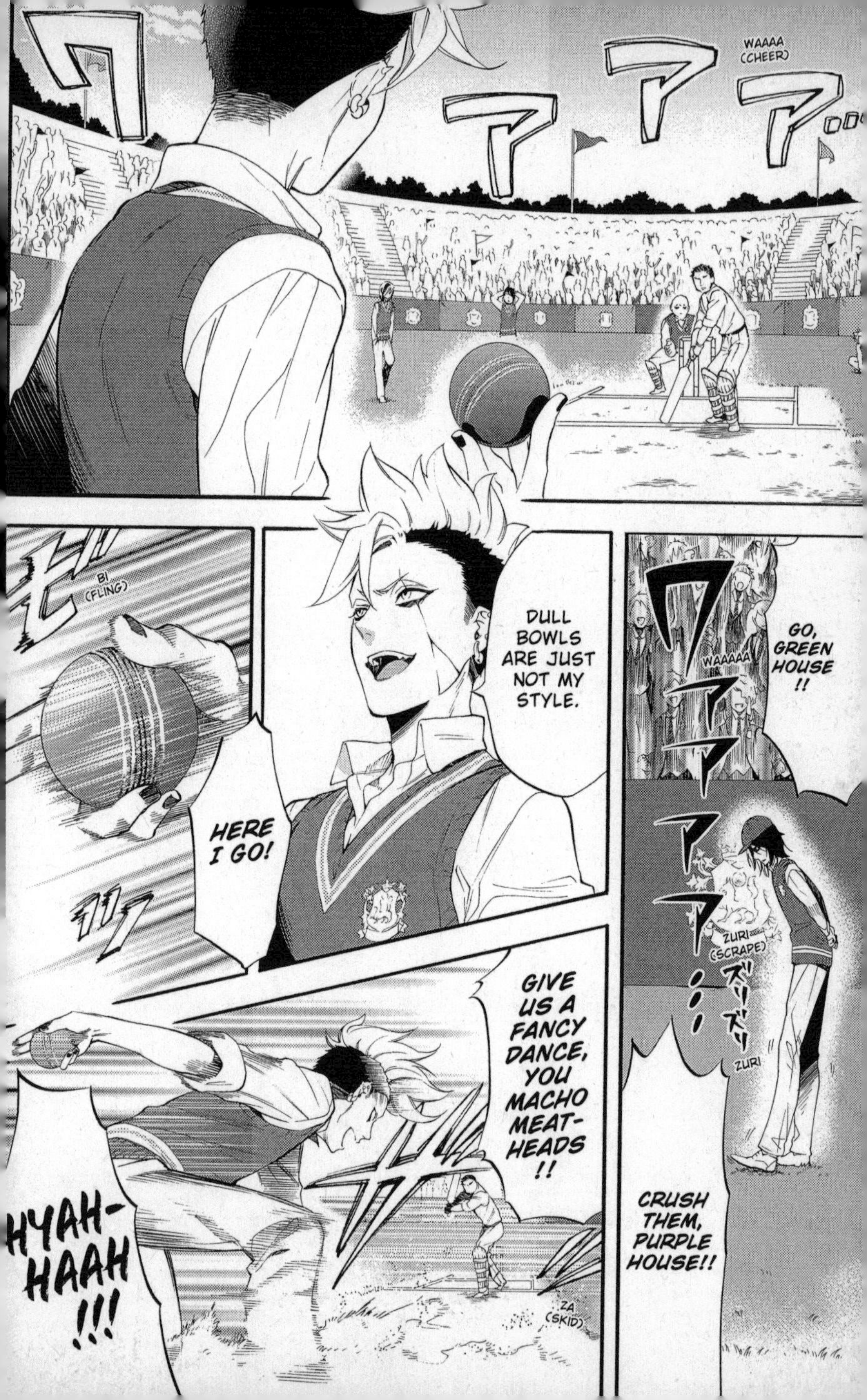
WAAAA (CHEER)
WAAAAA
GO, GREEN HOUSE!!
DULL BOWLS ARE JUST NOT MY STYLE.
HERE I GO!
BI (FLING)
ZURI (SCRAPE)
ZURI
CRUSH THEM, PURPLE HOUSE!!
GIVE US A FANCY DANCE, YOU MACHO MEAT-HEADS!!
ZA (SKID)
HYAH-HAAH!!!

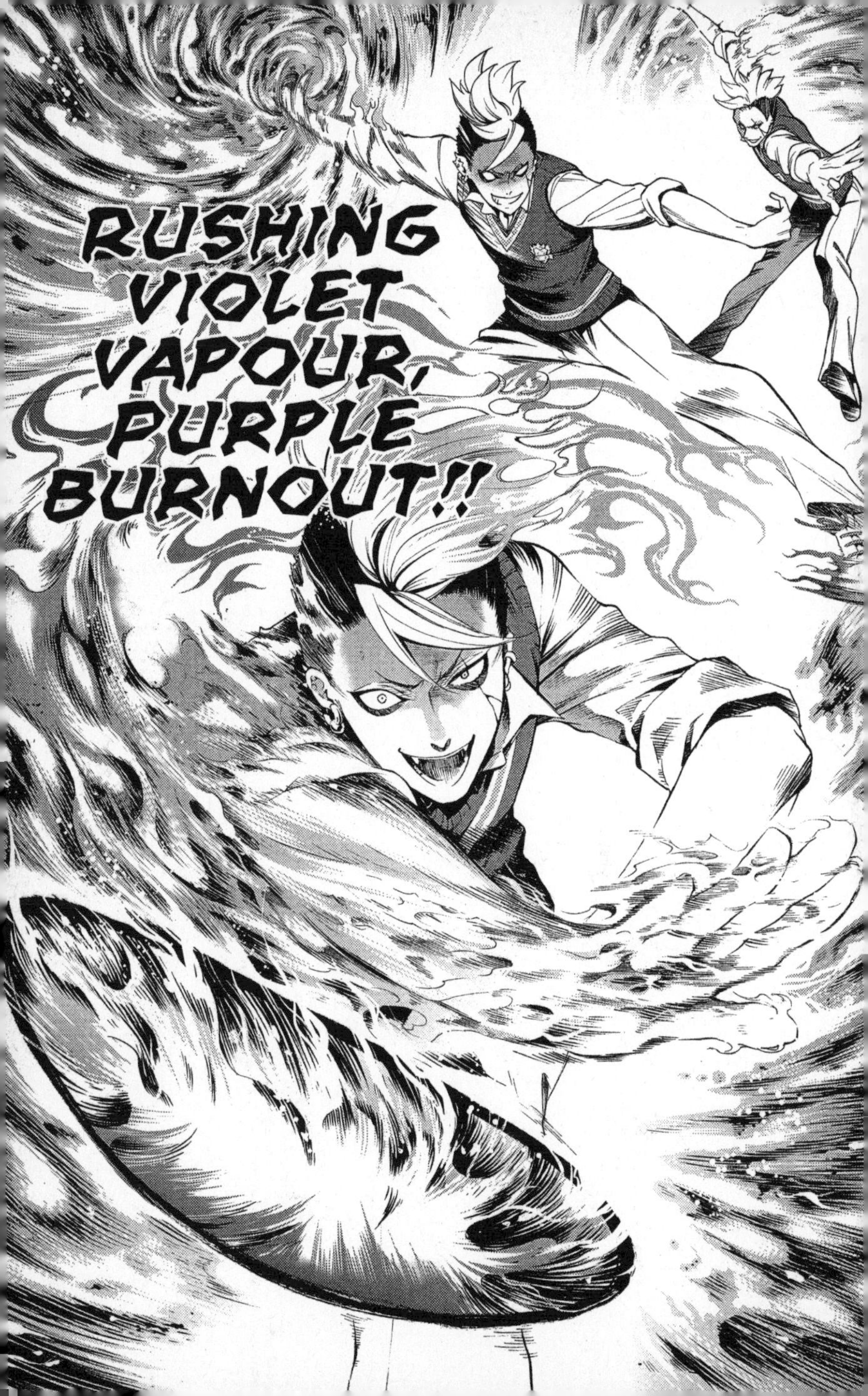
RUSHING VIOLET VAPOUR, PURPLE BURNOUT!!

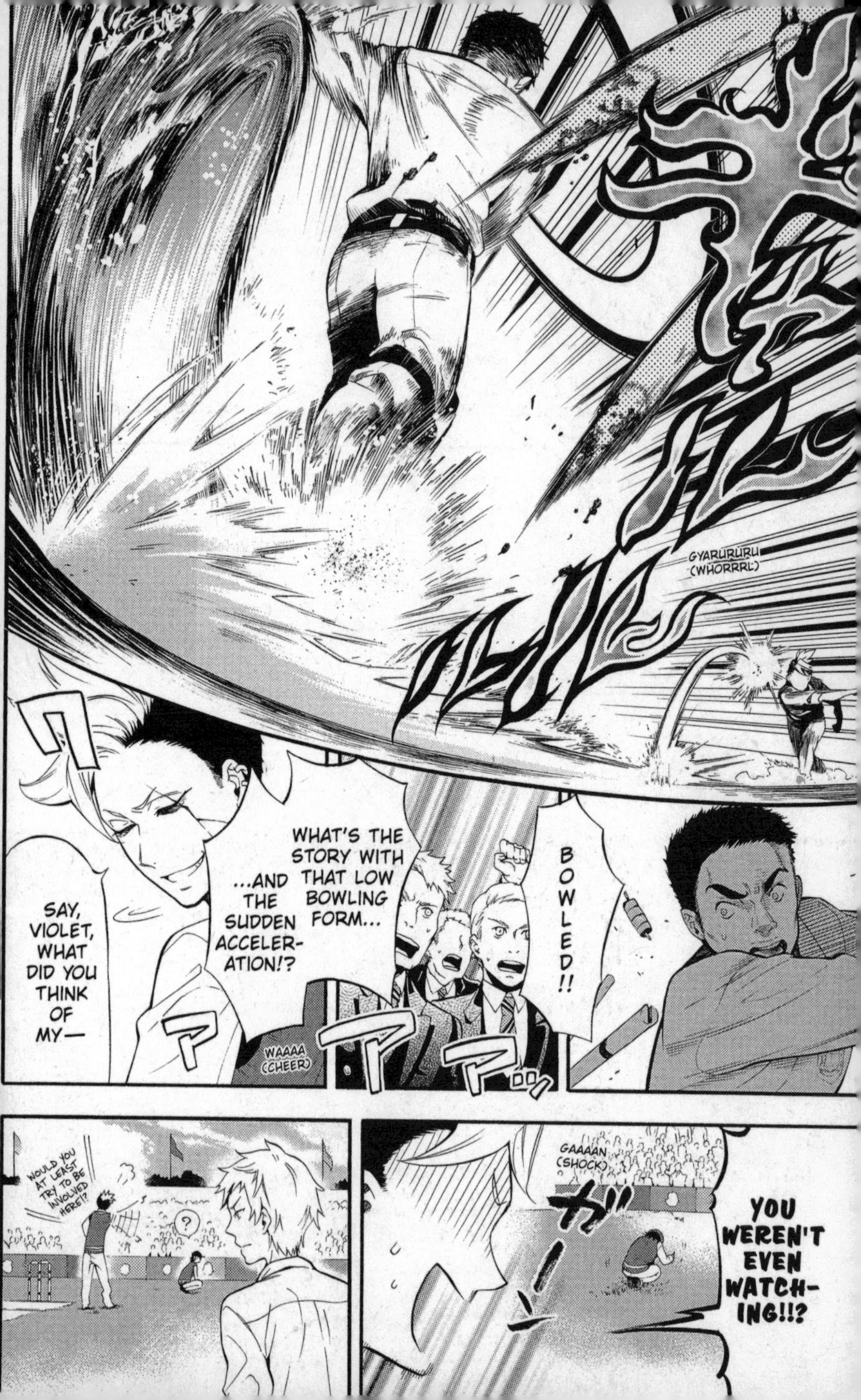
GYARURURU (WHORRRL)
BOWLED!!
WHAT'S THE STORY WITH THAT LOW BOWLING FORM...
...AND THE SUDDEN ACCELERATION!?
WAAAA (CHEER)
SAY, VIOLET, WHAT DID YOU THINK OF MY—
GAAAAN (SHOCK)
YOU WEREN'T EVEN WATCHING!!?
WOULD YOU AT LEAST TRY TO BE INVOLVED HERE!?
?

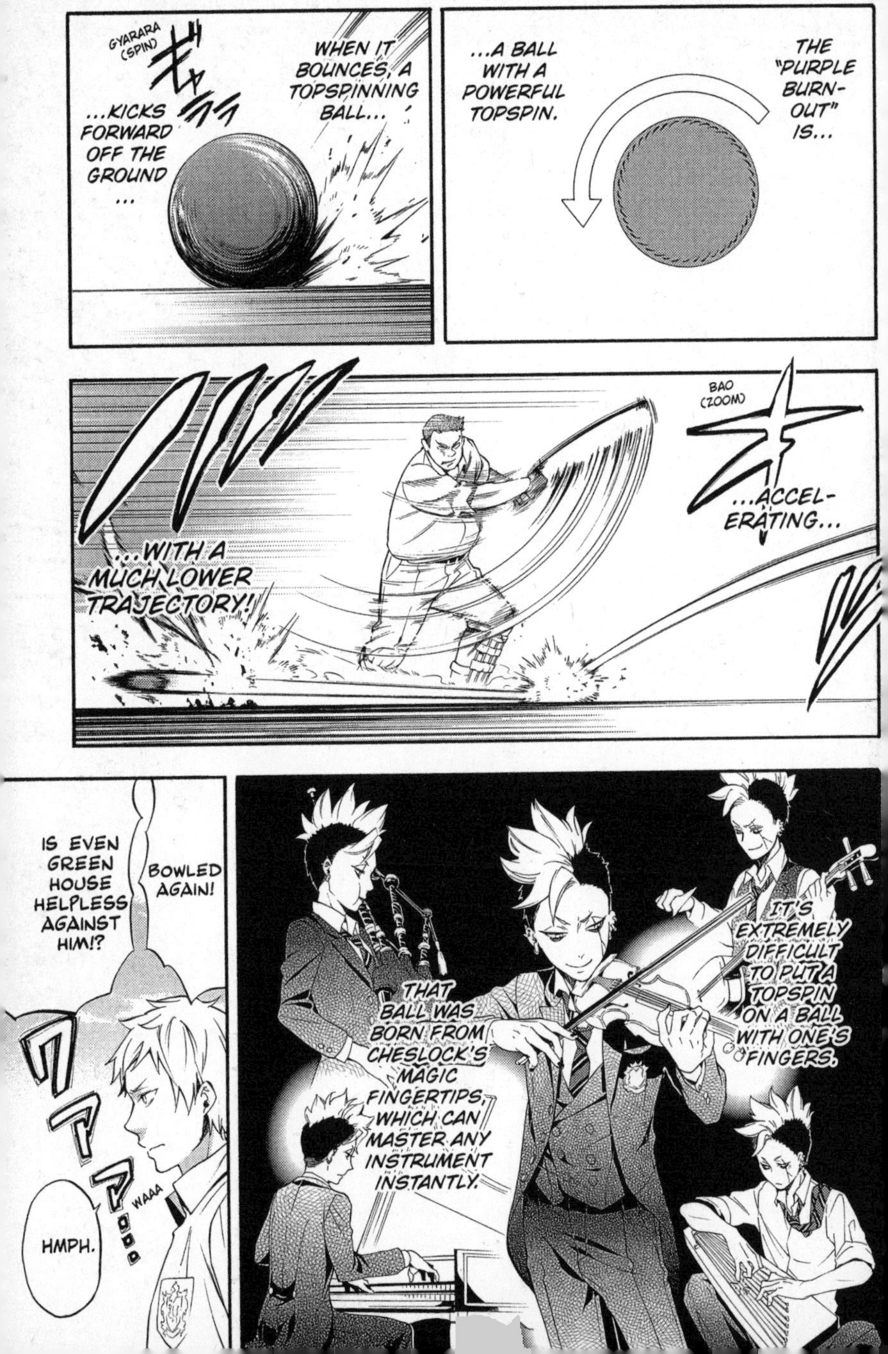
THE "PURPLE BURN-OUT" IS...
...A BALL WITH A POWERFUL TOPSPIN.
WHEN IT BOUNCES, A TOPSPINNING BALL...
GYARARA (SPIN)
...KICKS FORWARD OFF THE GROUND ...
BAO (ZOOM)
...ACCEL-ERATING...
...WITH A MUCH LOWER TRAJECTORY!
IT'S EXTREMELY DIFFICULT TO PUT A TOPSPIN ON A BALL WITH ONE'S FINGERS.
THAT BALL WAS BORN FROM CHESLOCK'S MAGIC FINGERTIPS, WHICH CAN MASTER ANY INSTRUMENT INSTANTLY.
BOWLED AGAIN!
IS EVEN GREEN HOUSE HELPLESS AGAINST HIM!?
WAAA
HMPH.

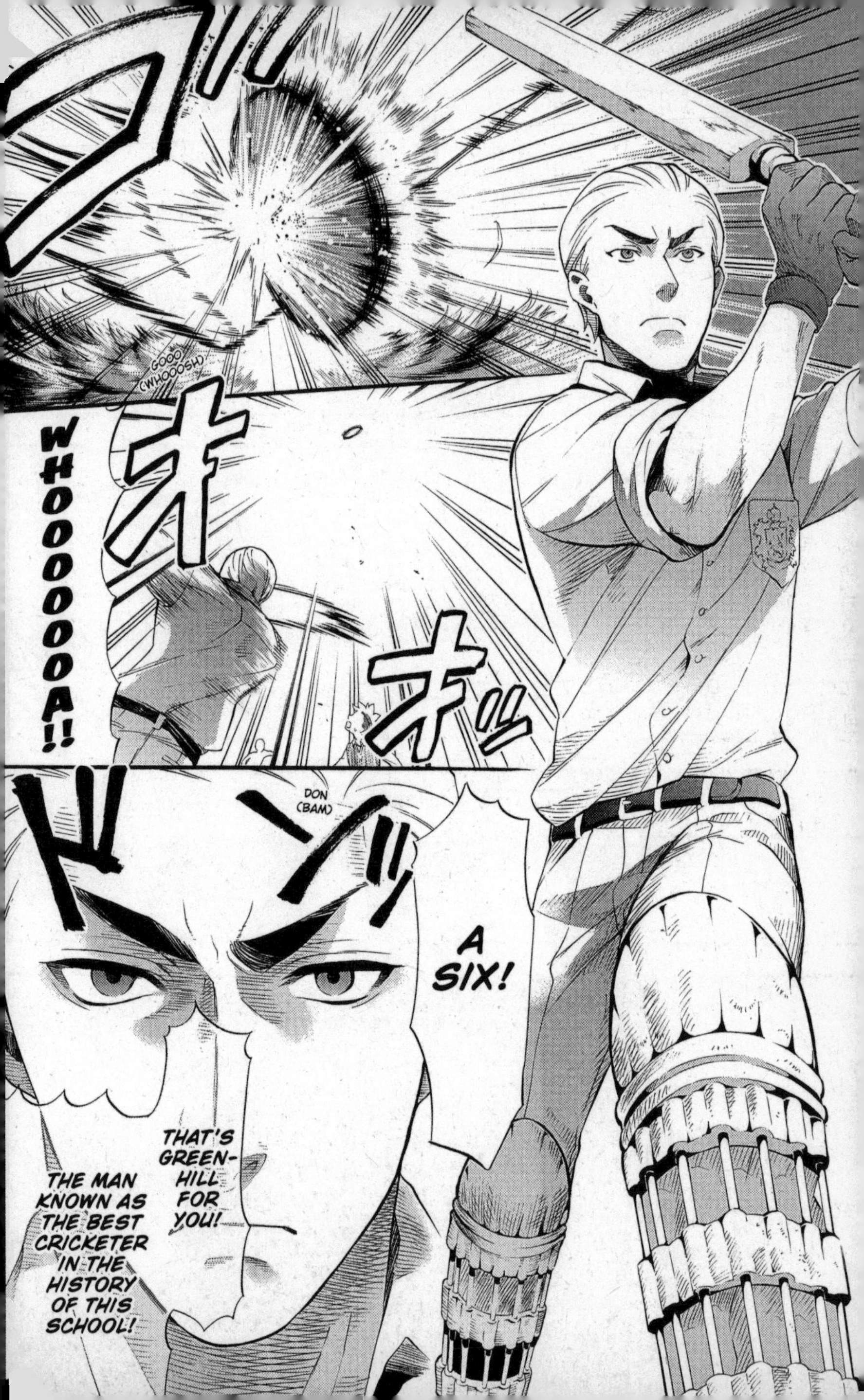
GOOO (WHOOOSH)
WHOOOOOOOOA!!
DON (BAM)
A SIX!
THAT'S GREEN-HILL FOR YOU!
THE MAN KNOWN AS THE BEST CRICKETER IN THE HISTORY OF THIS SCHOOL!

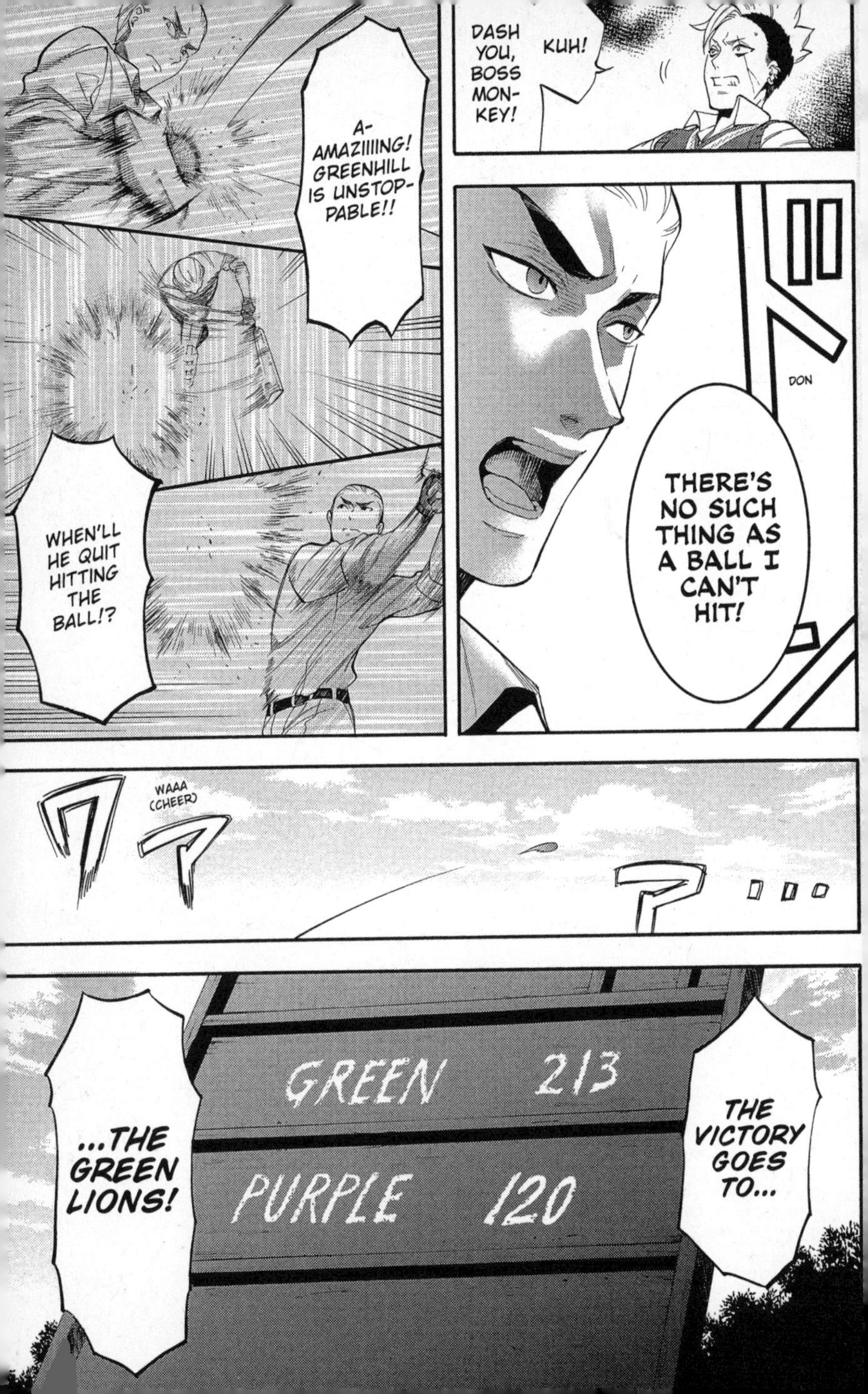
KUH!
DASH YOU, BOSS MON-KEY!
DON
THERE'S NO SUCH THING AS A BALL I CAN'T HIT!
A-AMAZIIIING! GREENHILL IS UNSTOP-PABLE!!
WHEN'LL HE QUIT HITTING THE BALL!?
WAAA (CHEER)
THE VICTORY GOES TO...
GREEN 213
PURPLE 120
...THE GREEN LIONS!

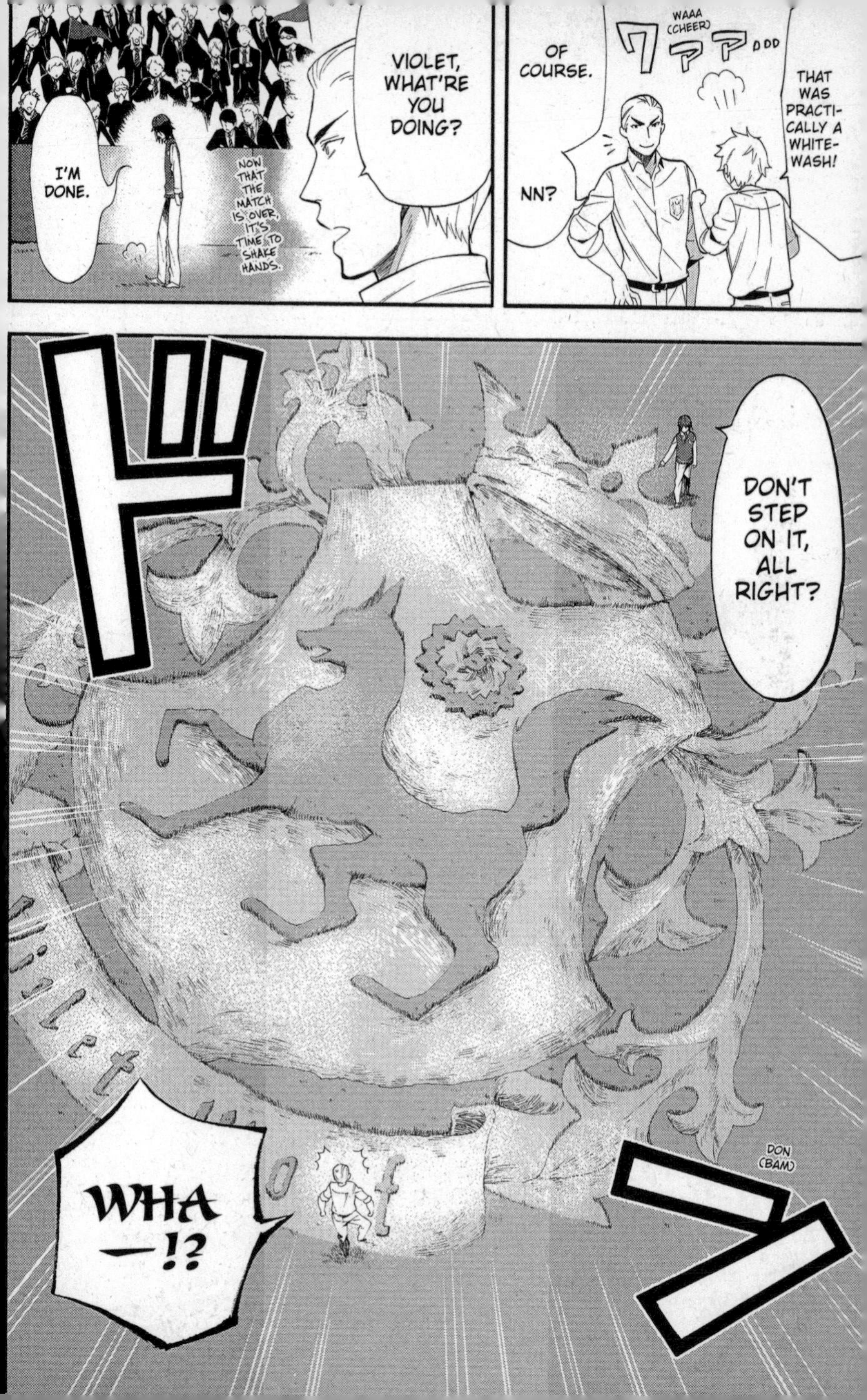
THAT WAS PRACTICALLY A WHITE-WASH!
ワアア
WAAA (CHEER)
OF COURSE.
NN?
VIOLET, WHAT'RE YOU DOING?
NOW THAT THE MATCH IS OVER, IT'S TIME TO SHAKE HANDS.
I'M DONE.
DON'T STEP ON IT, ALL RIGHT?
ドン
DON (BAM)
WHA—!?

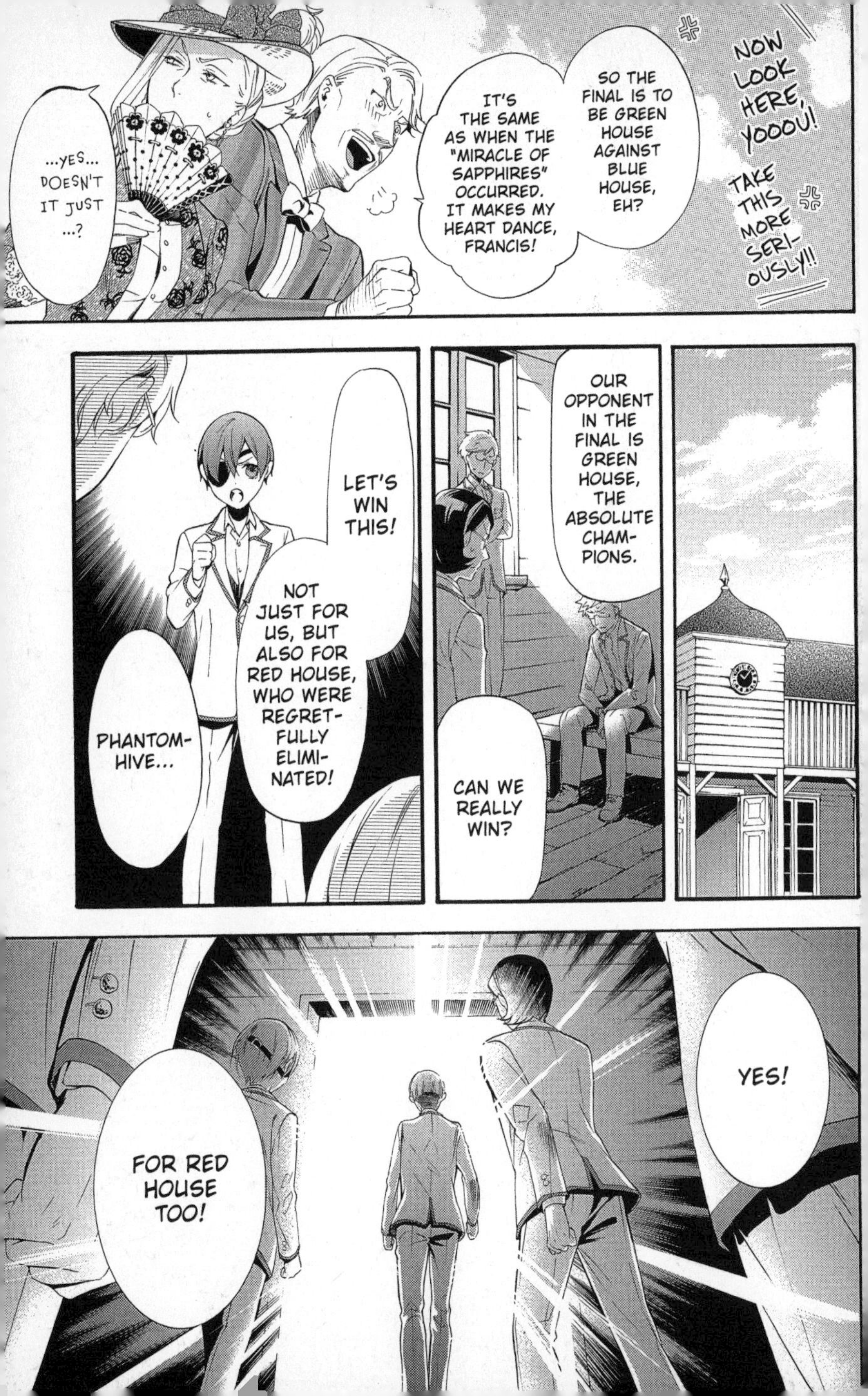
NOW LOOK HERE, YOOOU! TAKE THIS MORE SERI-OUSLY!!
SO THE FINAL IS TO BE GREEN HOUSE AGAINST BLUE HOUSE, EH?
IT'S THE SAME AS WHEN THE "MIRACLE OF SAPPHIRES" OCCURRED. IT MAKES MY HEART DANCE, FRANCIS!
...YES... DOESN'T IT JUST ...?
OUR OPPONENT IN THE FINAL IS GREEN HOUSE, THE ABSOLUTE CHAM-PIONS.
CAN WE REALLY WIN?
LET'S WIN THIS!
NOT JUST FOR US, BUT ALSO FOR RED HOUSE, WHO WERE REGRET-FULLY ELIMI-NATED!
PHANTOM-HIVE...
YES!
FOR RED HOUSE TOO!

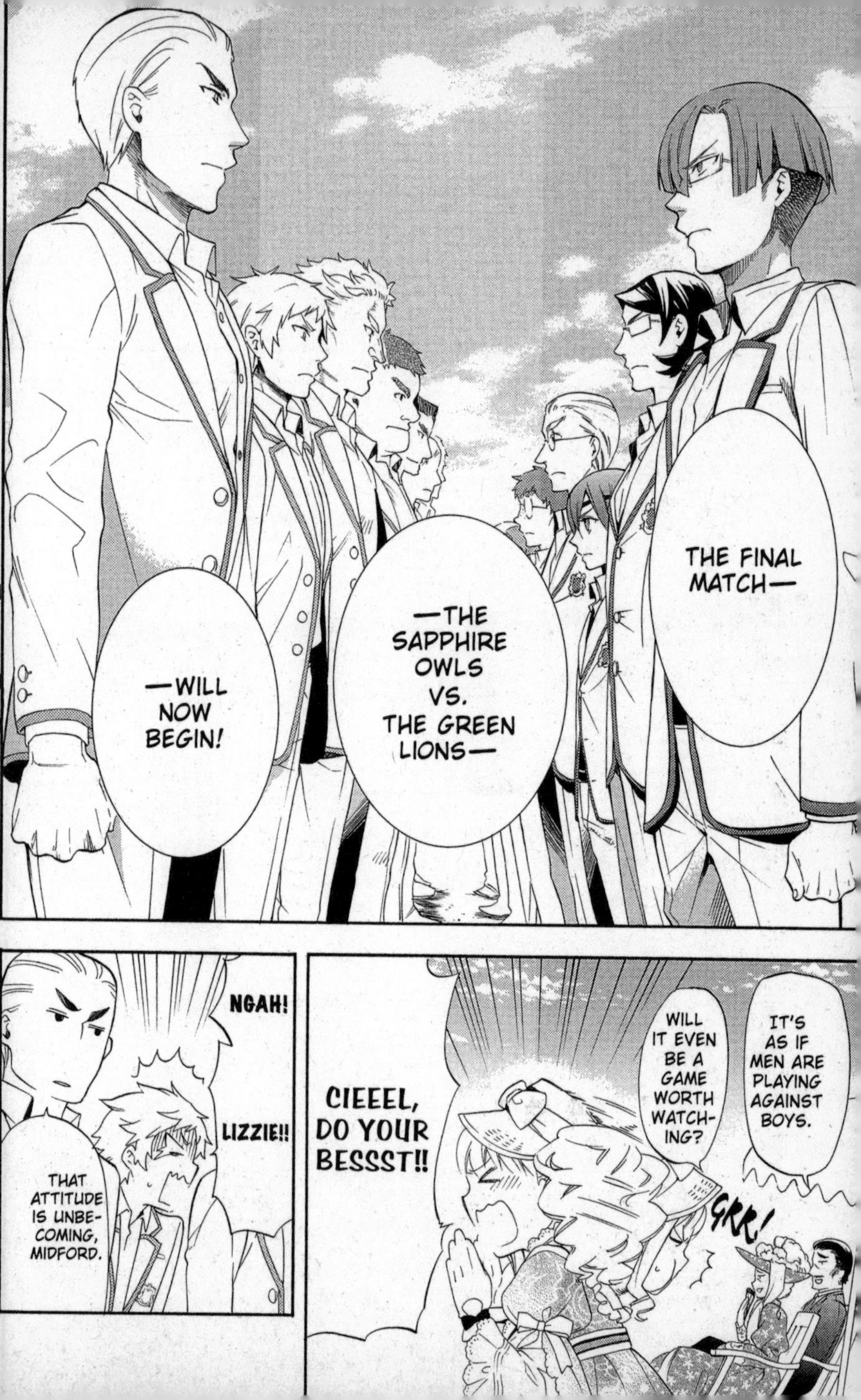
THE FINAL MATCH—
—THE SAPPHIRE OWLS VS. THE GREEN LIONS—
—WILL NOW BEGIN!
IT'S AS IF MEN ARE PLAYING AGAINST BOYS.
WILL IT EVEN BE A GAME WORTH WATCH-ING?
GRR!
CIEEEL, DO YOUR BESSST!!
NGAH!
LIZZIE!!
THAT ATTITUDE IS UNBE-COMING, MIDFORD.

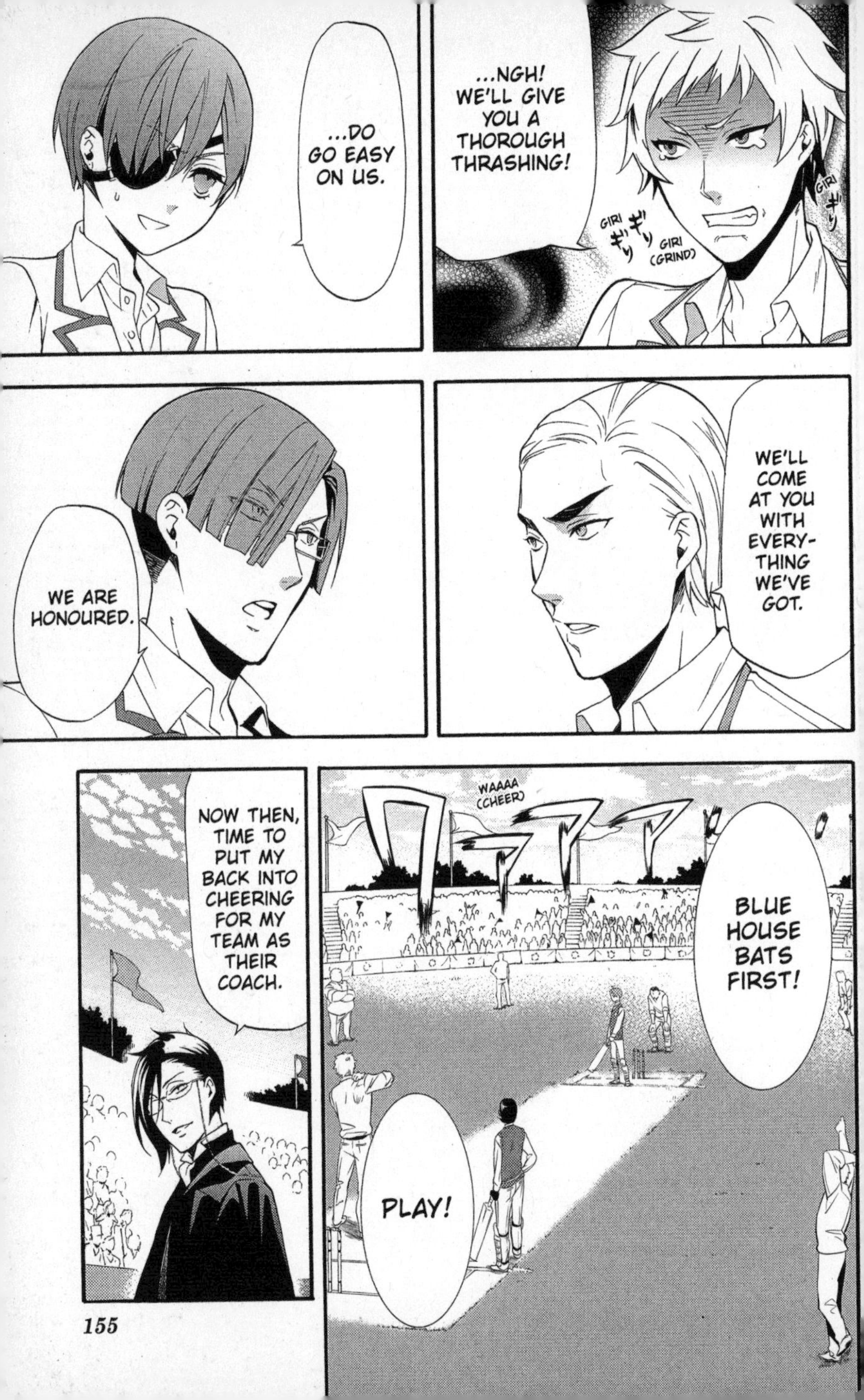
...NGH! WE'LL GIVE YOU A THOROUGH THRASHING!
GIRI
GIRI
GIRI (GRIND)
...DO GO EASY ON US.
WE'LL COME AT YOU WITH EVERY-THING WE'VE GOT.
WE ARE HONOURED.
WAAAA (CHEER)
BLUE HOUSE BATS FIRST!
PLAY!
NOW THEN, TIME TO PUT MY BACK INTO CHEERING FOR MY TEAM AS THEIR COACH.

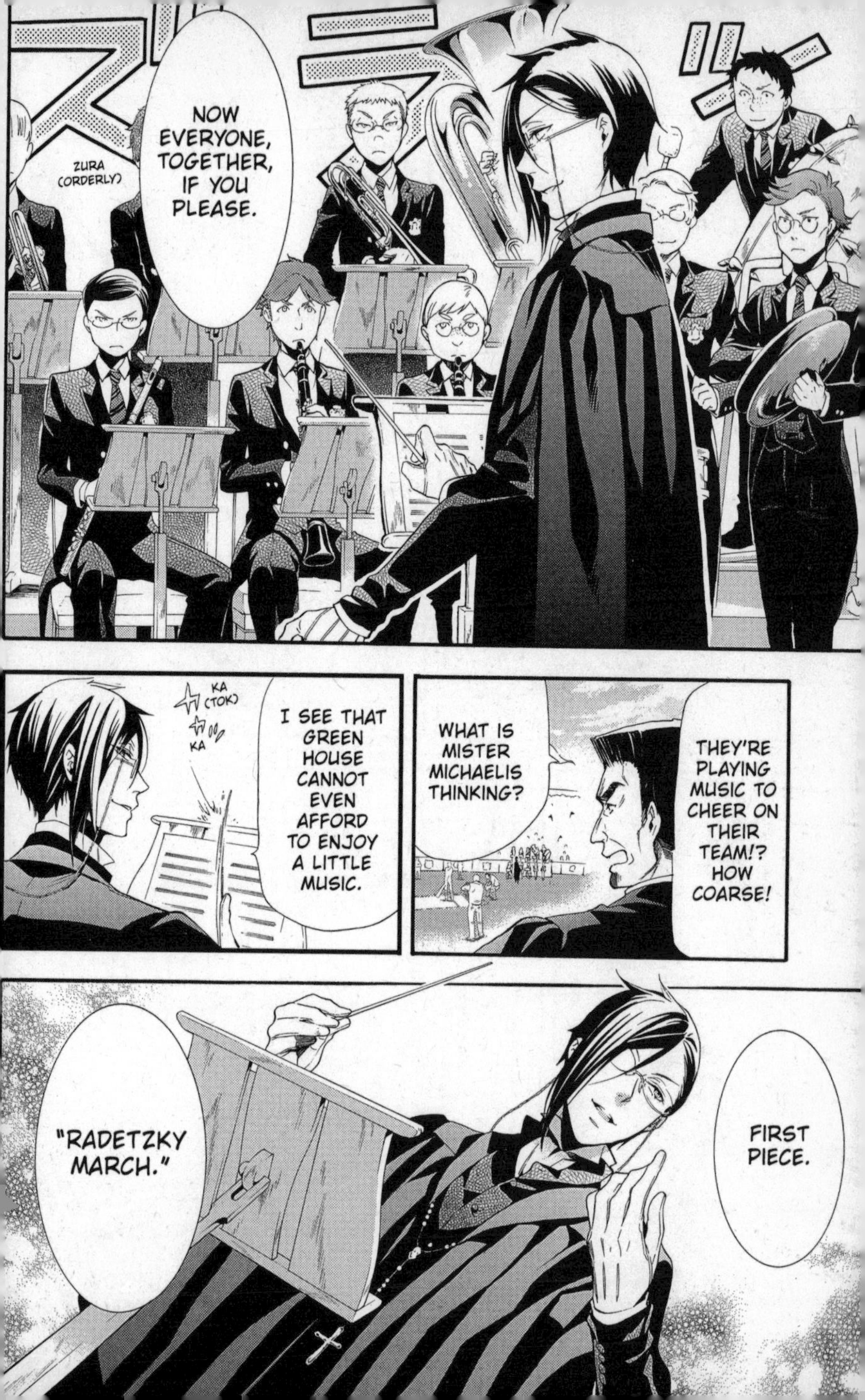
NOW EVERYONE, TOGETHER, IF YOU PLEASE.
ZURA (ORDERLY)
THEY'RE PLAYING MUSIC TO CHEER ON THEIR TEAM!? HOW COARSE!
WHAT IS MISTER MICHAELIS THINKING?
I SEE THAT GREEN HOUSE CANNOT EVEN AFFORD TO ENJOY A LITTLE MUSIC.
KA (TOK)
KA
FIRST PIECE.
"RADETZKY MARCH."

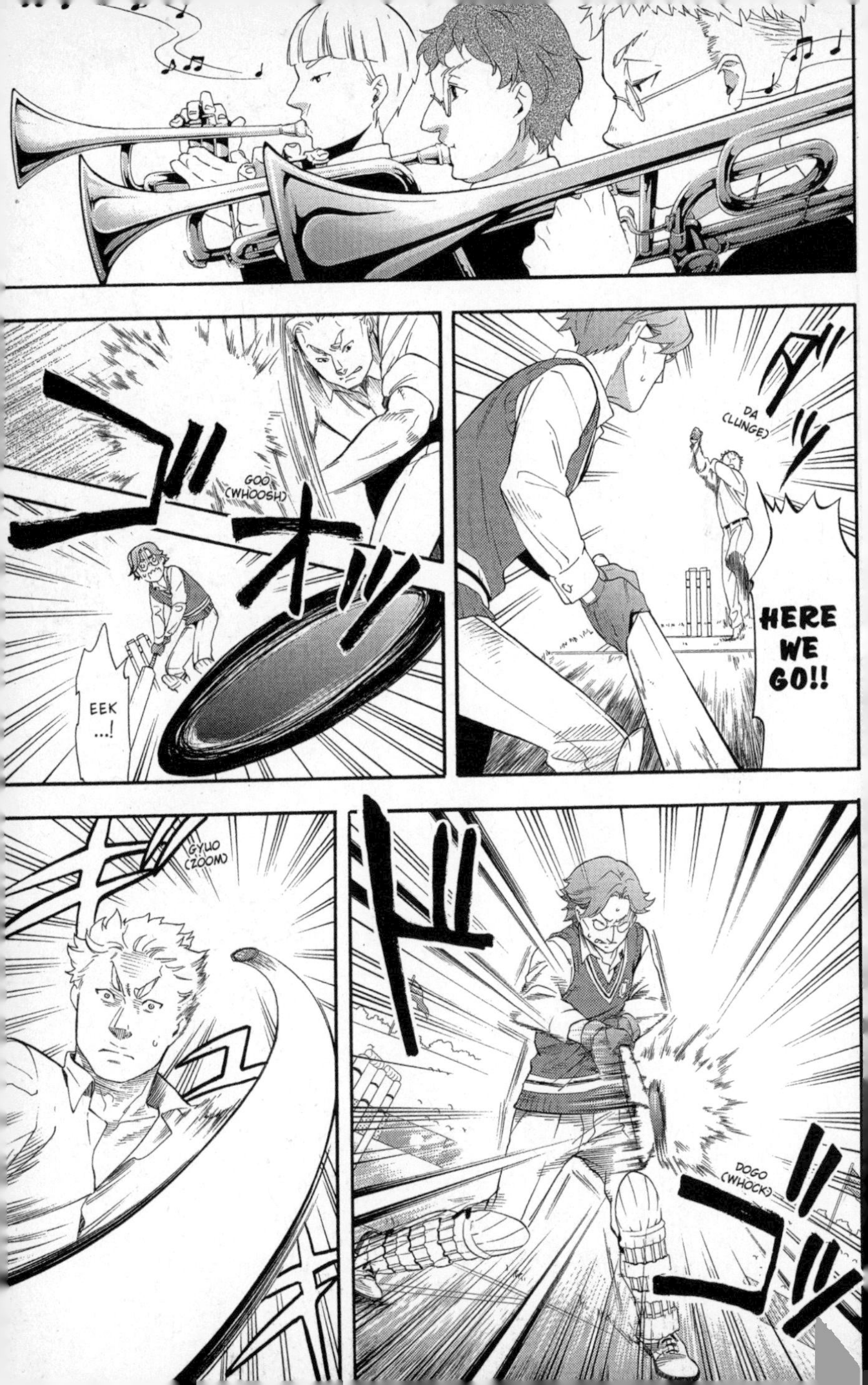
DA (LUNGE)
HERE WE GO!!
GOO (WHOOSH)
EEK ...!
DOGO (WHOCK)
GYUO (ZOOM)

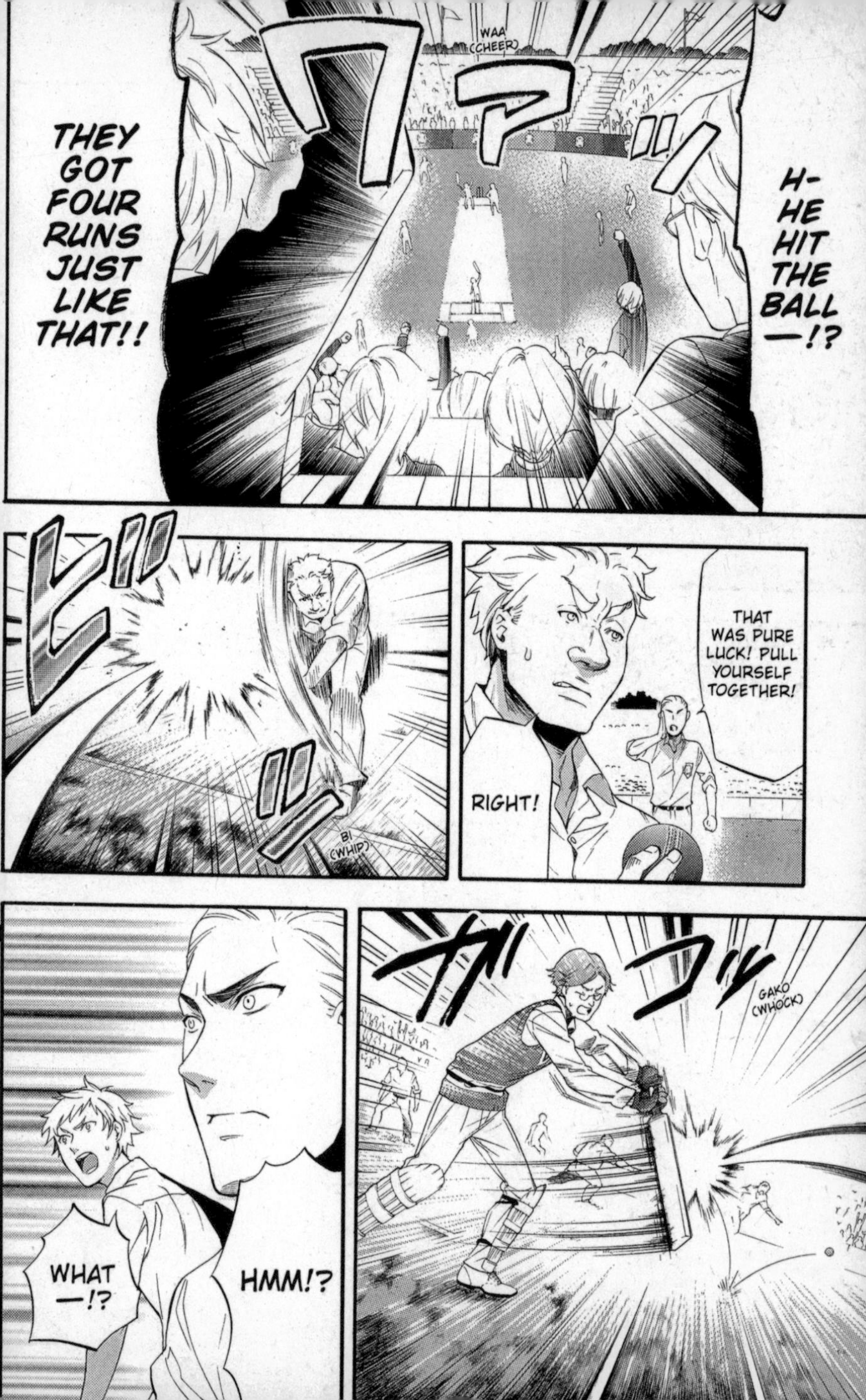
WAA (CHEER)
H-HE HIT THE BALL—!?
THEY GOT FOUR RUNS JUST LIKE THAT!!
THAT WAS PURE LUCK! PULL YOURSELF TOGETHER!
RIGHT!
BI (WHIP)
GAKO (WHOCK)
HMM!?
WHAT—!?

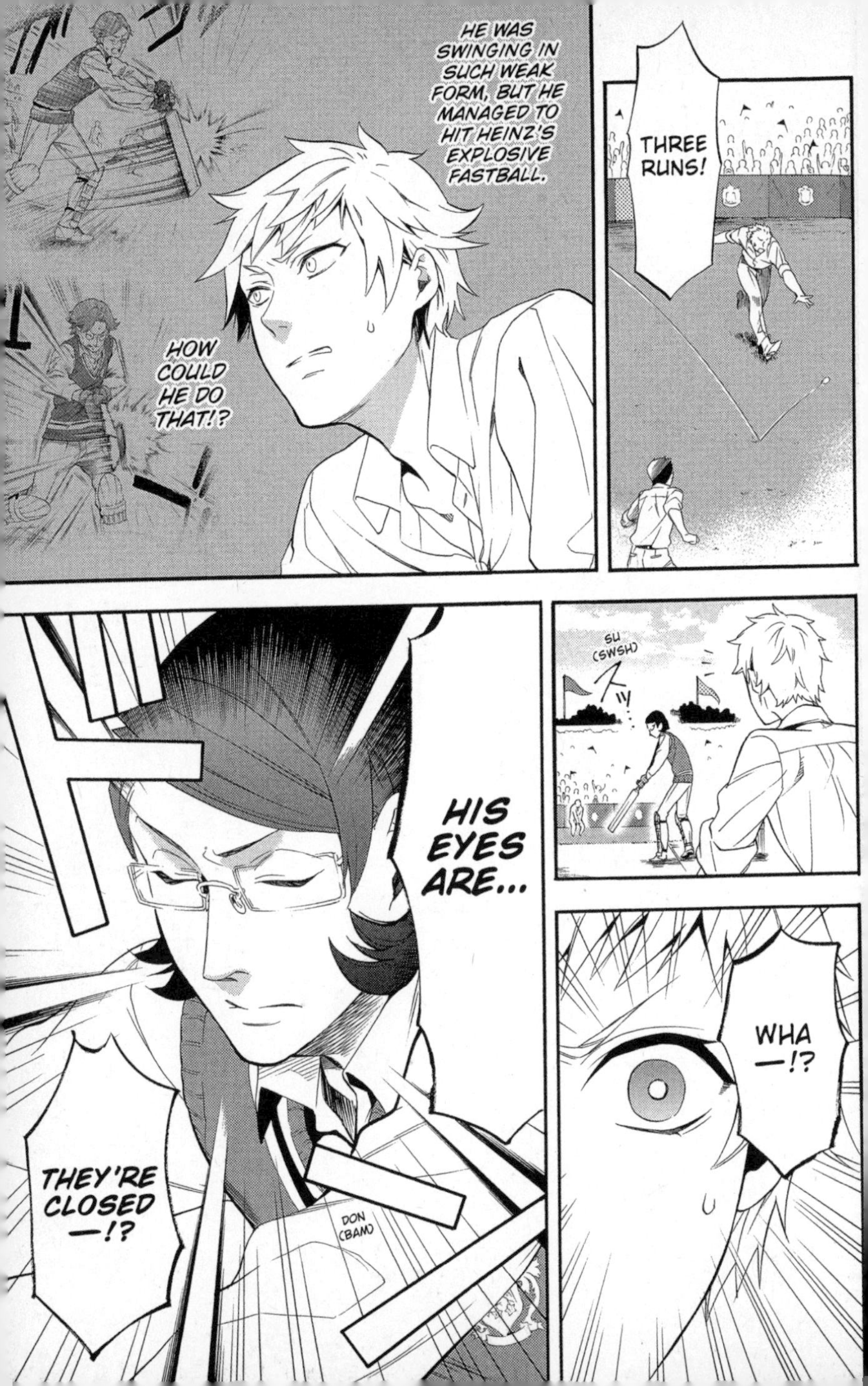
THREE RUNS!
HE WAS SWINGING IN SUCH WEAK FORM, BUT HE MANAGED TO HIT HEINZ'S EXPLOSIVE FASTBALL.
HOW COULD HE DO THAT!?
SU (SWSH)
WHA—!?
HIS EYES ARE...
THEY'RE CLOSED—!?
DON (BAM)

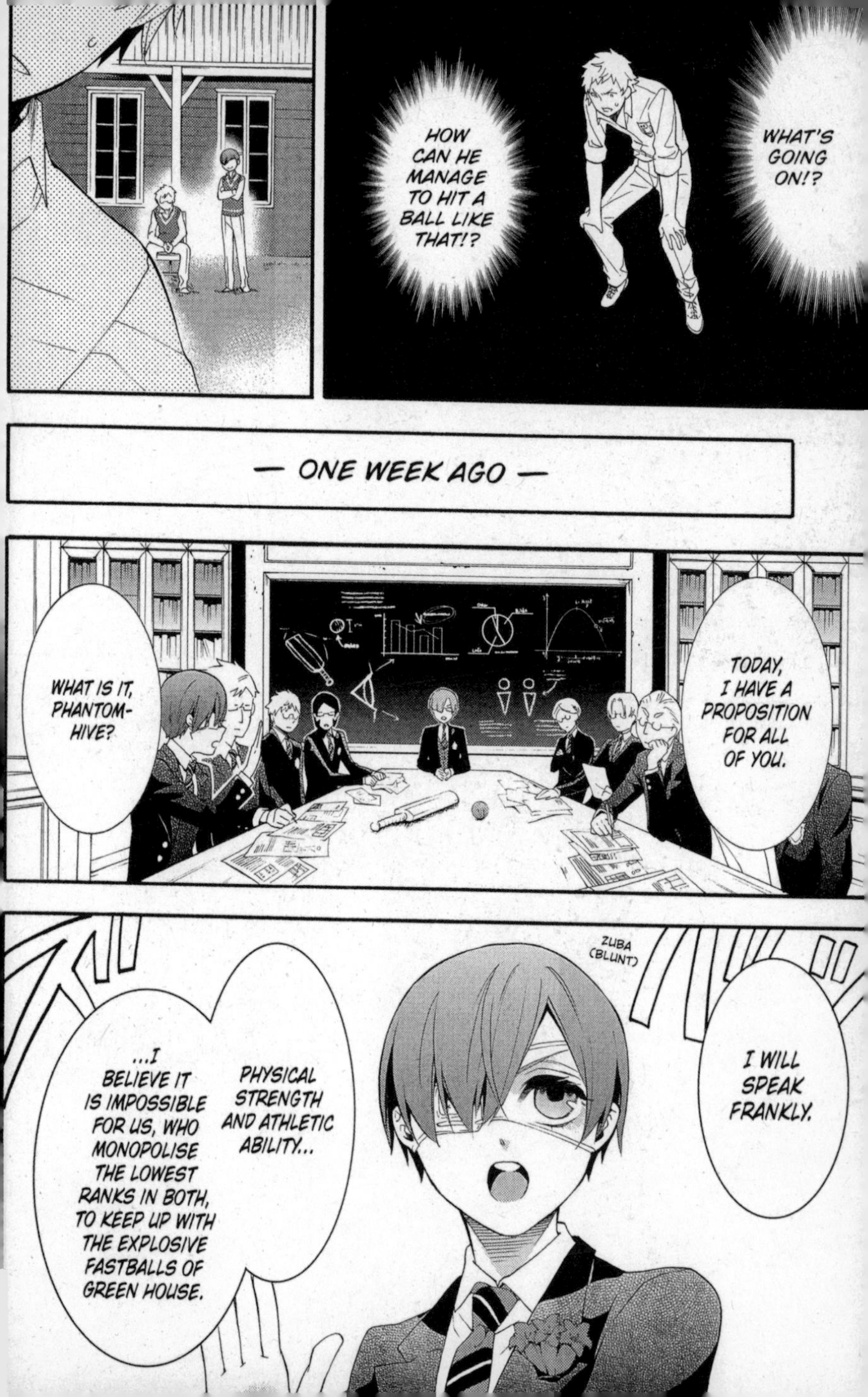
WHAT'S GOING ON!?
HOW CAN HE MANAGE TO HIT A BALL LIKE THAT!?
— ONE WEEK AGO —
TODAY, I HAVE A PROPOSITION FOR ALL OF YOU.
WHAT IS IT, PHANTOM-HIVE?
ZUBA (BLUNT)
I WILL SPEAK FRANKLY.
PHYSICAL STRENGTH AND ATHLETIC ABILITY...
...I BELIEVE IT IS IMPOSSIBLE FOR US, WHO MONOPOLISE THE LOWEST RANKS IN BOTH, TO KEEP UP WITH THE EXPLOSIVE FASTBALLS OF GREEN HOUSE.

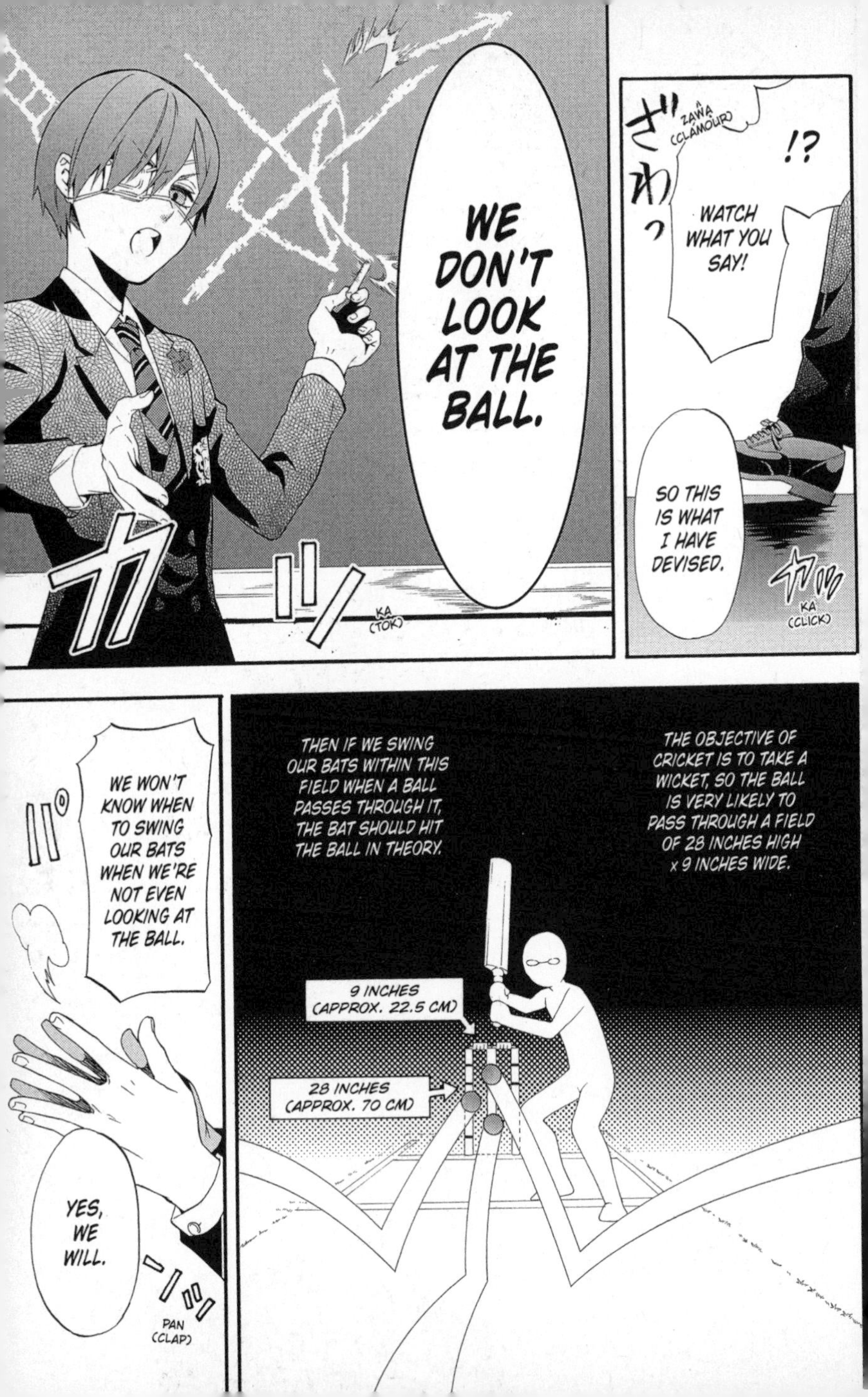
ZAWA (CLAMOUR)
!?
WATCH WHAT YOU SAY!
SO THIS IS WHAT I HAVE DEVISED.
KA (CLICK)
WE DON'T LOOK AT THE BALL.
KA (TOK)
THE OBJECTIVE OF CRICKET IS TO TAKE A WICKET, SO THE BALL IS VERY LIKELY TO PASS THROUGH A FIELD OF 28 INCHES HIGH x 9 INCHES WIDE.
THEN IF WE SWING OUR BATS WITHIN THIS FIELD WHEN A BALL PASSES THROUGH IT, THE BAT SHOULD HIT THE BALL IN THEORY.
9 INCHES (APPROX. 22.5 CM)
28 INCHES (APPROX. 70 CM)
WE WON'T KNOW WHEN TO SWING OUR BATS WHEN WE'RE NOT EVEN LOOKING AT THE BALL.
YES, WE WILL.
PAN (CLAP)

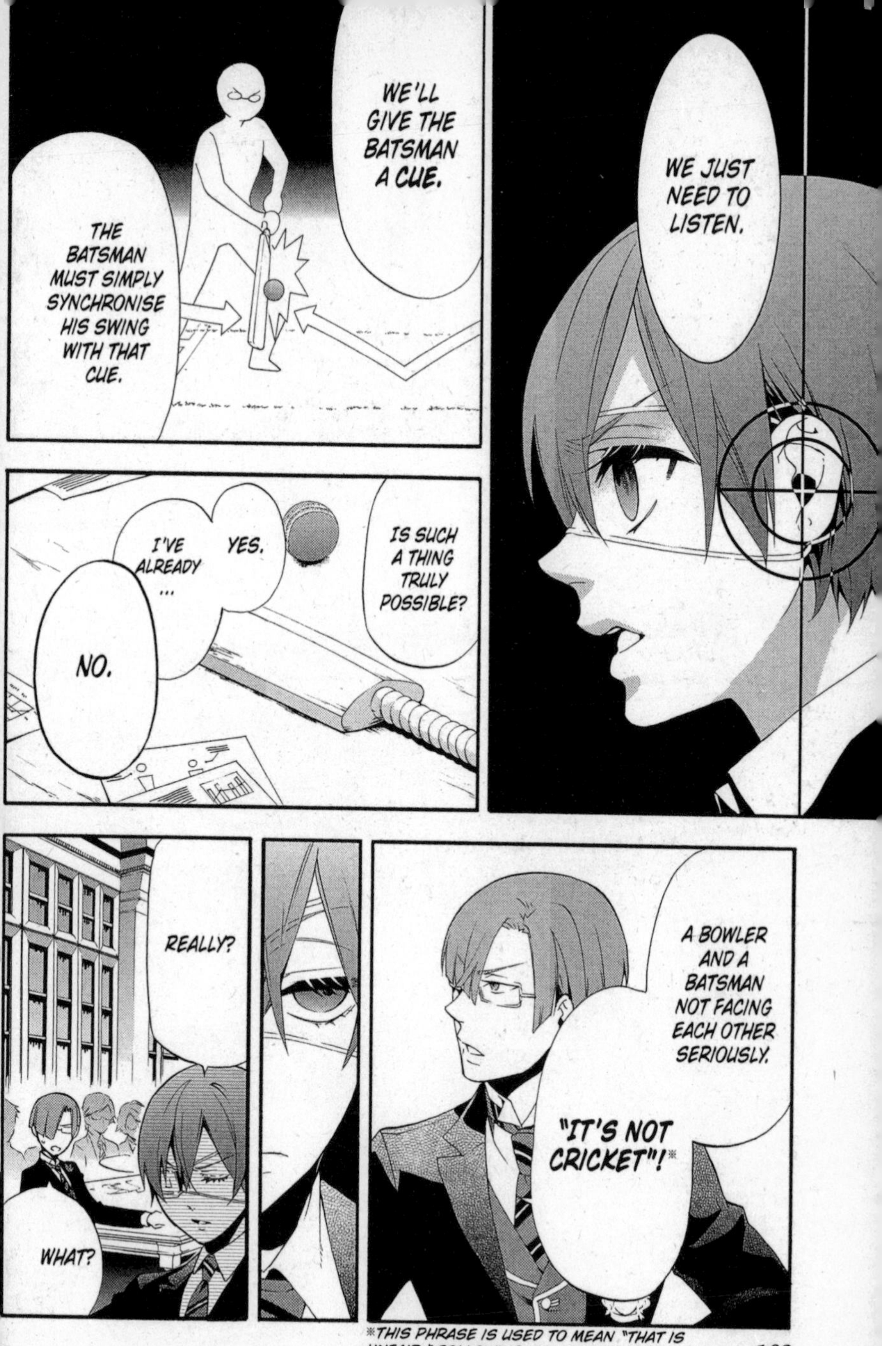
WE JUST NEED TO LISTEN.
WE'LL GIVE THE BATSMAN A CUE.
THE BATSMAN MUST SIMPLY SYNCHRONISE HIS SWING WITH THAT CUE.
IS SUCH A THING TRULY POSSIBLE?
YES.
I'VE ALREADY ...
NO.
A BOWLER AND A BATSMAN NOT FACING EACH OTHER SERIOUSLY.
"IT'S NOT CRICKET"!※
REALLY?
WHAT?

※THIS PHRASE IS USED TO MEAN "THAT IS UNFAIR," FOLLOWING THE SPIRIT OF CRICKET THAT PUTS A HIGH VALUE ON FAIR PLAY.

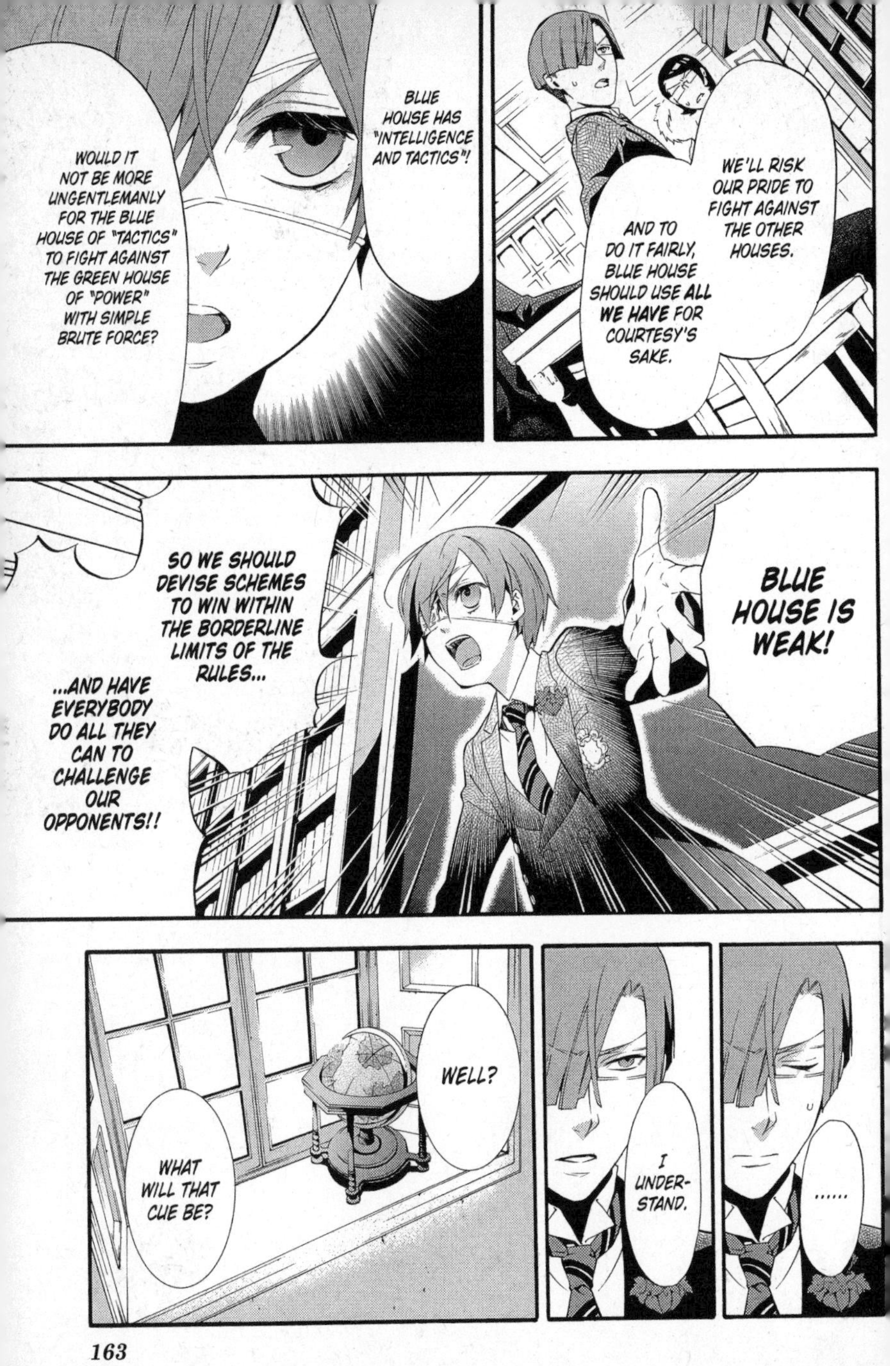
WE'LL RISK OUR PRIDE TO FIGHT AGAINST THE OTHER HOUSES.
AND TO DO IT FAIRLY, BLUE HOUSE SHOULD USE **ALL WE HAVE** FOR COURTESY'S SAKE.
BLUE HOUSE HAS "INTELLIGENCE AND TACTICS"!
WOULD IT NOT BE MORE UNGENTLEMANLY FOR THE BLUE HOUSE OF "TACTICS" TO FIGHT AGAINST THE GREEN HOUSE OF "POWER" WITH SIMPLE BRUTE FORCE?
BLUE HOUSE IS WEAK!
SO WE SHOULD DEVISE SCHEMES TO WIN WITHIN THE BORDERLINE LIMITS OF THE RULES...
...AND HAVE EVERYBODY DO ALL THEY CAN TO CHALLENGE OUR OPPONENTS!!
......
I UNDER-STAND.
WELL?
WHAT WILL THAT CUE BE?

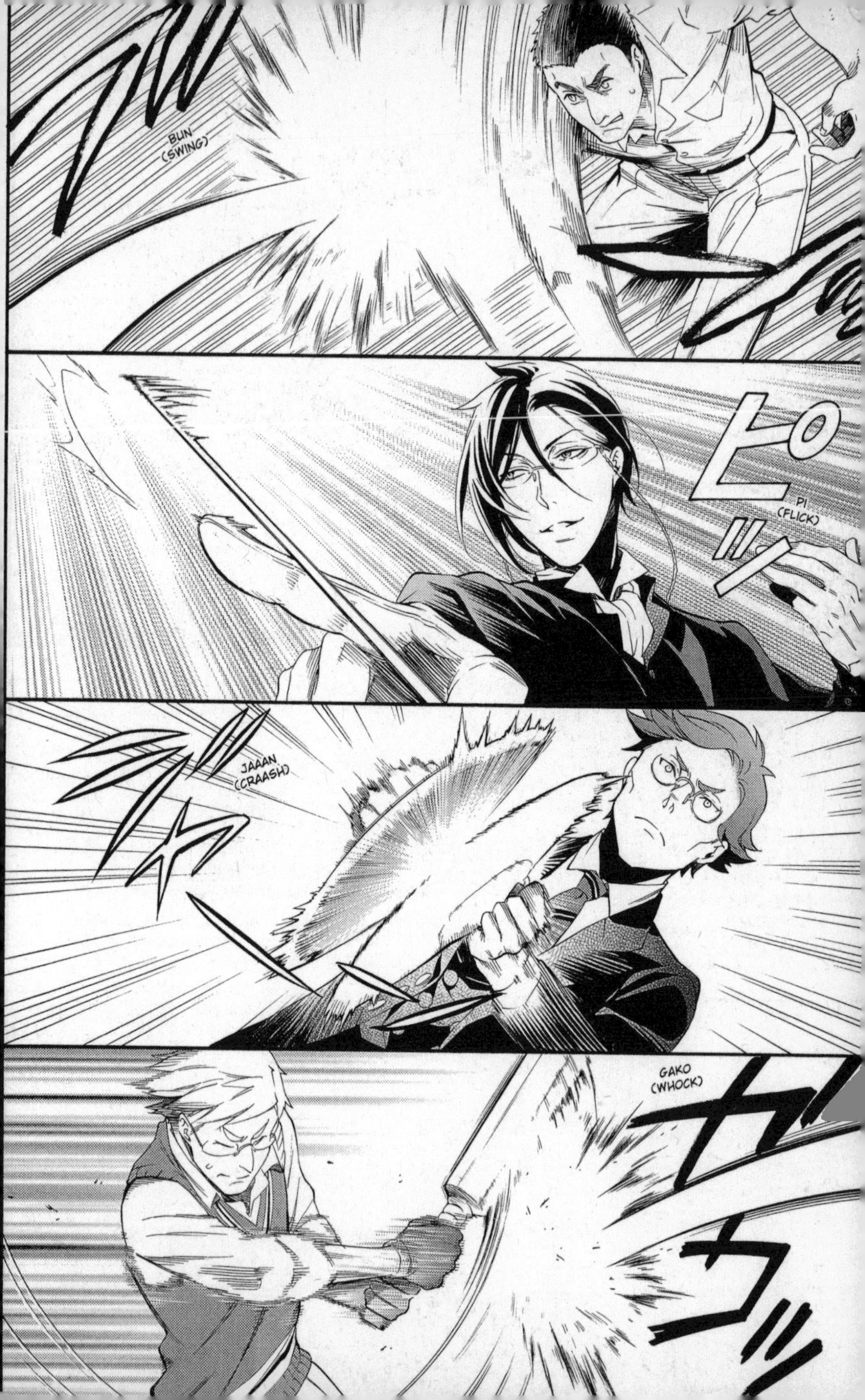
BUN (SWING)
PI (FLICK)
JAAAN (CRAASH)
GAKO (WHOCK)

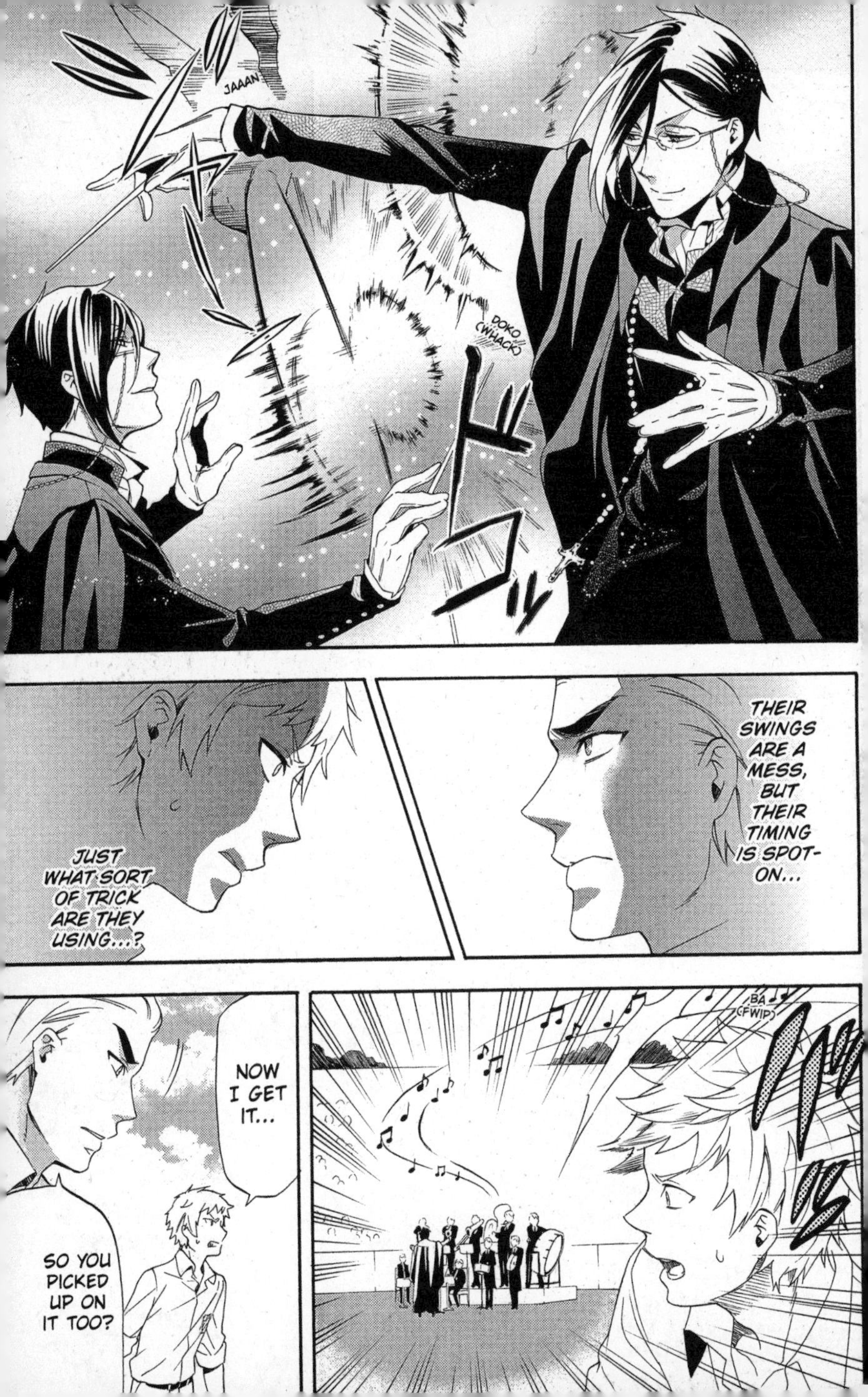
JAAAN
DOKO (WHACK)
THEIR SWINGS ARE A MESS, BUT THEIR TIMING IS SPOT-ON...
JUST WHAT SORT OF TRICK ARE THEY USING...?
BA (FWIP)
NOW I GET IT...
SO YOU PICKED UP ON IT TOO?

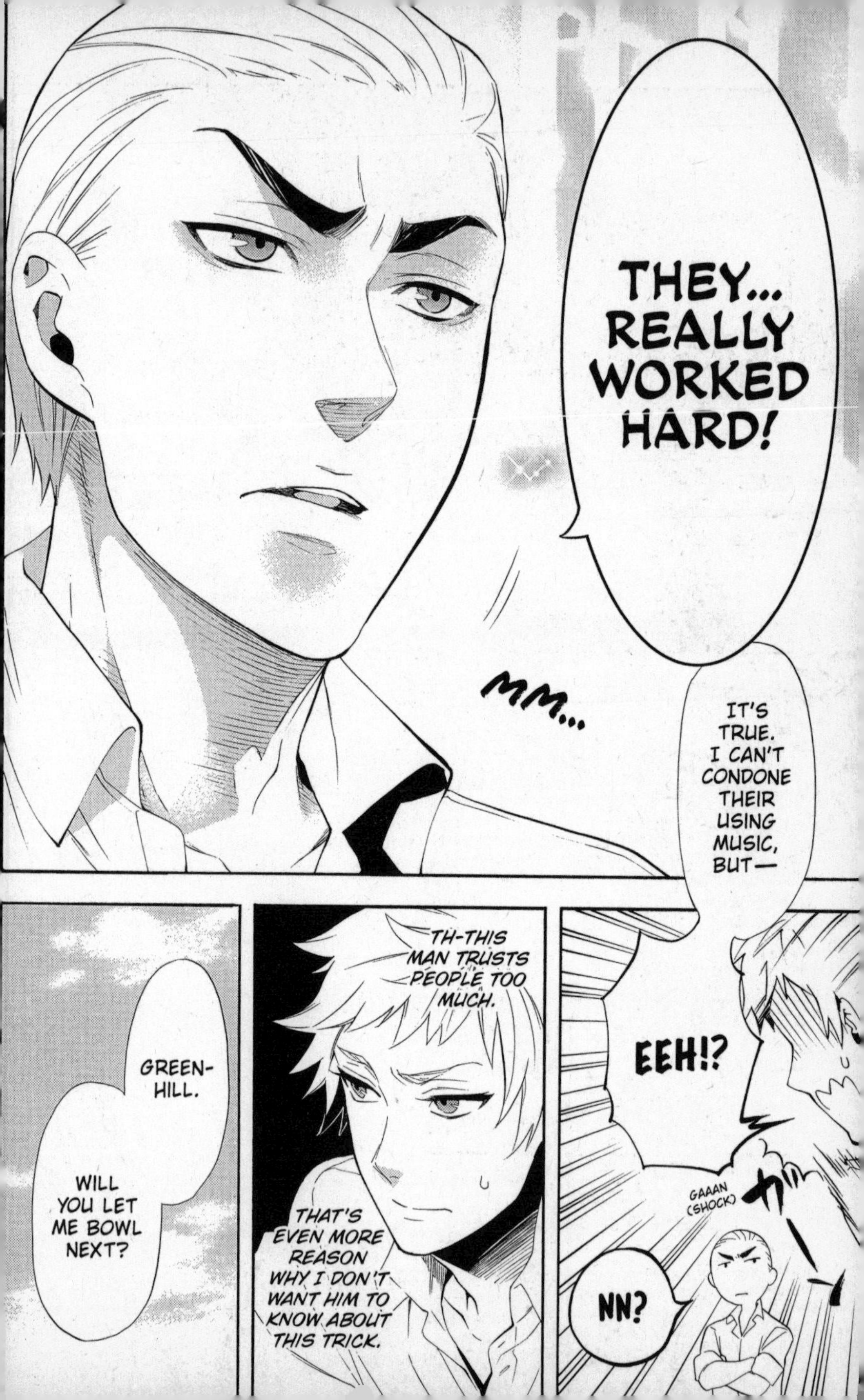
THEY... REALLY WORKED HARD!
IT'S TRUE. I CAN'T CONDONE THEIR USING MUSIC, BUT—
MM...
EEH!?
GAAAN (SHOCK)
NN?
TH-THIS MAN TRUSTS PEOPLE TOO MUCH.
THAT'S EVEN MORE REASON WHY I DON'T WANT HIM TO KNOW ABOUT THIS TRICK.
GREEN-HILL.
WILL YOU LET ME BOWL NEXT?

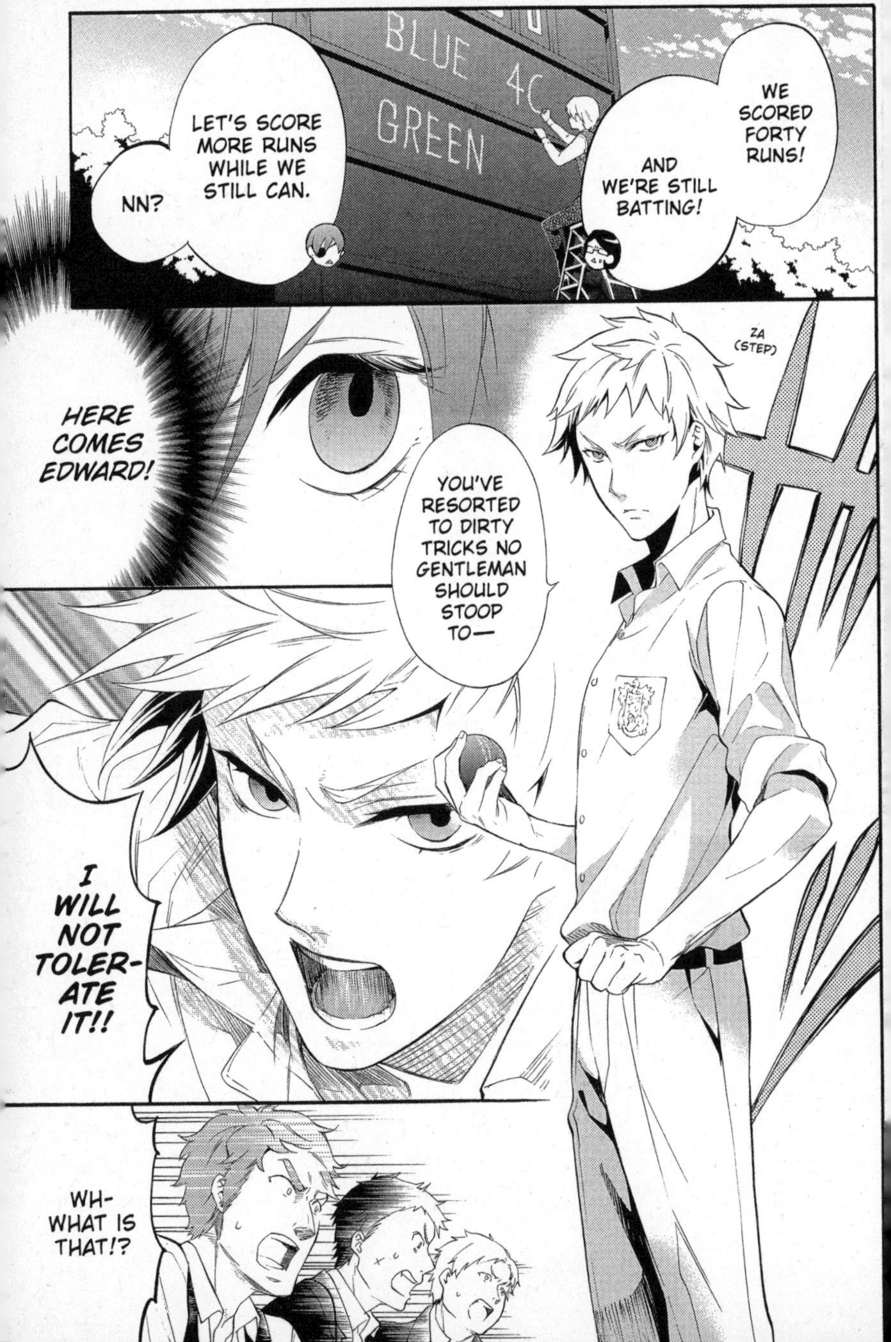
WE SCORED FORTY RUNS!
AND WE'RE STILL BATTING!
BLUE
GREEN
LET'S SCORE MORE RUNS WHILE WE STILL CAN.
NN?
ZA (STEP)
YOU'VE RESORTED TO DIRTY TRICKS NO GENTLEMAN SHOULD STOOP TO—
HERE COMES EDWARD!
I WILL NOT TOLER-ATE IT!!
WH- WHAT IS THAT!?

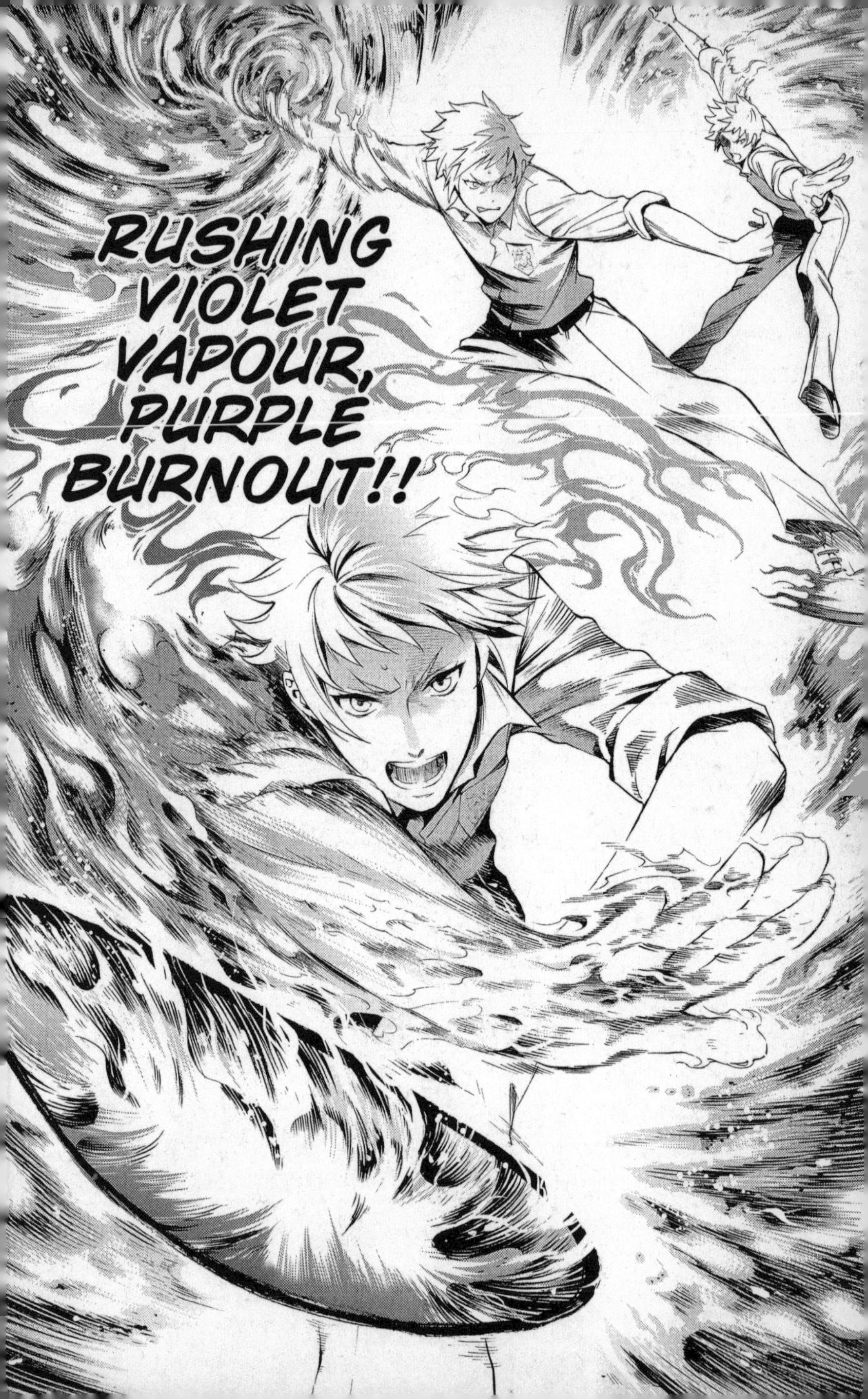
RUSHING VIOLET VAPOUR, PURPLE BURNOUT!!

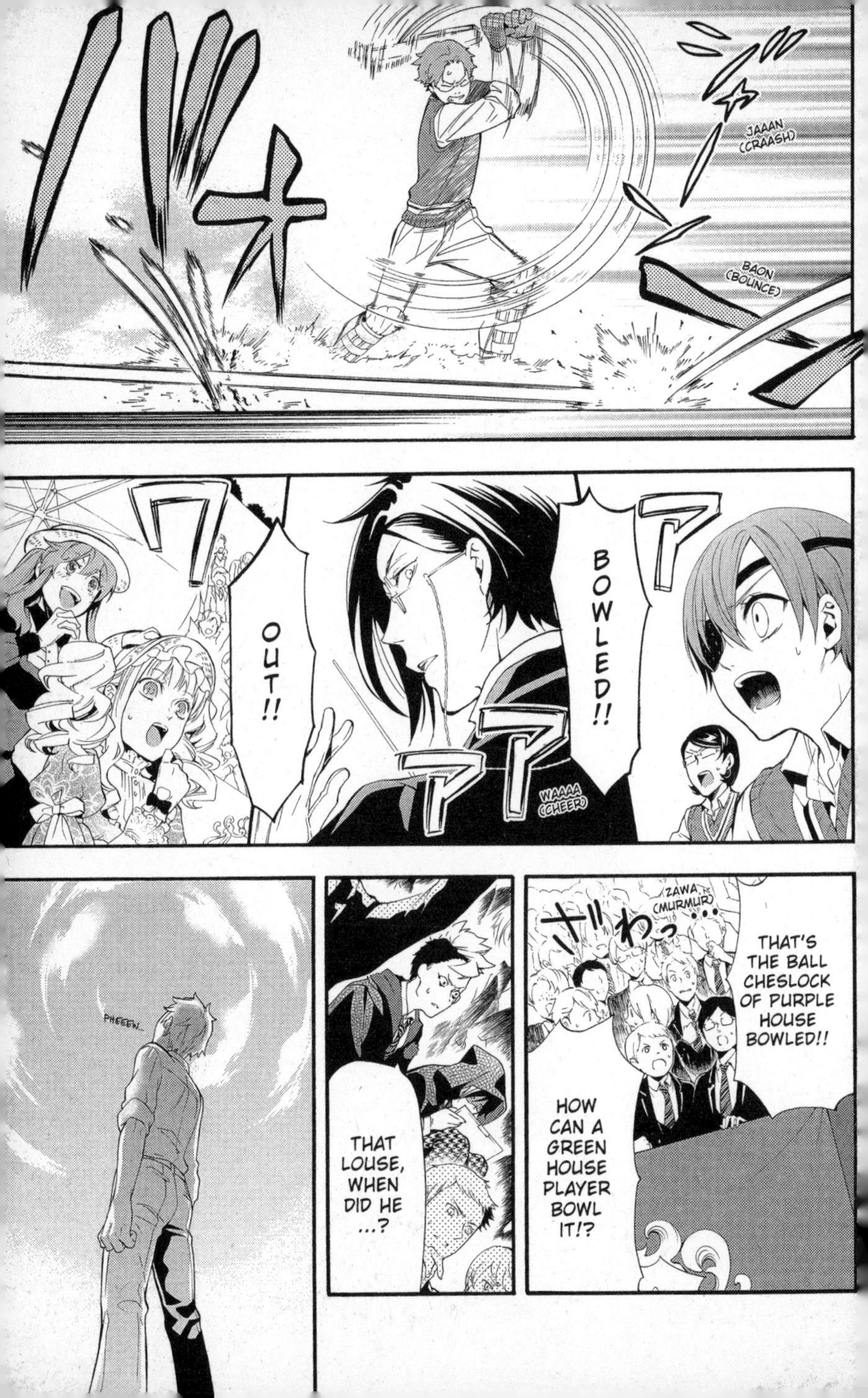
JAAAN (CRAASH)
BAON (BOUNCE)
BOWLED!!
OUT!!
WAAAA (CHEER)
ZAWA (MURMUR)
THAT'S THE BALL CHESLOCK OF PURPLE HOUSE BOWLED!!
HOW CAN A GREEN HOUSE PLAYER BOWL IT!?
THAT LOUSE, WHEN DID HE ...?
PHEEEW...

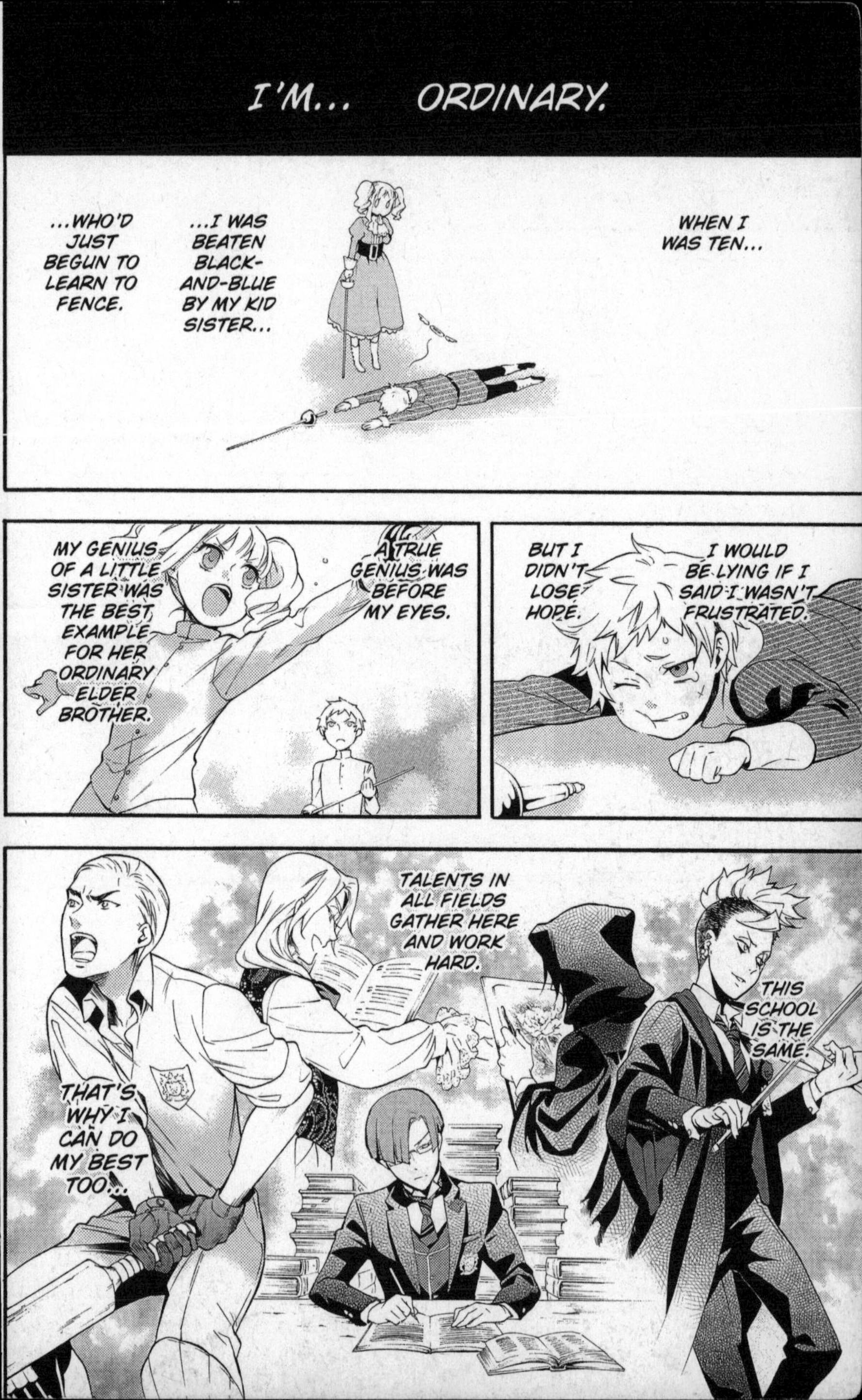

I'M... ORDINARY.
WHEN I WAS TEN...
...I WAS BEATEN BLACK-AND-BLUE BY MY KID SISTER...
...WHO'D JUST BEGUN TO LEARN TO FENCE.
I WOULD BE LYING IF I SAID I WASN'T FRUSTRATED.
BUT I DIDN'T LOSE HOPE.
A TRUE GENIUS WAS BEFORE MY EYES.
MY GENIUS OF A LITTLE SISTER WAS THE BEST EXAMPLE FOR HER ORDINARY ELDER BROTHER.
THIS SCHOOL IS THE SAME.
TALENTS IN ALL FIELDS GATHER HERE AND WORK HARD.
THAT'S WHY I CAN DO MY BEST TOO...

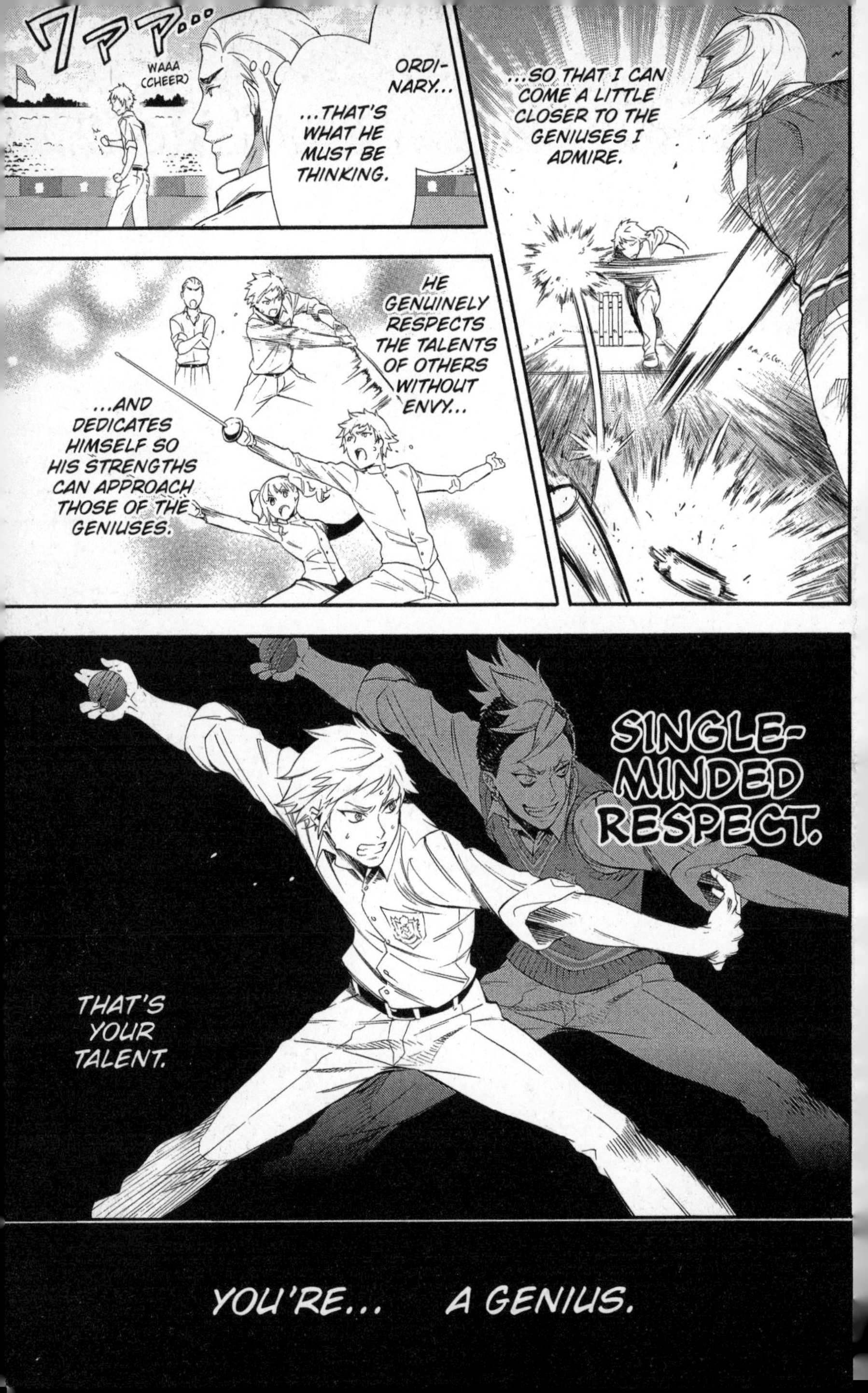
...SO THAT I CAN COME A LITTLE CLOSER TO THE GENIUSES I ADMIRE.
ORDINARY...
...THAT'S WHAT HE MUST BE THINKING.
ワァア...
WAAA (CHEER)
HE GENUINELY RESPECTS THE TALENTS OF OTHERS WITHOUT ENVY...
...AND DEDICATES HIMSELF SO HIS STRENGTHS CAN APPROACH THOSE OF THE GENIUSES.
SINGLE-MINDED RESPECT.
THAT'S YOUR TALENT.
YOU'RE... A GENIUS.

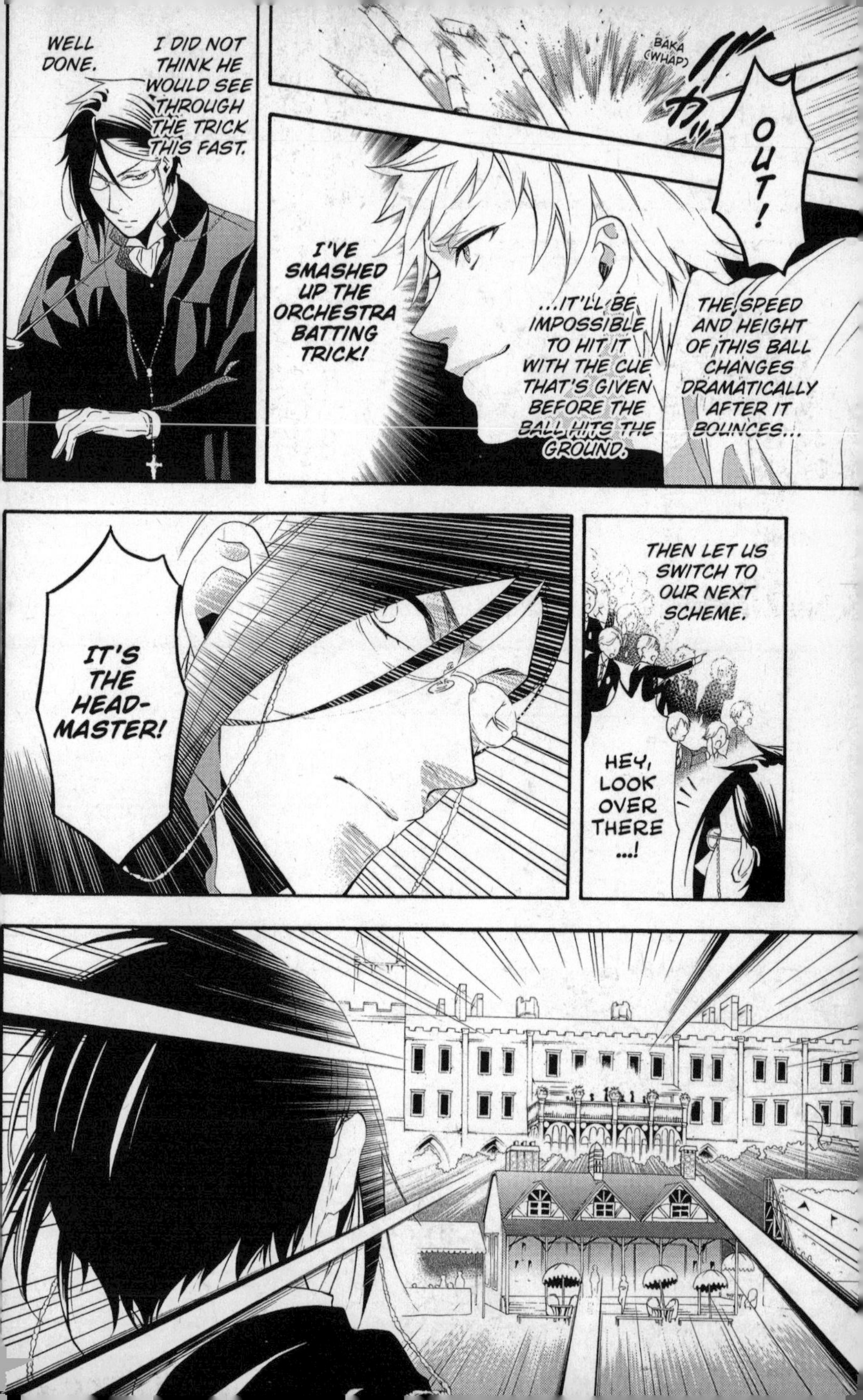
BAKA (WHAP)
OUT!
THE SPEED AND HEIGHT OF THIS BALL CHANGES DRAMATICALLY AFTER IT BOUNCES...
...IT'LL BE IMPOSSIBLE TO HIT IT WITH THE CUE THAT'S GIVEN BEFORE THE BALL HITS THE GROUND.
I'VE SMASHED UP THE ORCHESTRA BATTING TRICK!
I DID NOT THINK HE WOULD SEE THROUGH THE TRICK THIS FAST.
WELL DONE.
THEN LET US SWITCH TO OUR NEXT SCHEME.
HEY, LOOK OVER THERE ...!
IT'S THE HEAD-MASTER!

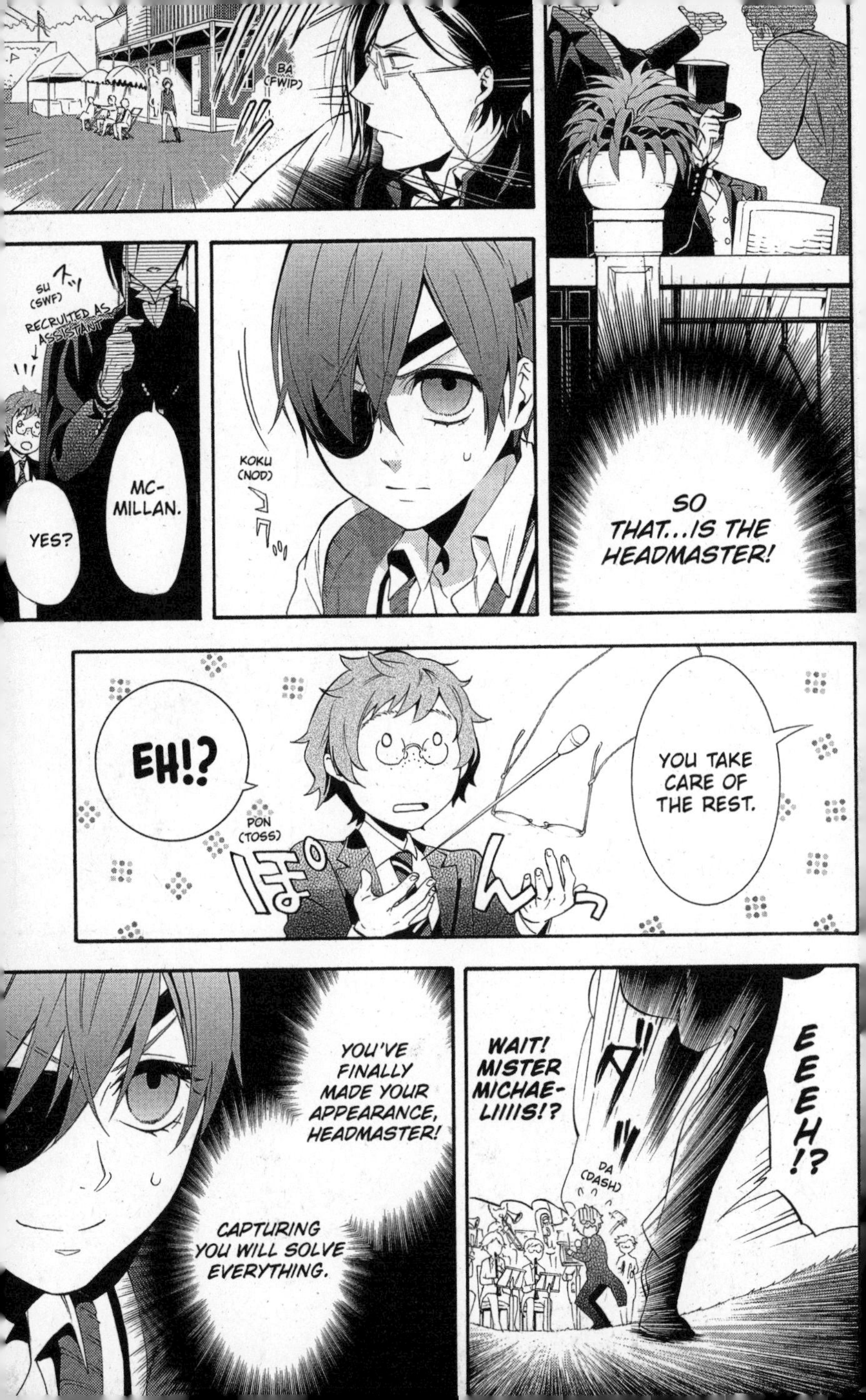
BA (FWIP)
SO THAT...IS THE HEADMASTER!
KOKU (NOD)
SU (SWF)
RECRUITED AS ASSISTANT
MC-MILLAN.
YES?
YOU TAKE CARE OF THE REST.
EH!?
PON (TOSS)
EEEEH!?
WAIT! MISTER MICHAE-LIIIIS!?
DA (DASH)
YOU'VE FINALLY MADE YOUR APPEARANCE, HEADMASTER!
CAPTURING YOU WILL SOLVE EVERYTHING.

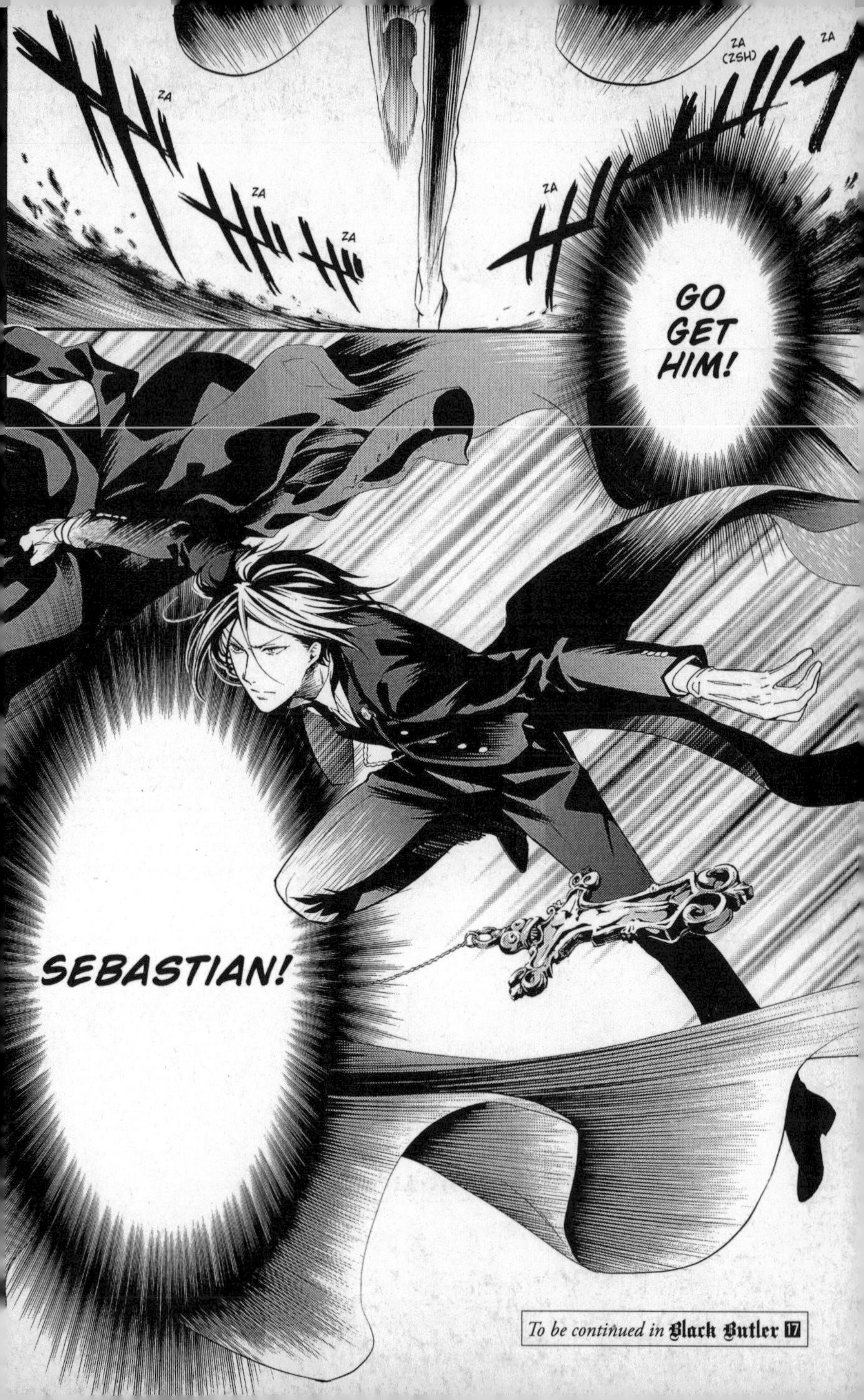
ZA
ZA (ZSH)
ZA
ZA
ZA
ZA
GO GET HIM!
SEBASTIAN!

To be continued in Black Butler 17

⇛ Black Butler ⇚

黒執事

❖

Downstairs

Wakana Haduki
7
Saito Torino
Tsuki Sorano
Chiaki Nagaoka
Asakura
*
Takeshi Kuma
*
Yana Toboso

❖

Adviser

Rico Murakami

Naoki Miyaji
(Japan Cricket Association)

Special thanks to You!

Translation Notes

INSIDE FRONT AND BACK COVERS
Do you want to go to New Delhi!?
There used to be a Japanese TV quiz show called *Trans America Ultra Quiz*, where challengers travelled across the U.S. while answering various trivia questions en route to New York, their final destination. The host of the show used to shout, "Do you want to go to New York!?" during the preliminaries.

PAGE 21
Sunt aliquid manes … amoris.
The Latin poem that the students are reciting in this scene is Elegy No. 7 from Part 4 of *Cynthia Monobiblos* by the Latin poet Sextus Propertius (54 BC–16 BC).

PAGE 106
Tournament cricket format
The type of cricket being played in the interhouse tournament is known as limited overs cricket.

PAGE 152
Whitewash
A sporting term used in cricket when one team sweeps all the matches in a series.

PAGE 156
"Radetsky March"
This famous patriotic march was composed by Austrian classical composer Johann Strauss I in 1848.

Yana Toboso

AUTHOR'S NOTE

My assistants, who help me with my *Black Butler* manuscripts, are all extremely competent.

They're wonderful, supporting me by drawing delicate teacups, gorgeous stained glass windows, decadent castles, sophisticated long-reach pruners, stylish *sotoba*, and intensely burning miracle balls, all under my instructions.

It was in just such a merry environment that Volume 16 came into being.

BLACK BUTLER ⑯

YANA TOBOSO

Translation: Tomo Kimura • Lettering: Alexis Eckerman

KUROSHITSUJI Vol. 16 © 2013 Yana Toboso / SQUARE ENIX CO., LTD. All rights reserved. First published in Japan in 2013 by SQUARE ENIX CO., LTD. English translation rights arranged with SQUARE ENIX CO., LTD. and Hachette Book Group through Tuttle-Mori Agency, Inc.

Translation © 2014 by SQUARE ENIX CO., LTD.

Yen Press
Hachette Book Group
237 Park Avenue, New York, NY 10017

www.HachetteBookGroup.com
www.YenPress.com

Yen Press is an imprint of Hachette Book Group, Inc. The Yen Press name and logo are trademarks of Hachette Book Group, Inc.

First Yen Press Edition: January 2014

ISBN: 978-0-316-36902-2

10 9 8 7 6 5 4 3 2 1

BVG   3 1901 05417 8266

Printed in the United States of America